D0558434

Chile
Recent Policy Lessons and Emerging Challenges

Edited by

Guillermo Perry
Danny M. Leipziger

The World Bank
Washington, D. C.

The World Bank Institute (formerly the Economic Development Institute) was established by the World Bank in 1955 to train officials concerned with development planning, policymaking, investment analysis, and project implementation in member developing countries. At present the substance of WBI's work emphasizes macroeconomic and sectoral economic policy analysis. Through a variety of courses, seminars, and workshops, most of which are given overseas in cooperation with local institutions, WBI seeks to sharpen analytical skills used in policy analysis and to broaden understanding of the experience of individual countries with economic development. Although WBI's publications are designed to support its training activities, many are of interest to a much broader audience.

This report has been prepared by the staff of the World Bank. The judgments expressed do not necessarily reflect the views of the Board of Executive Directors or of the governments they represent.

Library of Congress Cataloging-in-Publication Data

Chile : recent policy lessons and emerging challenges / edited by
    Guillermo Perry, Danny M. Leipziger.
        p.   cm.—(WBI development studies)
    Includes bibliographical references
        Contents: Empirical puzzles of Chilean stabilization policy /
    Guillermo A. Calvo and Enrique G. Mendoza—Another look at Chilean
    stabilization policy / Roberto Zahler—Chile's take-off : facts,
    challenges, lessons / Klaus Schmidt-Hebbel—Capital markets in
    Chile, 1985–97 / Nicolas Eyzaguirre and Fernando Lefort—Education
    reform in Chile / Christián Cox—Poverty and income distribution in
    a high-growth economy / Alberto Valdés—Effectiveness of the State
    and development lessons from the Chilean experience / Mario Marcel—
    privatizing and regulating Chile's utilities / Eduardo Bitrán,
    Antonio Estache, J. Luis Guasch and Pablo Serra—The governance of
    the Chilean economy since 1990 / Claudio Sapelli.
        ISBN 0-8213-4500-1
        1. Chile—Economic policy. 2. Chile—Economic conditions—1988–
    I. Perry, Guillermo. II. Leipziger, Danny M.   III. Series.
    HC192.C513 1999
    338.983—dc21   99-29537

Contents

Foreword

The chapters in this volume were prepared for the conference "Chile: Development Lessons and Challenges," held in Washington, D.C., December 17–18, 1997. They have since been extensively revised and updated. The conference was organized jointly by the government of Chile, the Latin America and the Caribbean Regional Office of the World Bank, and the World Bank Institute (formerly the Economic Development Institute). Among the 115 participants were senior government officials from ministries of finance, education, and health; academics; and experts from the World Bank, the International Monetary Fund, and the Inter-American Development Bank.

As one of the first countries to conduct a broad front of economic reforms and to build well-functioning institutions, Chile has been the subject of enormous study. Moreover, it successfully made the transition from authoritarian to democratic rule in a way that balanced economic, political, and social expectations. The success of Chile's economic reforms and the subsequent dramatic increase in real income are well known. Although 41 percent of the population lived in poverty in 1987, by 1994 this figure had fallen to 23 percent, while indigence fell from 13 to 5 percent during the same period. Reforms took place in pensions, education and schooling, health and nutrition, low-income housing, and banking. Decentralization of government occurred along with a wide-ranging privatization program, so that today the private sector is the driving force in the economy. The strength of Chile's institutions in confronting change is noteworthy. They have played a critical role in promoting development and economic integration.

This volume focuses on lessons learned in Chile—its successes and failures—and in the process examines policy issues that must be addressed in the future. It is hoped that this account will be valuable to policymakers contemplating similar efforts.

Vinod Thomas
Director, World Bank Institute

Acknowledgments

This volume was a combined effort of many people. The authors thank Belle Lamdany, who transformed the papers into a manuscript and coordinated the preparation of the volume. Karen Lashman, who had a key role in the design and management of the conference, gave freely of her advice. John Didier provided oversight and guidance, and Barbara de Boinville did an excellent job of editing. The authors also wish to thank Luca Barbone, Daniel Lederman, Saul Lizondo, Claudio Sapelli, and Donald Winkler for their assistance, as well as the Chilean authorities for their support.

Contributors

Eduardo Bitrán
Director General
Fundación Chile

Guillermo A. Calvo
Distinguished University Professor
Center for International Economics
University of Maryland

Cristián Cox
National Coordinator, Ministry of Education, MECE Program
Government of Chile

Antonio Estache
Principal Regulatory Economist
World Bank Institute
World Bank

Nicolas Eyzaguirre
Executive Director, Argentina, Bolivia, Chile, Paraguay, Peru, and Uruguay
International Monetary Fund

Alejandro Foxley T.
Advisor to Secretary General
Organization of American States

José Luis Guasch
Lead Economist
Latin America and the Caribbean Regional Office and
Development Economics Research Group
World Bank

Osvaldo Larrañaga
Professor of Economics
Department of Economics
University of Chile

Fernando Lefort
Professor of Economics
Universidad Católica de Chile

Danny M. Leipziger
Director
Finance, Private Sector and Infrastructure
Latin America and the Caribbean Regional Office
World Bank

María José Lemaitre
Executive Secretary
Council of Higher Education
Government of Chile

Mario Marcel
Executive Director for Chile and Ecuador
Inter-American Development Bank

Enrique G. Mendoza
Professor, Department of Economics
Duke University

Guillermo Perry
Chief Economist, Latin America and the Caribbean Regional Office, and
Director, Poverty Reduction, Economic Management, Public Sector Reform,
and Gender Issues
World Bank

Claudio Sapelli
Professor of Economics
Universidad Católica de Chile

Klaus Schmidt-Hebbel
Chief, Economic Research
Central Bank of Chile

Pablo Serra
Associate Professor, Universidad de Chile
Chair, Department of Industrial Engineering, Universidad de Chile

Alberto Valdés
Agricultural Advisor, Rural Development
World Bank

Roberto Zahler
President, Zahler and Co.
Former President, Central Bank of Chile

Introduction

Guillermo Perry
Danny M. Leipziger

Between 1985 and 1997 the Chilean economy clearly outperformed the rest of Latin America and the Caribbean (LAC). During this period Chile's gross domestic product (GDP) grew at an annual average of 7 percent, more than double the LAC average of 3.3 percent and higher than any other country in the region (figure 1).[1] Chile's strong growth performance relative to the rest of the region was successfully accompanied by a gradual decline in inflation to single digits. Its annual inflation rate was 6.0 percent in 1997 and 4.7 percent in 1998. Although the inflation rate is not the lowest in the region today (Argentina and Brazil did better in 1998 with respective rates of 1.5 percent and 2.7 percent), Chile has been the Latin American country with the most consistent record over the last 15 years (figure 2).

Chile also outperformed its neighbors on a host of macroeconomic and financial indicators—saving and investment rates, consolidated fiscal balances, real exchange rate stability, degree of openness, financial depth, and development of the capital market. At the same time it achieved a substantial reduction in poverty levels, exhibited some of the best indicators in

---

1. There were a few countries that also grew quickly during segments of the period, such as Argentina from 1990 to 1994.

1

Figure 1. Percent Change in GDP in Selected Latin American and Caribbean Countries, 1980–97

(annual average, constant prices, local currency)

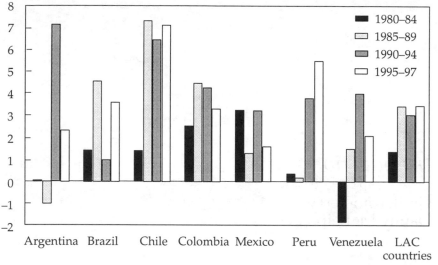

Source: World Bank data.

Figure 2. Percent Change in Consumer Price Index in Selected Latin American and Caribbean Countries, 1980–97

(annual average, December–December)

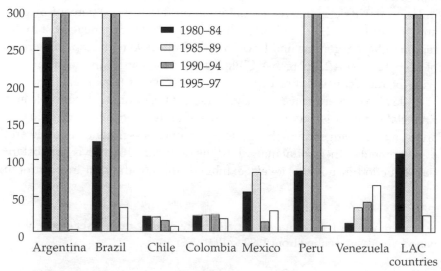

Source: World Bank data.

education and health, and ranked at the top on indicators of the quality of institutions, rule of law and governance.[2] These are no small achievements for a country that was in a deep economic crisis in 1983.

The "Chilean model" has been expostulated for some time in the region and elsewhere because it appeared that the country, despite terrible political and economic turmoil, embodied important lessons about economic management. Arenas often cited include banking crisis management, pension policy innovation, new export market development, privatization, and targeted social policies. More broadly, the dominance of market solutions in the country, its public policy discipline, and social policy advancements have promoted the Chilean case to the forefront of replicable lessons. The sustainability of policies has been just as important as discrete policy actions. For this reason the contributors take a long-term view of Chile's economy in order to draw out lessons of implementation and policy consistency.

This book presents a series of papers analyzing different aspects of Chilean public policy; they cover economic and social policies as well as regulatory and governance issues. The authors were asked to assess the contribution of Chilean policies and structural reforms to favorable outcomes and to discuss the general applicability of their findings. Secondarily, they were asked to examine policy limitations and unresolved issues. What distinguishes this volume of essays, however, is its focus on institutions. The pervasive theme is that Chilean policymakers managed more frequently than not to "get it right," and in so doing they set institutional examples of good public policy. This theme is analyzed explicitly in the final essay by Alejandro Foxley and Claudio Sapelli, and it is perhaps the key lesson of Chilean experience. As noted by Burki and Perry (1998), institutional rather than policy impediments are now Latin America's greatest challenge.

Good Macro Policies or Good Luck?

The first three chapters analyze the contribution of macroeconomic policies to superior outcomes. Chapter 1, by Guillermo Calvo and Enrique Mendoza, notes that favorable copper prices and high capital inflows con-

---

2. Chile ranked lower than expected on only one index, income inequality, although the lowest deciles have improved their position absolutely. In this volume see chapter 6 by Alberto Valdés.

tributed significantly to Chile's economic performance during the 1990s. Both factors helped boost growth and reduce inflation by producing an appreciation of the real exchange rate. Calvo and Mendoza, writing at the end of 1997, consequently point out that the real test for Chilean macroeconomic policies was still to come. The depressed prices for copper in 1998 and the international financial turmoil that followed the East Asian and Russian crises have certainly made macroeconomic management in Chile more difficult and slowed down the rate of growth of the economy, as has happened elsewhere in the region. However, so far, macroeconomic stability has not been threatened in a serious way, nor do we have any reason to believe that the economy will not recover its previous high growth rates in the near future.

Although the essays by Calvo and Mendoza, Roberto Zahler, and Klaus Schmidt-Hebbel emphasize the significant contribution of good policies, there are some discrepancies about the effectiveness of monetary policies and capital controls. Nevertheless, several aspects of economic policy stand out as clear examples of "best practice."

First, Chilean authorities consistently kept a tight fiscal stance, producing consolidated surpluses in most years during the 1985–97 period, a unique accomplishment in LAC (figure 3). Such fiscal surpluses were maintained in spite of the very heavy burden on the budget from the social security reform of 1981 (about 4.5 percent of GDP per year). The combination of social security reform and fiscal tightening contributed significantly to the rapid increase in savings rates, the highest in the region. Fiscal surpluses facilitated the absorption of capital inflows, so consumption booms and overheating were avoided without requiring excessively tight monetary policies. This, in turn, facilitated high sustained growth and limited the appreciation of the currency.

It is true that revenues derived from high copper prices during most of this period contributed greatly to the balance of payments and fiscal results. But it is also true that other countries in the region and elsewhere have systematically overspent whenever they had a boom in commodity and fiscal revenues; consequently, they later were faced with sharp commodity contractions during downturns. To a considerable extent, Chile's positive fiscal outcomes have been the result of sound policies as well as sound fiscal institutions. While fiscal surpluses may have been supported by revenues from high copper prices, it is also clear that institutions like the Copper Stabilization Fund and a very strict expenditure policy made important contributions, as did the tax reforms of 1984 and 1990. In particular, the Copper Stabilization Fund, which requires the saving or accu-

Figure 3. Nonfinancial Public-Sector Balances as a Share of GDP in Selected Latin American and Caribbean Countries, 1980–97

(annual average percentages)

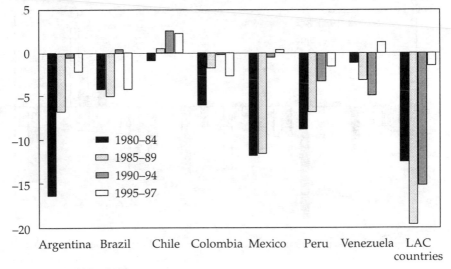

Source: World Bank data.

mulation of revenues derived from prices above a moving average of past prices,[3] helped to overcome the political economy problems that have impeded many developing countries from capturing fiscal surpluses in times of revenue booms. Chile also shows some of the best budgetary institutions in LAC, according to the indexes derived by Alesina and others (1996) and the Inter-American Development Bank (1997), as is stressed in the Foxley-Sapelli chapter.

Second, high and growing capital inflows were common to most LAC countries during the 1990s, so they cannot explain the differences in performance between Chile and the rest of Latin America. As a matter of fact, several countries permitted such inflows to be translated into consumption and credit booms that created both external and financial vulnerabilities. The Mexican peso crisis of late 1994 and the financial crisis suffered by

---

3. The first US$0.04 above the projected price (based on a moving average of past prices) go directly to the state, the following US$0.06 cents are divided between the state and the fund, and anything above that amount goes entirely to the fund.

Figure 4. Current Account Balance as a Share of GDP in Selected
Latin American and Caribbean Countries, 1980–97

(annual average percentages)

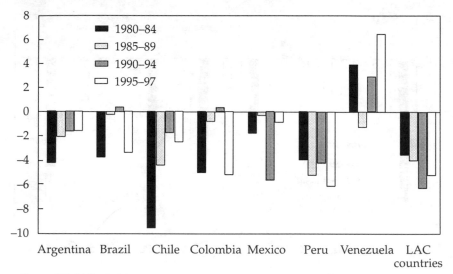

Source: World Bank data.

several countries in the region during 1994–95 were costly reminders of
such facts. Sound macroeconomic, financial, and debt management policies in Chile lowered these risks and led to favorable consequences. The
recent East Asian crisis highlights the dire consequences when high capital
inflows are not accompanied by sound policies and institutions (Leipziger
1998; Furman and Stiglitz 1998; and Perry and Lederman 1998).

Chile learned the lessons of the costly financial and currency crisis of
1982–83, with total fiscal costs estimates ranging from 30 percent to 50 percent of GDP and sharp recessions in 1982 and 1983 contracting output by
15 percent. Since then the authorities have implemented a mix of policies
to avoid prolonged credit and consumption booms, sharp appreciations
and misalignments of exchange rates, excessive current account deficits
(figures 4 and 5), excessive accumulation of short-term debt (external, public or private, or internal), and bank exposures. Tight prudential regulation
and supervision of financial markets accompanied a successful process of
financial deepening and capital market development, enabling the country to borrow at rates close to those of major OECD countries, at least until
the recent contagion in emerging markets.

Figure 5. Twelve-Month Moving Standard Deviation of the Bilateral Real Exchange Index

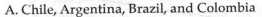

A. Chile, Argentina, Brazil, and Colombia

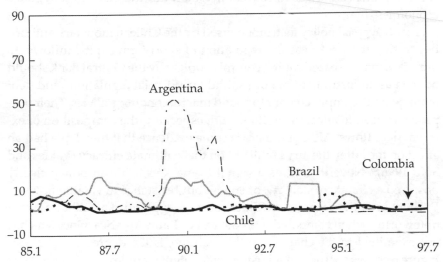

B. Chile, Mexico, Peru, and Venezuela

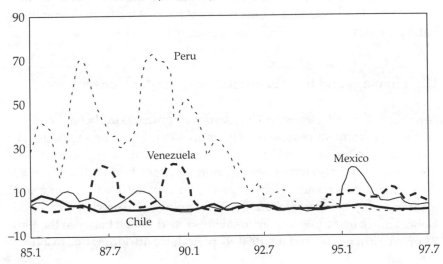

Source: Authors' calculations based on IMF data.

There is also evidence that Chile was probably the only LAC country that maintained an *undervalued* rather than overvalued real exchange rate (RER) for most of this period (Broner, Loayza, and Lopez 1998). Moreover, Chile experienced lower RER volatility than did the rest of the region's economies (figure 5).

A controversial policy instrument used by the Chilean monetary authorities during the 1990s was the regulation of short-term capital inflows. In our view, market-based capital controls applied by the Central Bank should be seen as an instrument of both sound "prudential regulation" and debt management, complementary to sound macroeconomic policies. Their purpose has been to affect the volume and, especially, the composition of external debt flows. Although there is some evidence that they have had an effect on the latter, the jury is still out on their ultimate efficacy (Valdés and Soto 1996).[4] Nevertheless, as a signal to markets, Chilean policy clearly postured a climate of stability, openness but resistance to volatile flows.

There are other aspects of Chile's economic performance that make it noteworthy when compared with the rest of Latin America. One, which is not examined in the chapters in this volume, is the degree of openness. Figure 6 shows a structure-adjusted trade intensity index (Burki and Perry 1997). This index takes into account (or subtracts) the effects of structural factors like population size, the size of a country's territory, the effect of being a developing country, and transportation costs on the trade-to-GDP ratio. Over time Chile has become the most open of the large economies in Latin America.

High Savings and Investment Rates: Cause or Consequence?

Another noteworthy aspect of Chilean development is the behavior of savings and investment rates, shown in figures 7 and 8. Chile's savings rates increased substantially and are well above the rest of the region today, and investment rates also have been growing very fast. Part of this increase in the savings rate is related, of course, to growth, but the quick pace of growth in savings suggests that something else was going on. In his chapter Schmidt-Hebbel notes that Chile's national savings rate doubled between the 1961–74 pre-reform period and the 1990–97 period. He attributes this to a rise in

---

4. On the evidence regarding the composition of external debt flows, see Agosin and French-Davis (1997).

Figure 6. Structure-Adjusted Trade Intensity in Selected Latin American Countries, 1985–95

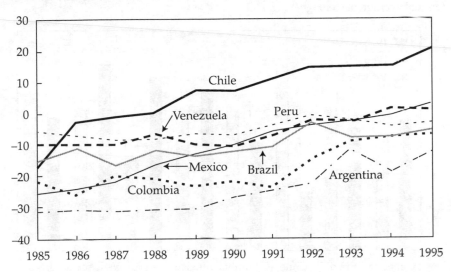

Note: The structure-adjusted trade intensity is the difference between the actual and the "structural" ratio of exports plus imports to GDP. This structural ratio (STI) is the estimated value of a regression that includes the following variables: population, area, FOB/CIF (as a measure of transportation costs), and an industrialized-country dummy. The estimated regression is the following: STI = -7.273*ln(area) -5.212*ln(population) + 2.663*(CIF/FOB)* 100 -14.260*industrialized-country dummy.

Source: Burki and Perry (1997).

nonfinancial public-sector saving (from 4.9 percent to 6.6 percent of GDP), to the emergence of mandatory private pension saving (at an average 3.7 percent of GDP), and especially to the large increase in voluntary private saving (from 7.7 percent to 14.4 percent of GDP). The latter increase is attributed by Schmidt-Hebbel mostly to the tax reforms of the 1980s (3.5 percent of GDP), and then in equal measure to increased growth and to changes in the dependency ratio because of demographic factors (each adding 2 percent of GDP).

Financial Deepening

In figure 9 we present an index of the development of banking sectors in Latin American countries. The index is composed of three indicators: the

Figure 7. Gross National Savings as a Share of GDP in Selected Latin American and Caribbean Countries, 1980–96

(annual average percentages)

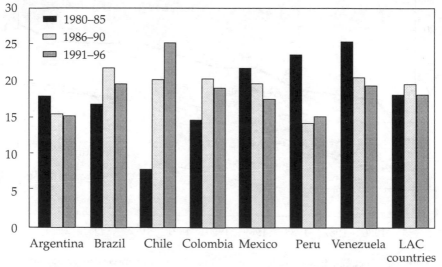

Source: World Bank data.

Figure 8. Gross Domestic Investment as a Share of GDP in Selected Latin American and Caribbean Countries, 1980–96

(annual average percentages)

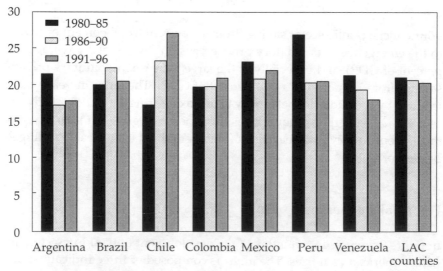

Source: World Bank data.

Figure 9. Banking Development Index for Selected
Latin American Countries, 1985–95

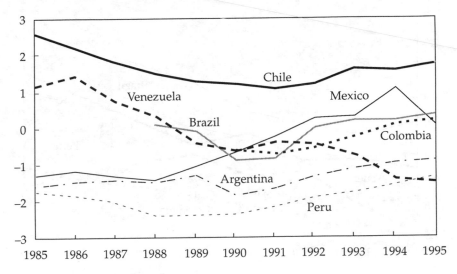

Note: The Banking Development Index includes the following indicators: the ratio of
quasi-liquid liabilities to GDP, the ratio of credit allocated to private sector to GDP, and the
ratio of credit allocated by deposit money banks to GDP. The index is a weighted average
of the principal components of its corresponding indicators, where the weights are given
the share of the indicators' variance explained by each principal component.
Source: Burki and Perry (1997).

ratio of quasi-liquid liabilities to GDP, the ratio of credit allocated to the
private sector to GDP, and the ratio of credit allocated by deposit money
banks to GDP. By these measures, Chile clearly has the most developed
banking sector in the region. Figure 10 shows a similar composite indicator
of stock market development, which includes market capitalization as a
share of GDP, the value traded as a share of GDP, the turnover ratio, market concentration, and an index of capital market regulations. At the end of
the 1980s, Chile's stock market was not the most developed in the region.
Since the early 1990s, however, it has experienced dynamic development,
and today it is probably the most developed in the region for a country of
its size. Even though we do not have an index of the quality of the institutions in the financial sector, we know from different studies that Chile has
a system of financial regulations that is very well regarded.

Nicolas Eyzaguirre and Fernando Lefort's chapter shows that Chile's
credit growth relative to GDP was moderate when compared with Asian
countries with similar macroeconomic performance, a phenomenon that is

Figure 10. Stock Market Development Index for Selected
Latin American Countries, 1988–95

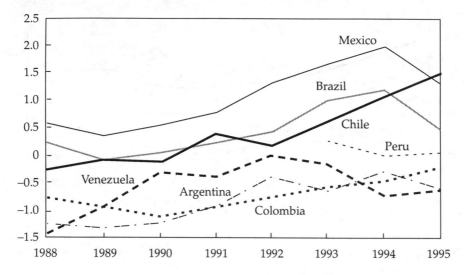

Note: The Stock Market Development Index includes market capitalization as a percentage of GDP, value traded as a percentage of GDP, turnover ratio, market concentration, and an institutional index. The index is a weighted average of the principal components of its corresponding indicators, where the weights are given by the share of the indicators' variance explained by each principal component.
Source: Burki and Perry (1997).

largely explained by the regulatory and supervisory framework established in the 1986 banking law. Moreover, this legislation contributed to the avoidance of financial bubbles after the financial integration of the Chilean economy during the early 1990s. Indeed, the close supervision and tight regulation of the banking system, a conservative monetary policy, and controls on short-term capital inflows kept asset price bubbles in check, albeit perhaps at a cost of 100 to 200 basis points of higher interest costs.[5]

---

5. In 1998 Chile's stock market showed signs of vulnerability. It was one of the most affected in Latin America by spillovers from the recent Asian crisis. During the first five months of 1998, Chile's stock market index fell 10.5 percent, while daily trading in the Santiago stock exchange reached an average of around $8 million, compared with as much as $50 million in 1995.

Social Policy: As Many Challenges as Lessons

In other areas Chile also performed better than other Latin American countries. Table 1 shows education expenditures per pupil (Inter-American Development Bank 1996). What you see is that Chile is the country in the region that at the beginning of the 1990s was spending more per pupil in basic education, especially in primary education, while others were spending much more in tertiary education. Table 2 shows that in terms of the level of educational attainment, Chile is relatively high in the region, but much remains to be done since the region's educational performance is relatively low by international standards. This is clearly an area where much still remains to be done, and today Chile is engaged in substantial reforms of its education system.

In 1990 Chile spent more per capita on health than did Argentina, Brazil, Colombia, Mexico, Peru, or Venezuela (table 3). The table also shows that Chile had the best indexes of access to health and infant mortality.

Chile has actively experimented with new incentive structures in social policy, getting the private sector into education and health, and stimulating competition among different providers. Cristián Cox and María José Lemaitre discuss education reform in their chapter, and Osvaldo Larrañaga covers reform of the health sector. According to them, these early reforms of the 1980s markedly improved coverage and efficiency but did less well in terms of quality.

The health system has evolved as a dual private-public system that will likely become unsustainable. The private part has experienced increasingly high costs and severe problems of adverse selection. At the same time, the

Table 1. Education Expenditures per Pupil by Level of Schooling: Selected Latin American and Caribbean Countries, 1990

(purchasing power parity dollars)

Country	Primary level	Secondary level	Tertiary level
Argentina	421	562	796
Brazil	526	621	5,258
Chile	619	557	1,795
Colombia	297	495	1,782
Costa Rica	438	877	3,166
Peru	163	245	n.a.
Uruguay	480	600	1,680

Source: Inter-American Development Bank (1996).

Table 2. Education Indicators for Selected Latin American and Caribbean Countries, 1992

Country	Mean years of schooling of adults age 25 and over	Primary net enrollment (percent)
Argentina	9.20	95
Brazil	4.00	90
Chile	7.80	86
Colombia	7.50	83
Costa Rica	5.70	87
Peru	6.50	88
Uruguay	8.10	93

Source: Inter-American Development Bank (1996).

public part of the system, which suffers from quality problems, has been left to care for the poor, the very sick, and the elderly. The big challenge, both for efficiency and equity reasons, will be to move from a dual system to an integrated system by using appropriate regulation and incentives.

In education we have witnessed a change from the experiments of the 1980s, which produced wider coverage and improvements in efficiency, to new programs in the 1990s that were specifically geared to improving quality. The latter programs include pilot programs that finance schools with innovative projects and targeted programs in the educational system to reach the very poor. They have been implemented without reversing the

Table 3. Health Indicators for Selected Latin American and Caribbean Countries

Country	Total health expenditures per capita, 1990 (US$)	Access to health, 1993 (percent of population)	Mortality rate of children under five, 1993
Argentina	418	92	27
Brazil	296	72	63
Chile	433	93	17
Colombia	250	75	19
Mexico	335	77	32
Peru	82	44	62
Venezuela	274	76	24

Source: Inter-American Development Bank (1996).

initial reforms, which had decentralized and changed the incentive structure in the educational sector by transferring schools from ministerial to municipal control, channeling public resources to private schools, and linking subsidies to student enrollment (and attendance) in both municipal and private subsidized schools.

Chile's remarkable economic performance has resulted in a significant reduction in poverty, as the chapter by Alberto Valdés shows. However, like in other Latin American countries, the crisis at the beginning of the 1980s worsened poverty rates dramatically, and therefore the situation at the beginning of the 1990s was probably not better than it was at the beginning of the previous decade. Table 4 ranks Latin American countries in terms of moderate poverty rates, as calculated by Londoño and Székely (1997). There are, however, problems with the ranking of poverty indexes and problems of comparability, so these figures should be interpreted with caution.

In terms of equality of income, the results for Chile are definitely not good. Compared with other LAC countries, it has had a high degree of inequality since 1980. Table 5 shows the rankings of those countries in terms of inequality, which is represented by the Gini index. Although it has mildly improved its position relative to the other countries in the sample, Chile has not shown a major improvement in Gini coefficients. (There continues to be some debate within Chile on the data and its international compara-

Table 4. Rankings of (Moderate) Poverty Indexes of LAC Countries, 1980, 1989, and 1990s

1980		1989		1990s	
Country	*Index*	*Country*	*Index*	*Country*	*Index*
Bahamas	3.3	Bahamas	6.8	Bahamas	8.9
Venezuela	11.1	Venezuela	14.3	Venezuela	13.4
Mexico	18.8	Mexico	21.4	Costa Rica	22.1
Chile	23.5	Colombia	23.5	Mexico	22.3
Peru	24.2	Costa Rica	25.3	Chile	23.5
Guatemala	26.0	Jamaica	28.9	Colombia	23.8
Colombia	27.9	Chile	31.3	Jamaica	25.1
Brazil	28.2	Dominican Rep.	35.7	Peru	35.0
Jamaica	29.1	Peru	37.6	Dominican Rep.	39.5
Costa Rica	29.6	Guatemala	45.0	Guatemala	42.5
Dominican Republic	37.3	Brazil	45.4	Brazil	43.5
Panama	40.6	Panama	50.0	Panama	48.4
Honduras	65.5	Honduras	69.2	Honduras	65.6

Source: Londoño and Székely (1997).

Table 5. Rankings of Income Inequality of LAC Countries, 1980, 1989, and 1990s

1980		1989		1990s	
Country	*Index*	*Country*	*Index*	*Country*	*Index*
Dominican Rep.	42.1	Jamaica	43.3	Jamaica	37.9
Bahamas	42.2	Peru	43.7	Peru	44.9
Peru	43.0	Bahamas	44.5	Bahamas	45.0
Venezuela	44.7	Venezuela	46.1	Costa Rica	46.5
Jamaica	45.6	Costa Rica	46.1	Venezuela	47.1
Mexico	47.4	Colombia	48.3	Colombia	48.2
Costa Rica	47.5	Dominican Rep.	50.7	Dominican Rep.	51.6
Panama	47.5	Mexico	53.7	Mexico	54.2
Colombia	48.8	Panama	56.8	Chile	56.5
Guatemala	49.7	Chile	59.0	Honduras	56.9
Chile	53.1	Guatemala	59.9	Panama	57.4
Brazil	57.1	Honduras	59.9	Guatemala	59.9
Honduras	61.1	Brazil	60.7	Brazil	61.4

Source: Londoño and Székely (1997).

bility.) The high inequality levels are still related to educational differences. One of the main challenges facing Chile, both from the point of view of economic results and social and political stability, is how to tackle efficiently this issue of inequality.

Regulatory Policy: The Costs of Being First

Chile is known as a pioneer in regulatory reforms. It was the first country in the region to undertake a massive privatization of public utilities and the first to implement new regulatory systems and create autonomous regulatory agencies. The chapter by Eduardo Bitrán, Antonio Estache, José Luis Guasch, and Pablo Serra shows that privatization paid off handsomely in terms of increased coverage, investment, and efficiency. But it did not necessarily yield great benefit in terms of lower prices for some of these services. A substantial part of the benefits from increased efficiency was not passed on to the consumers. This result is related to high levels of concentration and vertical integration in these sectors—in the end, to insufficient competition.

Some countries, like Argentina and Peru, that have followed Chile's footsteps in privatizing utilities have benefited from this experience and have been very careful to promote competition in these sectors, in order to ensure not only the benefits of increased coverage and investment efficiency, but also lower prices for consumers. In the future, regulatory policymakers in Chile need to reduce abnormal profits associated with regulated rather than competitive service sectors, as well as disincentives to increased concentration. What is revealed is that Chile has not been immune to the normal behavior of interest groups and regulatory capture that characterizes the experiences of other countries.

Public Sector Efficiency, Consensus Building, and Good Governance

The chapter by Mario Marcel presents further evidence on the effectiveness of Chile's public sector. In particular, the essay shows that the Chilean "state" has successfully contributed to the country's international competitiveness. It has efficiently mobilized relatively large amounts of resources (equivalent to 23 percent of GDP) with a relatively small work force (less than 6 percent of the country's economically active population). Important challenges, however, remain. The Chilean experience of the past 25 years suggests that there is no systematic relationship between the reduction of "state" participation in some areas and its strengthening in others. For example, the effectiveness of the privatization process was lessened by the insufficient autonomy and inadequate resources of the regulatory agencies. As shown by Marcel, the democratic administrations of the 1990s tried to match the capabilities and resources of the state to its new functions in a context of deregulation and privatization. This, however, is an ever-expanding task. The development process itself perpetually creates new demands and challenges for the state, especially in a democratic and open economy such as Chile's.

Following its actions to reduce the absolute size of the state via privatization, Chile undertook limited decentralization, first through regionalization and then by empowering municipalities. These basic principles have dominated its public policy since 1980: pressures to limit the size of the bureaucracy, full disclosure of public sector liabilities, and strict public financial management. These principles were accompanied by strong budgetary institutions that limited congressional expenditure powers, allowed the Minister of Finance to wield unusual discretion, provided for structured fiscal contingency financing, and maintained a strong and independent Comptroller General to oversee financial management matters.

Figure 11. International Country-Risk Guide Index

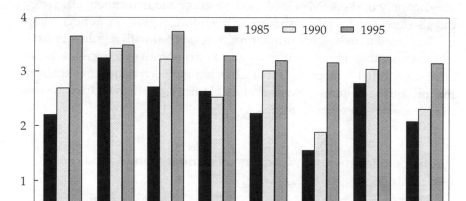

Note: The International Country Risk Guide Index includes indicators on rule of law, repudiation of contracts by government, expropriation risk, quality of the bureaucracy, and corruption in government. The higher the score, the better the governance of the country.
Source: International Country Risk Guide (ICRG).

Chile's experience demonstrates the virtues of strong fiscal controls and depoliticization of public policy.

In a concluding essay Foxley and Sapelli point out the process by which political consensus during the transition to democracy led to a constellation of policies that appears to have served the country well since 1990. Beginning with the establishment of credible key institutions, such as the autonomous Central Bank, and innovative "win-win" policies, such as pension reform, the government was able to lay public policy foundations. Economic management, as well as overall policymaking, have been aided by the coalition that formally linked major parties into the "concertación." Combining a strong executive branch with effective public institutions (such as the Central Bank, tax authority, and Comptroller General) under a broad consensus of what economic and social policy should provide has proven successful. Since no public policy model is static, further reforms are needed to maintain Chile's record and enable it to respond effectively to public demands.

Figure 12. Business Environment Risk Intelligence Index

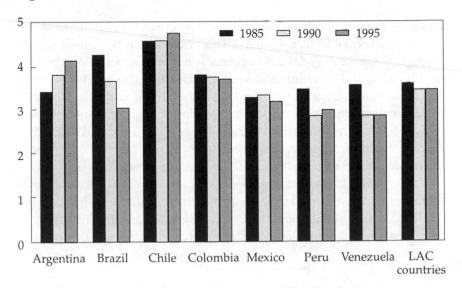

Note: The Business Environment Risk Intelligence Index includes indicators on bureaucratic delays, contract enforceability, and nationalization risk. The higher the score, the better the governance of the country.
Source: Business Environment Risk Intelligence (BERI).

The result of Chile's institutional and governance stance is the favorable perception of its business environment by private domestic and international investors and country-risk analysts. Figure 11 shows the evolution since 1985 of a composite institutional index that synthesizes several indexes published by the International Country Risk Guide (ICRG), and figure 12 shows another composite index based on information published by Business Environment Risk Intelligence (BERI). These two private agencies provide independent country-risk evaluations that assess the quality of public institutions and services as they are perceived by businesspeople and others who deal with various government branches on a daily basis. The ICRG provides ratings on five variables: *rule of law, expropriation risk, repudiation of contracts by government, corruption in government,* and *quality of the bureaucracy.* Similarly, the BERI index is based on three underlying variables: *enforceability of contracts, nationalization risk,* and *bureaucratic delays.* Both indexes show that investors consider Chile to have the least risky business environment of the large Latin American countries.

Conclusion

This book highlights the critical role played by institutions in the outstanding performance of Chile's economy. This is a critical lesson, since achieving high growth and social development is not only a matter of economic reform and sound economic and social policies, but also a result of sound and efficient institutions. A society's formal and informal rules and their enforcement mechanisms shape the behavior of organizations and individuals. Indeed, institutions are absolutely essential (Burki and Perry 1998, chap. 1). Sound institutions, however, take time to construct. Prolonged efforts are needed to achieve the full benefits of a predictable and credible economic policy. In particular, it takes time for institutional innovations to take place and mature and to create and maintain a good "policy culture" and good "policy environment." During the transition in Chile from an authoritative regime to democracy, coalition building was a difficult and painful process, but it led to policies and institutions with wide public support.

Several of the well-documented successes of the Chilean economy can be traced to sound and innovative institutions and organizations, often built upon previous experience. Examples are the decentralization process in the delivery of public services, the establishment of the Copper Stabilization Fund, the norms governing the autonomy of the Central Bank, and the budgetary institutions. Similarly, many of Chile's development challenges (such as reduction of income inequality, improvement of the health, education, and pension systems, and better regulation of the privatized public utilities sectors) are, in fact, institutional challenges that will require a great deal of technical and political creativity from Chilean policymakers and civil society.

What has distinguished Chile in recent years has been its consensus-reaching ability as symbolized by its formalized political coalition. The allocation of ministerial and subministerial posts, for example, has made unified policymaking possible. As Chile grapples with its poverty pockets, the balance between social safety nets and the need for greater efficiency in labor markets, a rebalancing of regulatory powers, and other thorny issues, it will need to rely on its institutional experience in public policy and conflict resolution. This, more than anything else, epitomizes the Chilean model.

References

Agosin, M. R., and R. Ffrench-Davis. 1997. "Managing Capital Inflows in Chile."
    Estudios de Economía 24: 2 (December).

Alesina, A., and others. 1996. "Budget Institutions and Fiscal Performance in Latin America." National Bureau of Economic Research Working Paper 5586, Cambridge, Mass.

Broner, F., N. Loayza, and H. Lopez. 1998. "Misalignment and Fundamentals: Equilibrium Real Exchange Rates in Seven Latin American Countries." World Bank, Washington, D.C.

Burki, S. Javed, and Guillermo Perry. 1997. *The Long March: A Reform Agenda for Latin America and the Caribbean in the Next Decade.* World Bank Latin American and Caribbean Studies. Washington, D.C.: The World Bank.

————.1998. *Beyond the Washington Consensus: Institutions Matter.* Latin American and Caribbean Studies. Washington, D.C.: The World Bank.

Furman, Jason, and Joseph E. Stiglitz. 1998. "Economic Crises: Evidence and Insights from East Asia." *Brookings Papers on Economic Activity* 2: 1–136.

Gavin, M., and others. 1996. "Managing Fiscal Policy in Latin America and the Caribbean: Volatility, Procyclicality, and Limited Creditworthiness." Working Paper 326. Inter-American Development Bank, Office of the Chief Economist, Washington, D.C.

Gavin, M., and R. Perotti. 1997. "Fiscal Policy in Latin America." In J. Rotemberg and B. Bernanke, eds., *Macroeconomics Annual.* Cambridge, Mass.: MIT Press.

Inter-American Development Bank. 1996. *Economic and Social Progress in Latin America, 1996 Report.* Washington, D.C.

————. 1997. *Latin America after a Decade of Reforms.* Washington D.C.: Johns Hopkins University Press.

Leipziger, Danny. 1998. "Public and Private Interests in Korea: Views on Moral Hazard and Crisis Resolution." Economic Development Institute Working Paper (Stock No. 37138). Washington, D.C.

Londoño, Juan Luis, and Miguel Székely. 1997. "Persistent Poverty and Excess Inequality: Latin America, 1970–1995." Working Paper 357. Inter-American Development Bank, Office of the Chief Economist, Washington, D.C.

Perry, Guillermo, and Daniel Lederman. 1998. *Financial Vulnerability, Spillover Effects, and Contagion: Lessons from the Asian Crises for Latin America.* World Bank Latin American and Caribbean Studies. Washington, D.C.: The World Bank.

Talvi, E., and C. A. Vegh. 1996. "Can Optimal Fiscal Policy be Procyclical?" Inter-American Development Bank, Washington, D.C.

Valdés, S., and M. Soto. 1996. "¿Es el Control Selectivo de Capitales Efectivo en Chile? Su Efecto sobre el Tipo de Cambio Real." *Cuadernos de Economia* 33 (April).

Part I

Economic Management

1

Empirical Puzzles of Chilean Stabilization Policy

Guillermo A. Calvo
Enrique G. Mendoza

> Central bankers and even some monetary economists talk knowledge-
> ably of using high interest rates to control inflation, but I know of no
> evidence from even one economy linking these variables in a useful
> way. . . .
>
> <div align="right">Robert E. Lucas, Jr.
Nobel Lecture: "Monetary Neutrality,"
<i>Journal of Political Economy</i> (August 1996): 666</div>

The performance of the Chilean economy during the 1990s was impressive. After recovering from the severe recession that followed the financial
crash of 1982, Chile sustained high economic growth in an environment of
controlled public and current account balances, tight fiscal and monetary

We thank Alejandro Izquierdo for valuable research assistance, and Sebastian
Edwards, Jose De Gregorio, Saul Lizondo, Roberto Zahler, Andres Velasco, and
other participants in the conference "Chile: Development Lessons and Challenges"
for their helpful comments.

policies, low and declining inflation, high saving rates, and low unemployment. During this period Chile also continued with its pioneering program of economic reform by building on the far-reaching reforms introduced in the previous two decades.[1] Thus, in sharp contrast to the ongoing struggle of other Latin American nations to stabilize their economies and escape recession, Chile seems to have attained what has proved elusive for most countries in the region: sustainable high growth.

In light of this impressive performance, there is growing interest in studying Chile's experience, with the aim of identifying the driving forces behind the strength of the Chilean economy and determining whether Chile's main accomplishments can be reproduced in other countries. There has been a natural tendency to attribute the Chilean success to the country's macroeconomic policies (Dornbusch, Goldjfan, and Valdes 1995 and Williamson 1997), but at the same time there has been a tendency to oversimplify the issue and make the argument that the economic problems of other developing countries can be solved simply by adopting Chile's policies. While the merits of Chile's sound policies should not be undervalued, there is little formal empirical evidence linking Chile's stabilization policy framework to the gradual deceleration of inflation. Little also is known about the extent to which the cyclical performance of the economy was influenced by important exogenous developments—particularly the large and persistent increase in the world price of copper and the surge in private international capital inflows. Without a clear understanding of the role of policy vis-à-vis exogenous factors in explaining Chile's economic performance, it is difficult to establish whether the dynamics exhibited by the Chilean economy were the outcome of a policy-led process of smooth convergence to sustainable growth or of the stages of an endogenous process triggered by exogenous shocks.

In this chapter we argue that (a) there is an important flaw in the conventional wisdom that views the management of indexed interest rates by the Central Bank of Chile as a means of conducting monetary policy by directly managing real interest rates, (b) factors other than stabilization policies have played an important role in Chilean economic performance, and (c) the dynamics exhibited by key macroeconomic aggregates can be interpreted in part as an endogenous process of adjustment triggered by exogenous shocks. In making this case, we document statistical analysis and

---

1. Corbo, Ludders, and Spiller (1996) provide a detailed review of Chilean stabilization and structural reform policies since the 1970s.

explore briefly some complex analytical issues that may help broaden our understanding of the Chilean experience.

We conduct our analysis in the light of a statistical framework that aims to integrate key elements of policy management, the external environment, and the endogenous dynamics of macroeconomic variables. This framework is an application of the identified Vector Autoregression (VAR) econometric technique introduced for the analysis of U.S. monetary policy by Sims (1992). In particular, we adopt a variant of this technique recently developed by Christiano, Eichembaum, and Evans (1998): the recursive identification approach. This approach proposes a straightforward method to isolate the effects of exogenous policy shocks on macroeconomic dynamics from the endogenous response of policy instruments to systematic changes in the economic environment. We view the characterization of the observed dynamics of the Chilean economy produced by this analysis as the set of empirical regularities that a macroeconomic model should aim to explain, and we provide some rough guidelines discussing the minimal elements of such a model. In particular, we argue that some features of the Chilean experience could be consistent with a model of forward-looking, staggered-price setting under conditions of widespread (but imperfect) indexation, although the formal development and testing of this model are beyond the scope of this chapter.[2]

The chapter is organized as follows. The next section reviews the most salient features of Chilean stabilization policy in the 1990s. We then discuss basic flaws in the conventional interpretation of the Chilean policy framework and develop the statistical model that helps us interpret the role of policy variables vis-à-vis exogenous factors in explaining Chile's macroeconomic performance. We conclude by drawing some policy lessons.

Chilean Stabilization Policy and External Factors, 1990–97

The general strategy of stabilization policy implemented in Chile in recent years was consistent with long-run objectives developed in the aftermath of the 1982 crash. In particular, the primary goals at the center of the Chil-

---

2. Note also that the need to keep the study focused on stabilization policy in the 1990s forced us to set aside several key aspects of the Chilean experience—such as the strategy for resolution of the 1982–83 banking collapse and the privatization of the pension system.

ean strategy were (a) to attain a high and sustainable GDP growth rate with a gradual decline in inflation, while ensuring that (b) the fiscal and current account deficits were kept under control, and (c) the international competitiveness of the economy was preserved. The actual policies implemented to achieve these goals, the priority assigned to each one, and their quantitative interpretation have varied over time, depending on the performance of the economy and changes in the world environment and in the views and preferences of policymakers. For example, between 1985 and 1989 inflation was contained but did not decline significantly (it oscillated around 20 percent), and after that it declined gradually. The current account as a share of GDP averaged 4.5 percent in 1985–89, while in 1990–96 it averaged 2 percent of GDP. The real exchange rate *depreciated* in 1985–89 by about the same amount that it *appreciated* between 1990 and 1996 (about 4.7 percent).

Monetary and Exchange Rate Policies

Monetary and exchange rate policies were the key instruments used to make progress in the gradual deceleration of inflation, and in maintaining the real value of the Chilean peso within limits regarded as consistent with Chile's external competitiveness. The preferred instrument of monetary policy was the management of short-term interest rates imperfectly indexed to the monthly change in the CPI through daily adjustments in an artificial unit of account known as the Unidad de Fomento (UF). The mechanism for managing interest rates changed over the years. In the late 1980s the aim was to influence short-term interest rates so as to produce desired targets of monetary aggregates. In the early 1990s there was a switch to a system of direct sales of 90-day bills that constituted liabilities of the central bank (and hence should not be given the same interpretation of a conventional open market operation, in which liabilities from the central government are bought or sold by the central bank in a secondary market). In 1996 and 1997 there was a switch to a regime of inflation targeting: the aim was to manage monetary policy by influencing overnight interbank interest rates to conform with preannounced annual inflation targets.

The central bank built a strong reputation and gained credibility by pursuing active monetary tightening to fight inflationary pressures and cool down the economy when clear signs of overheating emerged. One episode of this tightening is particularly notable: the so-called Sobreajuste (overadjustment) of 1990. Indexed interest rates were increased by an unprecedented magnitude, from about 8 percent to 16 percent. The real economy reacted to the change in policy, but inflation was very slow to respond. In fact, for several months inflation increased instead of falling. This is particularly notable because in Chile any small surge in inflation is rapidly magnified by the extremely high degree of indexation of the economy. All prices of durables are regularly quoted in UF and even some services, like school fees, are also quoted in UF. This period is suggestive of Chile's recent experience: monetary policy has not been very effective in influencing the price level, and a key determinant of the decline in inflation has been the appreciation of the real exchange rate.

Exchange rate policy was set with the general aim of maintaining the peso within a band that allows fluctuations around an indexed midpoint rate. Until 1998 the band was set to allow depreciations or appreciations of up to 12.5 percent before triggering central bank intervention. The midpoint rate was indexed to the productivity-adjusted monthly differential between Chile's CPI inflation and the CPI inflation of Chile's largest trading partners (through daily adjustments as in the case of the UF). The productivity adjustment was set to favor Chile at a rate of 2 percent annually. Intervention within the band generally was avoided, except at times when severe pressure for appreciation of the exchange rate built up as a result of short-term capital inflows.

It is important to note that the Chilean authorities managed both monetary and exchange rate policies within a flexible setting that allowed them to adjust these policies as necessary in view of new, relevant information and that envisaged a role for supplementary policies. For instance, monetary policy included close monitoring of the evolution of narrow monetary aggregates by comparing them to predictions of money-demand models. Monetary policy was supported by a very efficient and strict system of commercial bank supervision. Similarly, exchange rate policy adjusted to allow for widening of the band and step adjustments of the midpoint rate when too much pressure built up in the currency as a result of the surge in capital inflows. Exchange rate policy was complemented by policies aimed at weakening inflows of short-term capital by introducing and tightening taxes and timing restrictions on these inflows. The management of the two policies also reflected the central bank's assessment of the stance of fiscal policy, which was generally kept secret by the fiscal authorities. In this context, assessing the response of the economy to unexpected, exogenous shocks to the central bank's reaction function was particularly important.

The basic indicators that reflect monetary and exchange rate policies are illustrated in figure 1-1. This figure plots the 12-month inflation rate, the

Figure 1-1. Chile: Inflation, Interest Rate, and Real Exchange Rate, 1987–97

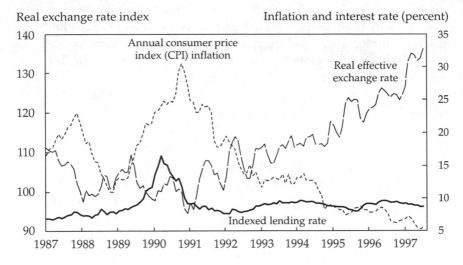

Source: Authors' calculations with data from the Central Bank of Chile.

90-day-rate interest rate in indexed bank loans, and the real effective exchange rate index. The real effective exchange rate index is the IMF's measure, according to which a real appreciation is an increase in the index.

Fiscal Policy

Chile's primary fiscal objective was to keep a small surplus in the trend level of the overall fiscal accounts, net of cyclical fluctuations—particularly those driven by the fluctuations in the world price of copper, which still have an important direct effect on total government revenue and total export revenue. A key instrument in the attainment of this goal was the Copper Stabilization Fund, which is designed to save a fraction of the windfall gains expected from temporarily high copper prices. Just as important was the government's strong commitment to the rules of this fund. The government abstained from engaging in a fiscal expansion fueled by temporarily higher export receipts.

Nevertheless, significant fiscal distortions remain in Chile. First, standard measures of the public deficit are misleading. To date, the central bank still suffers significant losses as a result of the low-yield assets it acquired as part of the process of rescuing the banking system in the mid-1980s, and to some extent also on account of partial sterilization of large capital inflows in the 1990s. Details on the amount of these losses are not publicly available, but it is estimated that they have ranged between 3/4 and 1 percentage point of GDP annually throughout the 1990s. Second, the Ministry of Defense still collects directly 1/10 of the revenue of the government's copper company, and there is virtually no accountability on the use of these resources. Third, the government still plays a major role in the banking system as owner of the Banco del Estado, one of the country's largest financial institutions.

The External Environment: Copper Prices and Capital Inflows

Two major developments characterize changes in Chile's external environment during the 1990–97 period: the large and sustained increase in copper prices and the surge in private capital inflows. To appreciate better the impact of high copper prices on Chilean production, we focus on Chile's core terms of trade. Because Chile relies heavily on oil imports, we compare the relative price of copper to oil in world commodity markets.

The top panel of figure 1-2 plots the actual and trend levels of the core terms of trade during the period 1986–97 at a monthly frequency—both copper and oil prices are taken from *International Financial Statistics*. This figure shows that Chile's successful efforts at stabilizing the economy and attaining high growth in the 1990s coincided with a large and persistent increase in the relative price of Chile's most important exportable commodity relative to its most critical imported input. The bottom panel of figure 1-2 suggests that this large and persistent rise in Chile's terms of trade is closely related to the country's strong economic performance. It plots the 12-month rate of change in the seasonally adjusted monthly indicator of economic activity (IMACEC) and the 12-month change in the core terms of trade (the latter plotted with a 6-month lag). Granger causality tests show that the hypothesis that 6 lags of the terms of trade help predict the current IMACEC cannot be rejected at the 5 percent significance level, without any evidence of reversed causality. Moreover, variance decomposition analysis shows that after two years about 1/4 of the variability in the growth of IMACEC is attributable to the core terms of trade.

In addition to the direct evidence from the Chilean case, cross-country studies of growth and business cycles in developing economies provide further evidence of the key role that terms-of-trade shocks can play both for short-run fluctuations in output and expenditures and in long-run

Figure 1-2. Chile's Economic Activity and Core Terms of Trade, 1986–97

Index

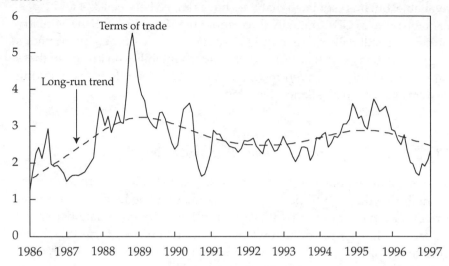

Percent

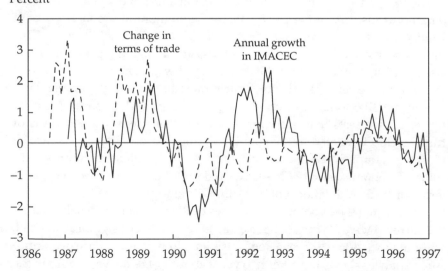

Note: The terms of trade are measured as the price of copper in terms of oil in world markets. IMACEC is the seasonally adjusted monthly indicator of economic activity. The change in terms of trade is a 12-month growth rate and is plotted with a 6-month lag.

Source: Authors' calculations with data from the International Monetary Fund's *International Financial Statistics* and the Central Bank of Chile.

growth and saving rates (Mendoza 1995, 1997). In particular, Mendoza (1997) argues that the high volatility of commodity prices can result in high saving and growth rates driven by precautionary saving, in which case the benefits of faster growth can be much less than under normal circumstances. Easterly, Pritchett, and Summers (1993) also document the key role that the terms of trade play in influencing long-run growth. They find that economic policies, educational attainment, and political stability contribute little to the observed lack of persistence in growth performance, while terms-of-trade changes are highly correlated with growth changes.[3] Barro and Sala-i-Martin (1995) do find that country characteristics contribute to growth differentials, but the terms of trade play a key role. Their panel regressions show that the growth effects of terms of trade compare with those of educational attainment, public spending on education, human capital, and political instability.

The second key development in Chile's external environment was the surge in capital inflows. This phenomenon has been documented widely for a large group of emerging economies (Calvo, Leiderman, and Reinhart 1993; Corbo, Ludders, and Spiller 1996; and Williamson 1997). There is some debate as to whether these inflows were caused by world phenomena or by the domestic investment climate favored by Chile's stability and structural reforms. However, as Calvo, Leiderman, and Reinhart (1993) have documented, there is strong statistical evidence that a large fraction of the surge of private capital inflows into emerging economies can be attributed to a temporary decline in industrial-country interest rates.

Stabilization Policy and Monetary Transmission

In this section we explore the transmission mechanism of Chilean stabilization policy. We begin with a discussion of financial indexation under Chile's UF system that identifies a key flaw in the conventional wisdom on Chilean monetary policy: interest rates quoted as premia over the UF monetary correction factor *do not* correspond to the real interest rate of the economy. With a clear understanding that the presumed instrument of monetary policy *is not* the real interest rate—the macroeconomic effects of which

---

3. Pooled regressions in Easterly, Pritchett, and Summers (1993) show that if the terms-of-trade gain as a share of GDP rises by 1 percent per annum, annual growth rises by 0.42 percent in the 1970s and by 0.85 percent in the 1980s.

should be easily predictable—we assess the connection between the Chilean policy setting described earlier and the performance of the Chilean economy. Like other authors before us, we failed to identify a systematic connection between monetary tightening via increases in UF interest rates and the observed deceleration of inflation, even though the real economy does respond to changes in UF rates. If the monetary policy framework is interpreted instead as being influenced by the evolution of the exchange rate, there is some evidence of a systematic, dynamic connection between the appreciation of real and nominal exchange rates and the fall in inflation. The latter is true in both a conventional unrestricted Vector Autoregression and in the case of policy shocks to a recursively identified VAR with a hypothetical policy reaction function for the exchange rate. The statistical analysis begins with a short discussion of technical issues related to identified VAR estimation.

Chile's Management of Indexed Interest Rates

As noted earlier, monetary policy in Chile has been conducted throughout the 1990s by influencing the interest rates on indexed financial instruments—the UF rates. Policy is set to influence most directly an anchor short-term rate (the rate on 90-day promissory notes of the central bank until 1995 and from then on the overnight interbank interest rate). Once this key rate is set, the term structure of interest rates on government obligations is market determined in auctions of longer term paper.[4] Through these operations the Bank influences the level of indexed lending and deposit rates at various maturities in the financial system. The value of the anchor interest rate is set to a target estimated to be consistent with objectives for growth and inflation, including since 1995 a publicly announced inflation target, and monetary aggregates are allowed to adjust accordingly. Consequently, the growth of narrow money has been highly variable over time, as documented below.

The Unidad de Fomento is a unit of account that represents an exchange rate between Chilean pesos and an index number linked to CPI inflation with a delay of roughly one month.[5] Interest on indexed contracts is charged with respect to balances denominated in UF. Because the UF is linked to

---

4. More recently, the Central Bank has aimed to gradually shift the main instrument of policy to nonindexed instruments.

5. For details on the operation of indexed contracts in Chile and implications for market efficiency between short-run indexed and nonindexed assets, see Mendoza (1992).

inflation, the UF interest rate is often viewed as identical to the real interest rate. However, we follow Mendoza (1992) to suggest that this view may be incorrect.

The UF begins to be adjusted in the 10th day of month t by a proportional amount each day, so that by the 9th day of month $t + 1$ it has increased in value by as much as the CPI did in month $t - 1$. The imperfection of this backward indexation rule is reflected in the fact that the interest rate as quoted in UF and the standard measure of ex post real interest rates are not equivalent, as they would be under perfect indexation (the changes in the UF and in the CPI would be exactly identical each month). More precisely, there is a differential between UF interest rates and ex post real interest rates determined by the ratio of the growth observed in both the UF and the CPI between the date a UF-indexed contract is signed and the date it matures. Note that this differential is thus approximately equal to the difference between inflation in the month before a loan is contracted and inflation in the last month of the contract. The differential between ex post real interest rates and UF interest rates at the three-month frequency relevant for monetary policy is illustrated in figure 1-3. As the figure shows,

Figure 1-3. Differential between UF Interest Rates and Inflation in Chile, 1986–97

Percent

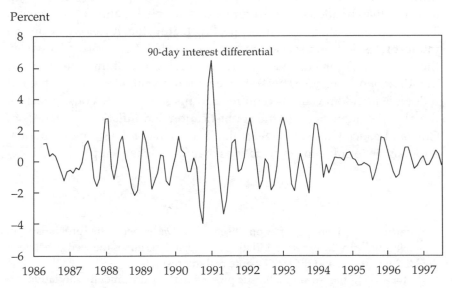

Note: Quarterly differential between interest rates quoted in UF and ex-post real interest rates computed as Ln[(UF + 3/UFt)*(CPIt/CPIt + 3)].

Source: Authors' calculations with data from the Central Bank of Chile.

imperfect indexation left a significant wedge between ex post real interest rates and UF interest rates, particularly when annual inflation rose or fell, or when monthly inflation fluctuated significantly. In August 1990, for instance, a 90-day indexed loan charged a quarterly UF rate of about 3 percent, but the ex post rate was near 9 percent.

In principle, one could expect that at longer maturities the imperfection of the indexation mechanism could play a smaller role, reflecting a tendency for the wedge between inflation and UF growth to be smaller. Although the variability of the indexation error is smaller at 12 than at 3 months (the standard deviation of the former is 1.69 compared with 1.75 for the latter), the error does not always fluctuate less with the lengthening of maturity. In fact, the error over 1 month has a smaller standard deviation (0.97) than either the 3- or 12-month errors. The 3-month maturity, which is the one relevant for the instrumental rate of monetary policy, displays the largest deviations, on average, from perfect indexation.

These comparisons between UF and ex post rates may also be questionable because the relevant real interest rates are ex ante rates, which incorporate expectations of inflation. The key expectation agents formulate when assessing 90-day loans in January of any year, for example, is a forecast of inflation in April given what is known in January.[6] Thus, ex ante real interest rates require a three-step-ahead forecast of inflation conditional on information available at t. One simple model of these expectations of inflation assumes that inflation expected for $t + 3$ is simply inflation observed at t. This static rule of thumb has the appealing feature that it yields ex ante real interest rates that correspond, on average, to UF interest rates.[7] However, there are two arguments that question the relevance of this rule. First, as Mendoza and Fernandez (1994) showed, monthly inflation in Chile has not followed a random walk, as required for this static rule to constitute a rational expectation. Second, the sophistication and inflation awareness of Chilean financial markets suggest that agents may follow a more rational approach in formulating expectations of inflation than simply expecting it

---

6. Particularly given the inflation observed in December of the previous year, which jointly with the expected inflation for April determines the wedge between the UF interest rate and the true ex ante real interest rate.

7. Moreover, if the true probabilistic process that governs monthly inflation is a random walk, the difference between the two rates follows a moving average with two lags.

to remain unchanged.[8] This view is also supported by results of tests of market efficiency and rational expectations applied to interest differentials between indexed and nonindexed deposits (Mendoza 1992).

Since one can view the ex post real interest rate as the ex ante rate of a perfect-foresight economy, and the UF rate as the ex ante rate of a naive economy with static expectations, it is perhaps more realistic to study an ex ante real interest rate based on rational expectations as a middle ground between those two extremes. In this case the expected value for inflation at date $t + 1$, conditional on information available at t, must be such that the forecasting error is zero on average and randomly distributed over time. For expectations of inflation at $t + 2$ or later, conditional on information available at t, the forecasting error of a rational expectation is still zero on average, but it may be autocorrelated over time reflecting unknown information emerging between t and the date for which the rational forecast applies. This is important because, as noted, the ex ante real interest rate at t of a 90-day indexed asset includes expected inflation for $t + 3$. Thus, in order to construct ex ante real interest rates based on rational expectations, one needs to examine the statistical process that governs monthly inflation and then use this process to compute three-step-ahead forecasts.

Mendoza and Fernandez (1994) constructed estimates of rational expectations of inflation for Chile using conventional Box-Jenkins techniques of time-series analysis. They found that monthly inflation follows a fourth-order autoregressive process, with seasonal dummies and two dummies to capture inflationary surges of September and October 1990, so as to prevent those surges from biasing end-of-sample forecasts. Inflation projections from this model were used to construct a time series of the ex ante real interest rate on 90-day to 365-day loans. The ex ante rate follows a path similar to that of the ex post rate, with the difference between the two being zero on average but displaying some time-dependence due to the nature of the three-step-ahead forecast error. Since ex ante and ex post rates differ only by a moving average error, it follows from figure 1-3 that the ex ante rate differs significantly from UF rates on a monthly basis. The UF rate is at best a rough approximation of the *averages* of ex ante and ex post rates. The approximation is not close because inflation is not a random walk.

---

8. The close attention paid to recurrent "signals" of monthly inflation sent by the central bank when agents compare interest rates for the bank's indexed and nonindexed documents is a clear example of this awareness.

Because of imperfections embodied in the UF indexation mechanism, monetary policy implemented by influencing UF interest rates cannot be interpreted as influencing the real interest rate, either in ex post or ex ante terms. By targeting UF interest rates, the monetary authority is likely to influence real interest rates depending on how actual or expected inflation reacts to UF interest rate targets. This is not substantially different from what occurs in the usual environment of nominal interest rates; in fact, as we show below in a basic theoretical model with staggered prices, price dynamics in the face of fully anticipated policy changes are exactly the same under UF indexation as under no indexation. Moreover, given the evidence on the variability of the differential between UF interest rates and ex post real interest rates, one can infer that the monetary authority may introduce unpredictable noise in real interest rates when inducing unanticipated changes in UF interest rates.

Identified VAR Estimation of a Chilean Model of Monetary Policy

We summarize the discussion of the recursive identification approach to Identified VAR policy models following Christiano, Eichembaum, and Evans (1997). The basic assumption of this analysis is that the policy instrument is governed by the following reaction function:

$$r_t = f(\Omega_t) + \sigma \varepsilon_t. \tag{1}$$

This specification of the reaction function embodies the following assumptions: Ω_t is the information set containing the variables known by the authorities when choosing the value of r_t, f is a linear function that describes the systematic reaction of the central bank to changes in the economic environment as reflected in indicators included in the information set, and ε_t is a unit-variance exogenous policy shock. In this approach, f is a function that embodies the central bank's strategy to conduct stabilization policy, including issues about priorities of various policy goals and preferences regarding inflation rates, exchange rates, and other variables. In contrast, the shock ε_t captures any nonsystematic factors that could affect policy decisions (political factors, subjective views of policymakers, changes in central bank staff, assessments of the unknown stance of fiscal policy, measurement error in the policy instrument, and any other unexpected exogenous shocks).

The recursive identification strategy differs from other identification approaches, such as those advocated by Sims and Zha (1995), in that it follows a straightforward method to isolate exogenous innovations to the policy reaction function. Recursive identification assumes that Ω_t includes lagged values of the relevant variables, as in an unrestricted VAR, plus certain contemporaneous variables. The contemporaneous variables in Ω_t include any variable that *does not* respond contemporaneously to the policy shock, while variables that do not enter contemporaneously in Ω_t are those that do respond at date t to date-t policy shocks. As a result, policy shocks are by construction orthogonal to the other right-hand-side variables in the policy reaction function and hence can be recovered directly as the residual from an OLS regression.[9] Thus, conditional on the specification of the policy reaction function, the dynamic response of any variable to a policy shock is measured by the regression coefficients of that variable on current and lagged values of ε_t. This is asymptotically equivalent to computing the impulse response function of a variable to an innovation in ε using a VAR model in which the policy reaction function enters "identified" by the right-hand-side contemporaneous variables.

Two observations are important regarding recursively identified VAR estimation. First, as Evans and Marshall (1997) showed, a general reaction function like the one specified above can capture in reduced form reaction functions that incorporate inflation targets, such as the well-known Taylor Rule relating the policy instrument to the output gap and conditional expected inflation in linear fashion (Taylor 1993). Second, recursively identified estimation does not require an explicit and complete structural model of the macroeconomy. What it requires is identification of (a) those variables that are endogenous and those that are exogenous, (b) those that enter in the information set of the monetary authority at the moment of setting policy, and (c) the subset of the variables in the information set of the central bank that responds contemporaneously to policy changes. Once these identifying assumptions are made, the dynamic relationship across the variables is data determined through VAR estimation. Clearly, considerations of theory, practical knowledge of the policy environment, and statistical limitations play a role in the identifying assumptions. As a result, the reaction function can only be specified at best as an approximation. Christiano, Eichembaum, and Evans (1998) describe the ongoing debate in

---

9. Sims and Zha (1995) used an alternative strategy that identifies the policy reaction function by imposing nonrecursive identification restrictions either in the matrix of autocorrelation of the VAR's errors or in the covariance structure of innovations

the case of the United States over the choice of the relevant right-hand-side variable of the policy reaction function and the set of variables (and their timing) in the left-hand-side.

Recursively Identified VAR Models for Chilean Stabilization Policy

We examine first a benchmark recursively identified VAR model of Chilean stabilization policy in which the reaction function is defined using the 90-day indexed lending rate (R90) as the policy instrument. The right-hand-side variables are logarithms of the consumer price index (P), the IMF's measure of the real effective exchange rate (RER), the seasonally adjusted monthly index of economic activity (IMACEC), the adjusted measure of narrow money supply (M1A), the stock of net international reserves (NIR), and the core terms of trade (TOT). We used monthly data for the period January 1986 to May 1997 obtained from various issues of the Monthly Bulletin of the Central Bank of Chile and from the IFS. To balance the tradeoff between minimizing omitted variable bias and the loss of degrees of freedom that multiplies as the variables added to the VAR increase,[10] we followed the same practice as Christiano, Eichembaum, and Evans (1998) and Evans and Marshall (1997) and restricted estimation to include only 6 lags of each variable. Thus, the usable observations actually entering into the VAR start in January 1987. Robustness of this restriction was tested using conventional tests such as Q and AIC (Akaike Information Criterion) statistics.

The variables that we consider to be unaffected on date t by a date-t policy innovation to R90 are P, IMACEC, RER, and TOT; the variables that are allowed to adjust immediately to the R90 shock are M1A and NIR. These settings are consistent with the view that prices and output respond with at least a delay of one month to policy innovations. Since RER in some sense is targeted too, because of the indexation rule on the nominal exchange rate, assuming that P is "sticky" forces the assumption that RER must also be "sticky." The assumption that TOT is unaffected by a date-t policy shock simply reflects the view that Chile is a small open economy, and hence the world relative price of copper in terms of oil is exogenous to developments within Chile. M1A and NIR are assumed to respond immediately to policy innovations reflecting the Chilean policy that allows money

---

10. If we include k lags and n variables in the VAR, estimation requires $k \times n^2$ free parameters.

supply to adjust without intervention to interest rate changes, and the limited effectiveness of sterilized intervention in an economy as open to trade and capital flows as Chile.

One can also view the variables we introduced in the reaction function as conveying information regarding other important variables that the monetary authority in Chile did consider to be critical, such as the current account, the growth of private expenditures, or labor market indicators. These variables can be interpreted as functions of the variables we included, which have the advantage of being available at a monthly frequency and with very short reporting lags, hence the notion of (1) as a "reduced form" relationship.

Figure 1-4 shows the model's impulse response functions in the presence of a 1-standard-deviation to the policy innovation. The results are striking.[11] The response of all macroeconomic variables to the policy innovation is in line with economic intuition, with the major exception that an increase in the indexed interest rate leads to a persistent increase in the price level. That is, a rise in R90, far from reducing inflation, results in a temporary surge in inflation and leaves the price level permanently higher. This occurs despite temporary declines in IMACEC and M1A, and a permanent increase in foreign reserves. Notice also that the R90 innovation hardly affects the real exchange rate. Therefore, implicit in these impulse response functions are adjustments of the nominal exchange rate (including adjustments within the band and adjustments of the band) in response to the increase in P that work to maintain RER constant.[12]

The analysis of the restricted VAR helps us identify the effects of exogenous monetary policy innovations, but it does not help us gauge the contribution of the endogenous systematic response of the policy instrument to changes in its determinants. Thus, one could argue that Chilean policy instrumented via R90 was an effective tool because of the way it reacted to changes in the right-hand-side variables of (1), and hence there was still an important contribution of monetary policy to the decline in inflation. As

---

11. The impulse response functions are plotted together with ±2 standard error bands calculated via Monte Carlo simulations using 100 repetitions.

12. These results are robust if only the price of copper instead of TOT is used in the estimation, and regardless of whether commodity prices enter in the analysis. Thus, unlike in the case of applications of restricted VAR techniques for the U.S. economy (Christiano, Eichembaum, and Evans 1998), the so-called "price puzzle" remains in the Chilean case despite the introduction of commodity prices.

Figure 1-4. Response to a One Standard Deviation Innovation in the UF Lending Rate: Modeled with the Relative Price of Copper in Terms of Oil

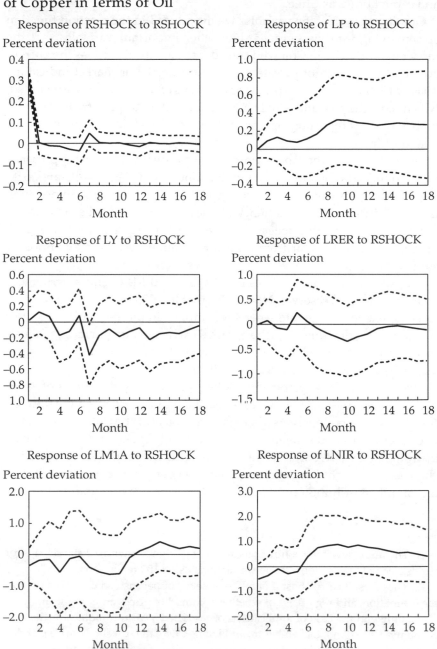

Source: Authors' research.

Christiano, Eichembaum, and Evans (1998) explain, the analysis of the systematic component of the policy reaction function is a difficult task that cannot be disentangled from the classic problem of interpretation of the exogeneity that goes into the ordering of variables in the Choleski decomposition of a VAR. However, in the framework presented here, one can shed some light on this issue by asking whether positive innovations to R90, due to exogenous policy shocks or to systematic responses to changes in other endogenous variables, result in declines in the inflation rate or the price level. As figure 1-5 clearly illustrates, the price level still increases and remains permanently higher in the impulse response function to a 1-percent shock to R90 of an unrestricted VAR.

We acknowledge that we are not the first authors who want to understand the mechanism of monetary transmission in Chile and are troubled by the puzzling implications of the data when the setting of monetary policy is modeled to capture the conventional wisdom presented earlier. The preceding results resemble those of other authors who used unrestricted VAR estimates and Granger causality tests (Mendoza and Fernandez 1994; Rojas 1993; and Rosende and Herrera 1991). More recently, Morande and Schmidt-Hebbel (1997) and Valdes (1997) experimented with nonrecursively identified VARs and obtained results very analogous to the ones we found. But unlike previous studies, these studies also estimated VAR specifications in which interest rate innovations did show some evidence of reducing the gap between actual inflation and the announced inflation target (both measured in terms of a redefined "core" CPI).

This is an interesting finding, but we were unable to make it consistent with the methodology we followed for two reasons. First, as Evans and Marshall (1997) suggest, inflation targeting does not produce a recursively identified VAR setting in which the inflation gap can be treated as a dependent variable. Instead, it implies that the reaction function must include the variables on which the monetary authority conditions its inflation target—which is analogous to the procedure we followed. Second, from a theoretical standpoint, introducing the inflation gap in the VAR presents nontrivial difficulties with the notion of a rational-expectations equilibrium. Hypothetically, if a fully credible target were set monthly, rational expectations imply that the inflation gap is a white noise error, and there would be no systematic link between this gap and interest rate innovations.

The purpose of these VAR experiments was to assess the operating hypothesis of the conventional wisdom regarding Chilean monetary policy: monetary policy manages real interest rates by influencing UF rates with the aim of reducing inflation via adjustments in the growth of output and expenditures. This view also considers lags in the monetary transmission

Figure 1-5. Response to a One Standard Deviation Innovation in the UF Lending Rate: Unrestricted VAR with Copper Price as Exogenous Variable

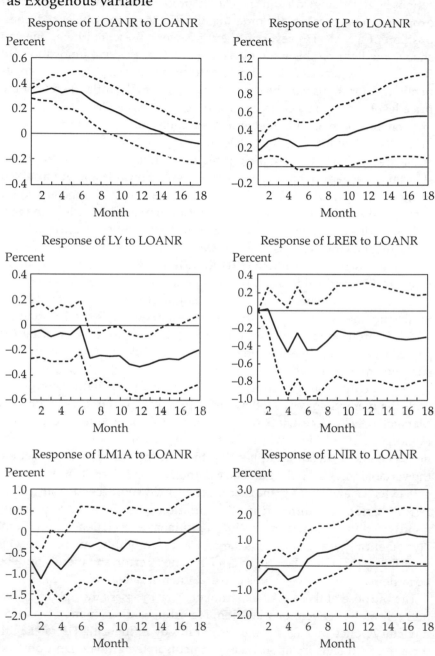

Source: Authors' research.

mechanism that could cause the decline of inflation to be slow and erratic. However, the fact that R90 does not correspond to Chile's real interest rate, the evidence of our restricted and unrestricted VARs, and the evidence from most of the other studies cited above seem to cast some doubt on the conventional wisdom.

The puzzling positive effect of increases in R90 on the Chilean price level is clearly fleshed out by the experience of the Sobreajuste period mentioned earlier. The large increase in the UF lending rate—characterized by a rise in the UF rate from about 7 or 8 percent to near 16 percent that started in 1989 and peaked in early 1990—was followed with some delay by a decline in economic activity. There was also a deceleration in money growth that was closer in time to the tightening of monetary policy. Indeed, by the end of 1990 the growth of M1A had fallen from near 40 percent in January 1989 to about 10 percent. However, for several months after the increase in R90 reached its maximum, inflation continued to increase and even accelerated, until it began to decline in 1991. Inflation did not return to the level before the tightening began in 1989 until December of 1992. The idea that the real interest rate could increase during this period as one would believe it did if one accepted the notion that UF rates are real interest rates is very hard to reconcile with the observed resilience of the inflation rate and the widely accepted view that Chile is a well-functioning market economy.

An Alternative View: Chile's Price Puzzle and a Reaction Function for the Exchange Rate

Chile's price puzzle—namely, that the response of the price level to tighter monetary policy can be the opposite of what the monetary authority expects—is not unique to the Chilean case. This so-called price puzzle is well known in the literature that examines VAR models of U.S. monetary policy (see the survey by Christiano, Eichembaum, and Evans 1998). In the United States the puzzle is resolved by introducing commodity prices in the information set of the monetary authority that enters in the reaction function. This, however, is not the case in our VARs for Chile. Still, the interpretation of the price puzzle given in the American literature is appealing. It suggests what might be affecting the analysis of the Chilean case: "the conjecture is that policy shocks which are associated with substantial price puzzles are actually confounded with nonpolicy disturbances that signal future increases in prices" (Christiano, Eichembaum, and Evans 1998, 36).[13]

---

13. Roberto Zahler provided us with an account of the aftermath of the *Sobreajuste* that can be nicely interpreted from this perspective.

In this section we propose one alternative for resolving Chile's price puzzle that specifies a policy reaction function in which the exchange rate is viewed as the dependent variable. This approach is motivated by (1) our observation that the gradual decline of Chilean inflation in the 1990s (figure 1-1) was associated with the real appreciation of the currency and (2) our discussion of Chilean stabilization policy in which we noted the flexibility of the exchange rate arrangement and the concerns for the real value of the currency and the size of the current account deficit. Note, however, that this reaction function for the exchange rate is largely hypothetical. There is no written evidence of an explicit strategy for influencing the exchange rate. The argument is based on anecdotal evidence of interventions within the exchange rate band and on the recurrent step adjustments to the width of the band and the formula for calculating the midpoint.

We examine first the unrestricted VAR estimated above to obtain impulse response functions to a 1-percent standard deviation shock to the real exchange rate (figure 1-6). A shock that appreciates the real exchange rate can account for the permanent decline in the Chilean price level and a persistent increase in output, with temporary fluctuations in interest rates and the quantity of money. Note, however, that a zero-to-slightly-positive response of the price level to the real appreciation remains within the 95-percent confidence interval. Thus, formally, the price puzzle is not fully resolved. Still, the position of the point estimates of the impulse response function of the price level relative to the bounds of the confidence interval suggests that, on average, the price level is most likely to fall as the real exchange rate appreciates. (For an analogous discussion of impulse responses of the price level and their corresponding confidence intervals, see Christiano, Eichembaum, and Evans 1998.)

We consider next a framework of a recursively identified VAR in which the policy reaction function is expressed in terms of the nominal exchange rate, E, in pesos per U.S. dollar, as the instrument of policy. In this framework we maintain that IMACEC and TOT are independent of current policy innovations, but we allow the consumer price index (P) to respond to contemporaneous innovations in the exchange rate. This assumption is consistent with the views that (a) there was an explicit policy to target the real exchange rate embodied in the rule that indexed the mid-point of the band to the lagged productivity-adjusted international inflation differential, and (b) while prices of nontradable goods can be relatively sticky, at least at a monthly frequency, P moves together with E because the price of imports in domestic currency moves together with the exchange rate. Thus, we wish to capture in the policy innovations to E any dynamic effects that go beyond the mechanical effects of changes in the exchange rate on the prices of

Figure 1-6. Response to a One Standard Deviation Innovation in the Real Exchange Rate: Unrestricted VAR with Copper Price as Exogenous Variable

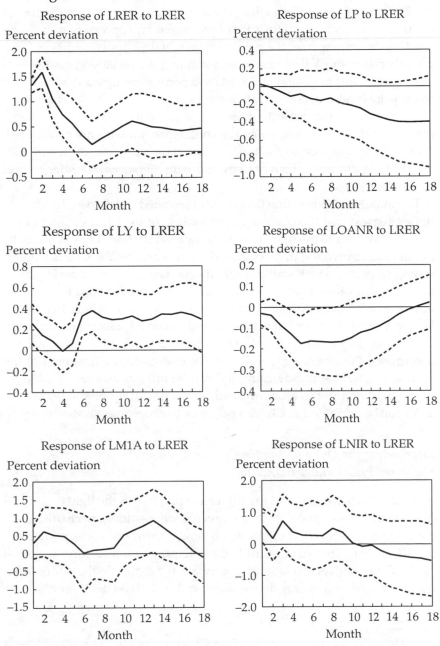

Source: Authors' research.

traded goods. M1A, R90, and NIR are also modeled as variables that can react contemporaneously to nominal exchange rate shocks.

Impulse response functions for this alternative policy scenario are plotted in figure 1-7. Note that in this case an increase in E is a depreciation, in contrast to an increase in RER that constituted an appreciation in figure 1-6. Clearly, judging from the point estimates of the impulse response functions, a policy shock that results in a nominal depreciation equal to a 1-percent standard deviation in E leads to a permanent upward adjustment in the price level, a persistent fall in output, and temporary fluctuations of foreign reserves, the quantity of money, and the indexed 90-day interest rate.[14] As before, however, when the confidence intervals are considered, the results are less robust; the hypothesis that the responses of all variables may be insignificantly different from zero at the 95-percent confidence level cannot be rejected.

The impulse response functions to the identified shock to exchange rate policy suggest that the observed appreciation of the Chilean peso might have contributed to the reduction in the rate of inflation. Thus, it might be possible to resolve the price puzzle if we re-interpret the Chilean policy setting as one in which stabilization efforts were concerned mainly with the evolution of the external sector, particularly the exchange rate. This, however, still leaves us with important unanswered questions. In particular, we do not know to what extent the systematic response of E (implicitly through the indexation rule of the mid-point of the band and the market-determined fluctuations around it) to the endogenous adjustment of the economy to terms-of-trade gains and capital inflows was responsible for the stabilization of the economy, and we do not study here whether the latter can be attributed to Chilean policy or to exogenous shocks.

Interpreting the Dynamics of the Chilean Economy: Staggered Prices under Indexation

In what follows we interpret the Chilean experience in the light of the predictions of a basic model with a staggered-price-setting mechanism; the environment of imperfect indexation is similar to the one corresponding to the UF system. The main result is that the same reduced-form equation establishing an inverse relationship between the change in the rate of inflation over time and excess demand derived in Calvo (1983), in a setting

---

14. The persistent output decline in response to a *nominal* devaluation represents another puzzle that deserves further examination.

Figure 1-7. Response to a One Standard Deviation Innovation in the Nominal Exchange Rate

Response of SHOCKEXR to SHOCKEXR

Percent deviation

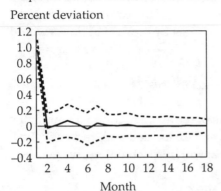

Month

Response of LP to SHOCKEXR

Percent deviation

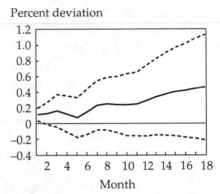

Month

Response of LY to SHOCKEXR

Percent deviation

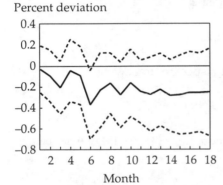

Month

Response of LOANR to SHOCKEXR

Percent deviation

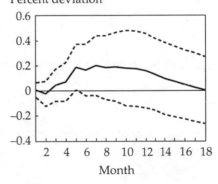

Month

Response of LM1A to SHOCKEXR

Percent deviation

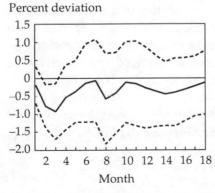

Month

Response of LNIR to SHOCKEXR

Percent deviation

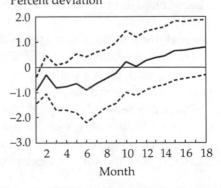

Month

Source: Authors' research.

without indexation, holds in the case of UF indexation. This inverse relationship also embodies a policy similar to the one followed to adjust the mid-point of the exchange rate band.

Let x_t denote the difference between the price set by firms that are setting the price at time t and the UF along the length of the contract. Thus, if the contract lasts until time $s > t$, then the price set by the firm at time s would be $UF_s + x_t$. We postulate:

$$x_t = \delta \int_t^\infty (P_s - U_s + Z_s) e^{-\delta(s-t)} ds \qquad (2)$$

where δ, P, U, and Z denote the inverse of the average contract length, the (log) of the price level, (log of) the UF, and excess demand, respectively.

Therefore, differentiating equation (2) with respect to time, we get:

$$\dot{x}_t = \delta(x_t + U_t - Z_t). \qquad (3)$$

On the other hand, the price level satisfies:

$$P_t = \delta \int_{-\infty}^t (x_s + U_s) e^{-\delta(t-s)} ds. \qquad (4)$$

Thus, differentiating equation (4) with respect to time, we get:

$$\dot{P}_t = \delta(x_t + U_t - P_t). \qquad (5)$$

Consequently, denoting $\pi = P$, from equations (3) and (5), we have:

$$\dot{\pi}_t = -\delta^2 Z_t \qquad (6)$$

which is the same expression of Calvo (1983) for a nonindexed economy. This reduced-form, perfect-foresight representation of inflation dynamics seems to be roughly in line with the Chilean experience, where the fall (increase) of inflation during the 1990s coincided with the acceleration (deceleration) of economic activity. This comparison is of limited relevance, however, since (6) is a perfect-foresight prediction that holds for fully anticipated policy changes.

The above result also implies that, in a rational expectations world, indexation with the UF system has no effect on price dynamics. Indexation, however, could have an effect on the level of inflation and uniqueness of monetary equilibrium. For example, let us assume that

$$Z_t = -b p_t, \ b > 0 \qquad (7)$$

where $p = P - E$, and $E = $ log of nominal exchange rate. Thus, assuming the international price level constant, p is the (log of the) real exchange rate (as computed by the IMF). Hence,

$$\dot{p}_t = \pi_t - \varepsilon_t \qquad (8)$$

where ε stands for the rate of devaluation.

Consider now the case in which the rate of devaluation is indexed to some lagged rate of inflation (as in Chile), such that:

$$\dot{\varepsilon}_t = \gamma(\pi_t - \varepsilon_t) \qquad (9)$$

$$\dot{P} = \delta x_t = \delta(P_t - U_t + Z_t). \qquad (10)$$

By (8) and (9), it follows that

$$\varepsilon_t = \gamma(p_t - p_0) + \varepsilon_0. \qquad (11)$$

Using equation (10) in (8), we get:

$$\dot{p}_t = \pi_t - \varepsilon_0 - \gamma(p_t - p_0). \qquad (12)$$

At steady state, $\dot{p} = p = 0$. Thus,

$$\pi_\infty = \varepsilon_0 + \gamma p_0. \qquad (13)$$

where the subindex ∞ denotes "steady state." An implication of equation (13) is that the steady state rate of inflation is a function of initial conditions. In particular, the more appreciated is the currency in real terms with respect to steady state initially, the higher is steady state inflation.

Conclusion

Our assessment of Chile's macroeconomic policy setting in the 1990–97 period shows that it is difficult to assign a very important role to interest rate or exchange rate policies per se in the notable accomplishments of the Chilean economy. One important conjecture in this assessment was that unusually favorable terms of trade and the surge in capital inflows were important elements in the Chilean success. Inasmuch as this is true, one can argue that the Chilean economy had not been "tried by fire" because ever since Chile took the high-growth track, the economy had not faced large adverse exogenous shocks or even fallen into recession.

The situation changed after the recent Asian crises, which brought about a sharp fall in copper prices and a wave of capital outflows. This has given us a chance to test the resilience of the Chilean economy to an adverse external environment. Interestingly, the first casualty of this change of luck was the entire monetary and exchange rate policy setting we described. In the summer of 1998, Chile narrowed sharply the exchange rate band and abandoned the indexation rule of its midpoint. Regulations oriented to limit capital inflows were also relaxed or abandoned.

The failure to find a systematic link between monetary policy and inflation is not an indictment of Chilean macroeconomic policy. First, weak and even paradoxical links of that sort have also been found for the U.S. economy (Christiano, Eichembaum, and Evans 1998), even though one must acknowledge that in Chile's case the "price puzzle" has proven more robust and is yet to be resolved. Second, our analysis has not examined the impact of other key policies that are hard to quantify (for instance, sound and efficient bank supervision and lengthening the maturity structure of public debt).

Nevertheless, our analysis calls into question the effectiveness of interest rate policy as an anti-inflationary device and suggests that some exchange rate anchoring could help to rein in the dreaded beast. These findings, particularly the first one, echo a view that is predominant in the economics profession, as represented by the quotation from Robert E. Lucas, Jr., at the beginning of the chapter.

Countries contemplating the use of the interest rate as a stabilization device should also be aware that taxation of capital inflows was a central policy instrument in Chile. This helped to insulate domestic interest rates from international ones and thus enhance the effectiveness of monetary policy. However, they can lead to domestic interest rates that substantially exceed international interest rates, inducing the development of tax-evasion loopholes. Moreover, as loopholes grow, domestic residents incur in foreign-exchange-denominated borrowing, which implies a virtual "dollarization" of the economy, and increases the economy's vulnerability to currency devaluation—as recently shown in Indonesia and Korea.

References

Barro, Robert J., and Xavier Sala-i-Martin. 1995. *Economic Growth*. New York: McGraw-Hill.

Calvo, Guillermo A. 1983. "Staggered Prices in a Utility-Maximizing Framework." *Journal of Monetary Economics* 12: 383–98.

Calvo, Guillermo A., Leonardo Leiderman, and Carmen M. Reinhart. 1993. "Capital Inflows and Real Exchange Rate Appreciation in Latin America." IMF Staff Papers, vol. 40, pp. 108–51. Washington, D.C.

Christiano, Lawrence J., Martin Eichembaum, and Charles L. Evans. 1998. "Monetary Policy Shocks: What Have We Learned and to What End?" *Handbook of Macroeconomics*. The Netherlands: North-Holland Publishing Co.

Corbo, Vittorio, Rolf Ludders, and Pablo Spiller. 1996. "The Foundations of Successful Economic Reforms: The Case of Chile." Catholic University of Chile, Santiago.

Dornbusch, Rudiger, Ilan Goldjfan, and Rodrigo P. Valdes. 1995. "Currency Crises and Collapses." *Brookings Papers on Economic Activity*, vol. 2.

Easterly, William K., Lault M. Pritchett, and Lawrence Summers. 1993. "Good Policy or Good Luck? Country Growth Performance and Temporary Shocks." *Journal of Monetary Economics* 32: 459–84.

Evans, Charles L., and David A. Marshall. 1997. "Monetary Policy and the Terms Structure of Nominal Interest Rates." Federal Reserve Bank of Chicago.

Mendoza, Enrique G. 1992. "Fisherian Transmission and Efficient Arbitrage under Partial Financial Indexation: The Case of Chile." IMF Staff Papers, vol. 39, no. 1. Washington, D.C.

———. 1995. "The Terms of Trade, the Real Exchange Rate, and Economic Fluctuations." *International Economic Review* (February).

———. 1997. "Terms-of-Trade Uncertainty and Economic Growth." *Journal of Development Economics* 54: 323–56.

Mendoza, Enrique G., and Fernando Fernandez. 1994. "Monetary Transmission and Financial Indexation: Evidence from the Chilean Economy." PPAA, No. 94/17, International Monetary Fund, Washington, D.C.

Morande, Felipe, and Klaus Schmidt-Hebbel. 1997. "Inflation Targets and Indexation in Chile." Central Bank of Chile, Santiago.

Rojas, Patricio. 1993. "El Dinero como un Objetivo Intermedio de la Politica Monetaria en Chile." Cuadernos de Economia 30, no. 90, pp. 139–78, Agosto.

Rosende, Francisco, and L. O. Herrera. 1991. "Teoria y Politica Monetaria: Elementos para el Analisis." Cuadernos de Economia no. 83, Abril.

Sims, Christopher A. 1992. "Interpreting the Macroeconomic Time Series Facts: The Effects of Monetary Policy." *European Economic Review* 36 (5): 975–1000.

Sims, Christopher A., and Tao Zha. 1995. "Does Monetary Policy Generate Recessions?" Department of Economics, Yale University.

Taylor, John. 1993. "Discretion versus Policy Rules in Practice." Carnegie-Rochester Conference Series on Public Policy, vol. 39, pp. 195–214. Rochester, N.Y.

Valdes, Rodrigo P. 1997. "Transmision de la Politica Monetaria en Chile." Banco Central de Chile, Santiago.

Williamson, John. 1997. "Mexican Policy toward Foreign Borrowing." In Barry Bosworth, Susan Collins, and Nora Lustig, eds., *Coming Together: US-Mexico Relations*. Washington, D.C.: Brookings Institution.

Comment:

An Alternative View of Chile's Macroeconomic Policy

Roberto Zahler

This comment analyses the core elements of Chile's macroeconomic policies during the 1990s from the perspective of the Central Bank of Chile. These policies had two main objectives: to reduce inflation and to keep the current account deficit of the balance of payments within an acceptable range. The underlying principle was to avert significant disequilibria in macroeconomically sensitive areas, whether in relation to the financial system's solvency and liquidity, the economy's external sector, employment, saving, and investment, or in real wages as they related to productivity.

Macroeconomic policy in Chile during the 1990s emphasized stability and sustainability of economic growth and attempted to minimize volatil-

The United Nation's Economic Commission for Latin America and the Caribbean distributed an earlier version of this comment in Spanish as part of a larger study, document no. LC/R 1771, December 1997. The views expressed herein are the sole responsibility of the author and do not necessarily reflect those of the Commission. The author wishes to thank Héctor Assael, Günter Held, and Andras Uthoff for their comments.

ity and vulnerability. An increasingly important—yet not exclusive—role was assigned to the market in determining key prices in the economy, and a medium- and long-term time horizon was used as a basis for the definition of policies. Considerations of timeliness, prudence, and gradualism prevailed.

Since 1989 the Central Bank has been an autonomous body functioning independently from the government. At first it had to grapple with an overheated economy. Later on, when the economy was working at full capacity, it had to cope with an extremely plentiful supply—some might say outright glut—of foreign exchange as a consequence of the country's strong export performance, copious inflows of risk capital, and heavy financial inflows.

The country's strategy was to reduce inflation from its 1989–90 annual levels of 25 to 30 percent to single digits by 1995–96 and, thereafter, to continue to chip away at the rate until reaching levels similar to those seen in industrial countries (that is, annual rates between 2 and 3 percent). A systematic, sustainable, and gradual decline was envisioned. The emphasis on a *systematic* reduction grew out of the need to boost the Central Bank's credibility. The focus on *sustainability* was in line with the proposition that price stability needed to have a solid foundation that would stand the test of time within a framework of general macroeconomic equilibrium. A *gradual* decline was viewed as important because of Chile's history of chronic inflation and its widespread practice of indexing prices and wages on the basis of past inflation. Under this practice, any sharp or sudden reduction in inflation was extremely costly in terms of economic activity and employment.

The Central Bank's commitment to achieving the progressively lower inflation targets it announced each year was used as an anchor by monetary policymakers. They relied chiefly on open-market operations based on the real interest rates for short-term Central Bank paper (initially for 90-day terms, but later primarily its one-day offer rate). This approach to monetary policy, in combination with the Central Bank's "treasury-style" management of domestic public debt, not only boosted policy efficiency, but also allowed the market to shape long-term interest rates and the yield curve for differing maturities. Chile did not use any monetary aggregate as an "anchor" or as an instrument of monetary policy because it was so difficult to find an aggregate that behaved in a stable, predictable manner. By the same token, monetary policymakers have refrained from using the exchange rate as an anchor because this would almost certainly lead to an excessive appreciation of the peso and would thus interfere with efforts to lower the deficit on the balance-of-payments current account to sustainable levels.

The offer rate on short-term Central Bank paper has been used to influence the cost of credit for the private sector and thereby—considering the exogenous nature of fiscal policy—align the trend in domestic demand with the level and rate of growth of potential GDP. The Central Bank started to use this instrument in a preventive way, even before signs that inflation was likely to overshoot its target level. The Bank was therefore able to institute a tight monetary policy in time. It was also successful in heading off an oversupply in production capacity by relaxing its monetary policy at the right point. In order to do this, the Central Bank needed to assess a series of indicators of aggregate supply and demand on an ongoing basis, including the rate of inflation, "underlying" inflation, the exchange rate, wages, the unemployment rate, levels of activity in manufacturing, commerce, and construction, imports, monetary aggregates, credit in the private financial system, and other sectoral indicators.

In the second half of the 1980s, foreign exchange was in extremely short supply and the stated objective was to achieve and maintain a "high" real exchange rate. During the 1990s, however, the chief objective of exchange rate policy was to back up fiscal and monetary policies so that the external sector of the economy could be brought into equilibrium over the medium term. More specifically, the objective was to keep the real exchange rate within a range (3 to 4 percent of GDP) consistent with a sustainable deficit on the current account of Chile's balance of payments.

A foreign exchange regime was established under which the exchange rate was neither fixed nor totally free floating. A fixed rate was rejected because it would have introduced considerable rigidity into the country's economic policy and would have subordinated it entirely to the maintenance of an external balance. Policymakers also shied away from a free float of the currency because they felt it was better to give the market some sort of signal as to the monetary authorities' best estimate of its long-term equilibrium value, which in Chile is referred to as the "agreed," or reference, exchange rate. This exchange rate was positioned at the center of a currency band that was widened to a range of plus or minus 10 percent. The decision to broaden the band, in conjunction with a series of measures to liberalize the foreign exchange market, allowed the market to play an increasing role in determining the rate. Meanwhile, the Chilean peso, which had been tied to the U.S. dollar, was linked to a basket of currencies that was representative of the country's foreign trade matrix. The purpose of this change was to make monetary policy more independent.

At first, an attempt was made to maintain a constant real exchange rate by correcting for (past) domestic inflation and for that component of external inflation relevant to Chile. Toward the end of 1995, however, a 2 percent appreciation in the trend rate for the peso was incorporated into the system. This was an effort to factor in the effect on the long-term real equilibrium exchange rate of the differential between economic growth and productivity, especially in the tradable sector, between Chile and its main trading partners.

During this period it became necessary to modify the exchange rate band on two different occasions in order to permit the peso to appreciate in response to market forces. These modifications were made only after the Central Bank had become convinced that the appreciation was necessary to bring the rate into line with its equilibrium level and that there was no sound reason for keeping the reference exchange rate out of alignment with the country's economic fundamentals. Indeed, there were many signs that Chile's position within the international economy was undergoing a structural change that demanded an adjustment in the exchange rate: its extremely strong export performance, the low level of its current account deficit, its hefty inflows of foreign direct investment, the liberalization of capital outflows originating from residents and nonresidents alike, and the steady improvement in all the indicators of credit worthiness. Yet the currency's real rate of appreciation—4.3 percent per year in 1992–96—was one of the slowest observed in Latin America during the period.

The Central Bank bolstered monetary and exchange policy by actively building up foreign exchange reserves. This was justified by the need to have sizable international reserves on hand as the country began to open up to the external economy. At the same time, it was important to prevent net capital inflows (which averaged 6.1 percent of GDP in 1992–96) from generating too large of a current account deficit. At one point the Central Bank's international reserves were actually equivalent to more than 25 percent of GDP and nearly 15 months' worth of merchandise imports. This was attributable to a highly favorable trend in the trade balance, the reinvestment of profits and additional flows of foreign direct investment, the reduction of the public sector's foreign debt, and net inflows of short-term capital. Short-term inflows were attracted by interest rate spreads between Chile and industrial countries, especially when they coincided with international rating agencies' progressive upgradings of Chile's country-risk rating and widespread expectations of an appreciation of the Chilean peso.

The sharp rise in reserves permitted the country to prepay the whole of the external debt it had renegotiated in the wake of the crisis of the early 1980s as well as its entire debt with the International Monetary Fund (IMF). It is important to point out that this build-up in reserves can only go so far, since it results in substantial losses for the Central Bank. These losses are generated by the differential between the interest rate at which these reserves are placed on the international market (in foreign currency) and the rate that the Central Bank has to pay on paper that it floats on the domestic market (in real pesos) in order to sterilize the monetary impact of that build-up.

The central dilemma facing macroeconomic policymakers in the 1990s was that, on the one hand, local interest rates had to be substantially higher than those of industrial countries in order to keep the domestic economy in equilibrium, while, on the other hand, Chile's country risk had been steadily declining, and expectations of a revaluation of the Chilean peso were rampant. In view of the fact that the public sector had posted an average annual surplus of 1.8 percent, that the increase in reserves had a significant quasi-fiscal cost, that capital outflows had been liberalized very rapidly, and that the peso had been appreciating at more than 4 percent per year in real terms (despite the Central Bank's efforts to counter this trend), macroeconomic policymakers had to make a choice. Should they allow domestic interest rates to fall into line with rates on the international market, or should they close, or at least narrow, that interest rate gap? The first option might lead to excessive expenditure, higher inflation, and/or a further appreciation of the peso and a larger deficit on the balance-of-payments current account. This would heighten the economy's external vulnerability. Accordingly, the government chose to narrow the interest-rate gap by moderating the pace of foreign borrowing by firms in Chile and discouraging short-term capital inflows by raising their cost.

The fifth component of Chile's macroeconomic strategy—complementing its fiscal, monetary, foreign exchange, and international reserve policies—relates to the opening of the capital account. In this sphere the strategy has also called for a gradual and selective liberalization process.

Capital outflows have been greatly liberalized for residents and nonresidents alike. Exporters are free to dispose of their foreign exchange, in Chile or elsewhere, as they please. Foreign investments by private individuals and business firms have been completely liberalized as well. But the liberalization process for the banking system, pension funds, insurance companies, and mutual funds has moved ahead more slowly because of legal restrictions and the need for caution. As a result, overseas investment by Chileans has gained momentum and now constitutes a highly significant and growing presence in quantitative terms, particularly in countries within the region where Chilean investment funds have been channeled into a wide range of activities.

Restrictions on capital outflows originating from nonresidents have also been eased: the lock in period required before the repatriation of foreign investment capital has been shortened from three years to one; restrictions on outflows of investment capital brought into the country in the course of external debt swaps (in the aftermath of the crisis of the early 1980s) have been eliminated entirely; and regulations have been relaxed with regard to the prepayment of foreign debts as well as the minimum percentage of external credit that must accompany inbound foreign direct investment. As for the situation with regard to capital inflows, a steep increase has been seen in foreign direct investment. New mechanisms for attracting external funds—American depository receipts (ADRs), convertible bonds, and other securities—have been authorized and developed.

This approach to the liberalization of the capital account has enabled the Chilean economy to establish a solid position for itself in international capital markets without heightening its external vulnerability or jeopardizing the autonomy of its monetary policy. The gradual and selective nature of the liberalization process as applied to the capital account has discouraged inflows to the stock market (because of the one-year lock-in period) and has thus warded off an asset price bubble. Furthermore, Chilean companies hoping to attract international capital have had to do so gradually, and this has helped to prevent a traumatic appreciation of the Chilean peso.

A one-year non-interest-bearing reserve requirement applies to most types of external credits and other sources of foreign currency finance. This discouraged short-term external borrowing by directly raising its cost and helped to ensure that economic agents would all be dealing with the same interest rate (set by the Central Bank) as the domestic economy moved toward equilibrium.

Chile was able to change the structure or composition of foreign financial claims by increasing the proportion of risk capital relative to overseas borrowing and, within the latter, the proportion of long-term funds relative to short-term capital. This helped to make the Chilean economy much less vulnerable to the vagaries of the world economy and to changes in the expectations of international economic agents.

Although some countries in the region have implemented seemingly more ambitious liberalization policies for their balance-of-payments capital accounts, they have had higher domestic interest rates than Chile, as well as wider spreads between domestic and international rates. This situation, which theoretically should have been just the reverse, reflects higher country risk or the expectation of steeper devaluations than in Chile. Thus, it is not a foregone conclusion that a country with a swiftly paced, comprehensive liberalization of its financial sector will achieve a solid or permanent form of integration into international capital markets. Chile's strong macroeconomic performance during the early 1990s has often been attributed to its high domestic savings rate rather than to its macroeconomic strategy. It should be noted, however, that domestic saving is not a constant that functions independently of macroeconomic strategy in general or of external finance strategies in particular. Empirical studies and experience both suggest that "naïve" policies regarding inflows of external finance usually lead to a situation in which external savings (often very short-term funds) end up financing excessive expenditure on domestic consumption and reducing domestic saving.

A final consideration is the favorable environment (except when the economy began to overheat in 1989–90) that existed for Chile's macroeconomy during the first half of the 1990s. Major structural reforms, the outcome of a costly process of trial and error, had been in place for quite a long time by then and were beginning to bear fruit. Another important factor—above and beyond the controversy over the growth rate of public expenditure and its impact on the fiscal and monetary policy mix—was the effort made to coordinate the work of the Central Bank and the Ministry of Finance in designing and executing macroeconomic policy in the first half of the decade.

GDP grew at an average annual rate of 7.5 percent in 1992–96, and unemployment stood at 7 percent. Real wages rose in step with average labor productivity (4.7 percent per year); gross fixed-capital formation surged upward at an annual rate of 14.2 percent (nearly twice as fast as GDP growth); and domestic saving averaged 25.1 percent of GDP. The fiscal surplus amounted to 1.8 percent of GDP, and fiscal saving totaled 5.1 percent of GDP. The real annual interest rate on bank loans for terms of between 90 days and one year averaged 8.9 percent. The domestic public debt (of the Central Bank) was lower than in the past, declining to 33.6 percent of GDP, while its maturity profile lengthened from year to year, reaching an average of 3.2 years for the five-year period. Annual inflation averaged 9.7 percent (Chile's lowest mean rate for any five-year period in over 50 years). From 27.3 percent in 1990, it slipped to 18.7 percent in 1991 and then descended at rates quite similar to the Central Bank's yearly inflation targets, reaching 6.6 percent by the end of 1996. The Chilean peso appreciated at a real annual rate of 4.3 percent, while exports grew by 10.4 percent per year in real terms (50 percent faster than GDP growth). The average annual deficit on the current account of the balance of payments amounted to 2.2 percent of GDP. Both inbound and outbound foreign direct investment hit record levels. Capital inflows represented 6 percent of GDP and net international reserves, which jumped by over US$12 billion during the period in question, were equivalent to 22.4 percent of GDP and to one year's worth of merchandise imports. The external debt totaled an average of 38.1 percent of GDP (15.7 percent net of international reserves).

In sum, the country's macroeconomic results for 1992–96 were highly satisfactory. Economic activity and employment, domestic saving and investment, and real wages and productivity all rose at a brisk pace. At the same time, inflation slowed significantly and headed toward industrial-country levels. Lastly, all of this was achieved without jeopardizing the economy's external equilibrium: on the contrary, Chile's position within the international economy was strengthened as its external credit standing improved and its vulnerability diminished. Equally importantly, none of the other key areas of the economy was thrown out of balance. Chile's macroeconomic performance in 1992–96 provides grounds for an optimistic view of the prospects for further economic progress.

2

Chile's Takeoff:
Facts, Challenges, Lessons

Klaus Schmidt-Hebbel

A major change in policies, economic structure, and performance has taken place in Chile during the past two decades. The clearest evidence of the country's better performance is its high and sustained economic growth, supported by similarly higher national saving and investment rates. But achieving sustained economic success has not been easy or without set-backs. Severe foreign shocks and serious domestic policy mistakes have punctuated the country's progress since the start of the reform efforts in the mid-1970s. Neither is the country's current growth path without risks.

This chapter presents the views of the author and does not reflect any position or opinions of the Central Bank of Chile and its Board of Directors. I thank Eduardo Lora for his data on policy reform indicators for Chile and Mita Chakraborty and Humberto López for providing crosscountry data from the World Bank's Saving Project. I am indebted to Gerard Caprio, Ricardo Hausmann, Andrés Velasco, Roberto Zahler, and participants at the December 1997 World Bank seminar on "Chile: Development Lessons and Challenges" as well as to Oscar Landerretche M. and an anonymous referee for their useful comments on a preliminary version. I also thank Claudio Soto for his useful discussions and very efficient assistance. The usual disclaimer applies.

Chile still faces significant policy challenges to reduce these risks and lock in high growth for the long haul.

In an international context, Chile joined the small number of takeoff countries that have been able to break away from the past by reaching sustained rates of high growth, saving, and investment. As a newcomer to the club and its only Latin American member to date, Chile can offer lessons in policy design and effectiveness that may be useful to other reformers, particularly in the Latin America and Caribbean region.

This chapter documents Chile's takeoff, focusing on the stylized facts of saving, investment, and growth. It presents a compact account of the main policy reforms implemented by Chile and estimates the empirical contribution of policy reforms to the recorded increase in saving, investment, and productivity growth. Both exogenous and endogenous growth models are used to provide a better understanding of Chile's historical growth and future growth prospects. The chapter then identifies major risks and policy challenges that need to be addressed to lock in sustained high growth. Final lessons from Chile's experience for other reforming countries are presented in the last section.

Chile's Saving-Investment-Growth Takeoff: The Facts

Overview of Chile's Takeoff

Chile's saving, investment, and growth (SIG) performance reflects high annual volatility and one major structural break during the past four decades. These salient features are reflected in figures 2-1 and 2-2 and summarized by relevant periods in table 2-1. The selected periods reflect distinct regimes of policies and performance. The prereform era is characterized by increasing macroeconomic instability and worsening economic performance (1961–74). Serious stabilization efforts and deep structural reforms were started in 1974–75 and have continued to date at varying speeds and intensities. It is useful to distinguish between the first reform period (1975–81) and the second reform period (1982–89) of the military regime; they coincide with two intense recession-recovery cycles. Continued macroeconomic stabilization but less intense structural reform initiatives characterize the high-employment period under democratic regimes (1990–97).

Chile's SIG performance suggests seven stylized facts.

- *Shocks, policy mistakes, and slow response to reforms.* The response of the economy to the deep stabilization and structural reform efforts started

Figure 2-1. Real GDP Growth, TFP Growth, and Unemployment Rates in Chile, 1961–97

Percent

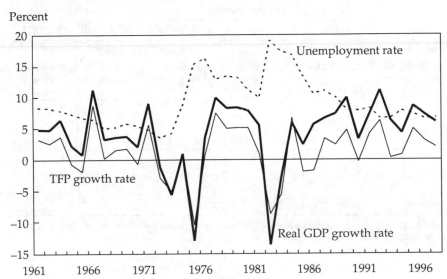

Source: Central Bank of Chile and author's calculations.

Figure 2-2. Gross Domestic Investment, National Saving, and Foreign Saving Rates in Chile, 1960–97

Percentage of GDP

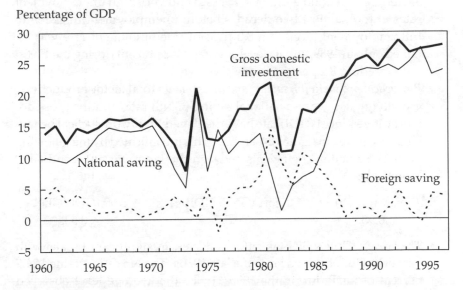

Source: Central Bank of Chile and author's calculations.

Table 2-1. Saving, Investment, and Growth in Chile, 1961–97
(percent)

Period	At current prices			At constant prices	
	GNS/GDP	FS/GDP	GDI/GDP	GDI/GDP	GFKF/GDP
1961–74	12.5	2.3	14.8	19.2	19.1
1975–81	11.4	5.6	17.0	17.8	16.0
1982–89	12.1	6.2	18.3	19.2	17.9
1990–97	24.7	2.4	27.0	29.2	25.5

	At constant prices			Per capita
	IA/GDP	TFP growth	GDP growth	GDP growth
1961–74	0.1	1.2	3.3	1.1
1975–81	1.7	2.0	4.4	2.9
1982–89	1.3	-0.1	2.6	0.9
1990–97	3.6	2.7	6.7	5.1

Note: GNS is gross national saving, GDP is gross domestic product, FS is foreign saving, GDI is gross domestic investment, GFKF is gross fixed capital formation, IA is inventory accumulation, and TFP is total factor productivity.
Source: Central Bank of Chile and author's calculations.

in the mid-1970s was delayed by the severe consequences of foreign shocks (in 1973–75 and 1980–82) and domestic policy mistakes (in 1979–82). Recessions of depression-like intensity hit Chile in 1975 and 1982–83, reflected in double-digit GDP losses and very high unemployment rates. It took almost two decades before unemployment rates fell to full-employment levels. An 8.0 percent unemployment rate was attained only in 1989, and its level averaged 7.2 percent during the 1990s, not exceeding 8.2 percent in any given year.

- *Procyclical productivity, saving, and investment.* Total factor productivity growth (g_{TFP}), the gross national saving (GNS) rate, and the gross domestic investment (GDI) rate have displayed highly procyclical behavior as suggested in figures 2-1 and 2-2. This is confirmed by the following partial correlation coefficients between the latter variables and GDP growth (g):

corr (g_{TFP}, g)	corr (GNS/GDP, g)	corr (GDI/GDP, g)
0.933	0.525	0.535

- *The takeoff.* Chile's SIG takeoff is reflected in significant breaks with past behavior observed since the late 1980s. The NS ratio attained 24.7 percent of GDP during the 1990s, twice the average level observed during the preceding three decades. The current-price (constant-price) GDI ratio reached 27.0 percent (29.2 percent) of GDP during 1990–97, exceeding substantially its historical level. The gross fixed-capital investment (GFKI) ratio rose by less, to 25.5 percent of GDP during 1990–97, as inventory accumulation jumped to 3.6 percent in the 1990s. TFP growth attained 2.7 percent per year in the 1990s, a figure that exceeds substantially the meager 1.2 percent recorded in 1961–74 or the 0.9 percent observed in 1975–89. As a result of higher investment and TFP growth, GDP growth attained 6.7 percent per year in the 1990s, twice its historical level.

- *Dating the trend break.* When does Chile's SIG takeoff start? Dating the trend break is not an easy task without controlling for saving, investment, and growth determinants other than economic policies—a task left to the next section. Figures 2-1 and 2-2 suggest that investment and TFP growth picked up modestly during the first reform period (1975–81), but gains were reversed during the bust-recovery years of 1982–86. The turning point was reached in 1987, when both GDI and NS ratios rose to historically unprecedented levels. From 1987 onwards, both ratios exceeded every year the levels recorded in every year of the 1961–86 period. TFP and GDP growth rates also attained higher levels from 1987 onwards. Sustained high growth is maintained after high (full) employment is reached in 1990.

- *Large foreign saving inflows.* Foreign saving (FS) played a crucial role during 1978–87, a decade when it exceeded 5 percent of GDP in each and every year. Voluntary private foreign resource inflows financed an exploding private investment-saving gap from the mid-1970s through early 1982. The debt crisis in developing countries triggered by the Mexican default in August 1982 dried up further private voluntary lending. Although the debt crisis implied a drastic regime change, Chile was able to secure substantial involuntary private capital inflows (as a result of debt rescheduling agreements) and loans from multinational financial institutions during 1983–87. Since 1988, foreign saving has fallen to less than 5 percent of GDP, declining to an average 2.4 percent during 1990–97. The latter level of current-account deficits, while similar to the 1961–74 average, is low if one considers that Chile had full access to foreign financing in the 1990s compared with the 1960s and early 1970s.

- *Significant foreign-national saving substitution.* The relations between GDI, GNS, and FS are distinctly different in 1961–77 (low FS, GNS, and GDI ratios) than they were in 1978–87 (high FS, very low NS, and moderate

GDI) and 1988–97 (low FS, and high NS and GDI). The 1961–97 partial correlation coefficients for FS and NS and GDI are the following:

corr (FS/GDP, GNS/GDP)   corr (FS/GDP, GDI/GDP)
        –0.566   –0.185

The large absolute correlation between foreign and national saving ratios reflects high substitution between both variables during the 1978–87 decade. The correlation between foreign saving and gross domestic investment ratios is low but surprisingly of a negative sign. This suggests that at times of foreign saving abundance, foreign saving is more of a substitute for national saving than a financing source for capital formation.

- *High saving-investment correlation.* Low saving-investment levels in the prereform period (1961–74) and high saving-investment levels in the postreform period (1990–97)—with basically unchanged foreign saving—suggest that Chile should be no exception to the well-known high saving-investment correlation that is observed internationally. This is confirmed by the following Feldstein-Horioka (1980) type of regression (t-statistics in parentheses):

$GDI/GDP = 7.906 + 0.719\ NS/GDP\quad R^2 = 0.76\quad 1961–97$
$\qquad\quad (10.43)\quad (6.93)$
$GDI/GDP = 3.855 + 0.899\ NS/GDP\quad R^2 = 0.92\quad 1961–97\ (excl.\ 1978–87)$
$\qquad\quad (16.65)\quad (3.95)$

The saving-investment correlation is much stronger when excluding the 1978–87 decade of high resource inflows. A number of explanations have been provided for the Feldstein-Horioka puzzle. They include national barriers to international capital flows, binding foreign source constraints, domestic policies targeted at low current accounts, home bias in international portfolio selection, and common factors affecting national saving and foreign investment in the same direction (Obstfeld and Rogoff 1996). Later in the chapter, when decomposing the rise in saving and investment according to causal factors, I identify common factors that provide part of the answer to the high correlation confirmed above.

International Comparison

Chile's SIG performance and takeoff can be compared with the relevant international experience, considering three country groups: OECD countries, nontakeoff developing economies, and nine (mostly East Asian) takeoff countries (figures 2-3a, 2-3b, 2-3c). The latter group includes countries

Figure 2-3. Saving, Investment, and Growth: Major World Regions and Chile, 1970–94

A. National Saving Ratio to GDP

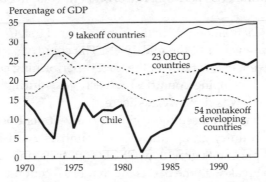

B. Gross Domestic Investment Ratio to GDP

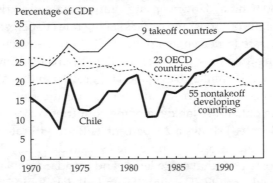

C. Per Capita Real GDP Growth

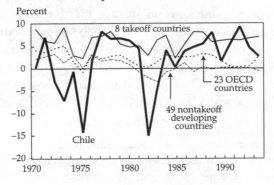

Note: The takeoff countries include eight Asian economies (China, Hong Kong, Indonesia, Korea, Malaysia, Singapore, Taiwan [China], Thailand) and one African economy (Mauritius).

Source: World Bank Saving Project Database and author's calculations.

that started as low-performing, developing countries in the 1960s but since then have been able to raise and sustain their saving, investment, and growth rates to levels that are unprecedented when compared with their own past and the contemporaneous performance of other developing and industrial economies.[1]

The following facts emerge from this comparison. First, Chile was a systematic underachiever until the mid-1980s. The country's saving and investment rates were below those of the lowest-performing country group (the nontakeoff developing countries) in each year during 1961–86. Per capita GDP growth was similarly mediocre.

Second, Chile has surpassed the saving and investment performance of the second-best country group (the OECD countries), and it has significantly exceeded per capita growth of OECD countries since 1989.

Third, Chile's break with the past is much more recent than the takeoffs started by the nine countries at different times between the early 1960s (Korea) and 1980 (China). However, large gaps remained during the 1990s between the takeoff countries' and Chile's saving rate (10 percentage points) and investment rate (6 percentage points). The gap between Chile's and the takeoffs' per capita growth rate is smaller (1 percent), suggesting that Chile's TFP growth is similar to average TFP growth in the takeoff economies. In the absence of TFP growth rates for the specific group of nine takeoff countries, the data for Asian developing countries (where most takeoff economies are located) shows a 2.9 percent TFP growth rate for 1982–91, the same figure Chile recorded during the 1990s (table 2-2).

Table 2-3 reports period average levels and standard deviations of SIG rates for the world, the OECD countries, and all developing countries, as well as for Chile, for 1965–92. A distressing fact to note is that SIG performance in developing countries is on average inferior to OECD countries not only with regard to first moments but also to second moments. In particular, average per capita growth in developing countries is half the size observed in OECD countries, but growth volatility is almost twice as large.

Chile's historical (1965–92) saving and investment volatility was equal to that observed in the world. However, Chile's growth volatility was much

---

1. Takeoff countries include eight Asian economies (China, Hong Kong, Indonesia, Korea, Malaysia, Singapore, Taiwan [China], Thailand) and one African economy (Mauritius). Another high-performing African country (Botswana) has been excluded from this sample because of incomplete data. A more detailed discussion of takeoff experiences in these countries is found in Schmidt-Hebbel and Servén (1997, 1999).

Table 2-2. GDP and TFP Growth in Developing Countries and in Chile, 1971–97
(percent)

Area and growth	1971–81	1982–91	1992–97
All developing countries			
GDP growth	6.0	4.2	
TFP growth	1.3	1.0	
Asia			
GDP growth	6.2	6.8	
TFP growth	1.9	2.9	
Latin America and the Caribbean			
GDP growth	6.2	1.6	
TFP growth	1.3	–0.7	
Chile			
GDP growth	3.0	3.2	7.2
TFP growth	1.1	0.3	2.9

Source: Agénor and Montiel (1996), Central Bank of Chile.

Table 2-3. Saving, Investment, and Growth in the World and in Chile: Average and Standard Deviations, 1965–92, unless indicated otherwise
(percent)

Area	Average			Standard deviation		
	GNS/ GDP	GDI/ GDP	Per capita GDP growth rate	GNS/ GDP	GDI/ GDP	Per capita GDP growth rate
World	15.4	21.4	1.8	6.3	5.0	4.6
OECD countries	23.3	23.8	2.8	3.1	3.2	2.9
All developing countries	13.3	20.8	1.5	7.1	5.5	5.0
Chile:1965–92	13.7	17.6	1.8	6.3	4.9	6.2
1961–74	12.5	14.8	1.1	3.8	2.9	3.9
1975–87	10.0	16.7	1.1	4.3	3.9	7.7
1988–97	24.3	26.4	5.4	1.4	1.8	2.3

Source: Schmidt-Hebbel, Servén, and Solimano (1996b) and Central Bank of Chile

larger than in the world at large and in developing countries in particular. But reaching a high SIG plateau allowed a significant reduction in Chile's instability. Standard deviations declined substantially from 1988 to 1997 for saving, investment, and growth rates, to values well below historical standard deviations observed in OECD countries. Higher levels and low volatility are reflected in a dramatic improvement in Chile's coefficients of variation. For instance, the coefficient of variation of per capita GDP growth fell from 7.0 during 1975–87 to 0.4 during the past 10 years. Lower volatility of investment and growth—a reflection of more stable macro policies, improved micro incentives, and more stable rules of the game—may reinforce the virtuous cycle of a high saving-investment-growth performance.

Policy Reforms and Saving-Investment-Growth Performance

A growing international literature analyzes the crosscountry evidence on Granger causality of saving, investment, and growth, and the relation between policy regimes and SIG.[2] Numerous studies assess Chile's policy reform experience and its relation to SIG performance.[3] A compact account of the main policy reforms implemented by Chile is presented next. Then the focus shifts to the determinants of Chile's SIG takeoff. I assess the empirical contribution of policy reforms to the recorded increase in saving, investment, and productivity growth. Both exogenous and endogenous growth models are used to provide a better understanding of Chile's growth takeoff and growth prospects. The use of an endogenous-growth model with transitional dynamics is particularly useful in understanding the likely future transition toward a lower level of long-term growth.

---

2. Among the crosscountry studies are Carroll and Weil (1994) and Attanasio, Picci, and Scorcu (1997). Reviews of causality issues and the relation between SIG performance and policies can be found in Schmidt-Hebbel, Servén, and Solimano (1996a, b).

3. Among the studies of Chile's policy reforms are Edwards and Edwards (1987), Bosworth, Dornbusch, and Labán (1994), Larraín (1994), Corbo, Lüders, and Spiller (1997), and Cortázar and Vial (1998). Among studies that focus more specifically on the relation between Chile's policies and SIG performance are Marfán and Bosworth (1994), Larraín and Rosende (1994), Morandé and Vergara (1997), and Marshall and Velasco (1998).

Policy Reforms

After decades of inadequate macroeconomic and microeconomic management by an ever-growing state that climaxed during the Allende government, the military regime started a program of macroeconomic stabilization
and structural reform in 1974–75. The first reform phase (1974–81) combined macroeconomic stabilization with deep and generally successful structural reforms that were unusually radical for the 1970s. However, major
policy mistakes (a fixed exchange rate with backward wage indexation,
and ineffective bank regulation and supervision) led to a classic "twin bank-
ing-cum-external crisis" (Kaminsky and Reinhart 1996) triggered by adverse foreign shocks in 1981–82. After the 1982–84 period of deep recession,
large macroeconomic imbalances, and partial reform reversals (including
government takeover of bankrupt financial institutions and a temporary
increase in tariffs), the military government started a second reform phase
that both corrected the macroeconomic and structural errors that led to the
preceding crisis and deepened reforms in other areas.

Since 1990 the democratic governments have maintained a strong fiscal
stance and the Central Bank of Chile—independent since 1989—has gradually reduced inflation to the lowest level in half a century. Public spending
on social programs has increased sharply. Structural reforms have proceeded
at a much slower pace, with gradual progress recorded in areas of trade
reform and privatization.

Summary indicators of macroeconomic stabilization, structural reform,
and tax reform will be used to assess the effect of policies on Chile's SIG
performance. The massive improvement in fiscal stance—started in 1976,
interrupted during 1982–85, and continued subsequently through 1997—is
reflected in significant nonfinancial public-sector surpluses (figure 2-4). In
fact, Chile has been able to record a systematic nonfinancial public surplus
of 1.7 percent of GDP since 1987.[4] With regard to inflation, Chile has pursued a very gradualist but effective price stabilization program: it has taken
23 years to reduce average annual CPI inflation from 375.9 percent in 1974
to a 6.1 percent in 1997.[5] Significant inflation progress was recorded during

---

4. The series of Chile's nonfinancial public surplus depicted in figure 2–4 excludes the amortization of implicit pay-as-you-go pension debt since 1981 and the
Central Bank's quasi-fiscal deficit. Inclusion of the first would raise the corrected
public surplus measure, while inclusion of the latter would reduce it.

5. Figure 2–4 presents a normalized measure corresponding to the cost of inflation (π), defined as $\pi/(1 + \pi)$.

Figure 2-4. Macroeconomic Stabilization and Structural Reform Indicators in Chile, 1960–97

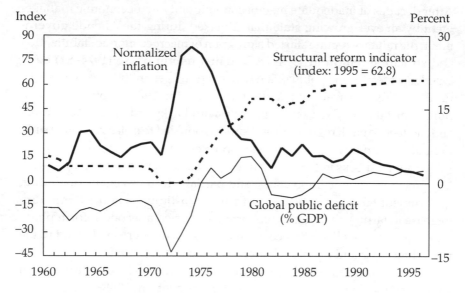

Source: Central Bank of Chile, Lora (1997), and author's calculations.

the first reform phase, but no further reduction was achieved during the 1980s. However, a gradual convergence toward international levels of inflation was successfully pursued during the 1990s.

Recent studies at the World Bank and the Inter-American Development Bank have evaluated policy reform progress and results in the Latin America and Caribbean region and put together a large set of country reform indicators.[6] Here I make use of Lora's (1997) aggregate index of structural reform progress. This measure combines reform progress in five areas: trade policy, tax policy, financial policy, privatization, and labor legislation.[7] Ex-

___

6. See in particular Burki and Perry (1997), Loayza and Palacios (1997), Lora (1997), and Inter-American Development Bank (1996).

7. Lora (1997) uses partial policy reform subindices (with equal weight) to construct each of his five policy reform areas. Partial and overall policy reform indicators are ranked from zero (lowest) to 100 (highest). I have extended for Chile Lora's five partial and overall policy reform progress indicators backward (for 1961–84) and forward (for 1996–97), based on available quantitative and qualitative information. The resulting 1960–97 time series for Chile's overall structural policy reform indicator is depicted in figure 2-4.

Figure 2-5. Individual and Corporate Tax Rates in Chile, 1973–97

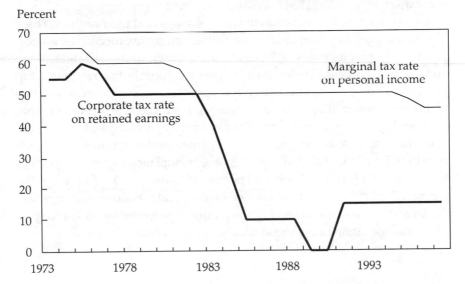

Source: Author's estimation based on Edwards, Flores, and Williamson (1996).

tending Lora's figures for Chile to the years before and after his 1985–95 time period yields the time series depicted in figure 2-4. The result shows a poor structural policy stance for the 1960s (at an average figure close to 10), a sharp deterioration in 1970–73 reflected by an index value of zero, and a massive improvement during the military government's first reform phase, reaching a value of 50 in 1980–82. After small partial reversals in the early 1980s, slower progress was made during the military government's second reform period, and it continued under democratic governments to the present.

Due to their importance for saving and investment behavior, the major tax reforms since the mid-1970s will be discussed briefly.[8] The reforms of 1974, 1984, and 1989 simplified and rationalized tax codes, reduced import duties, introduced value-added taxation, and lowered top marginal tax rates on personal income and corporate retained earnings (figure 2-5). Although the current tax base for individuals is their consolidated personal income, the dominance of VAT as the major revenue source in Chile, and tax incen-

---

8 For an account of the 1974–94 tax reforms, see Edwards, Flores, and Williamson (1996).

tives for personal saving, make the tax system a predominantly consumption-based regime. The 1984 tax reform provided tax exemptions and credits on various forms of personal financial savings and their returns. These personal saving incentives were complemented by tax incentives for corporate saving (or investment) by establishing generous depreciation allowances and significant differences between corporate tax rates and top personal income rates, and between corporate tax rates on retained and distributed profits. The 1991 tax reform reintroduced accrued total corporate earnings as the tax base at a 15 percent rate, which implied an increase of the tax rate on retained earnings from zero to the latter rate. The 1994 tax reform reduced top marginal tax rates on personal income from 50 percent to 45 percent. However, Chile's 30 percent difference in 1997 between the top marginal tax rate and the tax rate on corporate retained earnings was the largest in the world (Zee 1997), providing a powerful incentive for personal incorporation to postpone taxation to the future.

Saving

A major shift in the structure of national saving has taken place in Chile (figure 2-6). Large policy shifts and intense business cycles have been reflected in the saving rate of the central government, a variable that stabilized at an average 4.5 percent of GDP in the 1990s. Public enterprise rationalization adopted since 1974 did raise public enterprise saving to positive levels, but subsequent privatization led to a trend decline of state-owned enterprises (SOE) saving levels. Chile's radical 1981 pension reform led to a gradual increase in mandatory personal pension saving, standing at 3.7 percent of GDP in the 1990s. However, the most radical change is observed in voluntary private saving. After a dozen years of substandard saving performance—from 1975 to 1986—the private sector has raised quickly its voluntary saving rate, from 4.5 percent of GDP in 1986 to an average 14.4 percent of GDP throughout the 1990s. There is preliminary evidence that most of this increase has taken place in the corporate sector; households are saving little more than in the past.[9]

---

9. See Agosín, Crespi, and Letelier (1997). Because of the preliminary nature of their data and its limited time span, and my focus on the determinants of aggregate voluntary private saving (and not its composition), I make no further reference to the composition of aggregate private saving.

Figure 2-6. Sector Saving Rates in Chile, 1960–97

Percentage of GDP

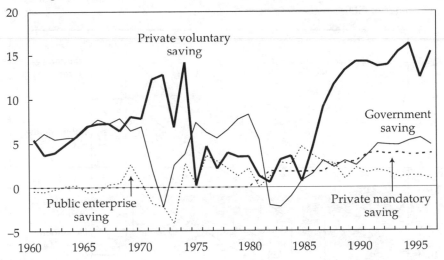

Source: Central Bank of Chile and author's calculations.

A number of recent studies have provided econometric evidence on Chile's private saving behavior.[10] Based on this literature and other empirical work on worldwide saving, I specify and estimate an equation for voluntary private saving for Chile.[11] The econometric results, reported in appendix 1, are used to decompose the rise in voluntary private saving between the 1961–74 prereform period and the 1990–97 period, by which time a significant part of the reforms had been completed and saving had taken off.

Figure 2-7 shows that the doubling in the national saving rate is due to a rise in nonfinancial public sector saving (from 4.9 percent to 6.6 percent of GDP), the emergence of mandatory private pension saving at an average 3.7 percent of GDP, and the large increase in voluntary private saving (from 7.7 percent to 14.4 percent of GDP). The latter increase is decomposed us-

---

10. These studies include Morandé (1996), Corsetti and Schmidt-Hebbel (1997), Agosín, Crespi, and Letelier (1997), Hachette (1997), and Haindl (1997).

11. Recent crosscountry studies on saving include Edwards (1995), Masson, Bayoumi and Samiei (1995), and Schmidt-Hebbel and Servén (1997, 1999).

Figure 2-7. Decomposition of Chile's Rise in National Saving
from 1961–74 to 1990–97

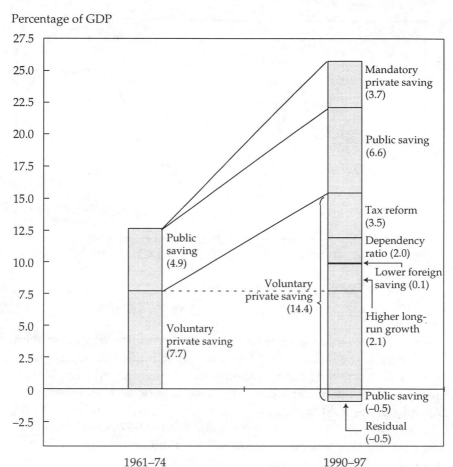

Percentage of GDP

1961–74   1990–97

Source: Based on author's regression reported in appendix 1, table A-1.

ing the regression coefficients reported in appendix 1 and the corresponding changes in saving determinants.

Fiscal adjustment—as reflected in the aforementioned increase in total
public saving—was offset only partially by lower private saving. The small
reduction in private saving (by 0.5 percent of GDP) is the result of a low
estimate for Chile's public-private saving offset coefficient, at 0.26. This
rejection of Ricardian equivalence implies that public saving is a very powerful tool to raise aggregate saving.

The substantial personal and corporate savings incentives provided by the tax reforms of the 1980s may have affected not only the composition of private voluntary saving but also its aggregate level. The tax incentives for corporate saving and investment discussed above lead to higher aggregate voluntary saving as long as firm owners do not offset the increase in corporate saving by lowering their personal saving levels. Further effects through higher personal saving may result from the substantial tax incentives provided to various forms of financial savings. The combined effect of the tax reforms and saving incentives is reflected in a 3.5 percent rise in voluntary private saving—a substantial amount.[12]

Now let's turn to nonpolicy saving determinants. Although foreign saving is a statistically and numerically significant private saving determinant with a 0.89 offset coefficient, the small increase in foreign saving from 1961–74 to 1990–97 contributes to a tiny 0.1 percent of GDP in private saving. Much more important is the effect of Chile's demographic transition. As baby-boom cohorts moved from childhood in the 1960s to mature adulthood in the 1990s, demographic dependency fell substantially, explaining 2.0 percent of the private sector's saving increase.

GDP growth (or the highly growth-correlated level of per-capita income) may raise private saving for many reasons: the declining share of people below subsistence consumption levels, the declining share of borrowing-constrained people, the presence of consumption habits, the rise in saving for offspring as bequests are valued as luxury goods, the rise in intertemporal substitution in response to higher income, or the income-responsive sub-

---

12. I have made use of a common tax reform dummy—dated at the important 1984 tax reform—that imposed the main changes in tax rates and saving incentives. Due to the high colinearity between top marginal income tax rates for individuals, corporate tax rates on retained earnings, and the provision of the 1984 saving incentives for individuals, the latter variables were not found to be individually significant in preliminary regressions (not reported in appendix 1). Exact offsetting of higher mandatory pension saving since the 1981 pension reform through lower voluntary personal saving is unlikely to occur when a fraction of pension savers are borrowing constrained, and household saving is as low as it is in Chile. Even additional voluntary saving could be observed as an effect of pension reform if the latter raises awareness about preparing for retirement. Preliminary evidence on the net effect of pension reform on voluntary saving is very mixed (Morandé 1996; Corsetti and Schmidt-Hebbel 1997; Schmidt-Hebbel 1998), but the latter study confirms that the overall effect of tax and pension reforms on voluntary saving has been positive.

stitution of wealth for consumption in individual preferences (Schmidt-Hebbel, Servén, and Solimano 1996a,b; Schmidt-Hebbel and Servén 1997, 1999). Whatever combination of reasons are behind Chile's rise in private saving, GDP growth is an adequate first-order proxy for these explanations. And the doubling of GDP growth from the 1960s to the 1990s explains a final 2.1 percent of GDP of Chile's private saving increase.

Investment

As in the case of saving, a major shift in the structure of gross domestic investment (at constant prices) has taken place in Chile (figure 2-8). Gross fixed-capital investment (GFKI) by the central government fell from 7.6 percent of GDP in 1960–74 to an average of 3.0 percent of GDP after 1974, with little further variations or structural breaks. Public enterprise GFKI shows a trend decline reflecting the decreasing share of public SOEs in GDP as a result of large-scale privatization. Inventory accumulation is highly erratic, close to zero until 1983, and then it stabilizes at a couple of percentage points of GDP afterwards. As in the case of saving, private GFKI shows a massive structural break. However, unlike saving, private investment in the late 1970s had already started to rise well beyond its historical level, probably in response to the early period of macroeconomic stabilization and structural reform. This progress was interrupted by the 1982–83 twin crisis and recession. From 1984 through 1995, private GFKI rises almost monotonically to reach a peak 22.5 percent of GDP. Throughout the 1990s private GFKI attained a historically unprecedented level of 20.8 percent of GDP.

A specification and regression result for private investment is provided in appendix 1, including a number of relevant economic and policy variables. It is based on empirical work on worldwide investment.[13] I use the empirical results to decompose the rise in Chile's private investment rate from 7.8 percent in 1961–74 to 20.8 percent in 1990–97.

Figure 2-9 shows that the 10.0 percent-of-GDP rise in gross domestic investment is due to an increase of inventory accumulation (from 0.1 percent of GDP to 3.4 percent of GDP), a large decline in overall public sector GFKI (from 11.3 percent to 4.7 percent of GDP), and the large rise in private GFKI.

Overall public investment enters with a negative sign the private investment equation reported in appendix 1. This suggests that the substitution effect of SOE investment dominates the complementarity effect of central government investment (public infrastructure). Therefore, the massive cut

---

13. See, for instance, Servén (1997).

Figure 2-8. Sector Gross Investment Rates in Chile, 1960–97
(at constant prices)

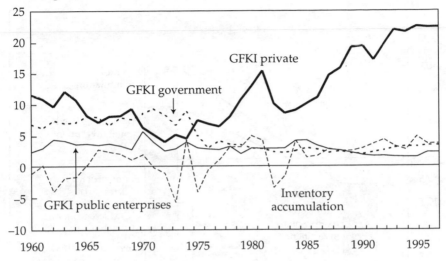

Percentage of GDP

Source: Central Bank of Chile and author's calculations.

in overall public investment has raised private investment by 1.6 percent of GDP. Separately, the large reduction in the corporate tax rate on retained earnings that took place between the 1960s and 1990s contributed to a 3.2 percent-of-GDP rise in private investment—similar in magnitude to the rise in private saving from tax reforms.

Macroeconomic stabilization, as measured by the decline in the volatility of inflation, contributed a meager 1.7 percent of GDP to higher private investment. Additional small benefits from macroeconomic improvement were reaped as a result of lower real interest rates (0.4 percent of GDP). However, this gain was more than offset by the negative effect of an external debt ratio to GDP in the 1990s that was slightly higher than in the 1961–74 period. This reflects a strong negative effect from debt overhang (–0.7 percent of GDP).

Better structural policies explain most of Chile's private investment takeoff. The investment ratio increased by 6.4 percent of GDP in the 1990s as a result of improved performance in the five policy areas included in the overall policy quality index. Indeed, almost half of the increase in private investment is attributable to structural and microeconomic policy reforms contributing to the improved incentive framework of private firms in Chile.

Figure 2-9. Decomposition of Chile's Rise in Gross Domestic Investment from 1961–74 to 1990–97

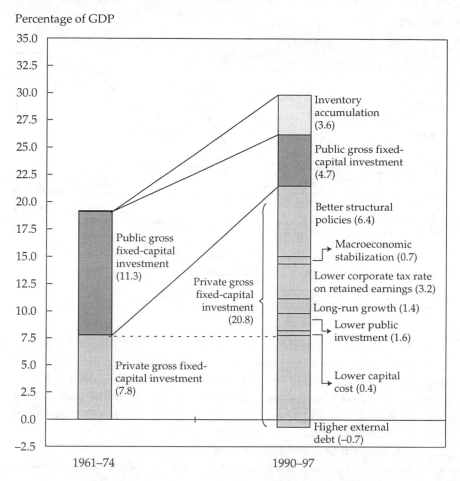

Percentage of GDP

Source: Based on author's regression reported in appendix 1, table A-2.

Finally, GDP growth has had a modest independent effect on private investment (+1.4 percent of GDP), a likely result of the positive influence of growth on private sector expectations about rates of return on their investment projects.

Growth

To assess Chile's recent takeoff experience and growth prospects, I use a production function that encompasses endogenous growth, the dynamic transition from current growth rates to sustainable stationary growth levels, a distinction between physical and nonphysical capital, and the role played by natural resources. Compared with other models, this growth model allows for a more powerful and realistic description of growth takeoff. Unlike the Solow growth model, it recognizes that stationary growth is affected by changes in policies and behavior. Unlike the simple endogenous growth model, it takes into account that transitional growth is different from steady-state growth.

As developed in more detail in appendix 2, output per unit of raw labor or per capita (y) is obtained as an aggregate of three production processes or sectors. The first embeds an AK-type endogenous-growth process with constant returns to broad capital per worker (k). The second sector reflects a Cobb-Douglas technology in broad capital and raw labor with declining returns to broad capital. The third represents a Cobb-Douglas technology in physical capital per capita (f) and nonreproducible natural resources per worker (nr) with declining returns to physical capital as well. Hence output per capita is determined by the following equation:

$$y = Z\,[Ak + Bk\alpha + Cf^{\beta}nr^{1-\beta}] \tag{1}$$

where broad capital per capita is defined as a Cobb-Douglas aggregate of physical capital per capita and nonphysical capital per capita (h). The latter is a combination of human capital, ideas, technology, and any other reproducible factor of production. Hence broad capital is defined as:

$$k = f^{\gamma} h^{1-\gamma} \tag{2}$$

where: $0 < \alpha, \beta, \gamma < 1$; and $A, B, C, Z > 0$.

Subsequently, I use different versions of equations 1 and 2 to assess Chile's takeoff and future growth prospects.

TRADITIONAL SOURCES OF GROWTH. Let's start by considering a conventional exogenous-growth version of equations 1 and 2 where output is produced by the second technology, and broad capital is restricted to physical capital only. This requires having $Z = 1$, $A = C = 0$, and $\gamma = 1$. An income share of physical capital (α) equal to 0.40 is used.[14] Coefficient B is reinterpreted as

---

14. This figure, consistent with the share of capital in Chilean national accounts, is widely used by other studies (Corbo, Lüders, and Spiller 1997; De Gregorio 1997; Roldós 1997; and Morandé and Vergara 1997).

Table 2-4. Sources of Growth in Chile, 1961–97

(percent)

Period	Capital growth	Labor growth	TFP growth	GDP growth
Unadjusted capital and labor				
1961–74	2.5	1.7	1.2	3.3
1975–81	1.3	2.9	2.0	4.4
1982–89	2.3	3.0	–0.1	2.6
1990–97	6.4	2.4	2.7	6.7
Quality-adjusted capital and labor				
1961–74	1.2	2.6	1.2	3.3
1975–81	1.3	4.6	1.0	4.4
1982–89	2.6	4.8	–1.2	2.6
1990–97	9.0	3.2	1.3	6.7

Source: Author's calculations.

a measure of total factor productivity (TFP), growing at an exogenous rate g_{TFP}. The latter rate—the standard Solow growth residual—is obtained by subtracting the contribution of the increase in physical capital and raw labor from GDP growth.

Table 2-4 reports standard growth accounting results—including the Solow residual—for relevant subperiods in Chile. The first set of results uses raw capital and labor data (not adjusted for changes in quality), while the second set is based on capital and labor series adjusted for estimated changes in quality.[15] Adjusting factor inputs for quality improvements reduced the contribution of TFP growth in the 1990s from 2.7 percent to 1.3 percent per year. The latter figure—a measure of "residual" Solow residual—is similar to residual TFP growth rates observed in the 1960s and 1970s (1.0 percent to 1.2 percent per year).

As the results confirm, it took Chile more than a decade of postreform experience before investment and TFP growth (or factor quality growth) responded significantly and on a sustained basis to the policy reforms started in the mid-1970s.

The Solow growth equation can be slightly restated by separating the growth rate of physical capital into the rate of physical investment (*inf*), the

---

15. The quality adjustment follows the methods and series reported in Roldós (1997).

average product of physical capital ($apf \equiv y/f$), and the rate of capital depreciation (δ):

$$g = \alpha \, [invf\, apf - \delta] + (1 - \alpha)n + g_{TFP} \tag{3}$$

where g is aggregate GDP growth, and n is employment growth.

Equation 3 explains Chile's growth takeoff—in the frame of the simple exogenous-growth model—in the following way (table 2-5). The significant increase in the rate of growth of physical capital—from 2.5 percent in the 1960s to 6.4 percent in the 1990s—is due to both a higher GFKI ratio and a larger average productivity of capital. The investment rate (GFKI/ GDP), after declining during the 1975–89 reform period, increased by 6.4 percent of GDP in the 1990s compared with its level in 1961–74. The average product of capital, which already started to rise during the reform period, was 14 percent higher in the 1990s compared with the 1960s.

Steady-state GDP growth is determined by the sum of exogenous TFP growth and employment growth in the Solow model. When using each period's observed values for the latter variables, one can conclude that actual GDP growth during 1961–74 (3.3 percent) was only slightly above the stationary growth level that could be achieved under prereform conditions (2.9 percent). This stands in contrast to the 1990s when actual growth (6.7 percent) exceeded significantly the steady-state growth level (5.1 percent). This larger difference can be attributed to the rather recent rise in the investment rate, which implies that Chile has still a long way to go before reaching its stationary growth rate if current postreform conditions are maintained.

By how much could Chile's growth rate increase if the country were able to raise its investment rate by, say, another 2.5 percent of GDP? The answer provided by the simple Solow growth model is straightforward: short-term GDP growth would increase by 0.4 percent to attain 7.1 percent (table 2-5). However, the long-term stationary growth level is unaffected by any change in the investment rate—a result of declining returns to capital in the Solow model.

Various authors have estimated Chile's potential growth rates. Most of them use a Solow growth decomposition exercise similar to the one presented above. Not surprisingly, their results (see table 2-6 for a summary) are also very close to those reported above.[16] For TFP growth rates in the

---

16. One should note that these results are short-term potential growth rates, not steady-state growth rates.

Table 2-5. Chile's Growth According to the Simple Exogenous-Growth Model, 1961–97

Period	GFKI/ GDP (invf) (%)	GDP/ capital (apf)	Depreciation rate (δ) (%)	Capital growth (gK) (%)	Employment growth (%)	TFP growth (g_{TFP}) (%)	Current GDP growth (%)	Steady state GDP growth (g^*) (%)
1961–74	19.1	0.393	5	2.5	1.7	1.2	3.3	2.9
1975–89	17.0	0.400	5	1.8	3.0	0.9	3.3	3.9
1990–97	25.5	0.447	5	6.4	2.4	2.7	6.7	5.1
Higher invest- ment	28.0	0.447	5	7.5	2.4	2.7	7.1	5.1

Source: Author's calculations.

range from 2.0 percent to 3.0 percent and investment rates from 24 percent to 30 percent of output, potential short-term growth rates are obtained in the range from 6.4 percent to 7.5 percent.

PRODUCTIVITY GAINS. As in the case of saving and investment, I specify and estimate empirical equations for TFP growth and the average product of capital—the two key productivity variables of the Solow growth model reported in table 2-5. Again I use the regression coefficients reported in appendix 1 to explain the rise in productivity variables (figure 2-10).

TFP growth (as measured by its three-year moving average) tripled during the past three decades, from 0.9 percent during 1961–74 to 2.9 percent in 1990–97 (figure 2-10). Controlling for the very negative effect of deteriorated terms of trade, TFP growth has been raised by macroeconomic stabilization (contributing 1.3 percent through lower inflation) and better structural policies (contributing 1.6 percent as measured by the large improvement of the overall policy index). Hence, by adopting better policies, Chile has been able to more than compensate for the effects of "bad luck" (the large permanent decline in the terms of trade suffered in the early 1970s) on productivity.

The quality of capital—as measured by the average productivity of physical capital—increased by 14 percent between 1961–74 and 1990–97 (figure 2-11). Most of this increase can be traced to better structural policies (the same variable that had the largest effect on raising the quantity of capital investment), controlling for the influence of labor quality and employment

Table 2-6. Potential Short-Term Growth Rates Estimated by Various Authors
(percent)

Author	Low growth	Key assumption	High growth	Key assumption
Marfán and Bosworth (1994)	4.2	Investment: 20	7.5	Investment: 27.5 TFP growth: 3
Chumacero and Quiroz (1997)	—	—	8.1	—
Rojas, López, and Jiménez (1997)	—	—	7.0	Investment: 30
De Gregorio (1997)	6.5	Investment: 25–30 Labor growth: 1.5 TFP growth: 3	7.0	Investment: 25–30 Labor growth: 1.5 TFP growth: 2.5
Roldós (1997)	6.4	Investment: 24 Labor quality: 0.6 Capital quality: 0.0 TFP growth: 1.9	7.5	Investment: 29 Labor quality: 0.6 Capital quality: 0.5 TFP growth: 2.4

levels. These results provide strong evidence that macroeconomic stabilization and structural reform have been the main determinants of Chile's productivity gains.

ENDOGENOUS GROWTH WITH TRANSITIONAL DYNAMICS. To overcome the limitations of the simple Solow model, I now make use of the full endogenous-growth model with transitional dynamics, broad capital, and nonreproducible natural resources, embedded in the production function of equations 1 and 2 above. The corresponding growth equation is the following:

$$g = \frac{mpf}{apf} [invf\, apf - (n + \delta)] + \frac{mph}{aph} [invh\, aph - (n + \delta)] + \frac{mpnr}{apnr} g_{nr} + n \quad (4)$$

where *mpf* (*mph*, *mpnr*) is the marginal product of physical capital (nonphysical capital, natural resources), *apf* (*aph*, *apnr*) is the average product of physical capital (nonphysical capital, natural resources), and g_{nr} is the rate of growth of natural resources per capita.

Chile's growth in the 1990s can be explained by the contribution of the growth determinants reflected in this model. This requires parameterizing production coefficients, sector shares, and factor growth rates. The full detail on parameter assumptions is provided in appendix 2. Here I briefly refer to key parameters. The current share of sector 2 (declining returns to broad capital) is fixed at 5 percent. The current share of sector 3 (produc-

Figure 2-10. Decomposition of Chile's Rise in Total Factor Productivity from 1961–74 to 1990–97

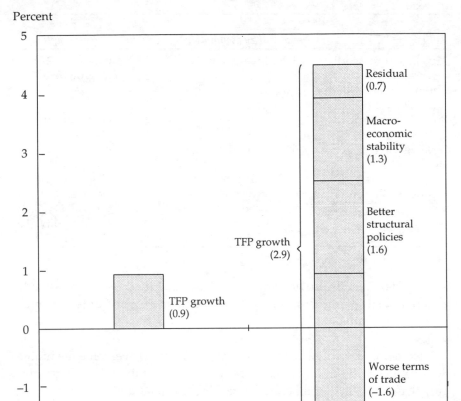

Percent

Note: The measure of TFP growth used here and in appendix 1 is a three-year moving average.

Source: Based on author's regression reported in appendix 1, table A-4.

tion based on nonreproducible natural resources) is 15 percent, equal to the sum of the current share of mining and fisheries in GDP (9.7 percent during 1990–97) and an estimate of the GDP share of manufacturing sectors based directly on natural resources (5.3 percent). The growth rate of use of nonreproducible natural resources (g_{NR}) is 7.2 percent, slightly above the current weighted average rate of growth of mining and fisheries (5.9 per-

Figure 2-11. Decomposition of Chile's Rise in Average
Productivity of Capital from 1961–74 to 1990–97

Index

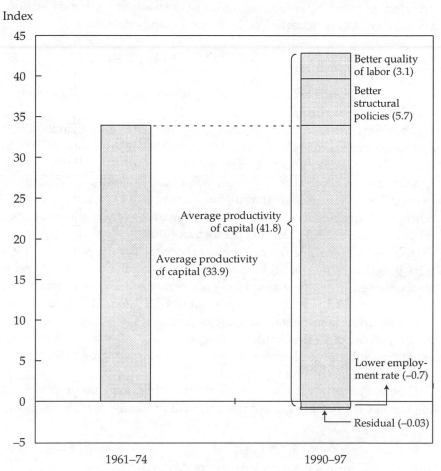

cent during 1990–97). The ratio of investment in nonphysical capital—human capital, R&D, ideas, and so on—to GDP is posited at 10 percent of GDP, which is twice the share of education and health in GDP during the 1990s (table 2-10).

Transitional growth exceeds stationary growth for two reasons. First, the marginal and average products of all factors of production are larger during the transition than at the final steady-state growth equilibrium. Second, by the very definition of nonreproducible natural resources (mostly mining deposits and fishing stock in the case of Chile), the transitional growth rate of the latter converges to zero in steady state. Hence, stationary GDP growth is characterized by the following equation:

$$g^* = \frac{mpf^*}{apf^*}\left[invf\,apf^* - (n + \delta)\right] + \frac{mph^*}{aph^*}\left[invh\,aph^* - (n + \delta)\right] + n \qquad (5)$$

where starred variables denote steady-state values of the corresponding variables defined above.

Table 2-7 reports the main variables governing GDP growth in the 1990s and its long-run convergence toward the steady-state level consistent with this model's structure and parameter values. Figure 2-12 depicts the corresponding interpretation of Chile's growth takeoff since the 1960s, growth in the 1990s, and subsequent transitional convergence to the stationary equilibrium. At current structural conditions, growth converges gradually from 6.7 percent now to 5.0 percent in the distant future.

How much more investment in physical capital and nonphysical capital is required to ensure that the level of GDP growth in the 1990s (6.7 percent) is maintained in the very long term? If the rate of GFKI is raised by 2.5 percent (from 25.5 percent to 28.0 percent of GDP) and, at the same time, spending on human capital, technology, and ideas is similarly expanded by 2.5 percent of GDP, short-term growth would increase to 8.5 percent, ensuring a subsequent convergence to a new stationary growth level of 6.7 percent (see table 2-7 and figure 2-12).

Therefore, natural resource–based growth, which explains 0.6 percent of the current 6.7 percent growth rate but will gradually vanish as a long-

Table 2-7. Chile's Growth Prospects According to the Author's Model
(percent)

Growth prospect	Physical investment rate (invf)	Non-physical investment rate (invh)	Nonrenewable natural resource growth (gNR)	Current GDP growth (g)	Steady-state GDP growth (g*)
1990–97	25.5	10.0	7.2	6.7	5.0
Higher investment	28.0	12.5	7.2	8.5	6.7

Source: Author's calculations.

Figure 2-12. Chile's Growth Takeoff and Future Growth Prospects According to a Model of Endogenous Growth with Transitional Dynamics

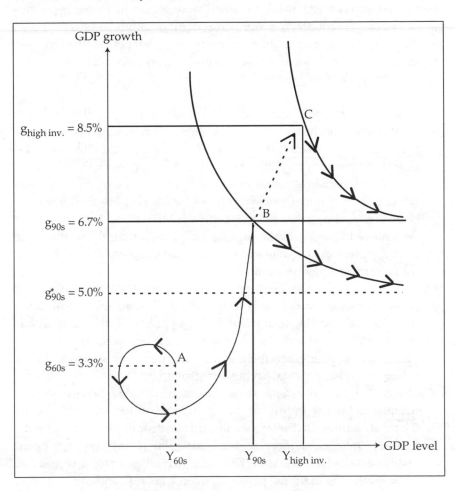

Source: Author's calculations.

term source of growth, provides a window of opportunity to shift the growth base toward reproducible resources. Further policy reforms to boost the growth of reproducible resources—physical capital, human capital, knowledge, and ideas—should be high on the policy agenda.

Ten Future Challenges

Chile has an extraordinary record: a decade of saving, investment, and growth that has enabled it to join the small set of successful emerging economies. How can the country's current growth momentum be extended well into the future? Chile's recent history and international experience suggest that the country's policymakers face 10 macroeconomic and sector policy challenges to make this possible.

1. *Ensure convergence to low inflation while attaining high price flexibility.* Continuation of the Central Bank's efforts to attain a successful convergence from current inflation levels close to 5 percent toward inflation levels prevalent in OECD countries is a necessary condition for maintaining high investment and growth rates. This should be achieved while attaining more flexible prices, including real wages, the real exchange rate, and nontraded goods prices. More price flexibility could be achieved as a result of adopting forward-looking wage and price contracts, deindexing monetary policy instruments, and preserving decentralized wage bargaining.

2. *Maintain a conservative fiscal policy stance.* While the public sector has shown consistent surpluses during the past decade, the consolidated nonfinancial and financial (Central Bank) public sector position has weakened recently. Ensuring maintenance of consolidated public surpluses would strengthen the macroeconomic policy stance and contribute to higher national saving and growth.

3. *Overhaul tax incentives for saving and investment.* Lower taxes have contributed to the rise in private saving and investment rates. However, the tax structure still displays significant shortcomings and distortions: excessive reliance on incentives for particular saving and investment instruments instead of across-the-board incentives, a world-record gap between the top marginal personal income tax rate and the corporate tax rate, a significant gap between tax rates on foreign and national investments, and low-yielding special taxes on particular activities or transfers. Several tax reform proposals have been put forward in anticipation of future action.[17]

4. *Keep the financial sector sound.* The ongoing Asian crisis suggests that banking fragility is typically a necessary and often a sufficient condi-

---

17. Among the tax reform proposals are Serra (1998) and Vergara and Fontaine (1997).

Table 2-8. Public Enterprise Output and Public Infrastructure Investment Shares in GDP
(percent)

Public enterprise and infrastructure investment	1990	1996
CODELCO value added	8.8	4.4
Other public enterprise value added	5.2	3.2
Public investment in infrastructure	1.0	1.6

Note: The shares are calculated at current prices, reflecting large copper price fluctuations affecting the state copper company, CODELCO.
Source: Ministry of Finance, Central Bank of Chile.

tion for causing a financial and external crisis with prolonged growth and welfare costs. Chile's strict financial regulation and supervision have contributed to the health of the country's banking sector. During a period of increasing bank competition and expansion into new services and regions, financial soundness can be promoted by complementing traditional banking supervision with market-based insurance mechanisms and lender-of-last-resort facilities, as implemented recently by Argentina.

5. *Privatize public enterprises and the provision of infrastructure investment.* The share of public enterprise output—8 to 10 percent of GDP, depending on the price of copper—is still quite large in Chile (table 2-8). Public investment in infrastructure represents another 1.6 percent of GDP. The government is involved in partial privatization of public water and sanitation companies and public ports. Building and/or operation of major infrastructure projects—including highways, tunnels, and airports—are currently transferred to the private sector through auctions and competitive concessions. Full privatization of all public enterprises and transfer of most infrastructure projects to the private sector—subject to adequate regulatory and supervisory frameworks in the case of natural monopolies—would boost growth significantly.

6. *Reform education.* Chile's indicators of educational attainment have improved since 1960 (table 2-9), but a large education gap separates Chile from East Asian high-growth economies and OECD countries. Insufficient human capital seems to be the Achilles' heel of Chile's growth prospects. What is needed is a massive rise in the quantity and quality of conventional primary and secondary education as well as in technical education and vocational training. The government is cur-

Table 2-9. Educational Attainment, 1960–95
(percent)

Year	Literacy rate	Student coverage Primary school	Student coverage Secondary school	Year	Average years of schooling
1960	83.6	n.a.	n.a.	1988	8.3
1970	89.0	93.3	49.7	1990	8.6
1980	90.8	95.3	65.0	1992	9.0
1990	94.6	98.2	79.9	1994	9.5
1995	95.4	95.7	79.3	1996	9.8

Source: National Institute of Statistics (INE); Ministry of Education.

rently implementing a major education reform to improve public and private education. Further improvements in the quality of education could be achieved by extending privately supplied education (currently 55 percent of total education expenditure, see table 2-10). Chile could raise the share of subsidies to private education or adopt a program of voucher-based education.

7. *Reduce poverty.* Chile made large strides in reducing poverty during the 1990s (table 2-11). This was largely the result of high growth and

Table 2-10. Spending on Public and Private Education and Health as a Share of GDP, 1990, 1995, and 1996
(percent)

Year	Education Public	Education Private	Education Total	Health Public	Health Private	Health Total
1990	1.60	1.75	3.35	0.69	1.46	2.15
1995	1.14	1.36	2.50	0.63	1.32	1.95
1996[a]	1.07	1.31	2.38	0.60	1.30	1.90

a. Estimated.
Source: Central Bank of Chile.

Table 2-11. Percentage of Chile's Population below the Poverty Line, 1987–96

1987	1990	1992	1994	1996
44.6	40.1	32.7	28.5	24.0

Source: CASEN.

Table 2-12. Income Distribution Indicators for Chile, 1968–97

Year	Gini coefficient	Year	Income distribution shares by quintiles		
			Lower 40%	Middle 40%	Upper 20%
1968	45.6	1969	11.7	31.3	57
1971	46.0	1978	9.7	29.5	60.8
1980	53.2	1987	7.5	24.0	68.5
1989	57.9	1991	10.1	28.8	61.0
1994	56.5	1994	10.5	30.6	58.9
		1997	10.0	30.5	59.5

Source: Gini coefficient: World Bank; income distribution shares: University of Chile; quoted in Marcel and Solimano (1994) for 1969–87, and kindly provided by Jaime Ruiz-Tagle (University of Chile) for 1991–97.

only partly the consequence of social expenditure programs (Larrañaga 1992). However, little progress has been achieved in reducing the relative gap between rich and poor (table 2-12). Significant poverty and large income differences put Chile at a significant distance from most other high-growth takeoff countries. The international experience suggests that overcoming widespread poverty—through improved access to better education and well-designed and targeted social programs—is a necessary condition for high private investment and growth.

8. *Reform the state.* To improve state efficiency, Chile has undertaken significant reforms. It established technical bodies (superintendencies) to supervise private enterprise behavior in sectors with externalities and market imperfections, and it adopted an independent Central Bank. However, areas of state administration (the judiciary in particular) are in urgent need of reform. Moreover, the distribution of authority and spending decisions between central and decentralized government levels needs to be reviewed, and the cabinet structure of the central government changed.

9. *Deepen trade opening.* During the 1990s, Chile followed a two-pronged trade reform strategy: unilateral reduction in external tariffs, and bilateral and multilateral trade agreements. While unilateral trade opening tends to yield larger output and welfare gains than do selective trade agreements, there could be hard-to-quantify additional market-accession gains from selective trade agreements.[18] Continuation of this

---

18. See the calculations by Harrison, Rutherford, and Tarr (1996) for Chile.

strategy is reflected in further unilateral tariff reduction enacted in late 1998 and continued work on bilateral and multilateral trade agreements (with the United States, Mercosur, APEC, and the European Union). This strategy puts Chile closer to the goal of complete free trade with the rest of the world.

10. *Address the political economy of remaining reforms.* Reforms that provide welfare and growth gains to a large but nonorganized population may be opposed by well-organized interest groups in the public sector (for instance, in health, education, public enterprises) and the private sector (for instance, sales agents of private pension management companies). They may attempt to block structural reforms that affect negatively their narrow interests. To overcome this opposition, the government must strike a difficult balance between conflict and negotiation with affected interest groups and the Congress in order to be able to implement the necessary reforms.

Ten Lessons from Chile's Experience

Chile's experience of broad and deep policy reforms since 1974 and its decade-long saving-investment-growth achievements provide valuable lessons to other reforming countries. The ten lessons that follow draw on reform evaluations for Latin America (including Burki and Perry 1997 and Inter-American Development Bank 1996) and for developing countries at large (Corbo and Fischer 1995; Rodrik 1996), as well as studies cited earlier in the chapter.

1. *Adopt sound policies.* Good policies—not good luck—trigger and sustain a growth takeoff. Chile's takeoff is mainly attributable to the massive macroeconomic and structural policy improvements achieved during the past two decades. In fact, the policy reforms more than compensated for the "bad luck" of Chile's permanent terms-of-trade loss suffered in the early 1970s. Saving mobilization, capital investment, and productivity gains have responded positively and strongly to a stable macroeconomic environment and the right incentive framework.

2. *Watch for hidden policy distortions.* Hidden build-ups of public liabilities—ranging from implicit public PAYG debts to increasing weaknesses in banking systems that require future bailouts—are often worse than explicit public deficits and debts. They hide sector distortions, cause moral-hazard behavior, and do not convey market signals that induce

the necessary corrections or reforms. Hidden relative price inflexibilities can be as bad as the former because their extent and costs are only apparent when the economy is hit by a severe adverse shock. Then it is often too late to adopt the necessary reforms. Chile's 1979–83 experience shows that the combination of implicit guarantees provided to a defaulting banking sector and inflexible exchange rates and wages is particularly costly.

3. *Invest in reproducible resources.* Trade opening often triggers a specialization of production and exports in natural resource–intensive sectors. The rents obtained from extracting nonrenewable resources—ideally at a sustainable rate—provide a window of opportunity for investing them in reproducible resources. This calls for a public policy that provides good incentives for investing in physical capital, human capital, knowledge, and ideas. A well-designed tax system is needed for a strong saving and investment response. Chile provides indirect proof that education is a key element in maintaining growth momentum.

4. *Avoid industrial policy.* Instead of pursuing an industrial policy, Chile has tried to provide symmetric treatment to all production sectors. It has focused on raising the overall supply of productive inputs instead of benefiting a particular resource or sector of production. This strategy—shared by many other Latin American reformers—seems to be paying off. The more activist industrial policies pursued by many East Asian economies have been less successful so far.

5. *Be prepared for the long haul.* Response lags to reforms should caution reformers to be prepared for the long haul. Depending on reform speed, reform mistakes, adverse shocks, and investment maturity lags in the new expanding sectors, the saving, investment, and growth response to reforms ranges from very short (as in Argentina after 1992) to very long (as in Chile).

6. *View reform optimality prescriptions with suspicion.* Most conventional recommendations on optimal reform sequencing, speed, and timing are irrelevant. This conclusion based on Chile's experience complements similar inferences reached by Corbo and Fischer (1995) for New Zealand and by the Inter-American Development Bank (1996) for other Latin American countries. Chile's experience and other real-world reform experiences cited in the preceding work strongly contradict the optimality prescriptions provided by the conventional literature. Those macroeconomic prescriptions are based on narrow models that abstract from the complexities of incentive structures, political-economy features, and reform processes. However, one remaining truth of the op-

timal sequencing literature is that macroeconomic stabilization should not come after structural reform—but it can be done in conjunction with price or financial liberalization. No other important recommendations on reform sequencing, speed, and timing have stood the test of successful real-world reforms.

7. *Reform broadly and quickly to take advantage of reform synergy.* Reformers should adopt as many reforms and as soon as possible—subject to at least some political support, the availability of competent technical teams for reform design and implementation, and certain preconditions on specific reforms (such as an adequate regulatory framework and an effective supervisory body). Governments should take advantage of reform synergy because there are declining marginal costs in planning reforms and selling them to the public. In addition, there are externalities of individual reforms for other reform areas; the sum of total reform benefits exceeds the sum of individual reform gains. Chile's experience confirms both points.

8. *Don't fear reform reversal and lack of credibility.* Expectations of reform reversals and lack of credibility are problems featured in the theoretical literature, but they do not seem to be very important in the experiences of many countries. Although some Chilean reforms (the 1975–79 trade reform and possibly the 1981 pension reform) faced initial problems of imperfect credibility, and some reforms were partially and temporarily reversed (trade reform and bank privatization during 1983–84), these were the exceptions rather than the rule. The lesson here is that weak reform credibility and the likelihood of policy reversal should not be taken as a hindrance to start strong reform programs.

9. *Reforms are feasible in democratic regimes.* Chile's post-1989 experience shows that continuation of macroeconomic stabilization and structural reforms are feasible under a democratic regime, although the pace of reform may be slower than expected. A crosscountry example is pension reform. The most radical pension reform to date is the one adopted by Chile's military government in 1981; all subsequent pension reforms adopted in the world—negotiated by democratic governments with their parliaments and often with affected interested groups—have been less radical in their substitution of pre-existing public pay-as-you-go systems.

10. *Use a careful strategy to overcome reform opposition.* In order to overcome opposition to growth-improving reforms by well-organized interest groups and lobbies that lose from the changes, democratic governments have to be careful in the design, marketing, and implementation of the

reforms. The literature on optimal reform strategies is split on this point (Rodrik 1996). While some authors argue that reforms should be adopted as a result of bottom-up consensus building and negotiation by all involved groups, other authors argue that it is more effective to impose or sell top-down reforms developed by technical teams without much negotiation with reform opponents. Chile's experience since 1990 suggests that a difficult balance has to be struck between both extremes. The actual mix of carrots (compensating reform losers) and sticks (denouncing the reform opponents' welfare-deteriorating actions) is determined by the relative political weight of the government, reform opponents, and reform supporters.

Appendix 1. Estimation Results

The subsequent regressions in tables A1–A4 are based on annual data for 1960 (1961) to 1997, available on request. Data sources are noted at the bottom of each regression table.

Table A1. Voluntary Private Saving Ratio to GDP (VPRSAV)

Variable	Definition	Coefficient	t-statistic
C	Constant	10.358	1.95
SGROWTH	Exponential smoothed growth	1.477	6.69
PUBSAV	Public saving ratio to GDP	−0.259	−2.64
FORSAV	Foreign saving ratio to GDP	−0.886	−6.07
DEPEND	Dependency ratio	−0.095	−1.50
D84	Tax reform dummy variable for 1984	3.508	2.98
D74	Tax reform dummy variable for 1974	7.292	3.94
R^2 adjusted		0.879	
F		40.19	
DW		2.12	

Note: Estimated by two-stage least squares.

Sources: FORSAV (Central Bank of Chile) has been instrumented by the following instruments: the private investment ratio to GDP (table A2), STRUCPOL (table A2), the terms of trade (table A4), the corporate tax rate (table A2), and the top individual tax rate (based on Edwards, Flores, and Williamson 1996). Other variables are VPRSAV (author's calculations based on Central Bank of Chile data and on PUBSAV), SGROWTH (author's estimation based on Central Bank data), PUBSAV (author's estimation based on Dirección de Presupuesto, various issues; Dirección de Presupuesto 1997, Larraín 1994), FORSAV (Central Bank of Chile), DEPEND (National Institute of Statistics), D84, D74.

Table A2. Private Investment Ratio to GDP (PRINV)

Variable	Definition	Coefficient	t-statistic
C	Constant	14.107	3.81
SGROWTH	Exponential smoothed growth	0.943	4.02
PUBINV	Public investment ratio to GDP	−0.243	−1.10
CORPTAX	Corporate tax rate	−0.076	−3.03
STRUCPOL	Structural policy indicator	0.118	3.20
UCK	User cost of capital	−0.218	−2.43
EXTDEBT	External debt ratio to GDP	−0.088	−5.54
INFVOL	Inflation volatility	−0.283	−3.18
R^2 adjusted		0.951	
F		101.58	
DW		1.59	

Note: Estimated by OLS.

Sources: PRINV (author's calculation based on Central Bank data and the public investment ratio to GDP), SGROWTH (table A2), PUBINV (Dirección de Presupuesto, various issues, Dirección de Presupuesto 1997, Larraín 1994), CORPTAX (author's estimation based on Edwards, Flores, and Williamson 1996), STRUCPOL (Lora 1997, extended by author's estimation), UCK (Central Bank of Chile), EXTDEBT (Central Bank of Chile), INFVOL (annual standard deviation of Consumer Price Index, Central Bank data).

Table A3. Average Productivity of Capital (y/k)

Variable	Definition	Coefficient	t-statistic
C	Constant	−45.572	−7.72
STRUCPOL	Structural policy indicator	0.106	4.07
E	Employment rate	0.743	9.72
LQI	Labor quality index	0.089	2.31
D7182	Dummy variable equal to 1 for 1971 and 1982; 0 otherwise	3.449	5.76
R^2 adjusted		0.913	
F		94.42	
DW		1.50	

Note: Estimated by OLS.

Sources: STRUCPOL (table A2), E (National Institute of Statistics), LQI (Rojas, López and Jiménez 1997).

Table A4. TFP Growth (gTFP)

Variable	Definition	Coefficient	t-statistic
C	Constant	0.101	0.05
STRUCPOL	Structural policy indicator	0.029	1.36
INF	Standardized CPI inflation rate	−0.074	5.91
TOT	Terms of trade	0.016	1.75
D7779	Dummy variable equal to 1 for 1977, 1978, and 1979; 0 otherwise	5.011	5.97
D82	Dummy variable for 1982	−6.177	−4.31
R² adjusted		0.713	
F		18.85	
DW		1.95	

Note: Estimated by OLS.

Sources: STRUCPOL (table A2), INF (author's calculation based on Consumer Price Index, Central Bank data), TOT (Central Bank data).

Appendix 2. Endogenous Growth with Transitional Dynamics, Broad Capital, and Nonreproducible Natural Resources

How can Chile's recent takeoff experience and future growth prospects be assessed? In order to encompass a richer growth process than the simple exogenous-growth case, I use a production function that allows for endogenous growth, transitional dynamics (as in the exogenous-growth case), broad capital, and nonrenewable natural resources. The subsequent model generalizes a framework for endogenous growth with transitional dynamics that allows for growth convergence (as in Barro and Sala-i-Martin 1995, chap. 1) by adding a nonreproducible natural–resource based production sector, which is most relevant for Chile.

The Model

Gross domestic product (Y) is obtained as an aggregate of three production processes or sectors. The first embeds an AK-type endogenous-growth process with constant returns to broad capital (K). The second sector reflects a Cobb-Douglas technology in broad capital and raw labor (L) with declining returns to broad capital. The third represents a Cobb-Douglas technology in physical capital (F) and nonreproducible natural resources (NR) with declining returns to physical capital as well. By contrast L is raw labor. Hence

$$Y = Z[AK + BK^{\alpha}L^{1-\alpha} + CF^{\beta} NR^{1-\beta}]. \tag{A1}$$

K represents here a broad form of capital that encompasses physical and human capital, as well as technology and ideas:

$$K = F^{\gamma} H^{1-\gamma} \tag{A2}$$

where $0 < \alpha, \beta < 1$; and $A, B, C, Z > 0$.

The advantage of this production process is that it nests four desirable features for characterizing Chile's current growth process: constant returns to capital in the long run (and hence endogenous growth), a convergence toward the steady state along which the returns to broad capital and hence growth decline until reaching the stationary growth level, a distinction between physical and other forms of nonphysical capital, and a role for nonreproducible natural resources in transitional growth.

Using small-case letters to denote variables per worker and after substituting equation (2) in (1), output per capita (that is, per unit of raw labor) can be written as:

$$y = Z\,[\,Af^\gamma h^{1-\gamma} + B(f^\gamma h^{1-\gamma})^\alpha + Cf^\beta nr^{1-\beta}].\tag{A3}$$

The growth rate of physical capital per capita g_f (nonphysical capital per capita g_h) is determined by the exogenous physical investment ratio to output *invf* (nonphysical investment ratio to output *invh*), the average product of physical capital *apf* (average product of nonphysical capital *aph*), and the rates of raw labor or population growth (n) and capital depreciation (δ):

$$g_f = invf\,apf - (n + \delta)\tag{A4}$$

$$g_h = invh\,aph - (n + \delta).\tag{A5}$$

The growth rate of aggregate output is:

$$g \equiv g_y + n = \frac{mpf}{apf}g_f + \frac{mph}{aph}g_h + \frac{mpnr}{apnr}g_{nr} + n\tag{A6}$$

where *mpf* (*mph, mpnr*) is the marginal product of physical capital (nonphysical capital, natural resources) per capita.

After substituting equations (A4) – (A5) into (A6), obtain output growth as:

$$g = \frac{mpf}{apf}[invf\,apf - (n + \delta)] + \frac{mph}{aph}[invh\,aph - (n + \delta) + \frac{mpnr}{apnr}g_{nr} + n\tag{A7}$$

Note that average products and marginal products (as well as their ratios) of physical capital, human capital, and natural resources can be written as functions of the shares of sector 2 (s_2) and sector 3 (s_3), as follows:

$$ap = \frac{ZA\,(h/f)^{1-\gamma}}{1 - s_2 - s_3}\tag{A8}$$

$$s_2 = \frac{ZA\,(f^\gamma/h^{1-\gamma})^\alpha}{y}\tag{A9}$$

$$s_3 = \frac{ZCf^\beta nr^{1-\gamma}}{y}\tag{A10}$$

$$\frac{mpf}{apf} = \gamma(1 - s_2 - s_3) + \gamma \alpha s_2 + \beta s_3 \qquad \text{(A11)}$$

$$aph = \frac{ZA\,(f/h)^\gamma}{1 - s_2} \qquad \text{(A12)}$$

$$\frac{mph}{aph} = (1 - \gamma)(1 - s_2) + (1 - \gamma)\alpha s_2 \qquad \text{(A13)}$$

$$\frac{mpnr}{apnr} = (1 - \beta)s_3. \qquad \text{(A14)}$$

Transitional growth exceeds stationary growth for two reasons. First, the marginal and average products of all factors of production are larger during the transition than at the steady-state equilibrium. Second, by the very definition of nonreproducible natural resources (mostly mining deposits and fishing stock in the case of Chile), the growth rate of the latter is zero in steady state. Hence stationary GDP growth is characterized by the following equation:

$$g^* = \frac{mpf^*}{apf^*}[invf\,apf^* - (n + \delta)] + \frac{mph^*}{aph^*}[invh\,aph^* - (n + \delta)] + n \qquad \text{(A15)}$$

where starred variables denote steady-state values of the corresponding variables defined above. Their stationary values are the following (recall that $s_2^* = 0 = s_3^*$):

$$apf^* = ZA(h/f)^{1-\gamma} \qquad \text{(A16)}$$

$$\frac{mpf^*}{apf^*} = \gamma \qquad \text{(A17)}$$

$$aph^* = ZA(f/h)^\gamma \qquad \text{(A18)}$$

$$\frac{mpf^*}{apf^*} = \gamma - 1. \qquad \text{(A19)}$$

Model Parameterization

Coefficient values: $\gamma = 0.5$, $\alpha = 0.5$, $\beta = 0.2$, $s_2 = 0.05$, $s_3 = 0.15$, $\delta = 0.05$.

Values of exogenous variables: $n = 2.4\%$, $invf = 25.5\%$, $invh = 10\%$, $apf = 0.447$ (hence $g_f = 4.0\%$).

Hence the following values for endogenous variables are obtained: $aph = 1.14$ (hence $g_h = 4.0\%$), $mph/apf = 0.4425$, $mph/aph = 0.4875$, $g_{nr} = 4.8\%$ (obtained residually from growth equation (A7), $apf^* = 0.358$, $aph^* = 1.083$.

Substituting the preceding values in the current growth equation (A7) and the steady-state growth equation (A15) allows us to obtain the corresponding values for 1990–97 and the higher-investment scenario, reported in table 2-6.

References

Agénor, P., and P. Montiel. 1996. *Development Macroeconomics*. Princeton, N.J.: Princeton University Press.

Agosín, M., G. Crespi, and L. Letelier. 1997. "Explicaciones del Aumento del Ahorro en Chile." *Documentos de Trabajo* 149, Departamento de Economía, Universidad de Chile, Santiago.

Attanasio, O., L. Picci, and A. Scorcu. 1997. "Saving, Growth, and Investment: A Macroeconomic Analysis Using a Panel of Countries." World Bank, Washington, D.C.

Barro, R., and X. Sala-i-Martin. 1995. *Economic Growth*. New York: McGraw-Hill.

Bosworth, B., R. Dornbusch, and R. Labán. 1994. *The Chilean Economy: Policy Lessons and Challenges*. Washington D.C.: The Brookings Institution.

Burki, S.J., and G.E. Perry. 1997. *The Long March: A Reform Agenda for Latin America and the Caribbean in the Next Decade*. World Bank, Washington, D.C.

Carroll, C.D., and D.N. Weil. 1994. "Saving and Growth: "A Reinterpretation." *Carnegie-Rochester Conference Series in Public Policy* 40: 133–92.

Chumacero, R., and J. Quiroz. 1997. "Ciclos y Crecimiento en la Economía Chilena: 1985–1996." In F. Morandé and R. Vergara, eds., *Análisis Empírico del Crecimiento en Chile*. CEP - ILADES/Georgetown University, Santiago.

Corbo, V., R. Lüders, and P. Spiller. 1997. "The Foundation of Successful Economic Reforms: The Case of Chile." Catholic University of Chile, Santiago.

Corbo, V., and S. Fischer. 1995. "Structural Adjustment, Stabilization, and Policy Reform: Domestic and International Finance." In J. Behrman and T. N. Srinivasan, eds., *Handbook of Development Economics*. Amsterdam: North-Holland.

Corsetti, G., and K. Schmidt-Hebbel. 1997. "Pension Reform and Growth." In S. Valdés-Prieto, ed., *The Economics of Pensions: Principles, Policies, and International Experience*. Cambridge, U.K.: Cambridge University Press.

Cortázar, R., and J. Vial. 1998. *Construyendo Opciones: Propuestas Económicas y Sociales para el Cambio de Siglo*. CIEPLAN - Dolmen, Santiago.

De Gregorio, J. 1997. "Crecimiento Potencial en Chile: Una Síntesis." In F. Morandé and R. Vergara, eds., *Análisis Empírico del Crecimiento en Chile*. CEP - ILADES/ Georgetown University, Santiago.

Dirección de Presupuesto. annual. *Balance Consolidados del Sector Público*. Ministry of Finance of Chile, Santiago.

―――. 1997. "Estadísticas de las Finanzas Públicas 1987–1996." Ministry of Finance of Chile, Santiago.

Edwards, G., T. Flores, and C. Williamson. 1996. "Análisis del Sistema Tributario Chileno y Evidencia Internacional." *Informe para la Cámara Nacional de Comercio*. Instituto Economía, P. Universidad Católica de Chile, Santiago.

Edwards, S. 1995. "Why Are Saving Rates So Different across Countries? An International Comparative Analysis." NBER Working Paper 5097. Cambridge, Mass.

Edwards, S., and A. Cox Edwards. 1987. *Monetarism and Liberalization: The Chilean Experience*. Cambridge, Mass.: Ballinger.

Feldstein, M., and C. Horioka. 1980. "Domestic Savings and International Capital Flows." *Economic Journal* 90 (June): 314–29.

Hachette, D. 1997. "Ahorro Privado en Chile." Universidad Católica de Chile, Santiago.

Haindl, E. 1997. "Chilean Pension Fund Reform and its Impact on Savings." Instituto de Economía, Universidad Gabriela Mistral, Santiago.

Harrison, G., T. Rutherford, and D. Tarr. 1996. "Opciones de Política Comercial para Chile: Una Evaluación Cuantitativa." *Cuadernos de Economia* 102: 101–37.

Inter-American Development Bank. 1996. "Economic and Social Progress in Latin America." Washington, D.C.

Kaminsky, G., and C. Reinhart. 1996. "The Twin Crises: The Causes of Banking and Balance of Payments Problems." Board of Governors of the Federal Reserve System, Washington, D.C.

Larraín, F. 1991. "Public Sector Behavior in a Highly Indebted Country: The Contrasting Chilean Experience." In F. Larraín and M. Selowsky, eds., *Public Sector and Latin American Crisis*. San Francisco, Calif.: ICS Press.

Larraín, F., ed., 1994. *Chile hacia el 2000: Ideas para el Desarrollo*. Santiago: Centro de Estudios Públicos.

Larraín, F., and F. Rosende. 1994. "Como mantener un Crecimiento elevado." In F. Larraín, ed., *Chile hacia el 2000: Ideas para el Desarrollo*. Santiago: Centro de Estudios Públicos.

Larrañaga, O. 1992. "Pobreza, Crecimiento e Igualdad: Chile 1987–1992." *Revista de Análisis Económico* 9 (2): 69–92.

Loayza, N., and L. Palacios. 1997. "Economic Reform and Progress in Latin America and the Caribbean." Policy Research Working Paper 1829. World Bank, Policy Research Department, Washington, D.C.

Lora, E. 1997. "Una Década de Reformas Estructurales en América Latina: Qué se ha Reformado y Cómo Medirlo." Inter-American Development Bank, Washington, D.C.

Marcel, M., and A. Solimano. 1994. "The Distribution of Income and Economic Adjustment." In B. Bosworth, R. Dornbusch, and R. Labán, eds., *The Chilean Economy: Policy Lessons and Challenges*. Washington, D. C.: The Brookings Institution.

Marfán, M., and B. Bosworth. 1994. "Saving, Investment and Economic Growth." In B. Bosworth, R. Dornbusch, and R. Labán, eds., *The Chilean Economy: Policy Lessons and Challenges*. Washington, D. C.: The Brookings Institution.

Marshall, J., and A. Velasco. 1998. "Otra Década de Crecimiento: Desafío y Perspectivas." In R. Cortázar and J. Vial, eds., *Construyendo Opciones: Propuestas Económicas y Sociales para el Cambio de Siglo*. CIEPLAN - Dolmen, Santiago.

Masson, P., T. Bayoumi, and H. Samiei. 1995. "Saving Behavior in Industrial and Developing Countries." In "Staff Studies for the World Economic Outlook." *World Economic and Financial Surveys*. Washington, D.C.: International Monetary Fund.

Morandé, F. 1996. "Saving in Chile: What Went Right?" *Documentos de Trabajo*. ILADES/Georgetown University, Santiago, April.

Morandé, F., and R. Vergara, eds., 1997. *Análisis Empírico del Crecimiento en Chile*. CEP - ILADES/Georgetown University, Santiago.

Obstfeld, M., and K. Rogoff. 1996. *Foundations of International Macroeconomics*. Cambridge, Mass.: MIT Press.

Rodrik, D. 1996. "Understanding Economic Policy Reform." *Journal of Economic Literature* 34 (1): 9–41.

Rojas, P., E. López, and S. Jiménez. 1997. "Determinantes del Crecimiento y Estimación del Producto Potencial en Chile: El Rol del Comercio Internacional." In F. Morandé and R. Vergara, eds., *Análisis Empírico del Crecimiento en Chile*. CEP - ILADES/Georgetown University, Santiago.

Roldós, J. 1997. "El Crecimiento del Producto Potencial en Mercados Emergentes: El Caso de Chile." In F. Morandé and R. Vergara, eds., *Análisis Empírico del Crecimiento en Chile*. CEP - ILADES/Georgetown University, Santiago.

Schmidt-Hebbel, K. 1998. "Does Pension Reform Really Spur Productivity, Saving, and Growth?" Working Paper 33, Central Bank of Chile, Santiago.

Schmidt-Hebbel, K., and L. Servén. 1997. *Saving across the World: Puzzles and Poli-cies.* World Bank Discussion Paper 354. Washington, D.C.

———. 1999. *The Economics of Saving and Growth: Theory and Implications for Policy.* Cambridge, U.K.: Cambridge University Press.

Schmidt-Hebbel, K., L. Servén, and A. Solimano. 1996a. "Saving and Investment: Paradigms, Puzzles, Policies." *The World Bank Research Observer* 11 (February): 87–117.

———. 1996b. "Saving, Investment, and Growth in Developing Countries: An Overview." In A. Solimano, ed., *Road Maps to Prosperity: Essays on Growth and Development.* Ann Arbor: The University of Michigan Press.

Serra, P. 1998. "Evaluación del Sistema Tributario Chileno y Propuesta de Reforma." Central Bank of Chile Working Paper 40, Santiago.

Servén, L. 1997. "Economic Uncertainty and Private Investment: An Empirical In-vestigation." World Bank, Washington, D.C.

Vergara R., and B. Fontaine. 1997. "Una Reforma Tributaria para el Crecimiento." *Documento de Trabajo* No. 269, Centro de Estudios Públicos, Santiago.

Zee, H. 1997. "Revenue, Efficiency, and Equity Aspects of Major Taxes in Chile: A Preliminary Assessment." International Monetary Fund, Washington, D.C.

3

Capital Markets in Chile, 1985–97: A Case of Successful International Financial Integration

Nicolas Eyzaguirre
Fernando Lefort

Progress in the 1990s

In 1997 the Chilean economy completed 14 years of continuous high growth, averaging 7.8 percent in the 1990s. This remarkable achievement encompassed other progress: inflation declined to a rate approaching industrial countries´ standards, the internal savings rate had tripled since 1985 (reaching 22 percent of GDP in the 1994–96 period), and the investment ratio—at current prices—climbed to 28 percent in 1996 from only 17 percent in 1985. External equilibrium has been carefully monitored. International reserves increased from dangerously low levels in the mid-1980s to more than nine months of imports of goods and services in 1997, while the current account deficit in the 1990s averaged a moderate 3 percent of GDP.

Another salient feature of Chile's economy has been the rapid deepening of its capital markets. Deposits in the banking sector increased from 30 percent of GDP in the mid-1980s to almost 45 percent in 1996; government bonds climbed from 13 percent to 33 percent of GDP and private bonds from 7 percent to 15 percent over the same period. Paid stocks, as low as 13

Table 3-1. Chile's Financial Assets, 1980–96

Year	Paid stocks[a]	Private bonds[b]	Government bonds[c]	M7 (less public bonds)	Total
	Market Value of Chile's Financial Assets in Millions of Dollars, 1980–96				
1980	10,287	282	1,501	11,069	23,139
1981	7,045	1,987	1,065	10,041	20,138
1982	6,847	2,430	3,700	4,714	17,691
1983	3,922	1,894	3,700	7,252	16,768
1984	3,783	2,090	4,271	7,606	17,750
1985	4,044	2,126	4,271	9,466	19,907
1986	7,854	2,183	5,389	10,032	25,458
1987	9,654	2,274	6,188	11,720	29,836
1988	11,889	3,009	7,464	13,657	36,019
1989	16,027	3,716	8,518	16,732	44,993
1990	20,520	4,341	12,131	16,379	53,371
1991	39,465	5,123	15,608	16,406	76,602
1992	37,835	5,542	17,656	18,609	79,642
1993	57,210	6,281	18,177	22,038	103,706
1994	74,669	7,835	20,436	22,744	125,684
1995	73,121	9,061	21,788	26,862	130,832
1996	66,215	10,455	23,292	30,814	130776
	Chile's Financial Assets as a Percentage of GDP, 1980–96				
1980	30.12	0.83	4.40	32.41	67.75
1981	20.85	5.88	3.15	29.72	59.61
1982	31.23	11.08	16.87	21.50	80.69
1983	13.27	6.41	12.52	24.54	56.74
1984	12.62	6.97	14.25	25.38	59.24
1985	12.96	6.81	13.69	30.34	63.80
1986	23.33	6.48	16.01	29.80	75.61
1987	25.89	6.10	16.59	31.42	80.00
1988	28.05	7.10	17.61	32.22	84.98
1989	34.78	8.06	18.48	36.31	97.64
1990	45.59	9.64	26.95	36.39	118.57
1991	82.36	10.69	32.57	34.24	159.87
1992	70.66	10.35	32.98	34.76	148.75
1993	101.17	11.11	32.14	38.97	183.40
1994	123.90	13.00	33.91	37.74	208.55
1995	107.79	13.36	32.12	39.60	192.86
1996	94.39	14.90	33.20	43.93	186.42

a. Includes both public and private stocks, excludes mutual fund shares.
b. Includes corporate bonds, commercial papers, financial sector bonds, and mortgages.
c. Includes corporate bonds, banks, mortgages, treasury securities, and Central Bank securities.
Source: Programa Interamericano de Macroeconomia Aplicada (PIMA).

percent of GDP in the mid-1980s, surged to 95 percent of GDP in 1996. The cumulative amount of these financial assets increased from 68 percent of GDP in 1985 to 187 percent in 1996 (see table 3-1).

These figures are impressive not only in terms of their growth rates. When Chile is compared with other Latin American countries, we find that Chile's banking intermediation in 1994, as measured by total loans as a percentage of GDP, almost doubled Brazil's, the second largest ratio in the region (table 3-2). In 1995 stock market capitalization in Chile as a percentage of GDP at least tripled capitalization in any other Latin American economy (table 3-3). Moreover, the level of securities outstanding as a percentage of GDP compares with the levels attained in industrial countries (with the exception of the United States, which exhibits deeper capital markets) and Asian emerging markets (with the exception of Malaysia). Another salient feature of Chile's economy is the relatively low value of the bank intermediation ratio. This is a clear sign of the maturity of capital markets and a positive development in terms of the variety of financing sources available to firms. Chile's favorable bank intermediation ratio may limit the potential emergence of systemic financial problems.

Although the capital output ratio of an economy that undertakes structural reforms is likely to increase substantially and therefore capital markets may deepen, the road to domestic financial deregulation and international financial integration is often full of bumps. It is today generally accepted that the development of financial markets enhances growth possibilities, and growth in turn promotes financial market development. How to achieve this synergy, however, is far from trivial. In fact, damaging effects of financial crises on the real economy, and on capital market developments in par-

Table 3-2. Banking in Latin America, 1994

Country	Total assets (billions of US$) (1)	Assets/GDP (percent) (2)	Loans/GDP (percent) (3)	Banking participation in intermediation (percent) (4)
Argentina	82	29	18	98
Brazil	338	61	26	97
Chile	54	104	47	62
Colombia	23	35	19	86
Mexico	158	47	—	87
Venezuela	16	28	9	92

Note: Excludes development banks
Source: Larraín (1995).

Table 3-3. Shares and Bonds in Selected Countries

Country	Listed enterprises (1995)	Capital-ization (as a % of GDP)	Shares (1995)		Bonds (1994)	
			Concen-tration[a]	Turnover[b]	Capital-ization	Turnover[b]
Argentina	149	13.4	47.7	28.1	7.0	600
Brazil	544	26.2	77.6	83.4	—	—
Chile	315	109.4	57.7	9.5	9.6	275
Colombia	190	23.9	52.5	17.8	1.6	—
Mexico	190	36.3	56.5	46.5	8.7	33
Venezuela	91	4.9	80.7	20.2	5.2	—
United States	—			69.7	108.3	1,460
Japan	—			32.4	78.0	250
Germany	—			97.8	70.1	2,120

a. Percentage of the 10 most active shares in the total transactions.
b. Transacted value as a percentage of capitalization.
Source: For listed enterprises: IFC, *Quarterly Review of Emerging Stock Markets*. For capitalization and turnover: Bank for International Settlements (1996).

ticular, have been far more devastating when they have included an international dimension (that is, a currency crisis). Recent experience suggests that the direction of crisis causality can run both ways: from a macroeconomic crisis to a financial crisis and from an initial disturbance limited to the banking sector to a full-blown macroeconomic crisis.

Chile's successful financial market and macroeconomic developments have rested on the interaction of three main pillars: (1) sound macroeconomic policies; (2) stringent banking and securities regulation and supervision; and (3) gradual capital account deregulation and international financial integration. The crucial word here is "interaction." Chile's orderly financial progress would not have been possible without solid macroeconomic fundamentals. But the maintenance of those fundamentals benefited from the strict framework of banking regulation and supervision in place since 1986. This framework prevented the emergence of a credit boom against a backdrop of rapidly increasing income levels and abundant external financing. In turn, the cautious and appropriately sequenced capital account deregulation sheltered the financial sector from the abundance of foreign funds and limited banks' credit risk through measures designed to discourage foreign exchange exposure in the balance sheets of nonbanks.[1]

---

1. Chile's sequenced capital account deregulation contrasts sharply with the sequences undertaken in the Southeast Asian economies.

The Hard Lessons of the 1980s and Subsequent Reforms

Chile learned the hard way. Premature domestic financial deregulation (without a suitable regulatory and supervisory framework) and abrupt capital account deregulation led to a massive collapse of the Chilean economy in 1982. GDP fell by 13.4 percent in 1982, declining again 3.6 percent in 1983, and the bailout of the financial system amounted to nearly 40 percent of GDP. The consequent accumulation of a stock of public debt issued to finance the bailout took years of growth and fiscal consolidation to be absorbed. Financial assets, which had reached more than 80 percent of GDP in 1982, scaled back and did not recover to that level until the late 1980s.

After the financial collapse a bold program of macroeconomic measures was implemented. Since the late 1980s there has been an overall fiscal surplus averaging close to 2 percent of GDP. The attainment of such a surplus is even more noticeable when considering that the pensions of the retirees have been mainly financed with current public income, while the contributions of the active employees have accumulated, as fresh savings, in the private pension funds. As is well known, Chile radically transformed its pension system in the 1980s, turning the old pay-as-you-go system into a capitalization scheme. The deficit from the old system has been fully accounted for in the budget, amounting to yearly expenses of some 3 percent of GDP. Private pension funds accumulated in 1996 around 40 percent of GDP in financial assets, with a sizable contribution, both in terms of amount and efficiency, to the development of capital markets.

Equally important was the radical transformation of the banking regulatory and supervisory scheme through the enactment in 1986 of a new banking law. This law, amended in 1989, was complemented by a securities law in 1993 that increased transparency in the capital markets and regulated conflicts of interest. At the end of 1997 a new law widened banks' activities and set rules for the internationalization of the banking system.

The 1986 banking law provided for stringent regulation and supervision of the banking system. The dedicated work of the supervisory authority, enhanced by a clear and powerful legal framework, has fostered sound development of the banking sector. Certainly, credit from the banking to the private sector has been growing since the economy began to recover in 1985. However, given the unusual and sustained high rates of growth of the economy and the flood of international funds into the country in the 1990s, banking lending growth can be considered prudent, especially when compared with the lending booms that characterized other emerging markets in the same decade.[2] Nonperforming loans, as a percentage of total loans, have decreased steadily, reaching 1 percent in 1996, a clear sign that the financial system is sound. Although a stable macroeconomic environment contributed to this progress, the careful design and strict implementation of the 1986 banking law and subsequent amendments are the real basis of the healthy condition of the banking sector and, no doubt, of the soundness of the economy at large.

The Current Economic Picture

The Chilean economy received enormous amounts of foreign capital throughout the 1990s. In fact, together with Malaysia, Thailand, and, until 1994, Mexico, Chile experienced the earliest, and cumulatively among the largest, surges in capital flows in the 1990s. The Chilean authorities reacted with measures aimed at reaping the benefits and minimizing the risks of the new environment. Those measures included a strong fiscal surplus, reforms in monetary policy, special devices to protect the integrity of the financial sector, a more flexible exchange rate regime coupled with a massive sterilized intervention in the foreign exchange markets, a continuous deregulation of capital outflows, and a gradual and selective openness to capital inflows.

These measures have not inhibited capital inflows (they were never intended to do so), but they have determined a favorable maturity composition of the capital account, which has improved the economy's resilience to adverse foreign shocks. The gradual strengthening of the domestic currency has given exporters time to adjust and improve competitiveness. The remarkable surge in the average product of labor (favored by the large and increasing rates of investment against a background of highly deregulated prices of goods and services) has enabled exporters to adapt to more stringent competitive conditions. In fact, exports in volume continued to grow well above output throughout the 1990s despite the significant, but gradual, appreciation of the peso.

---

2. Again, credit growth rates in Chile had been substantially lower than in Southeast Asia (Johnston, Darbar, and Echeverría 1997), a fact that is even more noticeable since capital inflows as a percentage of GDP as well as growth rates were similar in Chile and Southeast Asia before the crisis.

We resist the temptation to draw simplistic lessons from the Chilean experience. Given the current volatility of financial markets, it is hard to assert that the economy is protected against any level of international disturbance. Having said that, however, we seriously doubt that current events are going to affect the Chilean economy in any significant way, since they did not in the aftermath of the 1995 crisis in Mexico.

Although the size of the external shock was fairly large (about 2.5 percent of GDP solely measuring the terms-of-trade deterioration), the economy was projected to grow 4 percent in 1998 and 3 percent or more in 1999. The slowdown in growth has been determined mainly by the need to avoid an excessive current account deficit while export markets and prices remain depressed and external finance is scarce. The financial sector remains healthy, and the currency has depreciated moderately. Inflation continues to decrease, and transitory currency pressures have been abated through preemptive monetary and fiscal tightening. The profile of external debt amortizations is favorable given the policies that were undertaken to lengthen the external debt's maturity structure.

Some policies, especially the controversial reserve requirement described later in the chapter, have worked reasonably well because of the strength of the rule of law in Chile and the power and independence of the Central Bank. The gradual and cautious deregulation process has had some opportunity costs, especially in terms of the internationalization of the financial services industry and the diversification of residents' portfolios. Last but not least, the selection of what agents can and cannot do entails some degree of arbitrariness; regrettably, the less powerful firms and agents lacking access to sophisticated external sources of funding have been discriminated against. This may have had some adverse effects in terms of concentration of wealth.

Notwithstanding the above, we remain convinced that the Chilean road to domestic financial deregulation and international integration is going in the right direction. The case of Chile supports the idea that a stringent framework of banking regulation and supervision is critical, and that in the case of emerging markets such a framework may need to be even more stringent than the standards for industrialized countries given the volatility in some key variables. Indeed, international integration makes that stringent framework even more desirable, most probably as a precondition of capital account liberalization. Also needed are tight fiscal policies that contribute to internal savings and help stabilize domestic demand and monetary policies that dampen the volatility of inflation and output and provide a credible anchor for the domestic currency. If the country floats, the commitment of monetary policy to low inflation is likely to be tested by markets through occasional currency pressures. The magnitude and volatility of capital flows make it a necessity to avoid domestic elements that can enhance that unstable behavior (for example, implicit insurances, lack of transparency, poor disclosure requirements, and exchange rate rigidity). Given the difficulties of controlling the initial demand pressures stemming from capital inflows, and the possible occurrence of bubbles in asset prices, it is clear that it is necessary to take measures to "smooth" the process of financial integration. Special attention should be paid to designing an appropriate framework to deal with a higher level of currency and credit risk.

This chapter briefly describes some theoretical interactions between capital markets and growth. It then addresses measures in the macroeconomic arena that have affected, directly or indirectly, the development of capital markets and the sequencing and rationale of the capital account deregulation. We then examine the evolution of the banking sector and the structure of incentives provided in the law. In our discussion of the stock and bond markets, we pay special attention to the importance of internationalization and pension reform. The chapter concludes with an assessment of future challenges.

Capital Markets and Growth

It can be argued that part of the development and depth achieved by the Chilean financial sector during the past 20 years is a natural consequence of capital accumulation during Chile's transition to a higher stage of economic development. Many have written about the relationship between financial development and economic growth. On the one hand, under certain conditions, a growing economy can expect to see an increase in its financial assets. On the other hand, financial development can increase output growth by reducing the cost of capital and improving the allocation of funds in the economy.

These two channels between financial development and economic growth interact in a positive way. A positive productivity shock increases economic growth, enhancing financial development and improving, in turn, the prospects for economic growth. Also important is a diversified financial sector. It is not enough to increase the ratio of total financial assets to GDP. A country must be able to develop in a balanced way its stock, bond, and credit markets.

*Financial Deepening and the Liberalization
and Integration of the Economy*

An increase in asset holdings may be seen as a natural consequence of economic growth experienced by a developing economy in response to an increase in its steady-state level of capital. This simple fact is not always emphasized in the literature.

By the mid-1970s Chile's economy was closed and financially repressed. Interest rate ceilings, an almost nonexistent private financial sector, and financial assets accounting for less than 20 percent of GDP characterized its financial sector. Because a financially repressed economy is constrained by the supply side of funds, the elimination of interest rate ceilings tends to increase both the return to savings and the level of capital.

On the one hand, the higher return to savings offered by the financial sector shifts the composition of domestic savings toward financial savings (especially through the banking system) and away from less productive forms of savings such as jewelry. This increases any standard measure of the financial depth of the economy. If the removal of the interest rate ceiling increases the overall return on savings (and not only its composition), this price effect will increase savings. On the other hand, the financial liberalization will move forward the long-run steady-state level of capital of the economy. Since the new steady-state level of income is now farther away from actual income, this effect is equivalent to an increase in permanent income and will tend to increase consumption and decrease savings. Despite the indeterminacy of total savings, it is possible to show that financial depth, measured as the capital-output ratio, increases as a consequence of financial liberalization.

The same standard macroeconomic framework can be used to analyze what happens when a newly liberalized economy opens to international flows of trade and capital. If the rate of time preference of the economy is equal to the relevant world interest rate, there will be no changes in the steady-state level of per-capita income toward which the stock of capital is converging. However, the country is now able to borrow at the world interest rate. As a consequence, it will be optimal to smooth out the intertemporal path of consumption, borrowing during the first stages of the transition toward the steady state and paying back later. In other words, the country will carry a current account deficit for some time, one that will be reversed later. The amount of capital (the total level of assets) will follow the same path that would have been followed under a closed economy regime. The only difference is that a fraction of the claims issued against physical capital will be held by foreigners during part of the transition toward the steady state.

In normal circumstances, however, the rate of time preference of the small country will be higher than the relevant world interest rate. The open economy's steady-state level of capital will be higher than the closed economy's level, implying a process of capital accumulation. Given this relatively high rate of time preference of the economy, the new capital will be financed by borrowing from abroad. The extent and speed of capital accumulation depend on the imperfections of the international capital markets and the possibility that the rate of time preference of the most patient countries will change in time.

In Chile financial liberalization and economic reform triggered the increase in capital accumulation and growth. Of course, an increase in the savings rate would have had a similar effect on the rate of capital accumulation. This is the only case in which we should expect the savings rate to increase together with the increase in the asset holdings of the economy (financial savings). In general, the savings rate will be subject to two offsetting factors. Financial liberalization and the increase in the marginal product of capital raise the return on savings. Thus, this price effect tends to increase savings. However, the increase in the steady-state level of capital means that actual income is now farther away from the permanent income level and therefore consumption per-capita will tend to rise and savings to decrease as a result of the income effect. Consequently, there is no obvious relationship between the savings rate and financial deepening in the aftermath of financial and economic reform.

We also have assumed that the amount of financial assets in the economy equals the amount of physical capital. This is clearly an oversimplification. Specific reforms in the financial sector, such as the elimination of interest rates ceilings and adequate regulation of capital markets, might induce agents to alter the composition of their savings. It is expected that adequate reforms will increase the fraction of financial savings that can be used as funding for productive investment.

Financial Deepening and Economic Growth

The relationship between financial depth and economic growth has interested economists and policymakers for a long time. The early debate focused on the causal relationship between these two variables. Schumpeter argued that financial development improved the quantity and quality of investment projects, thus enhancing economic growth. On the other hand,

Joan Robinson postulated that as the economy develops and the level of activity increases, the demand for financial services expands; in her view economic growth leads to financial deepening. Finally, it is possible that a third variable, savings, causes both financial development and economic growth.

We have already explained how, under certain conditions, an economy growing toward its steady-state level of income will increase its financial depth. As we mentioned before, if the development of the financial sector has beneficial effects on economic growth, policies that strengthen the development of the financial sector will reinforce the general process of economic growth.

Financial development reduces the transaction costs of saving and investing, and the costs of adverse selection and moral hazard for firms. The reduction in these costs reduces firms' overall cost of capital and the relative cost of external funds, increasing the probability that they will undertake profitable investment projects, and hence increase output.

Many studies support a positive correlation between finance and growth.[3] Using cross-country data, King and Levine (1993) and De Gregorio and Guidotti (1995) find that the predetermined component of financial development is positively associated with future growth rates. Levine and Zervos (1996) find the same type of correlation between stock market development and economic growth. Moreover, Rajan and Zingales (1996) directly identify the effect of a decrease in the external cost of capital. They find that firms in need of external funding grow faster in countries with more developed financial markets. Using data for the United States at the state level, Jayaratne and Strahan (1996) show positive effects on state growth following allegedly exogenous intrastate-bank-branch reform. The authors identify the quality of bank lending as the key outcome of banking sector reform in enhancing economic growth.

Implicit in these findings is the importance of a good balance in financial instruments. What matters is not only the total amount of financial assets, but also the composition of those assets. The reasons for this are twofold: from the demand side for funds and from the supply side.

From the demand side for funds, the existence of a variety of securities means that firms raising capital will be able to choose more freely an optimal capital structure, minimizing the effective cost of capital. Considerations like asymmetric information, taxes, and agency problems are

---

3. Most of them appropriately address the endogeneity problem.

important when determining the optimal capital structure. A developed financial market will provide better information and monitoring devices, increasing investor confidence and reducing the cost of capital. This effect is especially important when the economy is growing, and firms are short of internal sources of funds. In summary, developed capital markets allow firms to raise capital more efficiently through corporate bonds and new equity issues.

From the supply side for funds, a liquid and developed capital market provides more liquidity and more options for diversification to investors. In general, investors will be able to diversify more risk as the availability of different financial instruments increases. This, in addition to better information, might increase the supply of funds available for investment purposes and contribute to economic growth.

Finally, agents in an economy with a relatively developed financial system open to international capital flows will be able to diversify their portfolios by investing in foreign securities. As the economy grows and domestic agents increase their wealth, this effect tends to become more important. However, during the transition to a steady-state level of income, returns to capital will be higher in the local economy, dominating those of alternative securities in the international market. As mentioned above, foreign investors will find domestic securities very attractive.

Macroeconomic Policy, Capital Account Deregulation, and Capital Market Developments

Since the mid-1980s Chile has sought a sustainable rate of growth through continuous control of internal demand expansion and an increasingly flexible exchange rate regime. It also has addressed traditional sources of macroeconomic instability, such as fluctuations in export receipts and capital inflows, as well as in the money supply. The positive results of this macroeconomic policy have fostered healthy capital market development, especially of the banking sector. In turn, the regulatory and supervisory efforts undertaken in both the banking sector and the bond and stock markets have contributed enormously to the sound macroeconomic evolution. It is precisely the interaction between these policy areas that explains, in our view, the emergence of synergy between growth and capital markets.

In this section we review Chile's macroeconomic policies since the mid-1980s, emphasizing capital account deregulation. We can distinguish two different periods. The first covers the economic recovery in the second half

of the 1980s; this recovery occurred against a background of severe constraints in the external balances. The second period began in the 1990s when
the Chilean economy started to receive enormous amounts of foreign capital. Abruptly the external condition of the economy switched from a regime of severe foreign exchange constraint to one of overabundance of
foreign financing (table 3-4).

In spite of the acute scarcity of foreign financing throughout the 1980s
after the eruption of the Latin American debt crisis, Chile's macroeconomic
policy has succeeded in achieving high and sustained growth since the
middle of the decade. This achievement is particularly remarkable considering the high fiscal costs that resulted from the crisis. The most important
feature of 1985–89 period is fiscal consolidation. The fiscal retrenchment
was large enough to cover the costs of the financial bailout and pension
reform, while managing to achieve overall fiscal surpluses toward the end
of the decade. Monetary policy was somewhat accommodative during the
period; coupled with growth it aided the banks' recovery.

Unlike in other regional economies, "dollarization" did not emerge in
Chile in the 1980s for several reasons. First, the Central Bank issued predominantly inflation-indexed promissory notes to finance the banks' bailout. This protected savers against inflation, a potentially volatile variable
given the currency crisis that accompanied the financial crisis. Therefore,
to some extent the incentives for agents to fly to foreign securities were
diminished. Second, the exchange rate was allowed to depreciate within a
band and at a rhythm that did not encourage arbitrage toward foreign securities, once interest rate differentials were taken into account. That policy
was complemented by discrete devaluations that were infrequent and
mostly unanticipated.[4] The above-mentioned combination of policies managed to achieve a large real depreciation of the currency, since the devaluations did not feed into domestic inflation given the depressed internal
demand. Growth was led by exports and later by investment, which was
pulled in turn by growth, competitiveness, and easier credit conditions.

The development of capital markets in that period was not spectacular,
but bank deposits recovered and began to grow (in absolute terms and as a

---

4. In light of the situation in Southeast Asia, it is somewhat surprising that the
recovery featured tight fiscal policies but an accommodative monetary stance. With
the current sophistication and globalization of financial markets, low domestic rates
combined with occasional discrete depreciations would probably not have been
sustainable.

Table 3–4. Chile's Balance of Payments, 1979–96
(in millions of US$)

Account	1979	1980	1981	1982	1983	1984	1985	1986	1987
Current account	-1,189	-1,971	-4,733	-2,304	-117	-2,111	-1,413	-1,191	-735
Goods and services	-594	-1,154	-3,378	-492	534	-193	484	616	841
Merchandise	-355	-764	-2,677	63	986	363	884	1,092	1,309
Exports FOB	3,835	4,705	3,836	3,706	3,831	3,651	3,804	4,191	5,303
Imports FOB	4,190	5,469	6,513	3,643	2,845	3,288	2,920	3,099	3,994
Nonfinancial services	-239	-390	-701	-555	-452	-556	-400	-476	-468
Financial services and transfers	-595	-817	-1,355	-1,812	-1,651	-1,918	-1,897	-1,807	-1,576
Capital account	2,247	3,165	4,698	1,215	508	1,940	1,385	741	936
Foreign direct investment	233	170	362	384	132	67	143	313	885
Other capital	2,014	2,995	4,336	831	376	1,873	1,242	428	51
Nonfinancial public sector	33	199	664	650	-170	508	630	468	104
Central bank	305	-114	-400	322	1,553	1,298	597	-82	31
Nonfinancial private sector	1,046	1,003	1,324	-537	-522	-96	6	325	789
Banking sector	630	1,907	2,748	396	-485	163	9	-283	-872
Errors and omissions	-11	50	102	-76	68	188	-70	223	-1,55.2
Balance of payments' balance	1,047	1,244	67	-1,165	-541	17	-98	-227	45

Table 3–4 (continued)

Account	1988	1989	1990	1991	1992	1993	1994	1995	1996
Current account	–231	–705	–538	111	–699	–2,098	–638	147	–2,919
Goods and services	1,505	1,006	–737	–229	–1,131	–2,447	–996	–163	–3,392
Merchandise	2,210	1,578	1,336	1,588	771	–982	725	1,481	–1,147
Exports FOB	7,054	8,080	8,373	8,941	10,008	9,199	11,604	16,136	15,353
Imports FOB	4,844	6,502	7,037	7,354	9,237	10,181	10,879	14,655	16,500
Nonfinancial services	–705	–573	–262	–8	–41	3	22	–163	–229
Financial services and transfers	–1,737	–1,711	–1,612	–1,469	–1429	–1,098	–1,385	–1,171	–1,543
Capital account	1,086	1,264	3,049	829	2,883	2,725	4,573	1,310	5,017
Foreign direct investment	952	1,366	941	425	652	1,104	1,754	1,007	4,114
Other capital	133	–102	2,107	404	2,230	1,621	2,819	303	9,03
Nonfinancial public sector	489	360	215	–683	157	–251	–227	–1,714	–1291
Central bank	–625	–825	–363	–73	9	–92	–55	–396	–396
Nonfinancial private sector	839	924	2,706	1,780	514	1,896	2,707	2,692	3,083
Banking sector	–570	–561	–450	–619	1,550	67	394	–279	–493
Errors and omissions	–122.5	–122	–143	298	315	–94	–741	–396	–917
Balance of payments' balance	732	437	2,368	1,238	2,499	578	3,194	1,061	1,181

Note: The methodology for the balance of payments was revised in early 1998, and it began to be calculated on an accrual basis from a cash basis. As a result, nonremitted profits of FDI were added both to the current account and to the capital account. Given the increasing stock of FDI, the methodological change enlarged the current account and FDI figures in around 1 percent of GDP since 1994. This table reports the old figures, since the new ones are not available for the whole period.

Source: Central Bank of Chile.

percentage of GDP) as did the stock market, fostered by privatization and fiscal incentives. It must be mentioned that Chile's fiscal adjustment was very costly in social terms and in terms of the country's infrastructure. Public investment was kept at a minimum. The way the privatization process was handled and the fiscal incentives launched to promote the public's acquisition of stock were, and still are, controversial.

Notwithstanding the above, the economy began to grow on a solid footing. The current account was reduced to manageable levels, and the banks, closely monitored by the supervisory authority, improved significantly their performance and health.

During the 1990s a set of crucial changes emerged. The country returned to its traditional democratic form of government in 1990, and the Central Bank was invested with strong autonomous powers. A huge amount of foreign private financing began to flow into the country. In this new context the government added to its goals of growth and external equilibrium the goals of greater social equity and the convergence of domestic inflation to industrial-country levels. To achieve the equity objective, the government significantly raised social expenditures. By that time, however, a true culture of fiscal soundness had emerged in the country. Each new spending measure was financed by new taxes, or it was offset by reductions in other expenditures. In this way the government surplus was maintained and even increased. (Between 1990 and 1998, the fiscal surplus averaged 1.8 percent of GDP.)

Inflation was controlled, with the support of strong fiscal accounts, through tough and preemptive monetary policy implemented by the powerful and now independent Central Bank. Two salient features of the anti-inflationary strategy are worth noting. First, the strategy was steadfast but gradual, given the high level of indexation of the economy. Second, even with the overabundance of foreign financing, the authorities resisted the temptation to converge rapidly to low inflation levels through a rapid and sizable appreciation of the currency. On the contrary, every effort was made to avoid an overappreciation of the currency.

With the renewal of capital inflows at the beginning of the 1990s, the objective of reducing inflation through monetary policy began to put increasing upward pressure on the currency, thus threatening the goal of keeping a moderate current external deficit. Although the initial response was to allow some appreciation coupled with sterilized intervention, soon the strength and continuity of the inflows made necessary the delineation of a complete policy framework. Here we summarize the main elements of that framework.

First, Chile took advantage of the sizable inflows to build a significant stock of foreign reserves. The abundance of foreign exchange and the fiscal surplus also allowed the authorities to buy back almost the full stock of the government's and the Central Bank's foreign debt. Instability stemming from terms-of-trade volatility continued to be tackled through the Copper Stabilization Fund (Fondo de Estabilización del Cobre), a device implemented in the 1980s that obliges the government to save extra earnings from the state copper industry when the price is above a certain benchmark.[5] Until 1997 the Fund had accumulated around 2 percent of GDP.

Through all of these measures the economy has been building buffer stocks, both in the fiscal arena and in the external sector, that have strengthened its resilience to internal and external shocks. This has helped in stabilizing output as well as monetary conditions, sheltering, to some extent, banks and other capital market participants from economic disturbances.

Second, Chile made the deregulation of direct foreign investment (FDI) a priority. To complement a very liberal foreign investment law designed in the 1980s, the government progressively eased limitations on repatriation of profits and capital. As a result, FDI flooded into the country, matching almost exactly the current account deficit in the 1989–98 period.[6]

Portfolio inflows, however, were not allowed to be registered as FDI and have been subject to different treatment. Foreign purchases of domestic stock were progressively allowed in the 1990s. First, investment funds of foreign capital (FICEs) began to be active. Because of the ten-year withholding period, these funds did not continue to be attractive to foreign investors. Regulations for issuance of American depository receipts (ADRs) were dictated in the early 1990s, with stringent conditions initially in terms of the international credit ratings of the issuer companies. Those conditions have been gradually eased. A similar policy has governed the issuance of bonds in the international markets.

---

5. This benchmark is intended to represent the long-term price, which sooner or later the actual price will reach.

6. Although the current account deficit has widened since the mid-1990s, in part because of the real appreciation of the currency, more than half of the deficit corresponds to the accrual of FDI profits. About 40 percent of FDI profits have been reinvested in the country. The priority given to FDI in Chile in sequencing the capital account deregulation contrasts sharply with the experience of Southeast Asia, where FDI inflows were severely restricted. Up to the first semester of 1998, FDI flows showed little volatility, confirming their long-run orientation.

Portfolio investments were liberalized gradually to smooth the adjustment of the domestic stock market. The high profit rates associated with
Chile's high convergence rate of growth easily could have fostered the
emergence of a bubble if the stock adjustment had been allowed to take
place instantaneously. The short record of Chilean companies in international markets, and the need to develop adequate accounting and disclosure standards, also influenced authorities to accommodate a gradual
adjustment. A negative externality for the economy as a whole can arise if
an unsettled company violates international standards and contaminates
other Chilean companies. Even with the restrictions that were adopted,
huge portfolio inflows (with record figures of over 3 percent of GDP in
1994) entered the economy throughout the 1990s (with a transitory inter-
ruption in 1995, the year of the Mexican crisis). These inflows were one of
the main forces behind the growth of the stock market in the 1990s (figures
3-1 and 3-2). Portfolio movements encouraged the issuance of ADRs by
domestic firms and also put upward pressure on stock prices through the
so-called secondary ADRs.

In spite of the dynamic growth of the stock market and stock prices, a
bubble did not emerge. Although price-earnings ratios increased from as

Figure 3-1. Stock Market Growth: Market Value, 1980–96

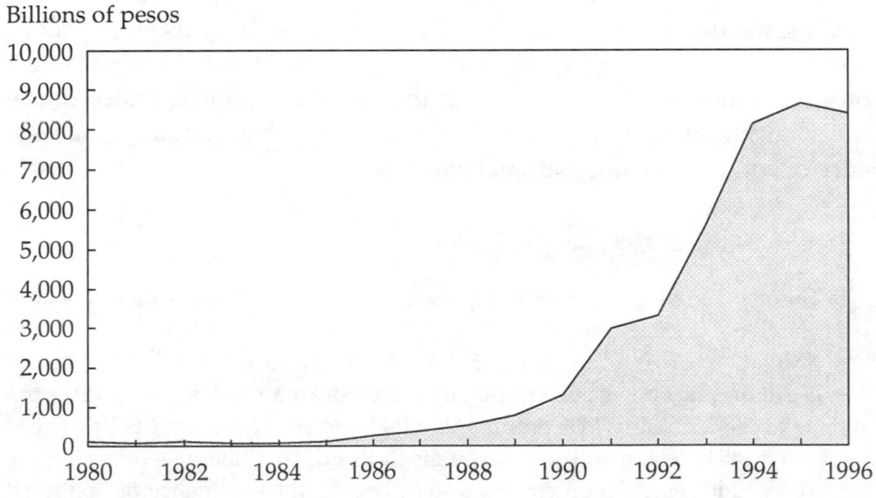

Billions of pesos

Source: Authors' calculations.

Figure 3-2. Stock Market Growth: Quantity Index, 1980–96

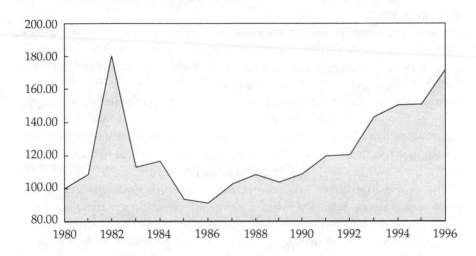

Note: Dividing the market value of stocks by a general stock price index gives the "quantity index."
Source: Authors' calculations.

low as 5 in 1989 to as high as 21.6 in 1993, they subsequently moderated, reaching levels of 13.4 in 1996. The fall in stock prices after 1994 is partially explained by the Mexican crisis, but also by the extension—until the end of 1998—of the reserve requirement of 30 percent (explained below) to secondary ADRs. This last measure is consistent with the philosophy of dampening volatile inflows, and mainly affects buy-and-sell practices with little effect on buy-and-hold decisions.

Third, Chile applied the more restrictive policy to foreign loans, especially the short-run ones. For that purpose a 30 percent (initially 20 percent) one-year unremunerated reserve requirement was established in 1991 for all foreign loans. The reserve requirement lasts one year (one can think of it as an up-front fee), regardless of the duration of the loan. The implied additional cost on the loan decreases with the length of the inflow, and therefore punishes especially short-run debt. It is worth adding that the reserve requirement is applied across the board to every type of foreign loan or foreign financial investment. Subsequent efforts have tried to close loopholes, and although there is some evidence of evasion, it has been largely avoided. In fact, Chile's stock of short-term external debt as a proportion of total external debt is one of the lowest in emerging markets (Eichengreen and others 1998).

The reserve requirement is only one of many policies that have been launched to smooth the international integration process, which has strong macroeconomic management at its core. In spite of its controversial nature, the reserve requirement appears to have been effective in altering the composition of the capital account (table 3-4) and in helping to maintain a wedge between domestic and international interest rates (particularly during episodes when the exchange rate has been somewhat fixed). Evidence on its capabilities to affect the overall size of inflows and the real exchange rate is, however, weaker (Valdés-Prieto and Soto 1997; Soto 1997).

The composition effect is deemed very important, especially with regard to the volatility of outflows, which in turn impinges on greater financial stability. As we will see in the next section, banks have been directly restricted in terms of foreign indebtedness through limitations on their menu of lending in foreign currency and through ceilings on currency mismatches. However, all too often banking crises emerge when changes in market sentiment lead to abrupt variations in capital flows and in the value of the domestic currency, even without significant mismatches at the banking level. If banks' debtors are not hedged against foreign exchange risk, a sudden devaluation will deteriorate sharply banks' assets and can lead to a financial crisis.

One of the merits of the reserve requirement is that it prevents currency and maturity (in foreign currency) mismatches all across the economy, and then protects financial stability against foreign shocks in a comprehensive way. Admittedly, the reserve requirement is not an ideal solution, but it is a prudent way to protect financial stability.[7] In the future, however, solutions are needed that address this problem at its root—that is, new banking regulations must be devised. It must be recognized that the external and inter-

---

7. The Chilean measures designed to dampen short-term inflows have been mostly discussed in the context of the transition to an open capital account regime. However, they may also prove useful when cyclical patterns in advanced economies determine massive flows of capital to emerging economies. Inadequate financial supervision in the creditor economies—for example, insufficient disclosure of investment and hedge funds coupled with high lending from commercial banks to those funds—or herd behavior caused by information asymmetries may warrant some restrictions to short-term inflows beyond the transitional phase.

nal volatility that characterizes emerging markets may need a set of prudent regulations in the financial system that go beyond those agreed to in the industrial countries.

Fourth, Chile's intervention in the foreign exchange market has attempted to smooth the currency appreciation process. Although exchange rate fluctuations are limited within a reference band, the authorities have progressively widened and even shifted that band whenever they have become convinced that the equilibrium exchange rate (the rate under full employment that will induce a current account deficit of 3 to 4 percent of GDP) is outside the band. When depreciation pressures have developed (notably in the aftermath of the Mexican crisis and currently with the turbulence in Southeast Asia), the domestic currency has been allowed to fall with very limited intervention and some monetary tightening. Chile has pursued this strategy to avoid extending signals of any kind of implicit exchange rate insurance, in order to dampen speculative pressures arising from interest rate differentials.

Fifth, Chile included in its policy mix strong fiscal surpluses to soften pressure for real exchange rate appreciation. Despite the strong fiscal surpluses, high demand pressures stemming from profitable investment opportunities and the abundance of foreign credit made it imperative to tighten monetary policy. This dangerous cycle of capital inflows, demand pressures, monetary tightening, and further capital inflows has been prevented, to the extent possible, through the already mentioned fiscal stance and by means of a continuous monitoring of bank lending policies.[8] We will come back to this last issue in the following section.

Sixth, Chile's monetary policy has been tough and preemptive. The newly independent Central Bank has built a solid reputation by fulfilling preannounced inflation targets for eight years in a row (1991–98). The continuous health of the banking sector has enabled the Chilean Central Bank to tighten monetary policy whenever that has been deemed necessary, and banks have had to adjust to the new monetary conditions. The inflation targets have served the economy well by providing a credible nominal anchor, which gradually replaced a more rigid exchange rate policy. There-

---

8. The strengthening of the currency in small, open, emerging economies is somewhat expansionary, at least in the short run, since the private sector is normally a net debtor in foreign currency. That feature notably complicates the task of monetary policy to maintain domestic equilibrium when huge capital inflows strengthen the currency.

fore, it has been possible to widen the exchange rate band significantly without leaving the economy vulnerable to nominal shocks. The credibility of Chile's monetary policy came under its first big test during the present financial turmoil, when the monetary authority reacted immediately and boldly to avert an overshooting of the exchange rate.

Finally, the Central Bank has taken advantage of the widening of the domestic financial markets to lengthen significantly the average duration of its internal debt and to place the securities issued to finance the purchases of foreign exchange. This strategy, coupled with the large stock of reserves, has enabled the emergence of a stable structure of monetary assets and liabilities. The ratio of M3 to international reserves has stayed at low levels. Monetary control has switched to open market operations, and monetary reserve requirements are quite low.

The above-mentioned elements have been decisive not only in terms of traditional macroeconomic indicators, but also in relation to key environmental indicators. Recent research cites output, exchange rate and terms-of-trade volatility, lending booms and bubbles in asset prices, maturity and currency mismatches, the size of the stock of short-term external debt, and the exchange rate regime as important factors behind banking and systemic crises (Goldstein and Turner 1996). Finally, capital account deregulation has not inhibited the increasing integration of the Chilean economy into world financial markets. The World Bank (1997) ranks the Chilean economy as one of the most financially integrated among developing countries.

The Banking Sector

After the collapse of the financial system in 1982–83, a number of bailout measures were launched to help rehabilitate financial institutions at a total cost in public resources of nearly 40 percent of the GDP during those years. The bailout measures included subsidies to debtors and the purchase of the delinquent and doubtful loans of the commercial banks by the Central Bank. Although the adopted measures were very controversial—in particular, the purchasing of loans by the Central Bank, which later give rise to the so-called subordinated debt problem—the new banking framework has proved to be quite resilient.

Since passage of a comprehensive new banking law in 1986, the results have been highly satisfactory. Delinquent loans as a percentage of total loans decreased sharply from levels as high as 9.65 percent in 1984 to just 0.95

Table 3-5. Selected Indicators of Chile's Financial System,
1980–96

Month/year	Return on capital[a] (percent)	Return on assets[a] (percent)	Delinquent loans as a percentage of total loans[a]	Regulatory leverage[a] No. of times	Portfolio risk[b] (percent)
Dec. 1980	13.91	1.12	1.21	—	—
Dec. 1981	7.71	0.70	2.34	—	—
Dec. 1982	−2.73	−0.18	4.05	9.66	—
Dec. 1983	−24.24	−1.39	8.43	11.46	—
Dec. 1984	−38.25	−2.00	9.65	12.88	—
Dec. 1985	19.64	0.74	3.51	11.76	—
Dec. 1986	13.47	0.74	3.53	9.17	—
Dec. 1987	16.99	1.23	2.70	9.84	—
Dec. 1988	23.03	1.65	2.02	9.90	—
Dec. 1989	23.61	1.82	1.79	10.62	—
Dec. 1990	22.93	1.91	2.10	9.82	4.08
Dec. 1991	17.64	1.45	1.81	10.20	3.72
Dec. 1992	17.61	1.39	1.20	11.14	3.53
Dec. 1993	22.11	1.65	0.81	11.18	2.05
Dec. 1994	20.05	1.53	1.02	11.44	1.57
Dec. 1995	20.97	1.48	0.91	12.06	1.28
Dec. 1996	18.27	1.35	0.95	11.80	1.26

a. Up to December of each year.
b. Up to October of each year.
Source: Superintendencia de Bancos e Instituciones Financieras.

percent in 1996 (table 3-5). The rate of return on capital has averaged 20 percent since 1987, with total loans increasing at an average annual rate of some 9 percent in the 1990s.

However, the recovery of loans/GDP has been extremely gradual. Banking credit to the private sector as a percentage of GDP decreased from the peak of 70 percent in 1982 to less than 40 percent in 1989 (figure 3-3). There are two principal reasons for that decline: first, the absolute decline in the amount of loans that were reprogrammed during the crisis and, second, the very conservative lending policies that banks adopted under the new banking law. Although the stock of credit to the private sector increased, private credit as a percentage of GDP recovered to slightly above 50 percent in 1997, a significantly lower percentage than in the 1980s.

Johnston, Darbar, and Echeverría (1997) compare the financial sector and capital account evolutions of Chile, Indonesia, Korea, and Thailand since the mid-1980s. The main difference between Chile and the Asian countries

**Figure 3-3. Banking Credit to the Private Sector
as a Percentage of GDP, 1976–97**

Percent

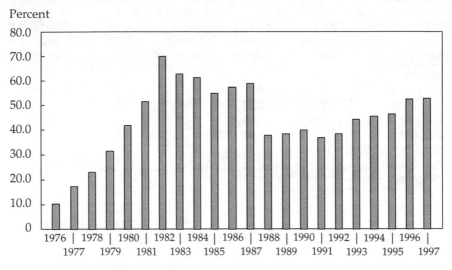

Source: Authors' calculations.

is the rate of growth of the credit to the private sector. Although the four economies share high rates of growth, declining or moderate rates of inflation, sound fiscal accounts, huge balance-of-payment surpluses, and moderate current account deficits (with the exception of Thailand), the behavior of credit is markedly different. Taking credit as a percentage of GDP for the periods 1985–90 and 1991–96, we see an increase of more than 100 percent in Indonesia, 60 percent in Thailand, and 20 percent in Korea. In sharp contrast, credit as a percentage of GDP actually decreases in Chile between the two periods by nearly 15 percent. Another important difference is the ratio of foreign direct investment to the current account deficit in the 1990s: about one in Chile, about 55 percent in Indonesia, and about 15 percent in Thailand. In Korea foreign direct investment was negative in the 1990s. In other words, Korea was a net investor in foreign economies.

Moderate credit growth in Chile is directly related to the Central Bank's tough and preemptive monetary policy, and to some extent to the regulation of capital inflows. Chile's achievements also can be attributed to the regulatory and supervisory framework, and its implementation, since 1986. Following is a brief summary of the main elements of that framework. In November 1997 Congress approved important legal modifications to the 1986 banking act. Since these modifications will affect the future of the banking sector but are not closely related to past developments, we leave their analysis for the concluding remarks.

One of the crucial elements the law tried to amend was the incentive structure. As Goldstein and Turner (1996) note, "bank owners, managers, and creditors each need to have something to lose if they fail to act in a manner consistent with their mandate." For that purpose, the new law implemented a clear and limited deposit insurance scheme. This scheme means that the payments system is protected through a full guarantee on demand deposits. However, those deposits are subject to a 9 percent reserve requirement and, if a bank receives demand deposits in excess of 2.5 times its capital and reserves, it is obliged to maintain the full excess in reserves, in an approximation to narrow banking. Interest payments on demand deposits are prohibited. To protect the small saver, the treasury gives a partial fiscal guarantee of 90 percent up to US$3,600 for time deposits.

To make banks internalize the risks associated with their portfolio decisions, financial investments are valued at market prices, and credit portfolio risk provisions are established. Loan provisions include self-regulation elements since the banks themselves evaluate their credit risk with subsequent supervision by the Superintendency of Banks. The market comes into the picture when it receives risk information from the evaluation, and when private risk-rating agencies evaluate the banks.

Disclosure obligations go further. Banks must share among themselves a monthly book containing the total amount of loans given by the banking sector to a person or a company. Information on individuals with delinquent loans is also provided. The Supervisor of banks is prohibited by law to delay the recognition of bank losses. Expected losses are quickly recognized in the monthly income statement by the bank. There is a complete classification procedure for commercial, mortgage, and consumer loans. Once the loan portfolio is evaluated, an estimated loss for the bank is calculated for setting provisions against profits. The loan portfolio of each bank is classified at least once a year. Finally, the Supervisor must publish a detailed report on the conditions of banks at least three times a year.

There are strict limitations on related lending. In the case of one person or one company, the maximum amount of loans is 5 percent of the bank's capital and reserves. The ceiling is raised to 25 percent if the credit has collateral. Loans to other financial institutions cannot exceed a ceiling of 30 percent of a bank's capital and reserves. Loans to persons or companies related to the ownership or management of the bank cannot be given in better terms of maturity, interest rate, and collateral than those given to other clients in similar transactions. It is forbidden to lend to members of the bank directory, their companies, and their direct relatives.

Table 3-6. Consolidated Balance of Chile's Banking Sector as a Percentage of GDP, 1976–97

	Assets				Liabilities			
					Reserves and capital			External debt commercial banks
Year	Net internal assets of Central Bank	Credit to the government	Credit to the private sector	Other assets	Central Bank	Commercial banks	M7	
1976	7.1	31.0	10.2	1.1	6.0	8.3	18.0	2.9
1977	3.7	28.1	17.3	6.4	7.1	6.0	18.9	3.2
1978	6.3	18.6	23.0	3.0	10.3	5.1	30.9	4.6
1979	7.9	12.1	31.5	5.1	15.2	6.2	29.1	6.1
1980	11.8	6.1	41.9	9.4	12.9	6.8	37.9	11.8
1981	10.6	3.6	51.5	3.5	9.6	7.2	30.6	14.8
1982	10.2	6.1	69.9	0.6	13.5	7.7	37.5	28.0
1983	2.9	10.3	62.9	5.7	11.4	5.3	35.5	29.5
1984	4.4	16.1	61.2	9.2	7.8	5.8	36.3	32.1
1985	14.5	25.7	54.8	21.2	0.9	9.5	38.5	40.3
1986	15.1	43.5	57.2	21.7	7.1	22.6	41.1	36.5
1987	14.1	37.8	58.9	21.8	11.1	25.1	42.6	25.7
1988	8.3	28.6	37.9	21.0	4.1	14.0	44.0	17.0
1989	1.3	23.1	38.6	13.4	5.3	12.3	45.1	11.2
1990	6.8	20.3	39.9	16.1	5.2	13.7	55.2	9.1
1991	12.2	17.5	37.1	11.3	4.2	9.9	58.6	5.4
1992	15.1	13.4	38.6	10.5	3.8	7.5	60.3	5.9
1993	20.7	11.4	44.2	7.6	3.5	7.9	65.0	7.5
1994	20.0	9.2	45.6	8.6	2.4	8.7	66.3	6.0
1995	21.4	6.2	46.2	8.1	0.9	10.1	66.6	4.4
1996	24.2	4.9	52.3	7.1	0.8	10.8	73.0	3.9
1997	24.6	4.0	52.8	10.6	1.1	13.6	77.3	2.3

Source: Authors' calculations based on Central Bank data.

On top of the self-regulation and market discipline elements, restrictions designed to limit exchange rate, interest rate, and credit risk have been issued. There are ceilings on maturity mismatches and exposure in mortgage letters. Banks are not allowed to keep shares in their portfolios, with a few minor exceptions. Finally, and most importantly, assets and liabilities in foreign currency differences cannot exceed 20 percent of a bank's capital and reserves. Moreover, banks cannot issue dollar denominated loans, except in the case of foreign trade loans. These last two restrictions, coupled with the reserve requirement policy on foreign inflows, significantly dampen banks' incentives to contract foreign loans. As a matter of fact, banks reduced their foreign indebtedness in the 1990s (tables 3-4 and 3-6), in sharp contrast with the 1978–82 period and with the recent experience in Southeast Asia. Under this regulatory framework the lending booms normally associated with capital inflow episodes have been avoided.

The 1986 banking law established a maximum debt-equity ratio of 20 for banks and 15 for financial societies. The 1997 law established a Basle coefficient of 8. Banks, however, can pursue internationalization in a more straightforward way if they exhibit a coefficient of 10. The average coefficient of banks in 1998 was 11, with a few falling below 8. A two-year period has been granted to the undercapitalized banks for recapitalization, with intermediate targets.

Finally, there is a clear procedure for corrective actions if any bank exhibits liquidity or solvency problems. Actions begin with a call to shareholders for preventive capitalization. Intermediate steps involve market solutions, like the sale of a portion of the loan portfolio or swaps of credits and deposits for capital. If these steps fail, liquidation may result. In the event of liquidation, creditors would be refunded according to a clear order of priority with the proceeds of the sale of the bank's assets.

In sum, early development of the so-called "best international standards" in the banking system, coupled with an augmented focus on exchange rate risk and early resolution of imbalances, have nurtured the health of the banking sector since the mid-1980s. Reforms have enabled Chile to avoid some of the undesirable side effects of capital account deregulation, particularly in periods of international lending booms.

Capital Markets in Chile

Since the mid-1980s, Chilean capital markets have boomed. While total financial assets were 67 percent of GDP in 1980, they reached almost 190 percent of GDP in 1996. This impressive development is partly explained by the natural process of capital accumulation experienced by the Chilean economy since the late 1970s in its transition to a new steady-state level of capital. The purpose of this section is to describe the main features of Chile's capital market since 1980 and to draw some lessons from this experience.

Since 1980 the composition of Chile's market portfolio has moved toward stocks and corporate and Central Bank bonds and away from certificate of deposits and other assets intermediated by the banking system (table 3-1). Financial assets issued by the banking system went from almost 50 percent of total assets in 1980 to 20 percent in 1996. On the other end, stocks moved from a bottom low of 20 percent of total assets in 1985, to almost 60 percent of total assets in 1994. By 1996, stocks were the single most important security in the Chilean capital market—reaching almost 70 billion dollars, which was more than 50 percent of total assets and almost 95 percent of GDP. In addition, corporate and government bonds increased in importance. They rose from 1 and 4 percent of GDP respectively in 1980 to 15 percent and more than 33 percent of GDP respectively in 1996.

Three main events help to explain the change in the composition of financial assets. First, the 1982 debt crisis implied a jump in government debt to around 15 percent of GDP, as the Treasury and later the Central Bank assumed responsibility for the bad loans made by the banking sector. The crisis also explained the fall in the market value of stocks, bonds, and financial assets; the reduction in new issues; and the decrease in transactions as a result of the fall in investors' confidence. Only after 1985 did capital markets start to show some sign of recovery. However, the very strict regulation of the banking system after the debt crisis reduced its role as financial intermediary. Second, the internationalization of the Chilean economy and the increasing globalization of the world economy fueled the explosion in the market value of stocks and private bonds since the early 1990s. They also explain the surge in Central Bank debt as a consequence of the sterilization of the monetary effects of international reserves accumulation. Finally, pension reform helped shape the Chilean capital markets, and pension fund managers have been crucial in determining the composition of financial assets from the demand side. This issue will be addressed in a separate section below.

In 1980 the main supervisory entity, the "Superintendencia de Valores y Seguros," was created. Since then it has supervised all market participants' compliance with the law. The Security Markets Law of 1981 (and its extensions to specific participants such as corporations, mutual funds, and investment funds) have regulated capital markets. In response to the increasing financial integration and sophistication of Chilean capital markets, the government amended the Security Markets Law in 1994. The amendments broadened the investment alternatives of institutional investors and improved regulation in matters such as conflict of interests and risk rating systems.

As of 1996 the main institutional investors in the Chilean capital market were pension fund managers with over 30 billion dollars in assets, insurance companies with almost 9 billion dollars in assets, mutual fund managers with more than 3 billion dollars, FICE managers with 1.3 billion dollars, and investment fund managers with 0.3 billion. Transactions take place both in a primary market and in a secondary market. Secondary transactions are made over the counter, but mainly through one of two main stock exchanges: the Santiago Stock Exchange and the Electronic Stock Exchange.

Financial Integration

In 1989 total assets were about 97 percent of GDP; by 1991 they had reached 160 percent. This increase was led by the increase in the total stock market value. The jump can be mainly explained by the fall in discount rates, a consequence of the reduction in country risk perception and foreign institutional investors' search for international diversification. The average price-earnings ratio was 4.9 in 1989, 14.7 in 1991, and 21.6 in 1993. As these figures illustrate, financial integration in countries with emerging markets can increase volatility, reduce the effectiveness of supervision, and, in some cases, produce financial bubbles. International integration can increase volatility, since the economy is more susceptible to external shocks. Yet financial integration implies more liquidity and less segmentation of the local market, and therefore firms gain access to cheaper funds as the higher price-earnings ratios indicate.

The Chilean stock market grew much faster after integration. On the one hand, this growth was the consequence of greater demand for funds. The sustained economic growth implied more investment opportunities for firms. On the other hand, financial integration and the sustained development of large domestic institutional investors increased the supply of funds. The market value of stocks exploded after 1990 (figures 3-1 and 3-2). Of course, as pointed out by the jump in price-to-earnings ratios, much of this increase was attributable to increases in stock prices. However, it was not only price. Figure 3-2 plots a quantity index of stocks: the market value of stocks divided by a general stock price index. Since 1989 there has been an important increase in the "real" amount of stocks. The index was around 100 in 1989 and reached more than 170 in 1996. This index indicates the increase in new stock issues. The number of listed firms went from 216 in 1990 to 290 in 1996.

In spite of the jump in price-earnings ratios observed during the early 1990s, those figures seemed to be conservative when compared with the ratios in other economies. By 1994 the price-earnings ratio reached almost 19 in Chile, and kept falling from then on. On the other hand, by 1994, it was 24 in the United States and 101 in Japan. In fact, it reached 18 in Hong Kong, one of the lowest ratios in Asia.

There are many possible reasons for the only moderate increase in asset prices in Chile. Three are worth explaining in detail. First, close supervision and strict regulations affecting the Chilean banking system after the 1982 crisis played a crucial role in avoiding the generation of financial bubbles fueled by large amounts of bank credit. Second, controls to capital movements, especially after their application to secondary ADRs, were very important in reducing portfolio capital and inducing direct investment. Finally, a restrictive monetary policy was also important in keeping asset prices from rising too much.

Most Asian economies that shared the macroeconomic stability and performance of the Chilean economy inadequately supervised the banking sector, and their capital account regulations adversely affected the composition of their capital inflows, in terms of fostering those of a short-run nature and obstructing the less volatile ones. Furthermore, their monetary policy accommodated most of the time the growing aggregate demand and, when it was tightened, the rigidity of the exchange rate policy severely undermined its contractionary effect.

Financial integration poses other challenges to emerging economies. The entrance of large foreign investors increases competition and demands more sophisticated financial markets. Competition has taken the form of ADRs. Almost 60 percent of firms included in our selective index IPSA are cross-listed as ADR in the United States, accounting for more than 7 billion dollars. Instead, foreign capital investment funds account only for 1.3 billion dollars. Most foreign investors would rather buy American depository receipts than Chilean stock directly. There may be several reasons for this. One has to do with information and disclosure practices in Chile. Firms cross-listing in the United States must go through the standard American process of creating a prospect, standardizing accounting practices, and disclosing all relevant information to investors. As long as disclosure practices are more demanding in the United States than in Chile, American investors will find it easier to invest in ADRs. Disclosure practices are important not only from a foreign investors' point of view, but also from the point of view of local investors.

Another challenge of financial integration has to do with the implementation of an adequate market infrastructure. Important components of the market infrastructure are a comparison system, a clearance and settlement system, and a depository system. The Chilean capital market provides adequate comparison and clearing systems with transactions being liquidated in approximately $T+2$. A major problem, however, has been a relatively high level of counter-party risk given the absence of a centralized clearing system.

The Chilean capital market has only recently created a relatively adequate depository system. In 1989 the legal framework for the operation of private entities for the deposit and custody of securities was established. In 1992 the "Depósito Central de Valores" was created. Before then, most securities were physically moved between investors, increasing the risk of loss and failed transactions. The establishment of the depository system has been slow. At present it handles most fixed-income transactions, but it has only slowly reached the stocks. Stock brokers have tried to avoid the costs of using the depository system, preferring to physically handle the securities themselves. In addition, banks have been reluctant to handle the funds liquidation to the depository agency, which only manages the securities.

Pension System Reform and the Capital Market

In 1981 the Chilean pension system changed from a traditional pay-as-you-go public system to a fully funded one with mandatory contributions. Private entities were put in charge of the funds' administration. There are at least three ways in which pension system reform is related to the development of Chile's financial sector. First, it helped make the case for higher public savings explicit by exposing the contingent liabilities of the former pension scheme. Second, pension funds helped finance the privatization process. Finally, pension funds helped to improve the efficiency of the Chilean capital market in general. In this subsection we will briefly discuss these three aspects.

The transition from a pay-as-you-go system to a fully funded system includes the government's obligation to the contributors of the old system. This obligation implies a fiscal problem that has two components: the actual payments to retirees and the recognition of the contributions made to the old system by active workers now contributing to the new system. The first component was expected to last between 10 and 15 years beginning in 1981, while the second will reach its peak in the year 2016. The Chilean government solved this fiscal problem not only by reducing other expenditures but also by issuing new public debt. In fact, the amount of public debt outstanding in the Chilean economy, measured in 1996 dollars, went from one billion dollars in 1981 to more than 23 billion dollars in 1996. These amounts represented a little more than 3 percent of GDP in 1981 and more than 33 percent in 1996.

Three things are worth noticing in this impressive expansion in public debt. First, the formal recognition of the obligation to contributors to the old pension system and the subsequent issuance of public debt implies an automatic increase in the financial depth of the economy (measured as the sum of outstanding shares, private and public bonds, and deposits in the financial system). Second, the increase in public debt did not necessarily have an important crowding out effect on investment, because a large fraction of the debt was automatically acquired by the pension funds. By the end of 1981 the pension funds had in their portfolios the equivalent of less than 0.2 percent of GDP in government bonds, but by the end of 1995 they had more than 16 percent of GDP, representing more than half the total stock of government bonds outstanding. In a sense, the new public debt generated its own demand. Finally and more importantly, the increase in the public debt during the early 1980s was in large part attributable to the rescue of the financial system by the government after the 1982 debt crisis.

Given the strong effort to increase public sector savings, the amount of debt issued to finance the pension reform was only a fraction of the new funds available to fund managers for investment purposes. The rest of those funds were, in fact, used to buy the government bonds issued to finance the financial debt crisis, and privately issued securities. A simple exercise of capitalizing the annual fiscal surplus and social security deficit using an approximately risk-free interest rate shows that by 1996 the conservative behavior of the public sector had freed resources equivalent to 43 percent of GDP. It can be argued that this amount represents the government's contribution to financial deepening.

Another important effect of pension reform on Chile's financial development is related to privatizations. There were two main reasons for privatizing public enterprises. First, an increase in efficiency was expected. Second, massive privatizations were an important source of financing for the government. With limited access to external funding during the 1980s, the government had few alternatives left to finance the privatization process. One of them was popular capitalism; the other was pension funds.

In 1985 pension funds were allowed to invest up to a 30 percent of their portfolios in stock shares. They were constrained, however, in the choice of firms and in the maximum amounts invested in specific firms. In particular, pension funds could only invest in firms with a relatively nonconcentrated ownership structure. State enterprises being privatized had specific targets in terms of achieving a high degree of ownership dispersion, and therefore they constituted a natural investment prospect for pension funds. In 1989, when some of the restrictions on stock investing were raised, as much as 94 percent of the stock shares in the pension fund portfolios belonged to eight recently privatized firms.

Pension fund reform improved the efficiency of capital markets. The proper development of domestic institutional investors in an emerging economy requires an adequate legal framework that considers aspects such as beneficial ownership, trusts, and investment management legislation. In the specific case of pension funds, the new legal basis must be able to guarantee the best interest of the contributors to the system, and in a framework in which the state has only limited responsibility. For that reason, the development of an adequate capital market where pension funds could efficiently channel retirement savings was crucial. The new legal framework can help detect weaknesses in the actual level of development of domestic capital markets. Supervisory institutions that ensure compliance with the new regulatory framework are essential. Obviously, the beneficial effects of this process permeate to all areas of capital market development.

In the Chilean case the development of a private pension system involved the creation of the "Superintendencia de Administradoras de Fondos de Pensiones." This entity is in charge of the supervision and control of the pension fund managers and their actions, in matters such as eligibility and portfolio composition. In addition, the "Comisión Clasificadora de Riesgo" determines the rating of different securities and issuers. Limits on types of securities and issuers are imposed based on risk ratings, portfolio diversification, ownership concentration, and other specific criteria. Regulations consider corporations' commitment to achieving a desirable level of deconcentration in order to allow pension funds to invest in their securities. In this way pension fund reform has had an important effect on corporate governance. Because of the limits imposed on ownership concentration of the target firms, pension fund capital discriminates in favor of less concentrated corporations. Also, pension funds usually contribute to the board of large corporations; at least one board member tends to represent the minority interest. The Superintendency supervises the behavior of fund managers in areas where conflict of interest might arise. For example, it restricts transactions with related parties and determines the composition of pension fund boards.

From the point of view of investors, pension funds as well as mutual funds have increased the risk-return combinations available to small and less sophisticated investors. Compared with long-term Central Bank bonds, pension funds have provided on average more return for about the same risk. Pension fund contributors were able to enjoy the beneficial effects of financial integration thanks to their long positions in domestic stocks whose price-to-earnings ratios significantly increased during the 1990s after the internationalization of the Chilean capital markets.

As mentioned before, from the point of view of security issuers, government, corporations and financial institutions, pension funds provided an invaluable source of funds. For corporations, the existence of pension funds allowed them to issue debt capital when equity capital was too expensive prior to the 1990s. Later on, after the process of financial integration, pension funds became a stable source of the now much cheaper equity capital.

The market value of pension funds increased from less than 1 percent of GDP in 1981 to more than 45 percent in 1996. Since 1985, pension funds have been allowed to invest in common shares of stock. By 1996, shares represented more than 30 percent of the total market value of pension funds and contributed significantly to the high real annual return obtained by the funds.

Future Challenges

The Banking Sector

The internationalization of Chilean banks has presented opportunities that have not been exploited so far. Until recent modifications, the banking legislation was, admittedly, over restrictive. Among the opportunities are further portfolio diversification advantages, economies of scale, enhancing the development of the services export industry, and synergies with the foreign direct investment of Chileans abroad and exports in general. New regulatory challenges also will emerge. Adequate country-risk assessment and knowledge of legal procedures and infrastructure as well as tax arrangements are crucial. Delays may prove costly. The 1997 law has set the framework for the initial steps.

The main shortcoming of the current legislation, in terms of the Basle core principles of banking regulation and supervision, is the absence of consolidated supervision. Since direct personal investment by Chilean bankers has been increasing, new risks have arisen that should be addressed. Furthermore, that risk will grow with the internationalization of banks under the new law. Fortunately, Chilean authorities favor further legislation on this issue, and it is hoped that they will find a window of opportunity in Congress to pass it.

Capital Market Development

Although much progress has been made, the Chilean capital market can still be improved. We have already mentioned the infrastructure problems and the need for better disclosure practices. In contrast to the high value of capitalization achieved by the stock market in the past few years, annual turnover remains low at less than 20 percent of total market value. There are several possible reasons for this phenomenon. One is a relatively high capital gains tax. Another is the large share of stocks in the portfolios of institutional investors; they tend to hold their positions for a longer time than individual investors. Finally, and probably more importantly, a high degree of ownership concentration of Chilean firms remains. In any case, the low turnover in the stock market signals a deficiency in liquidity that must be addressed.

Many firms that have recently gone public still maintain the structure of a family business. The reasons for going public were mainly to obtain cheaper funds for specific investment projects and to provide more liquidity to current shareholders. Control remains in the hands of a small group of shareholders who do not hold their shares for portfolio reasons and therefore are not interested in selling them. Ownership concentration may discourage minority shareholders from investing in stocks because of potentially large agency costs. New regulations regarding agency problems, protection of minority shareholders, and conflicts of interest are now being studied.

Although transaction costs charged by stock brokers have been declining lately, there is room for collusion among stock brokers since they are the owners of the Stock Exchanges.

The development of the Chilean capital market has been slow regarding derivatives and other sophisticated financial instruments. In spite of the foundation in 1990 of the clearing house "Cámara de Compensación Agente de Valores SA," which is in charge of offering options, futures, and other derivatives, the market for this type of instrument is almost nonexistent with the exception of a short market for dollar futures.

Reforms in the private pension system are pending. Some of them are intended to improve the funds' role as financial intermediaries. Limits on certain kinds of investments, initially implemented to regulate the risk borne by pension funds, have constrained the optimal choice of portfolio, especially for the largest pension funds. The extent of diversification attained by those funds has been reduced. As market conditions change, the investment limits must be revised. In particular, investment in foreign assets that allow a greater diversification must be encouraged. Pension funds are priced at market value and their returns used by contributors to discriminate among pension fund managers. An indicator of the risk of funds' portfolios would help contributors to make a more informed choice. Finally, because of the minimum return requirement, most funds invest in very much the same portfolio, reducing the options available to contributors. Moreover, the composition of this portfolio is tilted, for historical reasons, toward sectors where large public sector companies were privatized. A healthier pension system should offer more alternatives to contributors and make better use of opportunities for diversification.

References

Arenas, A., and M. Marcel. 1993. "Proyecciones de Gasto Previsional: 1992–2038." Documento de Trabajo, Ministerio de Hacienda, Santiago.

Barro, R., and X. Sala-i-Martin. 1994. *Economic Growth*. New York: McGraw-Hill.

Blommestein, H. J. 1997. *Institutional Investors, Pension Reforms, and Emerging Securities Markets*. Conference on Development of Securities Markets in Emerging Economies.

Budnevich, Carlos. 1997. "Banking System Regulation and Supervision in Chile: Past, Present, and Future." Central Bank, Santiago.

De Gregorio, J., and P. Guidotti. 1995. "Financial Development and Economic Growth." *World Development* 23 (March): 433–48.

De la Cuadra, S., and A. Galetovic. 1997. "Una o más bolsas de valores?" Catholic University of Chile, Santiago.

Eichengreen, Barry, and Michael Mussa with Giovanni Dell'Aricia, Enrica Detragiache, Gian Maria Milesi-Ferretti, and Andrew Tweedie. 1998. "Capital Account Liberalization: Theoretical and Practical Aspects." Occasional Paper No. 172. International Monetary Fund, Washington, D.C.

Gavin, Michael, and Ricardo Hausmann. 1995. *Macroeconomic Volatility in Latin America: Causes, Consequences, and Policies to Ensure Stability*. Washington, D.C.: Inter-American Development Bank.

Goldstein, Morris, and Philip Turner. 1996. "Banking Crises in Emerging Economies: Origins and Policy Options." BIS Economic Paper No. 46. International Settlements, Basle.

Jayaratne, J., and P. E. Strahan. 1996. "The Finance-Growth Nexus: Evidence from Bank Branch Deregulation." *Quarterly Journal of Economics* 111 (August): 639–702.

Johnston, B., Salim M. Darbar, and Claudia Echeverría. 1997. "Sequencing Capital Account Liberalization: Lessons from the Experiences in Chile, Indonesia, Korea, and Thailand." IMF Working Paper No. 157. International Monetary Fund, Washington, D.C.

King, Robert, and Ross Levine. 1993. "Finance and Growth: Schumpeter Might Be Right." Policy Research Working Paper 1083. World Bank, Policy Research Department, Washington, D.C.

Larraín, Christian. 1995. "Internacionalización y Supervisión de la Banca en Chile." Estudios Públicos, CEP No. 60, pp. 117–43. Primavera.

Levine, R. 1998. *Napoleon, Bourses, and Growth in Latin America.* Conference on Development of Securities Markets in Emerging Economies: Obstacles and Preconditions for Success. Working Paper 365. Inter-American Development Bank, Office of the Chief Economist, Washington, D.C.

Levine, R., and S. Zervos. 1996. "Stock Market Development and Long-Run Growth." Policy Research Working Paper 1582. World Bank, Policy Research Department, Washington, D.C.

Rajan, R., and L. Zingales. 1996. "Financial Dependence and Growth." National Bureau of Economic Research, Working Paper 5758, Cambridge, Mass.

Ramírez, G., and Rosende, F. 1992. "Responding to Collapse: The Chilean Banking Legislation after 1983." In P. Brock, eds., *If Texas Were Chile: A Primer on Banking Reform.* San Francisco: Institute for Contemporary Studies.

Soto, Claudio. 1997. "Controles a los Movimientos de Capital: Evaluación Empírica del Caso Chileno." Central Bank of Chile, Santiago.

Superintendencia de Administradoras de Fondos de Pensiones. 1996. "Evolución del Sistema Chileno de Pensiones." Santiago.

Superintendencia de Valores y Seguros. 1996. "The Chilean Securities Market." Research and International Relations Division, Santiago.

Valdés-Prieto, Salvador, and Marcelo Soto. 1997. "The Effectiveness of Capital Controls: Theory and Evidence from Chile." Universidad Católica de Chile, Santiago.

World Bank. 1997. *Private Capital Flows to Developing Countries: The Road to Financial Integration.* Policy Research Report. Washington, D.C.

Part II

Social Sector Advances

4

Market and State Principles of Reform in Chilean Education: Policies and Results

Cristián Cox
María José Lemaitre

During the 1980s Chile's military government (1973–90) reformed the schooling system. It decentralized school administration, introduced a voucher system of financing, and used legal and market incentives to spur the growth of state-funded private schools. In 1990, after more than a decade and a half of authoritarian politics and neo-liberal economics, a democratic government inaugurated policies that focused explicitly on public investments in the quality and equity of education, the learning contexts and outcomes of the system, while maintaining the organizational and funding components of the system that were begun in the 1980s. The motives for the reforms in the 1980s and 1990s differed. The reforms of the 1980s were primarily fiscal, administrative, and linked to political power issues. The reforms of the 1990s focused on the nature of the educational opportunities the system was able to offer and their social distribution.

The authors express their thanks to Francoise Delannoy for her comments and suggestions.

The Chilean government's policies in education since the beginning of the 1980s have been heralded as perhaps the most (at that time) radical pro-market and pro-choice educational reform carried out on a national scale. Often, however, the discussion and analyses have been more concerned with the radical character of the reforms and their ideological underpinnings than with their implementation or concrete learning achievements. Most remarkably, little attention has been given to the ideological, political, and programmatic divide marked by 1990 and the inauguration in government of new political actors and new orienting principles. Our chapter attempts to redress this shortcoming. It brings into focus the contrasts as well as the continuities of two decades of strong state intervention in education under different paradigms. It suggests that *third way* policies characterize the present—policies that stand apart from the distant past of a highly centralized state-run educational system and the market-oriented reforms of the 1980s.

The chapter's main purpose is to describe the origins and key features of state and market institutions and mechanisms that frame, regulate, and orient the development of the Chilean education sector at present. After boldly sketching the main features of the country's educational system and its level of development, we describe the reforms of the 1980s, reviewing their rationale, measures, and outcomes. Secondly, we address the policies and programs of the 1990s, referring to their context, measures, and results. We then discuss evidence about learning outcomes of public and private schools during the 1990s. In a concluding section we refer to the main challenges that confront the sector and draw lessons for policymaking.

Educational Development: Historical Landmarks in a State System

Chile's schooling system was organized in the last third of the nineteenth century by the state, along centralist principles copied from Napoleonic France. It developed as a public service administered by a comparatively able central bureaucracy dedicated to the equal provision of educational opportunities in a society and culture that greatly valued education.

Throughout the first half of the twentieth century, the key issue was *access*, as state efforts gradually expanded the primary schooling system. A major reform crowned this push for universal coverage at the end of the 1960s. Coverage increased to all urban and most rural areas, in 1970 reaching more than 90 percent at the primary level. Secondary level coverage of just over 18 percent at the start of the decade rose to 49 percent of the 14–18 age group in 1970. This expansion of access was accompanied by an extension of compulsory education from six to eight years, provision of textbooks for primary school children, and upgrading of teachers' qualifications. The curriculum and pedagogical features of the system also were reformed in the 1960s. A system-wide attempt was made to change from a rigid formalism to teaching methods that focused more on problem solving and the activity of the learners.

President Allende's socialist government (1970–73) tried a reform that unsuccessfully attempted to weaken the boundaries between school and work and sought to consolidate the various types of schools in the country into one centralized organization oriented according to collectivist principles. In circumstances of profound political division and upheaval, the *Escuela Nacional Unificada* (ENU) proposal contributed to the crisis of Chilean democracy. After the military coup of 1973, the Armed Forces government applied doctrines of "national security" to education, focusing on the control of teachers and the curriculum of history and social sciences.[1] The institutional, funding, and administrative framework of the schooling system, however, was not affected. Then in 1980 the government started a major reform that decentralized the administration of the schools (box 4-1) and introduced a voucher-based system of financing public education.

Thus, Chile accomplished:

- A reform focused on the *expansion of access* during the 1960s, implemented by a highly centralized state system in a democratic context;
- A reform focused on *efficiency* during the 1980s, implemented by an authoritarian military regime that effectively decentralized and introduced competition and private incentive mechanisms on a national scale;
- A reform of education focused on *quality and equity* during the 1990s, implemented through means that combined state and market principles; centrally driven (*push*) and decentralized (*pull*) strategies.

In 1970 close to universal access to primary education was reached, and in the 1980s and 1990s, despite political conflict and contrasting govern-

---

1. A month after the coup the Ministry of Education issued new guidelines for the teaching of history, including an order "that the industrial revolution should be treated, as its name indicates, in terms of changes in science and technology, eliminating the theories and conflicts attending political and social discussions that are now sufficiently well-known" (quoted in Gauri 1996, 150).

Box 4-1. The Chilean School System: Structure, Size, and Administrative Categories

Chile's school system is organized into primary and secondary levels. Eight years of education are compulsory at the primary level for pupils ages 6 to 13 years. Four years of education are not compulsory at the secondary level for pupils between the ages of 14 and 18. Secondary education is divided into two tracks: one follows a general academic curriculum in the humanities and sciences and is intended to lead on to studies at the higher education level; the other track is vocational (technical-professional) in orientation, and it is intended to prepare pupils for the labor force.

The preschool education system serves children up to the age of 5 through a variety of institutions, both public and private. It is noncompulsory, and enrollment consists for the most part of children ages 4 and 5: coverage in 1996 was 25 percent.

Total enrollment in the primary and secondary levels of the school system stood at 2.97 million pupils in 1996: 2.24 million in the primary level, representing 96 percent coverage for the 6-to-12 age group, and 739,316 pupils at the secondary level, representing 82 percent coverage for the 14-to-18 age group. There are 120,000 teachers in the system, working in approximately 10,000 schools at the primary level and 1,700 at the secondary level.

In terms of administrative and funding relationships, the institutional categories (created by the 1981 reform) are the following:

ment policies, enrollments in secondary schools grew substantially (table 4-1). The average years of schooling of persons 15 years of age and older also increased. There can be little doubt about the social and cultural valuing of education as a prime tool for expanding opportunities and social mobility. By the end of the 1980s, access had ceased to be the main challenge for policy in the sector. Efficiency, quality, and equity issues then took center stage.

Decentralization and Competition: The Search for Efficiency in the 1980s

The reforms in the early 1980s had financial, efficiency, and power distribution arguments as their main rationales for intervention. The focus was administrative; the key functions of the sector, related to learning, remained

- *Municipal schools* are administered by the more than 300 municipalities of the country through two forms: Administrative Departments of Municipal Education (DAEM) or Municipal Corporations. The Administrative Departments answer directly to the mayor and are subject to more rigid rules regarding management of personnel. The Municipal Corporations are nonprofit and are governed by less strict rules regarding hiring of personnel and use of resources. Eighty percent of municipalities manage education through DAEMs.
- *Private-subsidized* schools are financed through an attendance-based per-pupil public subsidy, or subvention. *Private-paid* schools accept no government subsidies and operate entirely on parental contributions.
- *Corporation schools* correspond to technical-professional secondary schools administered by business corporations with fiscal funding especially established for this purpose (which is not a per-pupil subsidy).

The relative sizes of the mentioned categories, in terms of 1996 enrollments, are:

Municipal education	55.9%
Private, state-subsidized education	33.0%
Private-paid education	9.4%
Corporations	1.6%

Source: Ministry of Education, *Compendio de Información Estadística, 1996.*

throughout the decade in the background.[2] Its key measures were established in 1980 and 1981 in the already mentioned context of authoritarian politics and neo-liberal economics.

The principles of the reform combined decentralization and competition criteria as prime tools for improving the allocation and use of resources by the school system. Amongst its key goals were:

- To improve the budget mix of the sector, transferring resources from higher education to preschool and primary education.

---

2. This can be stated in spite of, firstly, changes in the *official* curriculum, which were not accompanied by any significant effort to make it an *implemented* curriculum, and, secondly, the setting up of a national assessment system of educational results.

Table 4-1. Educational Attainment, 1970–96: Primary and Secondary Level Schooling

Year	Enrollments		Coverage		Average years of schooling (15+ years old)	Literacy rate
	Primary	Secondary	Primary	Secondary		
1970	2,200,160	306,064	93.3	49.7	4.3	89.0
1982	2,116,397	565,745	95.2	65.0	7.7	91.1
1990	2,022,924	719,819	91.3	80.0	8.6	94.6
1996	2,241,536	739,316	96.0	82.3	9.8	95.2

Source: Ministry of Education, *Compendio de Información Estadística* (1991, 1995, 1996).

- To improve efficiency in the use of resources, through competition among schools for the enrollment of pupils;
- To transfer functions traditionally carried out by the Ministry of Education and its central bureaucracy to local control represented by the municipalities;
- To reduce the negotiating power of the teachers;
- To increase participation of the private sector in educational provision, which would supply the basis for competition and provide consumers with more and better options;
- To bring technical secondary education closer to industry;
- To make the curriculum more flexible and modern.

Adopted Reforms

STATE EXPENDITURES IN EDUCATION. The implementation of the reform coincided with a decade of decreasing public expenditure in education. Total government spending in education declined 19.4 percent between 1985 and 1990: from 4.0 to 2.5 percent of GNP (table 4-2).

The composition of public expenditure in education also changed; preschool and primary education were favored over secondary and higher education. Government spending in tertiary education was reduced from close to 38 percent in 1980 to 19 percent in 1990, while government spending on primary education went from 57 to 78 percent in the same period (Prawda 1992; Brunner 1992).

In spite of the favorable budget mix, total expenditure in primary and secondary education fell sharply; per-student subsidies were not adjusted

Table 4-2. Ministry of Education Total Expenditure and Per-Student Subsidy, 1982–97

(Millions of CH$, average 1997 value)

Year	Ministry of Education total spending (includes higher education)	Index Ministry of Education expenditure 1982 = 100	Education budget as a percentage of total state budget	Education budget as a percentage of GNP	Monthly subsidy per student (in pesos)
1982	646.542	100	17.6	4.9	11.582
1983	599.666	93	14.8	4.3	9.955
1984	583.726	90	15.0	4.2	9.351
1985	583.148	90	14.1	4.0	8.784
1986	530.378	82	13.4	3.5	9.827
1987	487.771	75	12.4	3.0	9.226
1988	504.710	78	12.7	2.7	9.329
1989	492.615	76	11.8	2.6	9.345
1990	469.688	73	13.1	2.5	8.874
1991	511.120	79	13.4	2.6	9.159
1992	578.827	90	13.6	2.7	10.016
1993	646.871	100	13.8	2.8	10.904
1994	702.094	109	14.2	2.8	12.145
1995	810.308	125	14.9	2.9	14.346
1996	925.529	143	15.6	3.1	15.936
1997	1.032.262	160	15.5	3.3	17.214

Source: Ministry of Education, Planning and Budget Division, 1997; Ministry of Finance, Budget Office (1998).

to inflation. The initial reduction can be explained as a result of the economic crisis of 1982 and 1983. Nevertheless, after 1985 the economy grew steadily by more than 6 percent on average each year; therefore, the drop in expenditure can only be interpreted as the consequence of a political decision about the relative unimportance of education in the development strategy of the government.

TRANSFER OF SCHOOLS FROM MINISTERIAL TO MUNICIPAL CONTROL. The government transferred administrative responsibility for all public schools from the Ministry of Education to the municipalities in which they were located. The municipalities (325 of them in 1981) were given the authority to hire and fire teachers and manage buildings and facilities. The Ministry of Education kept its normative functions, namely, determining the curriculum and textbooks, providing technical supervision, and evaluating the system.

The declared rationale for this transfer of responsibility was to bring education closer to families and to local control, increasing citizens' participation and making schools more responsive to the needs of local communities. In practice, political conditions kept this from occurring. Municipalities were led by mayors and council members centrally appointed by a military government that was suspicious of participation and expressions of practically any *voice* mechanism (Hirschman 1973). Municipalization, therefore, was an administrative or bureaucratic decentralization (with some management and control functions shifted from the Ministry of Education to municipalities). Decentralization did not have democratic consequences; for example, power to make decisions about education was not given to citizens' and their elected representatives (Fiske 1996).

PER-STUDENT SUBSIDY FOR FINANCING EDUCATION. The reforms changed the traditional incremental budget allocation to public schools. A new system was instituted, one inspired by Milton Friedman's concept of an educational voucher that channeled public resources to municipal and private-subsidized schools on the basis of student enrollment. The subsidy was paid to every proprietor, whether private or municipal, on the basis of monthly attendance rates (rather than actual enrollment)—a strong incentive to develop strategies for keeping the pupils attending classes.

INCENTIVES TO THE PRIVATE SECTOR AND COMPETITION BETWEEN SCHOOLS. After the transfer of schools to municipalities, the subsidy paid to private schools was increased to equal that paid to municipal schools.[3] The new level of the subsidy paid per pupil to private schools was meant to encourage private providers to enter the sector and open new primary and secondary schools, thus enlarging the options for families.

This happened in urban, heavily populated areas, but the bigger subsidy did not increase, or diversify, the supply of schools in rural areas or in urban but less populated areas. In spite of the growth of private enrollment (from 19.6 percent in 1982 to 33.6 percent in 1996), about 27 percent of municipalities in 1996 had no private-subsidized schools, and over 70 percent had no private-paid schools (Carnoy and McEwan 1997). The same study shows a positive relationship between population density and private school coverage.

---

3. Private schools had always received subsidies from the government, but before the reforms they received roughly half the amount given to municipal schools.

LIBERALIZATION OF THE TEACHING LABOR MARKET. Intrinsic to the new model was a liberalization of the conditions regulating the teaching profession. Teachers lost their civil servant status; their unions were banned and their leadership politically persecuted; their wages were fixed by each individual employer, whether a municipality or a private proprietor. As public funding decreased, and schools lowered their costs, teachers' wages dropped by approximately one-third in real terms during the 1980s. About a fifth of the 100,000 teachers in the country lost their jobs at least once between 1980 and 1989 (Gauri 1996).

Salaries within the profession differed markedly. By the end of the decade, teachers' salaries ranged from a low of 8 times the individual student subsidy, typically in newly created private-subsidized schools not affiliated with churches or nonprofit organizations, to a high of approximately 20 times the subsidy, most frequently in municipal and older private-subsidized schools (Prawda 1992).

TRANSFER OF TECHNICAL-VOCATIONAL SCHOOLS. Responsibility for about 7 percent of public secondary technical-vocational schools (50 schools) was transferred from the Ministry of Education to specially set-up educational corporations, which were created in response to government directives to the country's main industrial, agricultural, mining, and commerce associations. These corporations were not funded by the per-pupil subsidy but through the traditional annual allocation, which was more (in some cases twice as much) than the subsidy.

CHANGES IN THE CURRICULUM. For all the subjects taught at the primary and secondary levels, a new curriculum and new syllabi were developed between the end of 1980 and 1983. Consistent with decentralization principles, government regulation of education content was relaxed. Schools were allowed to determine how many hours students would spend learning certain subjects, and secondary level students were permitted to choose some courses. In the case of technical-vocational education, state regulations were eliminated, and teachers in each school were asked to define their programs of study in accordance with their interpretation of labor market demands. Close to 400 technical courses of study were thus defined. In general, course content was simplified, giving teachers more say in what was taught. At the same time there was an attempt to make technical and vocational education more practical and less academically oriented (Cox 1992).

A NATIONAL TESTING SYSTEM. The government wanted schools to compete for pupils, and it wanted parents to choose schools based on learning outcomes. Consistent with this idea, it established a national testing system in order to measure student achievement in Spanish and mathematics. From 1982 to 1984, the *Programa de Evaluacion del Rendimiento Escolar (PER)* tested primary school children on both subjects; since 1988 the *Sistema de Evaluacion de la Calidad de la Educacion (SIMCE)* has tested all fourth and eighth graders in alternate years on Spanish and math, plus a sample of them on history and science.

Results

The reforms of the 1980s expanded the private provision of education (in its two forms, private-paid, and private-subsidized) from just below 25 percent of enrollments in 1982 to 40.1 percent of enrollments in 1990 (table 4-3).

Enrollments grew during the decade, from 2.8 million pupils in 1982 to 2.9 million in 1990. Enrollment in the private-subsidized sector grew at a much higher rate than total enrollment, from 19.6 percent in 1982 to 32.4 percent in 1990. Most of the transfer of pupils from municipal to private-subsidized schools took place in the 1982–86 period. Since the late 1980s there has been a steady albeit slow increase in the enrollments in both categories of private education and a decline in municipal school enrollments.

The number of private-subsidized schools increased by 50 percent, from fewer than 2,000 in 1980 to almost 3,000 in 1990. As mentioned, these schools were located mainly in urban areas, which was consistent with the incentives provided.

As a consequence of the reforms, municipal schools were organized along parallel lines of dependence and authority. On the one hand, the line of the

Table 4-3. School Enrollments (Primary and Secondary) by Administrative Categories, 1982–96

Year	Enrollments	National/ municipal schools (percent)	Private- subsidized schools (percent)	Corporation schools (percent)	Private- paid schools (percent)
1982	2,682,142	75.3	19.6	—	5.1
1984	2,710,369	68.2	26.3	—	5.5
1986	2,757,894	63.1	30.8	—	6.1
1988	2,771,932	59.6	31.4	1.9	7.0
1990	2,742,743	57.9	32.4	1.9	7.7
1992	2,741,624	57.7	32.3	1.8	8.2
1994	2,784,235	57.3	32.3	1.6	8.8
1996	2,980,852	55.9	33.0	1.6	9.4

Source: Ministry of Education, *Compendio de Información Estadística* (1996).

municipality referred to all administrative aspects, including human resources, budgeting, and facilities. On the other hand, that of the Ministry referred to curriculum, pedagogy, and evaluation matters, as well as control over the monthly attendance of pupils, a matter of critical importance for the subsidy mechanism.

It is important to evaluate not only the administration and financing of the school system during the 1980s but also its performance in terms of efficiency, quality, and equity criteria. The state intervention during the 1990s was closely related to what such an evaluation most directly reveals: arguably good results in terms of efficiency, absence of results, or negative ones, in terms of quality and equity criteria.

Efficiency

Educational inefficiency (wastage) was reduced during the 1980s in spite of the decline in available resources. Between 1980 and 1989, the primary school repetition rate dropped from 8.1 percent to 6.1 percent, and the primary completion rate improved from 12.2 years to produce a graduate to 10.6 years (Prawda 1992).[4]

Enrollments in secondary education expanded drastically. There can be little doubt about the per-pupil subsidy as an efficient mechanism for automatically adjusting demand and supply of school provision, at least in the most populated areas. Furthermore, the fact that the subsidy is paid on the basis of attendance motivated schools to improve students' attendance, an important enrollment factor, particularly in rural areas. Finally, a voucher system makes schools more responsive to parents and guardians, since "opting out" has an immediate impact on school finances.

Quality

The reforms of the 1980s did not have a positive effect on learning at the primary level. Nationwide measurements of fourth graders' cognitive achievements in language and math at the beginning and at the end of the decade show a decline (Morales 1991; Prawda 1992; and Carnoy and McEwan 1997).

The Ministry of Education applied nationwide standardized, low-stakes tests to fourth graders in 1983 and 1984 (Prueba de Evaluación del

---

4. The per-pupil subsidy created strong incentives for schools to pass pupils, regardless of their learning levels. Mark inflation was also a reason for schools to increase their enrollments. These factors may have artificially affected the primary repetition and primary completion rates (Espínola 1993).

Rendimiento Escolar, PER) and again in 1988 (Sistema de Información y Medición de la Calidad de la Educación, SIMCE). The measurements evaluated cognitive achievement in language, math, social sciences, and natural sciences. The samples included 3,200 primary schools (municipal, private-subsidized, and private-paid) in 1983–84, and 5,600 primary schools in 1988.

A comparison of the PER results of 1983 and SIMCE results of 1988 in Spanish and math shows a decline in the national average of 14.0 and 6.0 percent, respectively (Prawda 1992). These figures are probably overstated, since the sample in 1983 excluded rural schools (about 12 percent of the cohort); these schools have the poorest results. An analysis that compares only schools that were measured at the beginning and at the end of the decade found that the overall trend of decline is preserved, albeit reduced (Morales 1991). There is no guarantee, however, that the two tests are comparable in their level of difficulty across years, because a system of equating is not in place (Carnoy and McEwan 1997). In view of this evidence it seems a conservative hypothesis that learning results did not improve during the decade and probably declined.

The absence of improvements in learning results is not surprising. During the decade there were no significant investments in learning inputs. Indeed, the total number of school hours per year were allowed to decline as a consequence of the relaxation of the rules regulating school time and curriculum subjects (Cox 1992). Moreover, the essential teaching functions rested on a demoralized teaching force. In this context, competition for pupils undoubtedly produced the noted gains in efficiency and effectiveness: with less resources were obtained similar learning results, expanded coverage, and improvements in repetition and drop-out rates. National average learning results did not improve, however. They became the focal point of the policies of the 1990s.

Equity

The results for fourth graders in 1982 and 1988 show that the spread between the highest and the lowest scores in Spanish increased; the spread for mathematics remained the same, about 30 percentage points (Prawda 1992).[5]

---

5. Here the same caveat mentioned earlier applies. The sample of 1988 included more rural schools than did the sample of 1982. This biased the results, expanding the gap between the highest and the lowest scores.

The public subsidy was the same for all schools, but municipalities differ in their ability to supplement these resources. Poor areas are certainly less attractive to private providers of education. Therefore, the worst provision of education was concentrated in the poorest (both in a material and cultural sense) sectors of the population, and there were no mechanisms to counteract this situation.

Additionally, since competition was based at least partly on reported learning outcomes, schools had strong incentives to exclude pupils with low marks, who also tend to come from poor families (Rounds Parry 1996). This is especially significant in private schools, since municipal schools are obliged to accept all pupils living in the neighborhood. (The most prestigious municipal schools do not always do so.)

Government policies did not compensate for marked differences in the quality of educational services rendered or the exclusion from schools of children with low learning outcomes. The government did not refer to equity as a criteria for policy, and it did nothing to address the inequalities resulting from the competition between private-subsidized and municipal schools. Furthermore, it implicitly accepted, as the regulations on school time and subjects of the curriculum show, a publicly funded provision of education of different levels according to the material and cultural conditions in which the schools operated (Cox 1992).

Public Investments, Comprehensive Programs, and Reform: The Search for Quality and Equity in the 1990s

In 1990 the re-instatement of democracy brought a center-left coalition to government. Its main objective was national reconciliation. A second government of the same coalition was inaugurated in 1994. In accordance with a broad national consensus about the strategic importance of education for the country's economic and democratic development, it made its first priority substantial improvement in educational quality and equity.

The education policies designed and implemented in the 1990s were the result of more than a decade of research in academic centers opposed to the authoritarian government. These centers criticized both the pre-1980 "teaching state," deemed inadequate to meet the challenges posed by the quality and equity agenda, and the "Chicago" model applied during the 1980s, which they found singularly lacking in terms of equity criteria and the definition and achievement of national educational goals regarding citizenship and international competitiveness requirements. Neither precedent would improve quality or equity in the system.[6]

The educational reforms of the 1990s made the following shifts in strategic orientation:

- From a focus on inputs to one on learning processes and outcomes.
- From a view of equity as a nationally homogeneous provision of education to a provision that is sensitive to diversity and that discriminates in favor of the most vulnerable groups.
- From bureaucratic-administrative regulations to regulations based on competition, incentives, information, and assessment.
- From self-sustaining institutions relatively closed to society's needs and controlled by their own practitioners and bureaucracy to institutions that are connected to other institutional spheres and open to the demands of society.
- From policies that seek change through comprehensive reform processes (driven by linear planning concepts and/or mainly legal means) to differentiated strategies that resort to a range of "push, pull, and support" mechanisms, and a concept of incremental change based on making use of the innovative capacities of the schools.
- From policies subordinated to special or sectional interests to nationally defined strategic policies based on consensus among the main stakeholders.

The Goals of Educational Quality and Equity

State intervention in the educational sector in 1990 was a response to the main problems of the schooling system in the 1980s: low quality and unequal social distribution of learning results.

Regarding the goal of educational quality, the two governments in the 1990s attempted to substantially improve the learning outcomes of all (or most) students at all school levels. To this end policies endeavored to help

---

6. Two books summarize the vision that arose in these independent academic centers, funded throughout the 1980s by governmental and nongovernmental aid agencies in Europe and North America. The first is García-Huidobro (1989), and the second is PIIE (1989). Also influential was the World Conference on Education for All (1990) held in Jomtiem, Thailand, in March. At the beginning of the decade, the ideas developed within ECLAC and UNESCO played an important role. See ECLAC and UNESCO (1997).

students to think abstractly and systematically; to communicate, collaborate, and experiment; and to make moral judgments in a complex world.

The equity goal was to significantly improve the social distribution of educational outcomes, which in 1990 reproduced the socioeconomic stratification of the country. This required the provision of resources and supporting actions that favored schools and students belonging to the groups and communities most at risk. It also required a new approach to learning, one that accepted as the starting point of the school-learning enterprise the learner's viewpoint—the knowledge each student brings to the educational process and the cultural context in which he or she lives and works.

With these criteria and policy goals, the new authorities articulated a vision for the sector. The vision was not based on competition between two principles of ownership and management (state versus private). It considered Chile's prospects in an increasingly competitive world and the pressing need to defeat poverty and strengthen social cohesion and democracy. At the same time, the authorities sought to redefine the relationship between the state and the teaching profession. The military government had viewed teachers as nonstrategic and politically suspect. The new authorities viewed them as key actors deserving of public trust and support for accomplishing a process of change of vital importance to the country.

During the transition to democracy period, two important strategic decisions were made. The first was the decision not to reverse the municipalization process or to change the per-pupil subsidy mechanism. The second was the decision to upgrade the conditions, processes, and learning results of the schooling system as a whole. This state-led systemic intervention had explicit national-level goals both in terms of quality and equity. The policies of the 1990s integrated the means and mechanisms of the neo-liberal reform of the 1980s in a new, more vast context, producing a rich and complex pattern of continuity and change and the particular combination of institutions, principles of action, and incentive structures that characterizes Chile's educational system at present.

The policy measures of the 1990–97 period can be grouped in four domains: financing of education, regulation of the teaching profession, voluntary programs to improve educational quality and equity, and mandatory changes in the school day and curriculum.

Financing

INCREASED AND TARGETED SPENDING. The Ministry of Education's total expenditure steadily increased in the 1990–97 period: from 470 thousand millions of Chilean pesos to more than a billion of 1997 value, after a decade of decline of public expenditure in the sector. By 1990, the last budget defined by the military regime, the average per-student subsidy had dropped 23 percent since 1982; it was only in 1994 that the 1982 level of the average subsidy was surpassed, and in 1997 it was almost 50 percent larger than in 1982. If one includes spending on student welfare (food rations and scholarships), programs to improve the quality and equity of education, and investments in infrastructure, the monthly per-student expenditure in 1997 was CH$21,810 (approximately US$48), or practically twice the amount of 1982 (CH$11,582), the previous peak of the subsidy.

The government has tried to correct the most glaring imbalances between subsidies and normal operating expenses of schools of different sizes and in different locations. This has meant a significant increase in the subvention for rural schools and for adult education centers. Since 1995, special subsidies have been provided to schools in poor districts that have extended their hours of operation in order to offer remedial help to students who are slow learners.

SHARED FUNDING BEGUN IN 1993. As part of a broader tax reform in late 1993, private-subsidized elementary schools (not municipal schools) and *liceos*, whether municipal or private-subsidized schools, were allowed to charge families a fee. The proceeds could be used to top up the state subsidy, as a form of co-financing. After a certain limit in family fee revenues is reached, the state subsidy is reduced proportionately.[7] In 1996 co-funding of this kind resulted in revenues of US$80 million (equal to roughly 6.3 percent of total subsidy expenditures for that year). In 1997, 27 percent of enrollments (824,000 pupils) belonged to schools with shared-funding, with monthly payments that varied between CH$500 and CH$32,000.

The success of the co-funding formula in attracting private resources for education has been marred by the resulting segmentation in public education (differentiation by level of family income) and social segregation (exclusion of families that cannot pay). These tendencies undermine the principle of equity and demonstrate the need for mechanisms to neutralize such segregation. One such mechanism was a school-based scholarship fund

---

7. These discounts are applied progressively on the portions that exceed the value of the subsidy scale: if the fee is less than half the value of the subsidy, there is no reduction; if the fee is between 1 and 2 times the subsidy, the discount is 20 percent, and so on.

for students from poor backgrounds. It was created by the Full School Day Law of 1997. The fund increases with the level of the charges to the families, and it is financed from two sources: a) fiscal resources from reductions in the discounts applied to the student subsidy; b) private resources that correspond to a proportion of the charges made by the school to the families (5 percent if the fee does not exceed the equivalent of one unit of public subsidy, 10 percent if the charge is between 2 and 4 units of subsidy) (Gonzalez 1998).

Regulating the Teaching Profession

FIRST TEACHERS' STATUTE (1991). The government in 1991 revised the labor law governing the teaching profession. The law was moved out of the Labor Code, which governs private employment activities. This Teachers' Statute establishes national regulations covering conditions of employment (number of working days, maximum working hours, vacations). It provides for a common and enriched structure of wages; and bonuses for in-service training, professional experience, and service under hardship conditions. It also includes provisions that make it practically impossible to lay off teachers.

The Statute was controversial. It divided the government cabinet and won executive approval only because of the personal support of the president. In Congress the articles relating to the almost tenured nature of teachers' employment were stretched to exaggeration; for example, articles relating to the permanent status of principals were made more extreme than the original proposal by the Opposition. The 1991 Statute reversed the deregulation of the teaching labor market in the 1980s and partially contradicted the subsidy-based funding system. It made it virtually impossible for municipalities to change their teaching staff in response to shifting enrollment patterns. (In this respect the Statute did not affect the private system.)

The arguably regressive characteristics of the *Estatuto Docente* in terms of decentralization and adequate incentives criteria must be viewed in the political context of the times. The Statute originated in 1991, the first year of a democratic government after 17 years of authoritarianism. The teachers' union and body identified the return to democratic politics not only with a return to the public (fiscal) character of their contracts, but also with the reversal of the decentralization process of the 1980s. We suggest that the government chose to defend the decentralized institutional framework established during the 1980s and concede the *Statute*, in terms that did not risk confrontation and conflict with the key actors of the system.

By going a significant way toward meeting the expectations of the teaching profession, the government introduced rigidities for the municipal administrations, but it also laid an adequate political basis for the remainder of the change process. Between 1990 and December 1997, the schooling system suffered 12 days of work stoppage by teachers on a national scale, and there has been no opposition to the programs to enhance the quality of education, the heart of the educational agenda of the 1990s.

Was the 1991 Teachers' Statute beneficial? Or was the "peace" with the teachers' union obtained at too high a price in terms of management rigidities and distortions in the incentive structure? Both issues were addressed in a second round of legislation regarding the regulation of the teaching profession.

SECOND TEACHERS' STATUTE (1995). The 1991 Statute was revised for two main reasons: to increase mobility in the teaching body and to link teachers' wages to performance. Municipalities were empowered to adopt an Annual Plan for the Development of Municipal Education (PADEM). Under this plan they are allowed to reduce teaching staff according to variations in their enrollments.[8] In addition, the law establishes a National Performance Evaluation System (SNED). Schools are evaluated in light of the kind of students they have; incentives and premiums are given to teaching teams that show improvement in learning outcomes.

The SNED system gives an additional subsidy per pupil to the best-performing 25 percent of schools of each region of the country; the school owner or administrator cannot allocate the extra funding received from the state to any other use than teachers' salaries. The premium is to the school teaching team and not to individuals. The schools are selected according to the learning outcomes of their pupils and other criteria such as improvement of learning outcomes compared with outcomes in previous years; initiative in terms of innovations and projects; improvement of teachers' working conditions; equality of opportunity initiatives for pupils; and involvement of parents, teachers, and pupils in the school project. SNED gave premiums to 2,285 schools in 1996–97, benefiting 31,323 teachers who received an amount averaging approximately a month's wage.

The 1995 reform of the Teachers' Statute also provided for a further increase in teachers' salaries. Taken together with other salary increases that

---

8. The changes associated with PADEM have not yet passed their critical test, which is the reduction of the teaching force in municipalities that have experienced lower enrollments (Gonzalez 1998).

were awarded over the period 1990–97, teachers' earnings have risen by 100 percent in real terms since 1990. They now average about US$700 per month (CH$300,000 pesos) based on a 30–hour teaching week (Gonzalez 1998).

Comprehensive and Differentiated Programs to Improve the Quality and Equity of Learning Contexts

The policies of the 1990s tackled the double challenge of improving the quality and equity of educational opportunities through comprehensive and differentiated programs of intervention. The government invested in learning resources (traditional and new), provided direct pedagogical support to teachers attending poor groups, funded school-proposed improvement projects, and set up support networks and mechanisms. The foci of the programs varied according to the type of school and the needs defined as a priority during the decade.

Between 1990 and 1997 there were a succession of programs, each one covering a strategic need, and each one built on the implementation, efficacy, and efficiency lessons of the preceding ones. The government concentrated first on the 10 percent of the poorest primary schools, then on the entire state-supported primary education level, and subsequently on the secondary level (with two programs, one offering universal coverage and the other highly focused coverage).

THE "900 SCHOOLS PROGRAM." The transition to democracy government (1990–94) started its intervention in education with a program focused on the 10 percent of primary schools (900 schools) with the poorest learning outcomes. The program, begun in 1990, provides materials (infrastructure repairs, textbooks, teaching materials, classroom libraries) as well as technical support. Its aim is to improve reading, writing, and math skills, and enhance the self-esteem and communication skills of pupils in the first four years of primary school. The pedagogical strategy of the program is to offer new teaching methods for literacy and mathematics, hire young monitors from within the community who have completed their secondary education and who can provide supplementary tutoring for slow learners, and inject new textbooks and instructional materials in the schools. The program was extraordinarily fast in reaching the schools and started to show results by the end of its first year.

As noted, the "900 Schools Program" focuses on schools with the poorest performance. Schools that demonstrate improved learning levels—as measured in nationwide performance tests in the fourth grade—leave the program and move on to the Ministry of Education's universal coverage program for basic education, MECE-Básica.

Between 1990 and 1996, 2,099 schools participated in the program. In 1990 the average math and Spanish scores on the SIMCE test given to fourth graders in the P-900 schools was 52.11 (out of a possible 100); in 1996 their score was 64.06, indicating an improvement of 11.95 percentage points. Over the same period, the average improvement for all state-supported schools was 8.95 percentage points, which suggests that the quality gap between the lowest-ranking schools and the rest of the schools in the system narrowed.[9]

PRESCHOOL, PRIMARY, AND SECONDARY EDUCATION IMPROVEMENT PROGRAMS. These programs represent systemic intervention to change the conditions, processes, and outcomes of municipal and private-subsidized schools through investment in material inputs and innovations adapted to specific types of schools.

MECE-Básica was launched in 1992 with financial and technical support from the World Bank. Covering the whole of the primary level, it cost US$243 million, and it was concluded as an externally funded and supported program in 1997. All its actions have been institutionalized as part of the routine programs of the Ministry of Education.

MECE-Media (1995–2000) includes all secondary schools (municipal and private-subsidized); also supported by the World Bank, it takes advantage of the implementation lessons of MECE-Básica to advance new strategies of comprehensive intervention (Lemaitre 1998). It has a budget of US$207 million.[10]

MECE-Básica and MECE-Media include the provision of textbooks for all primary and secondary school students (6 million textbooks per year in primary education alone); libraries for all classrooms between 1st and 6th grade, and school-libraries for all secondary schools; teaching materials for

---

9. See Ministry of Education, *Programa P-900 Comparación SIMCE - Escuelas P-900*, Santiago, 1997. The P-900 program has been the subject of several external assessments. On this point, see the Swedish Development Agency's evaluation report on the Programa 900 Escuelas, "Pedagogía y Gestión," in Gajardo (1994).

10. Average annual spending under MECE-Básica, at US$40 million, was equivalent to 5 percent of total state expenditure in the primary level in 1992 and 1993. The MECE-Media program will invest an average of US$34.5 million per year from 1995 to 2000 in publicly supported *liceos*. That annual figure represented 13 percent of the total per-pupil subsidy to secondary education in 1996.

all classrooms between P–K and 4th grade, plus teaching equipment for all primary and secondary schools.[11] The largest in financial terms and most innovative of the in-puts acquired for primary schools and *lycées* alike are sets of between three and nine last-generation computers per institution (varying according to enrollments), hardware required for the functioning of a school network of communications (the ENLACES program).

MECE programs have improved buildings and facilities and funded a health program to detect and treat visual, hearing, or other learning impairments.[12] MECE programs also have provided direct pedagogical assistance to teachers in rural schools, funded teachers' and students' initiatives, and set up and financed support networks of different degrees of institutionalization. We shall briefly describe them.

There are more than 3,000 rural schools in Chile. *MECE-Rural* provides them with special textbooks, libraries, and teaching materials, plus a curricular and pedagogical framework especially designed for multigrade schools (where students belonging to different grades attend the same classroom). In-service teacher support includes the organization of rural teacher groups that meet once a month during a full day for mutual professional support and learning based on special materials. The program has made steady progress since 1992 (reaching roughly a fifth of its target group each year). MECE-Rural started in the regions with the largest rural populations and the most vulnerable schools. By 1996 the program had reached 3,338 schools, 5,121 teachers, and 96,540 students.

An educational computer network *(ENLACES)* connects students and teachers to other schools, to universities, and the world. The computer laboratory in each school has communication and multimedia capabilities and

---

11. Modern and complete libraries are being set up in all secondary schools. The Ministry of Education determines 20 percent of each library's collection, and teachers from each school select the remaining 80 percent of titles from catalogues decided by panels of experts. Each of the new libraries will acquire about 2,000 titles, plus newspapers and journals, at the end of a process that involves three procurement stages. The average unit cost of a library (size varies according to enrollments): US$26,000.

12. Between 1992 and 1996, the infrastructure component of MECE-Básica carried out repair work at 2,232 schools (89 percent of its original target). Its health component conducted exams on the entire student body from grades 1 to 4, reached 322,241 children with the help of specialists (ophthalmologists, ear, nose and throat specialists, and traumatologists) and treated 233,739 pupils (glasses, drugs, kinesitherapy, hearing aids, examinations), exceeding the original goals of the program.

user-friendly software (La Plaza) to access reference data, teaching materials, and communication tools.[13] Schools are connected to the Internet through the university network. By December 1997, 1,500 primary and secondary schools were connected to the network, with close to 600,000 pupils and 27,000 teachers involved. By the end of 1998, 3,000 schools were included in ENLACES. At least 50 percent of primary schools (85 percent of enrollments) will be connected by the year 2000.[14] The next step in the ENLACES network development is the integration of the computers and the communication facilities into the curriculum.

Educational Improvement Projects (EIPs) mobilize the professional capabilities of teachers to improve learning. They are short-term projects (one to three years) funded by the government on a competitive basis. EIPs are designed by the teachers in a school and evaluated by the provincial level of the Ministry of Education in terms of their expected impact on learning outcomes, management practices, or teaching proficiency. An important feature is the integration of centralized decisionmaking with grass-roots initiatives. Successful projects have improved communication among teachers in different subjects or grades; used a team approach to diagnose problems and design solutions; related EIP activities directly to school routines; enabled teachers to manage the process and not merely follow bureaucratic orders; and instituted innovative practices with respect to curriculum, instruction, and the production of teaching materials. In many cases when a school is awarded a project, the parents or the community as a whole contribute additional funds for its execution; this not only expands the resources available but also exposes the school and its teachers to their external environment in a unique way.

Between 1992 and 1998, primary schools presented more than 8,540 EIPs in six yearly contests, 4,850 of which were funded. In the 1996 and 1997 contests, 671 secondary schools participated; 391 of these schools (or 30 percent of all state-funded secondary schools) were selected for funding and their projects are being implemented. Each project involves public funds of about US$7,500 at the primary level and US$12,600 at the secondary level.

Probably the most important EIP risks are those of self-reference of school projects. But this may be counterbalanced by the rapidly growing use of

---

13. *La Plaza* means village square; space of encounter and communication.

14. Total investment in ENLACES for 1992 to 2000 is US$120 million. Average cost per school is US$24,000 (80 percent in hardware and software; 20 percent in training).

the ENLACES network for communication between teachers of different schools and regions, and by the higher order learning objectives defined by the new curriculum.

Two additional components of the MECE-Media program aim to change processes in secondary schools: professional work groups for teachers and optional curricular activities (OCAs) for students. Time has been allotted within the school schedule for teachers to meet and discuss their daily routines and practices. The Ministry of Education provides support in terms of materials and technical assistance. Work groups afford teachers an opportunity to select teaching materials, study innovations proposed by the MECE program, share their teaching experiences, and make use of the technical assistance provided.

OCAs are school-based activities that respond to students' interests (in the arts, sports, communications, and the environment, for example). Optional curricular activities help students re-define their relationship with the school and provide students—especially those from poor areas—with a protected environment and opportunities to develop special interests in their free time. Teachers learn to look at their students in a different context, which improves the relationship between them. OCAs operate in the schools on Saturday mornings and holidays.[15]

The MECE program publicly solicited proposals of technical assistance to schools. The university institutions and diverse consultancy groups that responded are listed in a *Directory for Technical Assistance*. Institutions included in the directory may act as consultants to the schools in several different areas related to educational improvement (curriculum, pedagogy, assessment, student development, management, and teaching resources). Funds are transferred to the schools in order to enable them to hire such consultants as they consider necessary. The contracts—limited to short-term projects—are established between each school and the technical assistance supplier they choose, with no involvement of the Ministry of Education. Each secondary school is given US$2,800 for spending on these contracts.

PROJECT MONTEGRANDE (1997). Out of 1,200 state-funded secondary schools, 221 schools submitted projects in a national competition to be selected as a model school of excellence. Fifty-one schools were selected. The projects (4 years, averaging US$150,000 per school per year) had to consider man-

---

15. In 1997, the first year total coverage of secondary schools by the MECE program was achieved, 160,000 students participated in OCAs (26 percent of total enrollment in publicly funded secondary education).

agement practices, teaching quality, and equity promoting measures. They also had to show that they were able to attract external financial support from the local community, business organizations, or other institutions. Selected schools represent the diversity of the system and thus will be able to provide transferable examples of teaching and management "good practices" to the rest of the schools.[16]

Montegrande schools were chosen through a two-step selection: (1) rigorous external assessment and ranking of eligible projects and (2) decisions on those projects by a politically pluralistic national board composed of persons from educational, scientific, and humanistic fields (Lemke 1998). The Board of the Montegrande project ranged from a leading figure of the Chicago-boys group of the reforms of the 1980s to an ex-senator of the Communist Party.[17] In its composition as well as in its intent, the Board effectively incarnates the national and state character (not only governmental) of the educational effort of the country in the 1990s.

Montegrande schools are the first in the public system to make use of an important legal change introduced by the Second Teachers' Statute. It allowed school directors, as an effect of *delegation of faculties* from the private or municipal proprietor, to administer public funds allocated to the school, thus carrying decentralization principles beyond the municipal level to the school level.

STRENGTHENING THE TEACHING PROFESSION (1997). As noted earlier, teachers' salaries have almost doubled in real terms since 1990, and the National Performance Evaluation System (SNED) instituted team-based merit pay. In addition, four new programs were set up in 1997 to strengthen the teaching corps: (1) national prizes for excellence in teaching; (2) international study tours for teachers to expose them to the best teaching practices (1,400 beneficiaries in 1997); (3) scholarships to attract good students into the profession; and (4) reform of teacher education in 17 universities and in-service training programs to adapt the whole teaching body to the demands of the new curriculum.

The most ambitious of the mentioned interventions is the last. Universities were selected in a national competition; on average just over US$2 million is

---

16. In 1997 Montegrande schools enrolled 40,000 pupils or 6.0 percent of all students in publicly funded secondary schools.

17. This is a reference to María Teresa Infante, a leading figure of the municipalization process, and Volodia Teitelboim, senior politician and intellectual of the Chilean Left.

spent per institution to fund reform projects lasting four to five years. The strategy is a clear case of state intervention through "remote-control" means, like competitive funding and support through institutional networking.

The Building of Political Conditions and Reform Initiatives: Changes in the School Day and Curriculum

We address here policy measures that affect the system as a whole, which in contrast to the programs of improvement are not voluntary but legally binding. They refer to *time* and *the curriculum*. A consensus-building initiative played an important role in terms of public articulation of key issues and political support for a change in the scale of the investments needed by the reform effort of the 1990s.

The current administration (1994–2000) offered a major technical and political initiative to articulate a political consensus on education policy and to make the public aware of the strategic implications that education had for the country's overall development. The president of the Republic convened a high-level Technical Committee on the Modernization of Education, with significant representation from the opposition parties. Its task was to prepare a full-scale proposal for education policy. Its report was submitted to a second body convened by the president, the National Commission to Modernize Education, which at the end of 1994 completed a plan for education reform at the national level.

The Technical Committee and the National Commission made a major contribution to informed debate among the country's political, business, and cultural leaders by offering a systematic diagnosis of the situation and a set of priorities for change that were highly consistent with policies already being implemented. They recognized the urgency of in-depth reform of secondary education and the need to extend the time spent in school, modernize teaching methods, and enhance the flexibility and management capacity of educational institutions.

In 1995 a "Framework Agreement for the Modernization of Chilean Education" was signed by the government and all political parties with seats in Congress. This agreement, consistent with the proposals of the National Commission, called for reforms in the management and financing of state-supported education, reforms that were to be subsumed in part under the Teachers' Statute of 1995.

EXTENSION OF THE SCHOOL DAY. In May 1996 the president of the Republic announced increased investments in education of approximately US$1,500 million between 1997 and 2002, in order to lengthen the school day to eight pedagogical hours on average. This extension of the school day provides an absolute increase in the time students devote to school work, plus a better use of school facilities. It means an additional 200 hours a year on average for students, through a 38-hour week for primary students and a 42-hour week for secondary students. Resources needed include additional pay for teachers (to cover their extended hours) and funds for the expansion of required buildings (20,000 classrooms) and school meals for the most vulnerable children (600,000).[18] The system will thus operate a total of 1,200 hours a year, in line with OECD countries. In May 1998, 3,932 schools (primary and secondary) with a total enrollment of 491,330 pupils (16 percent of total enrollments) were already functioning with a full school day.[19]

It is important to underline that the reforms implemented after 1990 required a longer school day. Indeed, "the road had become too narrow for the traffic." Extension of school time came to be seen as an answer to the emerging demands of the new pedagogy. A pedagogy that relies on the use of libraries and computers and attempts to pass the initiative for learning to pupils (and policies that motivate teachers to work in groups and resort to flexible trial-and-error methods) is time consuming. In this context the extension of school time was preceded by an assessment of educational needs.

CURRICULUM CHANGE (1996–98). A new curriculum for primary education was defined in 1996. Schools may determine their own syllabi within a framework of objectives and content. For Chile this is a major innovation in terms of curriculum organization, and it has important implications for decentralizing and strengthening the teaching profession: every school in

---

18. The expansion of enrollment during the 1970s and 1980s was carried out with practically no investment in infrastructure. The school system accommodated the increased number of students by working in two (and in some cases three) shifts, which greatly reduced the number of school hours per week for each shift.

19. In 1990 the school system operated on an annual basis of about 880 classroom hours (depending on the level of schooling). Decisions taken between 1991 and 1995 extended the school year by two weeks, which raised the annual total to about 940 hours, and provided special funding for low-income schools that extended the hours of student access (the school day reinforcement program). The extension of working time for students and teachers was a constant theme of reform policies throughout the 1990s in contrast to the 1980s, when it was not an issue, and schools in poor areas were allowed to shorten total classroom time (Cox 1992).

the country must decide whether to adapt the curriculum to its own educational plan or follow the course of study defined by the Ministry of Education. In addition, the new curriculum framework reflects the latest disciplinary and teaching standards.

A new curriculum framework for secondary education was officially approved at the beginning of 1998. From May to August 1997 there had been an unprecedented participatory process in which more than a hundred institutions and 95 percent of the secondary teachers answered detailed questionnaires on each of the school subjects and made suggestions on improvements. Additionally, a consultative panel of international experts was convened, and the new curriculum in math and science was subjected to a revision by experts from the Third International Math and Science Study (TIMSS).

The new official curriculum of Chilean education is more flexible and decentralized in its modalities of implementation and more demanding than the traditional curriculum in terms of learning objectives and standards. For example, it defines as learning objectives to be achieved by students before the end of their school experience: the ability to investigate, organize information, and suspend judgment in the absence of information; to communicate and resolve problems; to think analytically and interpret information; to design, plan, and implement projects; to monitor and assess one's own learning; to manage uncertainty and adapt adequately to change (Ministry of Education 1998).

RESULTS. Since 1990 there have been sustained improvements in the learning achievements of primary school students as measured by the SIMCE national assessment results. Although the primary education system as a whole is better, the gap is still too wide between the scores of the best and worst students.

Table 4-4 points to differences in the Spanish and math scores of fourth grade students in municipal, private-subsidized, and private-fee-paying schools between 1990 and 1996. Results show improvement in learning outcomes for all categories of schools. In relative terms, there was a slightly higher rate of increase for children in municipal schools (which enroll students from the lowest socioeconomic groups) compared with the national average; and a definitely higher rate of increase compared with children in private schools (highest socioeconomic level), significantly narrowing a gap between the two that remains substantial.

Figure 4-1 offers a synoptic view of the math and Spanish national averages in learning outcomes for fourth and eighth graders (the final grade at

Table 4-4. Learning Outcomes of Fourth Grade Students by Type of School, 1990–96

		Average percentage of correct answers: Spanish and math		
			Type of school	
Year of exam	*National average*	*Municipal*	*Private-subsidized*	*Private-fee-paying*
Spanish				
1990	61.2	57.2	64.7	80.0
1992	68.0	64.0	70.8	86.8
1994	67.5	63.5	70.0	83.7
1996	71.9	68.3	74.3	86.2
Increase	10.7	11.1	9.6	6.2
Math				
1990	60.1	56.2	63.1	79.9
1992	67.3	63.7	69.6	85.2
1994	69.3	65.4	71.3	86.4
1996	71.2	67.8	73.1	85.6
Increase	11.1	11.6	10.0	5.7

Source: Ministry of Education, SIMCE (National System of Measurement of the Quality of Education). SIMCE national standardized tests measure learning achievements in language, math, social sciences, and natural sciences for the majority of fourth graders in even years and eighth graders in odd years. In 1994, for example, 224,000 pupils took the tests in the fourth grade.

the primary level).[20] Though starting from different points, the learning outcomes in both grades show similar improvements sustained during the period.

A Comparison of Learning Outcomes in Public and Private Schools, 1990s

Learning outcomes are one of the best measures of the success or failure of interventions in the educational sector. Chile has been measuring learning achievements since 1983, and the results described in the previous section have been the object of many studies, with conflicting explanations of the

---

20. Tests taken in different years during the 1990s are comparable; the PER test results from the 1980s and the SIMCE results are not.

Figure 4-1. National Learning Outcomes of Fourth and Eighth Grade Students, 1990–97

Average percentage of correct answers: language and math

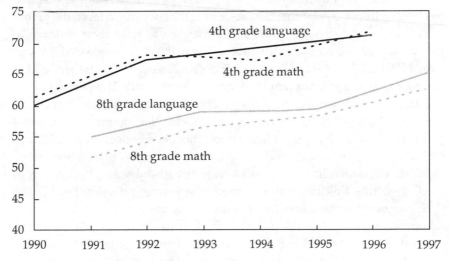

Note: Each year's average represents the unweighted average of the total number of schools.

Source: Sistema de Medición de la Calidad de la Educación, SIMCE (various years).

better results exhibited by the private-subsidized schools (Aedo and Larrañaga 1994; Lehmann 1994; Winkler and Rounds Parry, 1996; Medlin, 1996; Rounds Parry 1996; Carnoy and McEwan, 1997; Mizala and Romaguera 1998).

Most of these studies have focused on private schools' greater effectiveness and efficiency compared with public (municipal) schools. Unadjusted average scores are significantly higher in private-subsidized schools than in municipal schools (table 4-4), and private-subsidized schools operate at lower cost per pupil than do municipal schools.

These facts would seem to indicate that private-subsidized schools are not only more effective than municipal schools, but also more efficient, and that this quality is associated with the preference parents show for these schools. A closer look, based on convergent results from studies by Mizala and Romaguera, Rounds Parry, Medlin, and Carnoy and McEwan, reveals other facts, which define the larger framework of social and cultural conditions in which schools operate and qualify in important ways the advantages in the results of private-subsidized education and, more generally, the impact of choice and competition.

First, student distribution between municipal and private schools is closely linked to family income. Private-paid schools are, obviously, attended by children from high-income families, but at the subsidized level, the higher the income of families, the more likely they are to send their children to private-subsidized schools. Thus, according to the nationwide CASEN survey of 1994, 52.3 percent of the municipal enrollment that year belonged to the poorest two deciles of family income, whereas only 21.5 percent of the enrollments of the private-subsidized sector belonged to these deciles.

Second, parental choice is not the only factor that determines where a child goes to school. Private-subsidized schools use selection procedures, including diagnostic tests and parental interviews (Rounds Parry 1996; Espínola 1993; Medlin 1996; Gauri 1996). Private-subsidized schools also tend to exclude children with low grades or learning disabilities. Medlin (1996) argues that these selection practices produce a further effect, "intra-school socialization," or the positive effects on learning of more able and motivated students working in a comparatively homogeneous group. Further, Medlin found evidence in Lehmann (1994) that the only context in which private-subsidized schools' learning results were marginally inferior to those of municipal schools was in poor rural areas. This is highly consistent with the mentioned findings about selection and socialization effects: in sparsely populated and poor areas, private-subsidized and municipal schools educate a comparable student body, both in terms of socioeconomic background and heterogeneity in capacities and motivation.

The analysis of raw test scores must be adjusted in order to correct for these factors. Once scores are adjusted for differences in parental education and family income, private schools are not more effective than municipal schools. Analyzing results for fourth grade Spanish and mathematics in even years between 1990 and 1996, Carnoy and McEwan (1997) found that as finer measures of parental education are considered, the private-school advantage disappears.[21] They argued that Aedo and Larrañaga (1994)

---

21. When no attempts are made to take into account the socioeconomic status of students, the achievement gap in 1994 between municipal schools and private-paid schools is more than 20 points, and almost 6 points for private-subsidized schools. When simple controls are made for parental education levels and the type of city in which the schools are located, these differences decline to 4.95 and 1.43, respectively (Carnoy and McEwan 1997). They matched SIMCE data on students with the CASEN household survey and Junta Nacional de Auxilio Escolar y Becas

and Winkler and Rounds Parry (1996) did not accurately compare private-subsidized and municipal schools because they did not use sufficiently discriminating measures of parental education and socioeconomic status. Mizala and Romaguera (1998), using a comparable methodology in their analysis of the SIMCE results of 1996, arrived at the same conclusion as Carnoy and McEwan: private-subsidized schools do not achieve better outcomes than municipal schools when children from similar family backgrounds are compared. After comparing the main studies available in 1996, Medlin (1996) concluded that the differences in the SIMCE results of the two types of schools were not attributable to differences in quality produced by competition, but to selection and socialization effects instead.

We associate the improvement in the learning outcomes of primary school students during the 1990s with public investment and educational programs. High-quality delivery of education to primary school pupils is complex, requiring the confluence of a variety of factors and specialized knowledge that is not readily available. Competition among schools may not increase productivity because principals and teachers and institutions may not have the means and the knowledge to do so. Students may circulate between competing schools and the differences between the private-subsidized and the municipal schools may diminish (in terms of the students and families they cater to and the services offered), but without affecting the average levels of learning of both subsystems. This, it seems, is an adequate description of what happened during the 1980s. In the 1990s public investment and programs provided to both types of schools the inputs and knowledge required to upgrade the system as a whole. Competition may add pressures for better performance, but the latter could not have been obtained solely by competition.

If the most vulnerable schools are considered, there can be few doubts about the direct impact of public investment and programs. The "900 Schools" program provided material and technical support to schools with

---

(JUNAEB) survey, obtaining a better estimate than previous studies on the variance in parental education within the two poorest deciles. This variance is correlated with the type of school, which will tend to confuse private school effects and parental education effects. With this in view, Carnoy and McEwan refined the measurements of the parents' education variable and concluded (for fourth grade Spanish and math for 1990, 1992, 1994, and 1996) that the private school advantage declines and eventually dissapears as finer measures of parental education are added to the regressions.

the lowest learning outcomes in the system, most of which (but not all) belonged to municipalities. The gap in learning outcomes between private-paid and municipal schools with P-900 coverage closed faster (7 points between 1990 and 1996) than between private-paid and municipal schools without P-900 (3 points). When private-subsidized and municipal schools are compared, P-900 municipal schools closed the gap by almost 5 percentage points during the same period.[22]

In the case of MECE-Rural, the gains in learning outcomes are even more marked. In a sample of 196 rural schools (6.1 percent of those involved in the program) that were measured by SIMCE in 1992 and 1996, 34.3 percent of fourth graders had correct answers in math in 1992; 60.8 percent had the correct answers in 1996 (an improvement of 26.5 points). The same level of improvement occurred on the Spanish test: from 34.1 percent in 1992 to 59.4 percent in 1996 (a variation of 25.3 points).[23]

Private-subsidized schools are indeed more efficient than municipal schools (Winkler and Rounds Parry 1996; Medlin 1996; Mizala, Romaguera, and Farren 1998). They function with fewer administrative staff and have larger classes; they spend less per pupil with, as noted, comparable results. Greater costs in municipal schools are the result of several factors other than bureaucratic shortcomings.[24] First, municipal schools educate pupils in rural, thinly populated areas. (As mentioned, there is a positive association between population density and the establishment of private schools.) Therefore, class sizes tend to be smaller than in private schools. Second, many pupils attending municipal schools have special educational needs, which raises costs. These pupils tend to be excluded from private schools as a consequence of their selection procedures. Third, municipal schools are subject to greater legal constraints on teacher contracting and other management restrictions.

Parents have shown a preference for private-subsidized schools, as enrollment rates show. This suggests that private schools are offering a combination of services (including learning) that many (but not all) parents

---

22. If the national averages are compared in the 1990-96 period (table 4-4), the mentioned gap was reduced only 1.5 percent for Spanish and 1.6 for math.

23. Data provided by the Departamento de Estudio, División de Planificación y Presupuesto, Ministerio de Educación, 1998.

24. Carnoy and McEwan's estimate is that municipal schools spend about 12 percent more than private-subsidized ones, and that this figure drops to 6.8 percent outside the Metropolitan area.

prefer to those offered by municipal schools. This preference often is not related to effectiveness or efficiency-based criteria, but to peer effects, which may positively affect learning (Medlin 1996), status symbols, and processes of social and educational distinction (Espínola 1993; Gauri 1996; Bourdieu 1979). It is highly probable that in the near future many parents will continue to prefer private schools. Public policymakers should recognize that this external pressure on public and private-subsidized schools may improve school quality, and they should try to enrich the information basis and criteria for parents' choice. At the same time public policy should strengthen legal and public participation mechanisms to ensure the right to education, and it should seek ways to diminish the impact of student selection procedures by private-subsidized schools.

Lessons and Challenges

Lessons

The Chilean experience of reform in education during the 1990s teaches several policymaking and implementation lessons. They are as historical and context dependent as any national process of education reform can be.

First, a comprehensive effort to transform and upgrade the educational opportunities offered by a national schooling system can best be undertaken when four conditions, characteristic of Chile's situation during the 1990s, are present:

- Social consensus about the need for the changes;
- Political support at the highest level within the state;[25]
- Sufficient financial resources to fund changes in the level of functioning of systems;
- A time horizon that is longer than the term of the government.

The governments of the 1990s defined the transformation of the schooling system as a state issue (not only a governmental issue) based on the consensus in society about the sector's strategic importance to the devel-

---

25. The *investments cum reform* effort of the 1990s rested not only on the Ministry of Education and its authorities and professional leadership, but also on the political and personal commitment of two presidents of the Republic and two ministers of finance.

opment needs of the country. Consequently, the governments put all their political and financial clout behind the defined agenda; the time horizon has been a decade.

Second, no radical shifts were made but rather incremental change in spite of political and ideological divisions. The first democratic government made the important strategic decision not to reverse the municipalization process or change the funding criteria and mechanisms established in 1981. This decision was reached despite teachers' expectations and interests in that direction and despite the authoritarian origin and implementation of municipalization. Instead, it was deemed necessary to *build upon* both transformations, seeking to neutralize or change their negative impacts: namely, democratizing municipal control and complementing the pressures for performance intrinsic to competitive mechanisms with systemic state funded and led support strategies and mechanisms for upgrading the quality of national learning outcomes and narrowing the gaps of inequalities. The result is a cumulative combination of tools of government and market-like incentives. The learning results of the 1990s proved the positive impact of that combination.

Third, policy stability is essential. Despite the fact that there have been five ministers of education under two governments in the period 1990–97, the professional core responsible for design and implementation leadership within the Ministry of Education has been the same. This has had a direct positive impact on the consistency and synergy of the various educational programs.

Fourth, decentralization with national gains in quality and equity requires an able center. High-quality teaching and learning for diverse populations cannot be decreed; at the same time, the definition and evaluation of national goals with respect to learning, orchestration of public support for schools, and safeguarding of the right to education and equity criteria need an able Ministry of Education and other central institutions. The policies and results of the 1990s demonstrated an effective combination: an able center that defines goals and standards to be achieved and provides support to those who require it, and decentralized units responsible for developing their own answers.

Fifth, vouchers have their uses and their limits. The per-pupil subsidy helped expand educational access, prompted schools to keep pupils attending classes, introduced into the system cost-efficiency criteria, and produced variation in the offering of education. Further, during the 1990s, it facilitated the channeling of public resources to poor schools, as in the case of rural education. The per-pupil subsidy and the competition between schools for students were not in themselves sufficient to produce improvements in the quality and equity of education. In 1990, after close to a decade of application of a voucher-like scheme of incentives for performance, the national average learning results of the schooling system were unacceptably low, and strong inequalities in the social distribution of key cultural competencies remained.

Sixth, synergy is created by push, pull, and networking mechanisms. During the 1990s, Chile applied mechanisms of intervention that combined classic centralized, top-down approaches (push), with decentralized mechanisms of two types: incentives for grass-roots initiatives (pull), and networks of support to schools. This three-pronged approach has permitted a flexible and diversified strategy of intervention.[26]

Finally, the more profound the changes, the more gradual should be their implementation.[27] The reform experience of the 1990s has shown ways to deal with the tradeoff between political demands for speed and visibility of programs and their impact, and the slower pacing and less visible nature of the learning processes of people and organizations, intrinsic to qualitative changes. The lesson here is the usefulness of managing programs according to a concept of *double gradualness*: gradual increases in educational coverage and gradual changes in the scope of reform. A program may expand its coverage according to its own financial and institutional capacities, but it must order the entry of its more demanding components into the schools according to the rhythms of learning of the involved actors and institutions.

Challenges

EDUCATION AS A RIGHT: SHORTCOMINGS IN A COMPETITIVE CONTEXT. A most pressing challenge to Chilean education comes from the selection practices of schools, or the operation of competition-S mechanisms (Glennester and Low

---

26. For an insightful view of different "pressures for performance" in social programs, or of institutional, market, and "market surrogate" mechanisms, see Israel (1996).

27. For example, in MECE-Media, school libraries were acquired and set up in every *liceo* in the first year of the program, but the Educational Improvement Project, a component more demanding for the schools, was implemented only in the second year of the program.

1993): one of the means to improve the learning outcomes of a school is to exclude from it the pupils (and families) who have or may have low learning outcomes. Choice works here not for the families but for the schools. It increases the social segmentation of education and distorts the competition for quality. If the right to education and equity are to be protected, a challenge of the first order is to effectively counterbalance the negative effects of S-type competition without disrupting the "pressure for performance" effects of competition for quality in general. The current legal framework makes it difficult or impossible to reverse the practices whereby private-subsidized establishments, and some municipal schools, tend to reject or expel students on the basis of poor performance, the marital status of their parents, teenage pregnancy, and other similar causes.

EQUITY: INSUFFICIENT PROGRESS. Despite targeted policies through criteria of affirmative action, and despite the positive impact of P-900 and MECE-Rural programs, the most vulnerable schools have received insufficient resources to counteract the effect of poverty on learning results (Hopenhayn 1998; Espínola 1998). Much stronger action is needed, increasing resources and intensifying focused strategies of support to schools serving poor areas.

We believe that to improve educational equity it is of the utmost importance that the state set up mechanisms that neutralize or counterbalance the social segmentation effects of the shared-funding scheme. This scheme, while adding resources to the schools, is differentiating publicly supported education along income lines.

OPEN PEDAGOGY IN CLOSED INSTITUTIONS? The reforms of the 1990s were consistently aimed at the school institution and its educational practices, leaving comparatively untouched the normative framework regulating the school system and the structure of the Ministry of Education and the municipalities. There is a tension between the pedagogical, curricular, and management practices promoted by the different programs at the schools (which favor results over bureaucratic procedures, team work, horizontal communication, innovation, and open practices of trial and error) and the vertical, closed, and bureaucratic nature of much of the normative framework that regulates schools and teachers.

This tension between "structure" and "function" affects in similar ways the Ministry of Education and the municipal administration of education. Although it generates contradictions and blockages for a change in the organizational culture of the sector, it has not been tackled, partly because of its inclusion in the much wider issues of the modernization and reform of the state.

WEAKNESS OF VOICE AND ACCOUNTABILITY MECHANISMS. The innovations of the 1990s had a significant and positive impact upon the schools and their practices. It was not their focus, however, to build up participation by parents and the community. Such participation can counterbalance the power of the schools that select and restrict the right to education. The relative weakness of "voice" principles weakens the accountability of schools to society. As more information on the learning results of schools and the general performance of the education system is made public, the basis for accountability of schools to society expands.

COMMUNICATIONS AND TEACHERS' PARTICIPATION. There is a deficit of understanding between the discourse of the Ministry of Education and the publicly articulated vision of the teachers' union (Colegio de Profesores). The still outstanding issue is to build a new sense of partnership between the state and the teaching profession with respect to the organization and functional features of state-supported education. This partnership has to bridge meanings dear to the professional traditions of the pre-1980s, a centralized educational system, and the goals, means, and meanings of the reform of the 1990s.

There is a lack of symmetry between the concept of participation of the teachers' union and the authorities' concept of participation. The authorities value the EIPs and teachers' participation in the MECE-Rural; they value the new curriculum framework and the flexibility it gives to each educational community, as clear opportunities for effective and active participation for tens of thousands of teachers. The teachers' union, however, feels left out of the process, because it was not consulted on the reform of the school day, or because there has been no debate over the "type of human being" and the kind of society that education is supposed to create (Dastres and Spencer 1997). While one side is focused on the school and conceives of participation in terms of making the school more professional and autonomous, the other side is looking for public discussion and ideological debate.

During the 1990s, Chile's educational policies were relatively successful in implementing means and principles of change in education. In the near future the rhythm of the changes and the magnitude of their impact will depend more upon the learning processes of people and institutions at the bottom level than upon political and technical decisions made at the top. Such decisions, however, will continue to be particularly decisive for the equity goal, still on the debt side of the policy agenda of the sector. From a wider and longer term perspective, the social and political consensus in Chile regarding the importance and nature of the ongoing changes in education may ensure that they will have the time to develop and become comprehensive and profound enough to satisfactorily answer society's educational requirements for the twenty-first century.

References

Aedo, Cristián, and Osvaldo Larrañaga. 1994. "Sistemas de entrega de los servicios sociales: la experiencia chilena." In C. Aedo and O. Larrañaga., eds., *Sistema de entrega de los servicios sociales: una agenda para la reforma*. Washington, D.C.: Inter-American Development Bank.

Bourdieu, Pierre. 1979. *La Distinction: Critique Sociale du Jugement*. Paris: Editions du Minuit.

Brunner, José Joaquín. 1992. "La educación superior en Chile: 1960–1990." In J. J. Brunner, H. Courard, and C. Cox, eds., *Estado, mercado y conocimiento: políticas y resultados en la educación superior chilena, 1960–1990*. Santiago: Foro de la Educación Superior.

Carnoy, Martin, and Patrick McEwan. 1997. "Public Investments or Private Schools? A Reconstruction of Educational Improvements in Chile." Stanford University.

Comisión Nacional para la Modernización de la Educación, Comité Técnico Asesor del diálogo nacional sobre la modernización de la educación chilena. 1995. *Los desafíos de la educación chilena frente al siglo XXI*. Santiago: Editorial Universitaria.

Cox, Cristián. 1992 . "Sociedad y conocimiento en los 90: puntos para una agenda sobre currículo del sistema escolar." *Estudios Públicos*, No. 47, Santiago.

Cox, Cristián, and Pablo Gonzalez. 1998. "Educación: de programas de mejoramiento a reforma." In René Cortázar and Joaquín Vial, eds., *Construyendo Opciones: propuestas económicas y sociales para el cambio de siglo*. Santiago: Dolmen.

Dastres, Cecilia, and C. Spencer. 1997. "El proceso comunicativo de la reforma educacional." Instituto de Sociología, Universidad Católica, Santiago.

ECLAC (Economic Commission for Latin America and the Caribbean) and UNESCO (United Nations Educational, Scientific, and Cultural Organization). 1997. *Education and Knowledge: Basic Pillars of Changing Production Patterns with Social Equity*. Santiago.

Espínola, Viola. 1993. "The Educational Reform of the Military Regime in Chile: The System's Response to Competition, Choice, and Market Relations." Ph.D. diss., University of Wales, UK.

————. 1998. "Revisión de quince años de política educativa en Chile: ajustes en función de la equidad." In E. Cohen, ed., *Educación, Eficiencia y Equidad*. Santiago: CEPAL, OEA, SUR.

Fiske, Edward B. 1996. *Decentralization of Education: Politics and Consensus*. Washington, D.C.: The World Bank.

Friedman, Milton. 1955. "The Role of Government in Education." In R. A. Solo, ed., *Economics and the Public Interest*. New Brunswick, N. J.: Rutgers University Press.

Gajardo, Marcela, ed. 1994. *Cooperación Internacional y Desarrollo de la Educación*. Santiago: Agencia de Cooperación Internacional, Ministerio de Planificación (AGCI).

García-Huidobro, Juan Eduardo, ed. 1989. *Escuela, Calidad e Igualdad*. Santiago: CIDE.

Gauri, Varun. 1996. "Market Forces in the Public Sector: Chilean Educational Reform, 1980–1994." Ph.D. diss., Princeton University, Princeton, N.J.

Glennester, H., and W. Low. 1993. "Education." In J. Hills, ed., *The State of Welfare*. Oxford: Clarendon Press.

Gonzalez, Pablo. 1998. "Financiamiento de la educación en Chile." In *Financiamiento de la educación en América Latina*. Santiago: PREAL-UNESCO.

Hirschman, Albert O. 1973. *Exit, Voice, and Loyalty*. Cambridge, Mass.: Harvard University Press.

Hopenhayn, Martín. 1998. "El desafío educativo: en busca de la equidad perdida." In E. Cohen, ed., *Educación, Eficiencia y Equidad*. Santiago: CEPAL, OEA, SUR.

Israel, Arturo. 1997. *A Guide for the Perplexed: Institutional Aspects of Social Programs*, SOC No. 104. Washington, D.C.: Inter-American Development Bank.

Lehmann, Carla. 1994. "El sentido de pertenencia como catalizador de una educación de calidad." Serie Documentos de trabajo No. 222. Centro de Estudios Públicos (CEP), Santiago.

Lemaitre, María José. 1998. "Turning Improvement into Reform: Secondary School education in Chile, 1991–2001." In Lene Buchert, ed., *Educational Reform in the South in the 1990s*. Paris: UNESCO.

Lemke, Mariann. 1998. *A Study of the Selection Process of the Montegrande*. Santiago: CIDE.

Medlin, Carol Ann. 1996. *Applying Economic Logic to Education Finance: Chile's Experiment with the Per-Student Subsidy*. Santiago: CEPAL.

Ministry of Educación. 1991, 1995, 1996. *Compendio de Información Estadística*. Santiago.

————. 1998. *Objetivos Fundamentales y Contenidos Mínimos Obligatorios de la Educación Media*. Santiago.

Mizala, A., and P. Romaguera. 1998. "Desempeño y elección de colegios." Documento de Trabajo, Serie Economía N°36. Depto. Ingeniería Industrial, Facultad de Ciencias Físicas y Matemáticas, Universidad de Chile, Santiago.

Mizala, A., P. Romaguera, and D. Farren. 1998. "Eficiencia técnica de los establecimientos educacionales en Chile." Documento de Trabajo, Serie Economía N° 38. Depto. Ingeniería Industrial, Facultad de Ciencias Físicas y Matemáticas, Universidad de Chile, Santiago.

Morales, J. 1991. "Calidad de la Educación en la Década de los 80." MINEDUC-CPEIP, Documento de Trabajo, Santiago.

PIIE. 1989. *Educación y Transición Democrática, Propuesta de Políticas Educacionales.* Santiago.

Prawda, Juan. 1992. "Educational Decentralization in Latin America: Lessons Learned. A View from Latin America." Human Resources Working Paper 27. World Bank, Washington, D.C.

Rounds Parry, Taryn. 1996. "Will Pursuit of Higher Quality Sacrifice Equal Opportunity in Education? An Analysis of the Education Voucher System in Santiago." *Social Science Quarterly* 77 (4): 821–41.

Winkler, Donald, and Taryn Rounds Parry. 1996. "Municipal and Private Sector Response to Decentralization and School Choice." *Economics of Education Review* 15 (4): 365–76.

World Conference on Education for All. 1990. *Meeting Basic Learning Needs: A Vision for the 1990s.* New York: UNICEF.

5

Health Sector Reforms in Chile

Osvaldo Larrañaga

In the mid-seventies Chile introduced a set of reforms that radically transformed the country's economy. The liberalization of the economy to external trade in goods and capital flows, the deregulation of domestic markets, and the state's subsidiary role in favor of the private sector were the main features of these changes. At the beginning of the eighties, there was a second round of structural reforms, this time oriented to shifting the allocation of resources in the social sectors: education, health, housing, and social security. In these sectors, mechanisms of competition were introduced, private sector participation was motivated, and public subsidies were targeted to lower income groups.

The reforms at the beginning of the eighties introduced two major changes in the health sector. First, they brought about the development of the private sector by making possible the assignment of the compulsory contribution that workers and pensioners were required to make for health to private insurers—called Health Insurance Institutions (ISAPRES)—as an alternative to public insurance, the only option until then. Second, the reforms restructured the organization and operation of the public health system by separating the functions of sector management and policy from the provi-

---

This chapter is based on previous work by the author. See especially Larrañaga (1996), Larrañaga (1997a), and Larrañaga (1997b).

sion of health services to the hospital network. This network was then organized into 26 regional services. Furthermore, the reforms decentralized primary health care, entrusting municipalities with administering public clinics that provide ambulatory care at a low level of complexity, with technical oversight by the regional health services.

Before the reforms the Chilean health sector had already achieved significant advances regarding coverage of the population and health indicators. Key to these results was the early development of the public health system (in the twenties) and the subsequent creation in 1952 of the National Health Service, which unified the different public institutions in the sector and strengthened its development. During the seventies, a strategy was adopted that prioritized primary health care and the programs for vulnerable groups, especially mothers and children. This accelerated the improvement of health indicators, which at the end of 1970 had attained much higher levels than had been expected considering the country's level of economic development.

In 1997, seventeen years after the introduction of the reforms, the balance of the results was mixed. The reforms generated a dual health system that functions under different rationales, though retaining the usual strengths and weaknesses of individual insurance (partial coverage, high administrative and selling costs, lack of transparency in plans and benefits); the public system continues to provide health care to most of the country's population, but it operates with strong deficiencies relating to productivity and accountability as a result of the bureaucratic organization and financing based on supply.

Thus, Chile has a private system of competitive health insurance *and* a public scheme organized on the basis of a social security system that permits subsidized care to its beneficiaries. This combination creates a health system that segments the population according to socioeconomic and health risk variables between public and private alternatives.

The development of these sectors has been determined by changing public health policies. The period between 1981 and 1989 was characterized by a strong decline in public health expenditure as a consequence of the economic crisis of the first half of the decade and the probable strategic option of the military government to encourage the development of the private sector. In contrast, during the years 1990 to 1997, public health expenditure doubled as a result of the policy of "growth with equity" that inspired the democratic governments of this period.

The current situation finds the private system already consolidated, covering some 25 percent of the population and administering around half of the resources of the health sector. The public system has remarkably strengthened its infrastructure but faces tough opposition from workers' unions to the introduction of the reforms necessary to enhance productivity and quality of services rendered to beneficiaries.

The objective of this chapter is to evaluate the performance of the Chilean health system in the light of the reforms and the ensuing policies of public expenditure and regulation. The chapter has five sections. The first addresses early developments of the Chilean health system as well as the structure and financing of the health sector after the reforms. The second section analyzes the implications of the dual health system for the structure of insurance and the segmentation of the population between public and private alternatives. Specific aspects of the private and public health system are discussed in the third and fourth sections. My conclusions are presented at the end of the chapter.

The Chilean Health System

Early Developments

The view that health is a basic right of the population was established early in the history of the sector. The process of consolidation of the public sector begins in 1918 with the first Sanitary Law, which established public responsibility in sanitary programs and preventive health. In 1924 the Social Security Law was enacted, giving coverage via the provision of health services for workers and their families, and the Ministry of Hygiene and Social Security was created. This ministry's mission was the study of the population's health conditions and the subsequent creation of public health programs to improve those conditions.

The most important antecedent is the institution of the National Health Service (SNS) in 1952. It originated from the need to extend the health service to the poor segments of the population. The implementation of the SNS in many ways replicated the British health model, while financing more closely followed the German experience of taxes and contributions. Thus, a unified network of public establishments was gradually developed, including primary health care establishments and emergency posts. Improving maternal and child care was one of the main objectives.

The health model implemented through the SNS specified standards of behavior and protection that involved great discipline, which made it possible to cope successfully with the epidemiological problems of the period.

By the seventies it covered most of the national territory and exhibited very successful indicators in matters of health. Strongly unified in terms of the state and with great sanitary achievements, this system seems to endorse the arguments against the modernization of the sector.

On the other hand, during the forties public sector employees and those of the manufacturing industry lay the foundations for a separate health service (SERMENA) to fully meet their needs. In the sixties curative benefits were introduced under a system of free choice in which payment was made for each medical service (fee-for-service). This service was set up as a separate health system, perceived later as discriminatory against the workers who go to the SNS for services and do not enjoy freedom of choice regarding the provider of the services nor from the social security institution that they belong to. Those affiliated with SERMENA obtain outpatient care that is performed mainly by the private sector, via a system of preferred providers who have enrolled in the service. Hospital health care, in turn, is provided by the SNS.

The typical health indicators show that the Chilean population has considerably improved its health condition since the mid-sixties with regard to life expectancy, infant mortality, child malnutrition, and other indicators. Some of these indicators accelerated their positive trends toward the middle of the seventies.

The trend observed responds in part to the global phenomenon associated with progress in medical techniques and the development of new medicines. According to a World Bank (1993) report, all regions in the world experienced notable increases in life expectancy beginning in the sixties. However, Chile shows better indicators than the countries at a similar level of economic development, signaling the presence of country-specific factors contributing to such results.

The early development of the public health system in Chile and the ensuing impulse provided by the unification of the system into the National Health Service are the main factors in the country's health achievements. The strategy of prioritizing primary health care during the seventies, which led to the construction of multiple rural health posts as well as the targeting of health and nutritional programs to the most vulnerable groups, accelerated the positive trends in health indicators during the seventies.

Until the mid-seventies the Chilean health sector responded to a centralized system with no separation of functions. Such concentration was due to a strong organic structuring of health as a national system. This centralized system could function adequately in the context of the former epidemiological profile of the population, characterized by the prevalence of infectious diseases and the presence of strong externalities.

The Reforms of the 1980s

The reforms at the beginning of the eighties introduced two major changes in the health sector. First, they brought about the development of the private sector by making possible the assignment of the compulsory contribution that workers and pensioners were required to make for health to private insurers—called Health Insurance Institutions (ISAPRES)—as an alternative to public insurance, the only option until then. Second, the reforms restructured the organization and operation of the public health system by separating the functions of sector management and policy from the provision of health services to the hospital network. This network was then organized into 26 regional services. Furthermore, the reforms decentralized primary health care, entrusting municipalities with administering public clinics that provide ambulatory care at a low level of complexity, with technical oversight by the regional health services.

Structure of the Health System

The 1981 reforms established the present structure of the health system, which operates on the basis of the provision of public and private insurance and health services (figure 5-1). Oversight of the health system is the responsibility of the Ministry of Health, which is in charge of the supervision, evaluation, and control of all health policies.

As the leading entity of the public health system, the Ministry is in charge of the provision of those activities of a public goods character. The National Health Fund (FONASA) is the decentralized service responsible for collecting, administering, and distributing the financial resources of the public system. The productive base of the sector is comprised of 26 Health Services, autonomous entities with legal status and with their own financial assets and resources. They are responsible for providing secondary and tertiary health care through a network of hospitals—a total of 180 with different levels of complexity—as well as outpatient clinics (attached to hospitals).

Primary health care in the public system is the responsibility of primary health care centers that offer curative care services of low complexity via a modality of outpatient care; health promotion and prevention activities are

Figure 5-1. Structure of the Chilean Health System

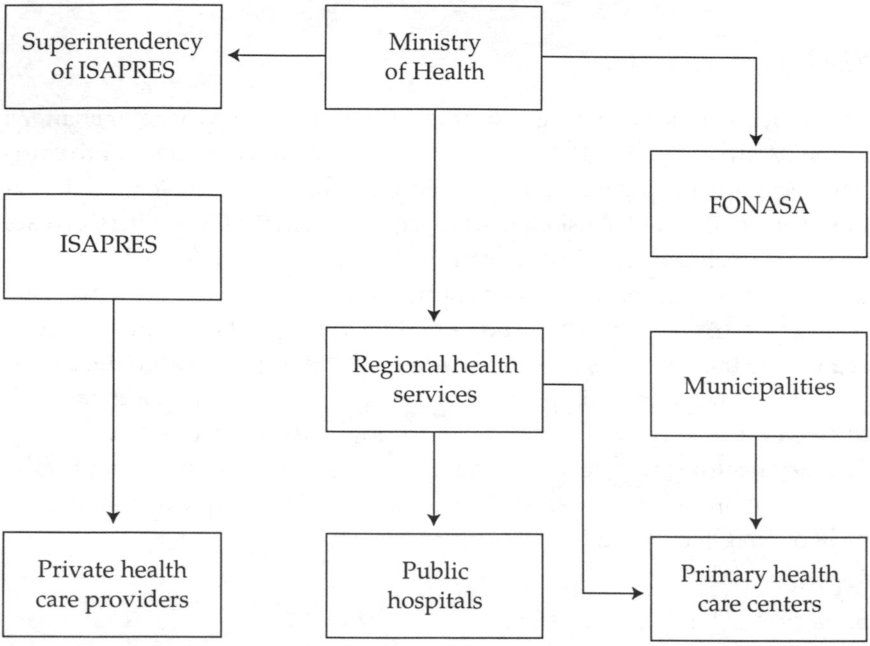

```
┌──────────────────┐        ┌──────────────────┐
│  Superintendency │◄───────│    Ministry      │──────────┐
│   of ISAPRES     │        │   of Health      │          │
└──────────────────┘        └──────────────────┘          │
                                     │                     ▼
┌──────────────────┐                 │           ┌──────────────────┐
│                  │                 │           │     FONASA        │
│     ISAPRES      │                 │           │                  │
└──────────────────┘                 │           └──────────────────┘
         │                           ▼
         │                  ┌──────────────────┐  ┌──────────────────┐
         │                  │  Regional health │  │  Municipalities   │
         │                  │    services      │──┐                   │
         │                  └──────────────────┘  └──────────────────┘
         ▼                           │                     │
┌──────────────────┐        ┌──────────────────┐  ┌──────────────────┐
│  Private health  │        │     Public       │  │  Primary health   │
│  care providers  │        │   hospitals      │  │  care centers     │
└──────────────────┘        └──────────────────┘  └──────────────────┘
```

Source: Author's information.

included. The primary care network consists of 376 clinics, in addition to 1,102 rural health posts and 720 rural medical stations. Most of these facilities are administered by the municipalities, with technical supervision from the respective Health Service.

The private health system consists of health insurance companies (ISAPRES) and private health care providers. ISAPRES were created under the 1981 social security reform and in 1997 included 21 institutions open to the public and 13 closed institutions serving employees of specific companies (self insurance). Private providers of health care are clinics, hospitals, and independent professionals that serve people insured by ISAPRES and those belonging to the public system through a modality termed freedom of choice. In some cases ISAPRES directly offer health care services, vertically integrating insurance and service provision activities.

Finally, the Superintendency of ISAPRES is a public autonomous organization created in 1990 to register and inspect private institutions that administer health insurance.

Access and Coverage

Access of the Chilean population to health care in Chile occurs via a system of compulsory affiliation. All workers in the country, as well as pensioners, are obliged to contribute 7 percent of their income to the health system. This payment can be made to FONASA, in which case the person and his or her family group (dependents) remain enrolled in the public system. The contribution can also be deposited with an ISAPRE, in which case the person and his or her family group become part of the private health system. Low-income nonsalaried people working in the informal sector of the economy are enrolled in the public system as indigents.

Persons subscribed to FONASA obtain access to two different types of health care providers. Under the institutional modality they can access the primary care clinics of the municipalities and, in the case of more complex care, they can be referred to public hospitals. The second modality of care, that of freedom of choice, is open only to beneficiaries contributing to FONASA, providing them access to a group of private providers associated with FONASA for this purpose. In practice, FONASA's freedom-of-choice modality is used mostly for ambulatory care rather than for more expensive complex care requiring hospitalization.

FONASA beneficiaries are entitled to free health care and pharmaceuticals in the public primary care clinics. However, access to hospitals requires an income-determined copayment that varies between 0 and 50 percent of the rate established for the service. Access to the freedom-of-choice modality is subject to a copayment structure according to the type of service provided (not income).

Private providers are reimbursed according to the service provided (fee for service). More restrictive modalities also exist, with preferred providers or within the health infrastructure belonging to the ISAPRE itself. Access of patients from the private system to public hospitals is restricted and cannot exceed 10 percent of beds at these facilities.

The ISAPRE system has been continuously growing since it was created in 1981 (table 5-1). In 1996 it represented 31.5 percent of the total population covered by the public and private health systems. Between 1983 and 1994 the beneficiary population enrolled in ISAPRES increased from 360,000 to 3,600,000 beneficiaries.

The coverage of the Chilean health system is practically universal. FONASA acts as a last resort insurance. That is, any persons, regardless of their income, can be affiliated with the public health system. The system's capacity to meet existing demand is another matter. In geographic terms,

Table 5-1. Private Health Sector Coverage, 1986–95
(Percentage of total population in public and private sectors)

Year	Beneficiaries	Contributors	Salaried contributors	Mean income of ISAPRE contributor[a]
1986	6.4	11.7	0.0	322.2
1987	9.8	15.2	21.5	284.6
1988	12.1	18.2	25.3	294.3
1989	13.9	21.8	30.0	313.5
1990	16.9	25.9	35.4	292.9
1991	19.8	31.0	42.0	280.2
1992	23.4	35.9	47.0	273.2
1993	24.3	40.7	52.7	265.2
1994	27.3	41.6	53.9	259.2
1995	30.4	42.6	55.2	277.3

a. Thousands of pesos ($ December 1995).
Source: Superintendency of ISAPRES.

almost the entire country is covered by the primary care network. According to the 1990 CASEN household survey, most of the population has access to a health center within a reasonable period of time (table 5-2). However, waiting times at different health centers can vary considerably; between 0.6 and 4.1 hours according to a recent survey of the Ministry of Health in a sample of 27 primary health centers in the city of Santiago.

Financing

The structure of revenues and expenditures of the public health sector in 1996 is shown in table 5-3. Total expenditures increased in that year to the equivalent of US$1,770 million, financed through compulsory contributions to FONASA (31.3 percent of total sector revenues), resources from the public budget (48.6 percent), copayments from public health services, fundamentally from the freedom-of-choice modality of FONASA (6.6 percent), payments by private patients (5.6 percent), and other revenues (7.9 percent).

Seventy-five percent of public sector resources are allocated to finance health care services supplied by the different providers: municipal clinics, public hospitals, and private providers that operate through the freedom-of-choice modality. The remaining 25 percent finances public health activities, sector investment, labor-related benefits (wages) for those who oversee medical licensing, care to private individuals, and other expenses.

Table 5-2. Travel Time to the Nearest Health Center
(percentage of total population)

Area and season	0–20 minutes	21–40 minutes	More than 40 minutes	Total
Urban areas				
Summer	72.6	13.3	1.8	100.0
Winter	67.9	22.0	10.1	100.0

	0–60 minutes	61–120 minutes	More than 120 minutes	Total
Rural areas				
Summer	87.2	11.3	1.6	100.0
Winter	79.4	17.5	3.1	100.0

Source: Based on Casen Household Survey database.

Table 5-3. Revenues and Expenditures in the Public Health Sector, 1996

Revenues and expenditures	Billions of 1996 Chilean pesos	Percent
Revenues	763.7	100.0
Contributions	239.5	31.3
Fiscal transfers	371.3	48.6
Copayment in free choice mode	50.1	6.6
Payment by private patients	42.6	5.6
Other revenues	60.2	7.9
Expenditures	737.6	100.0
Primary care	60.8	8.0
Secondary and tertiary care	415.3	54.4
Free choice mode	96.5	12.6
Public health activities	49.7	6.5
Medical leaves	24.4	3.2
Private patients' care	42.6	5.6
Investment	47.2	6.2
Other expenditures	27.2	3.6

Source: FONASA (1996).

Table 5-4. Revenues and Expenditures in the ISAPRES Sector, 1996

Revenues, expenditures, profits	Billions of Chilean pesos	Percent
Revenues	552.8	100.0
Mandatory contributions	432.1	78.2
Voluntary contributions	81.1	14.7
Other revenues	39.6	7.1
Expenditures	528.6	
Reimbursements to health providers	320.1	57.9
Medical leaves	83.2	15.1
Administration and sales	98.3	17.7
Other expenditures	27.4	4.9
Profits	24.2	4.4

Source: Superintendency of ISAPRES.

In turn, the private ISAPRES system's revenues in 1996 were on the order of 553 billion in 1996 Chilean pesos or US$1,340 million (table 5-4). This comes principally from the contributions paid by persons enrolled in that system. It is difficult to calculate total spending of the private sector because of the lack of statistics regarding copayments by users. Available estimates indicate that these payments are about 30 percent of operating expenses of ISAPRES (40 percent of reimbursement for health care services provision). If this is the case, total spending in the private sector increases to US$1,640 million in 1996.

Approximately 58 percent of the revenues of the ISAPRES system is allocated to the payment of medical services. Again, this figure does not include copayments, which would increase the expense for services provided to 66 percent. The second most important item in the expenditure structure is administrative and selling costs, which in the year 1996 represented 17.7 percent of the funds administered by ISAPRES. The expenditure on subsidies for medical licenses also is important in the private system, amounting to 15.1 percent of the total. Finally, the net income obtained by ISAPRES represented 4.4 percent of total revenues.

The evolution of health expenditures over the 1981–96 period is shown in table 5-5. There are three relevant facts here. First, spending in the private system continuously increased during the entire period, reflecting a trend similar to the coverage of the population enrolled in that segment of the sector. Second, public sector resources experienced a sharp decline in

Table 5-5. Spending in the Health Sector as a Percentage
of GDP, 1981–96

Year	Public sector	Private sector[a]	Total
1981	2.98	0.03	3.01
1982	3.57	0.14	3.71
1983	2.96	0.19	3.15
1984	2.84	0.32	3.16
1985	2.60	0.38	2.98
1986	2.60	0.38	2.98
1987	2.11	0.77	2.88
1988	2.17	0.90	3.07
1989	2.00	1.04	3.04
1990	1.96	1.27	3.23
1991	2.17	1.42	3.59
1992	2.27	1.51	3.78
1993	2.40	1.66	4.22
1994	2.49	1.73	4.22
1995	2.30	1.77	4.07
1996	2.45	1.77	4.22

a. Excludes private expenditures in medicines and copayments.

Source: Financial reports by FONASA, Superintendency of ISAPRES, and Ministry of
Finance.

the eighties and a significant recovery during the nineties. Third, global
spending by both sectors shows an increasing trend as a percentage of GDP.

The trends in public expenditure are accentuated when computed in terms
of per capita spending, that is, the expenditure per beneficiary. In particular, the recovery of the expenditure in the nineties is within the context of a
fall in the beneficiary population of the public system. Thus, real public
spending in per capita terms increased by 110 percent in the period 1990–
96. On the other hand, average spending per private sector beneficiary declined, a trend that suggests that the ISAPRES system has successfully
expanded to the lower income strata of the population.

The Dual Health System

The Dual Insurance Structure

The reforms of the eighties created a health system in Chile that is unique
in the world. It combines a social security scheme with a system of private
competitive insurance. Each person has the option of moving with few re-

strictions between these two systems, which operate with radically distinct rationales.

The public system operates via a modality of shared social security (solidarity) that offers a level of benefits that bear no relation to the contribution paid. That is, there is no relation between the price that is paid and the health coverage obtained. The sector is financed through compulsory contributions and public resources from general taxes. As noted in table 5-3, during 1996, the respective shares of these sources in financing health benefits were 31.3 percent and 48.6 percent.

The health coverage that the public sector offers to its beneficiaries is not well defined (in a contract). In principle, the public system offers comprehensive health care services with the exception of those of a luxury nature, such as aesthetic surgery for beauty purposes, personalized nursing care, and other such services. In practice, the resources available are allocated among users according to quantity rationing schemes: primary health care clinics operate on a first-come-first-served basis subject to daily ceilings, whereas hospitals have waiting lists, which can be rather long for surgical treatments.

The ISAPRES operate as a competitive insurance system. These companies compete for clients and do not receive public subsidies to provide health care to low-income persons or those at high health risk.[1] Therefore, they should charge insurance premiums related to the risk of the insured.

The insurance plans offered by ISAPRES are written in contracts, which specify reimbursement percentages for care and related services provided, as well as the ceiling on reimbursements.

The ISAPRE contract associates price and expected cost of the plan. The relationship functions via two variables: (i) the premium the ISAPRE charges for a health plan can legally vary between persons according to three factors related to the expected health expenditure: age, gender, and number of insured (dependents); (ii) the insurance operates with percentages of reimbursement and coverage ceilings (stop-loss), limiting the cost that the user entails for the ISAPRE.

ISAPRES offer numerous health plans. A more generous plan is more expensive and offers higher percentages of reimbursements and higher ceilings.

---

1. The exception is a 2 percent subsidy on the income of low-income people affiliated with ISAPRES. This transfer accounts for 5 percent of contributions paid to ISAPRES, and it will be suppressed in the future according to a proposal presented by the government.

The private insurance contracts offered by ISAPRES are of a contingent nature. This means that the company cannot void the contract, but the insured person can (one year after having signed it or by mutual agreement of both parties). The ISAPRE can modify a complete plan, but it must offer the people covered by this plan an equivalent level of benefits in an alternative plan.

The contracts of private insurance companies cannot exclude health care services other than those that FONASA also excludes. The coverage of pre-existing diseases is limited; when a person signs an insurance contract, there is a waiting period of 18 months for the treatment of such illnesses.

A variant to the individual insurance plan is a collective contract offered by ISAPRES to companies and other institutions. Like the rationale of individual insurance, this contract offers specific benefits according to the income of the people insured (supervisors, employees, workers). There is no information available on the proportion of insurance contracts of this collective nature, but anecdotal evidence places this figure as high as 40 percent of total beneficiaries.

The insurance structure of the public and private health sectors creates a dual system that segments the population into two groups. Coverage offered by private insurance depends on the premium paid, which in turn depends on the income level, whereas the demand for coverage depends on the risk level of the person or family group being insured. As a result, the higher the income or the lower the health risk, the greater the coverage offered by private insurance will be.

Coverage provided by public insurance, however, is a function of the average spending (per capita) available to the sector. In particular, the higher the fiscal spending in health, the greater the per capita coverage of public insurance will be.

The combination of these factors—personal income, health risk, and public subsidy—leads to a division of the population in terms of public and private health systems as shown in figure 5-2. In this manner the existing insurance system creates the dual structure that concentrates high-income and low-risk people in the ISAPRES system and low-income and high-risk people in the public system. The latter acts as an insurance of last resort and makes viable the dual insurance system. Table 5-6 shows this segmentation of the population into public and private health insurance according to the variables of per capita family income and age of the person (where age is used as a proxy of health risk).

When per capita income increases and fiscal spending remains constant, the percentage of the population subscribing to private insurance will in-

Figure 5-2. The Dual Health Sector System

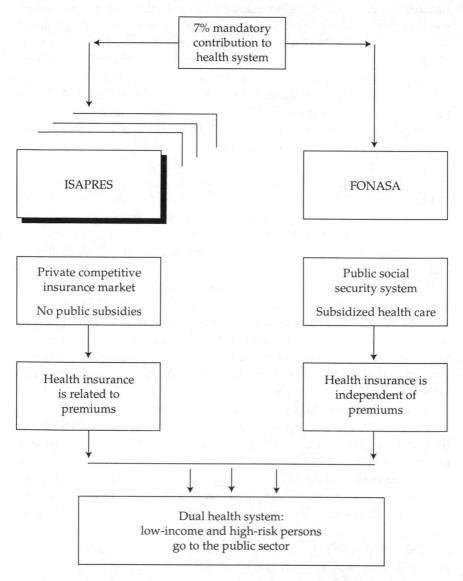

Source: Author's information.

crease. The opposite effect will happen if fiscal resources for the public system increase more than per capita income. The former assumes that the other factors that explain the election of health insurance remain constant, among others, the medical risk of the population and the relative efficiency

Table 5-6. Public and Private Health Sectors, Coverage by Income and Age
(in percent)

	\multicolumn{10}{c}{Household income quintile}								
	I		II		III		IV		V	
Ages (years)	Public	Private	Public	Private	Public	Private	Public	Private	Public	Private
0–20	93	7	82	18	69	31	51	49	30	70
21–50	92	8	82	18	69	31	53	47	34	66
51–64	97	3	94	6	88	12	81	19	51	49
65+	99	1	98	2	97	3	94	6	77	23
Total	93	7	84	16	74	26	60	40	39	61

Source: Encuesta Socioeconómica de Hogares Casen 1996 (own computations on survey data basis, computer files).

of both systems in the provision of health services. Table 5-7 presents the variables of per capita income, subsidy per beneficiary of the public sector, and coverage of the private insurance system over the total user population of both systems from 1984 to 1996. This information validates the hypothesis submitted on an overall basis.

A person of low income accesses the public insurance system because that is where subsidized health care can be obtained. The problem is not the failure of the private sector to take care of the poor. Rather, the problem stems from the design of the system that allocates public subsidies to those who subscribe to the public insurance modality.

Costs in the Chilean Health System

The most important problem that many health systems in developed countries have is the explosive increase in costs (Hoffmeyer and McCarthy 1994). This phenomenon has been especially acute in the United States, where private insurance has been a major factor underlying this trend (Weisbrod 1991). Has anything similar happened in Chile given the relative importance that private insurance has in financing its health sector?

Table 5-5 shows that health expenditures in Chile have increased considerably, from 2.88 percent of GNP in 1987 to 4.22 percent in 1996—a per capita increase of 241 percent. The figures presented exclude expenditures on pharmaceuticals, copayments made in the private sector, and individual health care.

The growth of health expenditures is explained by developments in both the public and private sectors. In the latter, the insurance premiums are

Table 5-7. Per Capita Income, Fiscal Transfers, and Health Sector Coverage, 1984–96

Year	ISAPRE beneficiaries as a percentage of total (1)	Per capita income (1984: 100) (2)	Per capita fiscal transfer to health (1984: 100) (3)	Ratio of (2) to (3)
1984	4	100.00	100.00	1.00
1985	5	102.00	90.67	1.12
1986	9	106.18	86.05	1.23
1987	12	111.60	88.63	1.26
1988	14	118.07	96.81	1.22
1989	16	127.99	82.47	1.55
1990	19	130.29	95.18	1.37
1991	23	137.85	125.05	1.10
1992	26	150.94	159.34	0.95
1993	30	158.19	191.73	0.83
1994	31	162.46	220.84	0.74
1995	32	173.83	231.16	0.75
1996	32	183.74	248.82	0.74

Source: Informe sobre Finanzas Públicas, Dirección de Presupuestos; Informe Estadístico del Fondo Nacional de Salud, FONASA (various years).

strongly determined by the 7 percent portion of income that must be devoted to the health contribution, which acts as an element of cost containment. Nevertheless, revenues from voluntary additional contributions have increased from about 10 percent in 1990 to around 19 percent in 1996. The information available on copayments points in the same direction. The ISAPRE Consalud estimated that per capita spending in copayments increased to an annual average rate of 12.9 percent between 1989 and 1993, making the ratio between copayments and operating expenses of the ISAPRES increase from 19.9 percent to 32.2 percent during this period.

As far as the public health sector is concerned, the expenditure per beneficiary has increased by more than 110 percent in the 1990–96 period. Such a trend is attributable to the political goal of recovering the operational levels of the sector that had been strongly affected by the decrease in fiscal resources during the previous years. It is probable that the input costs of the public sector depend on the level of activity of the private sector, which increases the demand (and prices) of health inputs.

The evidence shows a clear growth trend in health sector expenditures since 1990. This includes increases in the quantity of health services as well as in unit costs. However, there are two important features that make improbable a future explosion in health expenditures. First, public sector expenditures are constrained by global ceilings that are determined by the budgetary law, which in turn is subject to tight fiscal discipline (the last fiscal deficit occurred in 1986). Second, expenditures in the private sector are checked by the large copayments that internalize health costs among the beneficiaries and help to solve the problem of moral hazard in health insurance.

The Private Health Insurance System

In 1997 the system of ISAPRES administered about half of the health spending in the country and made possible a major development in the supply of private health providers. Nevertheless, the private insurance system has operational problems. Some of these are common to competitive insurance health plans around the world; others are specific to the design of the system in Chile.

Private Health Insurance

Competitive health insurance systems generally have equity-related problems, because the insurance premium that persons can pay is determined by their ability to pay, while the premium the insurance companies charge is related to the health risk of the insured person. In the absence of public regulation or subsidies, a competitive health insurance market will discriminate against low-income and/or high-risk persons.

This problem applies to the complete spectrum of goods and services produced in a market economy. Why should health care services be a special case? One important reason lies in the basic need of all persons for health care, which obliges governments to guarantee universal coverage of a package of basic health services. The random nature of health events, as well as the potentially high costs of health needs, have brought about the development of national social security systems, which typically are organized in terms of one public institution (or several institutions organized in a noncompetitive system).

To replace the traditional social security system with a competitive insurance scheme, governments must address the equity problems. One alternative is the public regulation of premiums and conditions for the population's access to care. However, this type of practice generates new problems. In effect, if governments try to regulate by setting premiums, the market will respond with practices of risk selection; it is profitable to exclude any person having higher health risks than those financed by the premiums. The government can enact laws to ensure that these people have access to health insurance, but companies will always find (hidden) mechanisms for practicing some degree of risk selection.

A second option is for the government to subsidize any persons who find it difficult to contract insurance because their incomes are too low or their health risks are too high. The subsidy can come from the public budget, or it can be financed from the contributions paid by the others insured. The latter case calls for a second floor insurance to make the adjustments between the amounts paid and those that the companies receive according to the risk pool. The difficulties with this type of mechanism are mainly operational, for example, how to adequately calculate the health risk of the individual to ensure that the subsidy provided is sufficient to prevent insurance companies from practicing risk selection.

A third alternative is to channel the subsidy toward high-risk and/or low-income persons by having a public system that provides them with health care directly. This is the case of FONASA in Chile.

Private health insurance in Chile is subject to a set of regulations: premiums can only vary in terms of three risk factors: age, gender, and number of dependents; insurance companies cannot void standing contracts (but the insured can); and there is a relatively short waiting period for coverage of preexisting illnesses. These regulations, coupled with the lack of public subsidies, help to explain the main problems with Chile's private insurance industry (such as lack of coverage of old age and inadequate coverage of catastrophic risks). In Chile the premium paid by the insured depends on the level of income, which generates problems in addition to those already mentioned.

On the other hand, the potential advantages of the ISAPRES system are those associated with competition and freedom of choice, such as variety of products, flexibility, allocative efficiency, and economic rationality. Such benefits are most relevant to the health care providers. Competition and freedom of choice also have associated costs (administrative and selling costs, as well as a lack of a medical reference system).

Compulsory Contribution for Individual Insurance

In order to participate in the private insurance system, a person must contribute 7 percent of his or her income. Depending on the amount of this contribution to the ISAPRE, a health insurance plan is offered relating expected expenditure to payments made. In economic terms, the quantity of the service supplied is the endogenous variable in the transaction, which is adjusted to a price that is determined in an exogenous way. An exception to this is the possibility of obtaining additional insurance plans in exchange for a contribution higher than 7 percent of income.

Individual insurance systems can be discussed on efficiency and equity grounds, but they have a distinctive rationality that defines their scope and function. The financing of this insurance via an amount expressed as a part of income introduces an element alien to such rationality and is an additional source of problems.

The public mandate that makes it obligatory to acquire health insurance is based on the beneficial nature of health care. However, the rationale of the insurance mandate is to make it compulsory to contract a basic health insurance and in no case to obtain a coverage that increases with personal income. Why should the more affluent be obliged to insure themselves more than the poor?

Before the reforms of the eighties, a unified public insurance system financed access to health care for the poor with crossed subsidies from the contributions of higher income people (as well as from funds from general taxes). Social security systems, such as the ones referred to earlier, have a logic of internal redistribution that does not apply to the competitive structure of the ISAPRES system. For this reason, the contribution of 7 percent of income to finance the competitive insurance health plans is an anachronism.

Furthermore, the compulsory contribution of 7 percent is inefficient. A segment of the population could have more insurance coverage than that indicated by public rationality. Such a situation creates negative externalities for the rest of the population. In effect, the segment of the population with a high ratio of contributions to expected expenditures for health services induces the ISAPRES to compete for this market by providing "superfluous" benefits, such as sophisticated medical technology and luxury infrastructure. This structure of demand may also have a general equilibrium effect on the prices for the entire range of health services if the inputs used are specific and have alternative uses in the sector (for example, doctors). This would imply a possible deterioration in quality—or an increase in price—of those products assigned to other segments of the market (for example, health services for the elderly).

Old Age

One feature of private insurance is the variability of the premium according to the age of the person insured. Typically, the premium charged by

ISAPRES to old people is three to five times higher than the one charged to young people insured. The premium gap simply reflects different expected costs in health care services across different groups of the population. Part of the payment associated with a health plan occurs in the form of copayments made at the time of access to medical care. The elderly will be affected by higher copayments because of the difference in the expenditures made and the ceilings that limit the reimbursement per service or per period of time (year) (see next subsection).

Persons affiliated with the ISAPRES system during their youth or middle age—when their expected health expenses are relatively low—may have to leave the system upon reaching old age, when the expected expenditures on health care substantially increase. The helplessness of the elderly in the private insurance system is one of the main reasons why ISAPRES get "bad publicity." One of the most valued objectives of health systems is the security of health care when needed. To what extent could a system that "abandons" those affiliated with it when they are most vulnerable and in need of health care depart from this objective?

An insurance structure that discriminates against the elderly also has a general equilibrium effect. The high health expenses expected for the elderly will be in part the endogenous result of the structure of the demand generated by the system. This will happen as the provision of health infrastructure for elderly people is lower—and the price of health services higher—than otherwise.

A small proportion of people older than 65 are beneficiaries of the ISAPRES system (see table 5-6). The ISAPRES Association argues that the current elderly population subscribed when they were young to the public insurance system and it is not the duty of the ISAPRES to provide them with health coverage now that they are old. But the relevant question is this: what will happen in the future with the current population that does belong to private insurance?

The coverage of the elderly population is a social security problem rather than an insurance problem. In the advanced period of the life cycle of persons, their need for health care increases. A natural mechanism to cope with this situation could be to finance the health coverage of old age with social security savings. The Chilean social security system operates on the basis of the capitalization of saving funds, so it could easily include a contribution for financing the health premium in old age. As a matter of fact, a related proposal was discussed in the country some years ago, but the initiative failed over the question of whether the contribution needed (0.9 percent of income) should be included in, or additional to, the contribution of 7 percent.

Fischer, Romaguera, and Mizala (1995) estimate that the higher insurance premium for elderly people could be financed by the income that they would obtain from the present pension funds, without the necessity of increasing the contribution rate. Their calculation takes into consideration the reduction of family dependents associated with old age and the high return that the social security funds have had. However, this study critically depends on the rate of return used, as well as on the assumptions made about the evolution in health costs.

Another possible solution to the problem of the elderly is the savings schemes that are being implemented by some ISAPRES. For example, one plan being developed establishes a basic health plan for old age with the following three requirements: (i) payment of an extra contribution of 1.5 percent of income; (ii) the insured must have subscribed to the ISAPRE for at least 10 years before becoming 65 years old; (iii) and the insured must carry out obligatory health prevention activities during this period and, if any illness is detected, follow adequate treatments.

Coverage of Catastrophic Risks

Another important problem of Chilean private health insurance is the lack of coverage against catastrophic risks. The higher expenses in health care are not covered by the insurance plans offered by ISAPRES.

This feature derives from the stop loss property of insurance plans. Figure 5-3 illustrates the relation between cost of service and the portion of it that is covered by health insurance (broken line). The diagonal of 45 degrees presents the case of complete coverage of the cost of the service. The distance between the diagonal and the broken line represents the copayment that the person has to make. The copayment is a constant portion of the cost until reaching the ceiling of the coverage (S'). For expenses over S' the copayment is complete. A catastrophic event is represented by the C cost level. The coverage of the insurance is the altitude OS', whereas the copayment increases to CS'.

Díaz, Valdés, and Torche (1995) had access to information on expenses for the major portion of ISAPRE users during 1994. Their work shows that copayments account for 31 percent to 45 percent of the cost of health care services (see table 5-8). For high-cost treatments, these figures can represent a large amount of money, supporting the lack of coverage of catastrophic risks in private insurance plans.

The lack of coverage of catastrophic expenses contrasts with the fact that the ISAPRES have not developed insurance plans with deductible amounts. The development of an insurance industry that does not offer alternative

Figure 5-3. Reimbursements and Copayments in ISAPRES

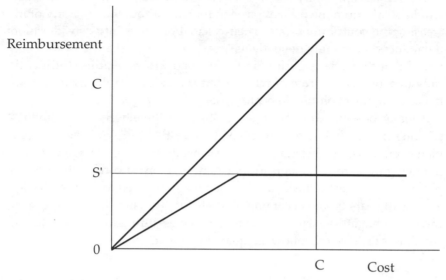

Source: Author's information.

plans with deductibles and higher coverage of higher expenses seems strange.

There are three possible explanations for the lack of coverage of catastrophic risks in ISAPRES' insurance plans. First, the majority of those in ISAPRES are people at low health risk. Therefore, the plans that will dominate the market will be those that cover the most demanded services such as medical consultations, laboratory exams, deliveries, and other services with similar frequency of use. Second, the stop loss property of the plans may constitute a natural response of the market to the present regulations. In particular, the contingent nature of the insurance contracts together with the prohibition against premiums according to medical risk (except for age and gender factors) foster coverage ceilings as a way of controlling losses in plans that have a concentration of people with high health risks. Third, the presence of FONASA as a last resort insurance makes it rational for many middle- and low-income people to subscribe to an ISAPRE so they will have lower cost services and later emigrate to the public insurance system when costs are higher. For this reason, the dominant plans in the private insurance market are those that preferably cover high-frequency and low-cost health care services (Díaz, Valdés, and Torche 1995).

Table 5-8. Lack of Coverage of Catastrophic Risk by Private Sector

Cost of the health service	Average copayment as percentage of total cost
Less than US$1,250	31.25
More than US$2,500	39.45
More than US$5,000	42.30
More than US$7,500	43.64
More than US$10,000	44.42
More than US$12,500	44.92

Source: Díaz, Valdés, and Torche (1995).

Competition and Freedom of Choice

For markets to cause an efficient allocation of resources, consumers must make informed decisions on the basis of the choices available. Diamond (1992) and Fuchs (1996) question the efficiency of outcomes based on competition and freedom of choice in the health sector because of the difficulties in providing information for the consumers to make an informed choice and to optimize their own well-being. Such criticism has been directed especially to information asymmetries between health providers and patients, but it also can be applied to health insurance.

The Chilean case adequately illustrates the difficulties that people have when facing the choice of private health insurance. In fact, consumers are faced with a great heterogeneity of health plans offered by ISAPRES, without having the necessary information to discriminate adequately between them. And even if they were to have this information, it is not clear that such a variety of plans is needed for welfare optimization. This contrasts with the usual case where having a larger choice set enhances consumers' welfare.

In 1995 there were around 8,800 different health insurance plans offered by the ISAPRES. Such variety partly responds to the diversity of existing "prices" that are determined exogenously by the compulsory contribution of 7 percent of income. This feature causes the market to generate a continuous range of insurance plans to respond to the also continuous structure of premiums related to the financing structure. The large variety of existing plans, each one with its own percentage of reimbursement and coverage ceilings, introduces confusion in the system rather than information.

The information difficulties that characterize the insurance market are compounded when one considers that each ISAPRE operates with a specific tariff structure, upon which the copayments for services are determined. Moreover, each type of service includes thousands of items. This information can be found by the user only within the physical plant of each ISAPRE. Under such circumstances, it is virtually impossible for consumers to make a rational evaluation of health insurance plans and choose wisely between them.

A common problem related to competition in private health insurance markets is the high administrative and selling costs of private plans. The empirical evidence on Chile supports this case. During the period from 1990 to 1996, the administrative and selling costs of ISAPRES increased to around 30 percent of the cost of medical services by the same institutions. The elevated expense on administration is related to the cost of operating individual accounts, whereas the sales expenses are related to the commissions for salespeople who subscribe new affiliates to an ISAPRE or obtain the transfer of people who belong to another insurance company.

The ISAPRES insurance system works through a free choice modality of suppliers. The insured person decides the provider of the health service according to his or her preferences and the copayments required in each case. With few exceptions, the health care provider is reimbursed retroactively via a fee-for-service modality.

The freedom of choice of health care providers is well appreciated by the users. People can seek different specialists in search of a diagnosis or the confirmation of one, choosing between a variety of establishments for examinations or more complex treatments. The service provider's remuneration depends on selection by the user; this promotes a careful and considerate service, contrary to the health care services provision prevalent in the public system.

Freedom of choice and retrospective payment have some problems associated with them, however. These problems could obscure the advantages in terms of the user's satisfaction.

In the first place, the theme of supply-induced demand recurs. If the demand for health care services is largely induced by the providers—which is not necessarily bad—the argument regarding the benefits of freedom of choice loses a lot of strength.

In the second place, there is a lack of entry doors within the ISAPRES system. The insured person chooses to go to a specialist (after having self-diagnosed the type of illness that afflicts him or her) instead of going to a general doctor who makes a reasonable diagnosis and refers the patient—

should it be necessary—to the type of specialist required. Under the current system the patient is likely to go to the wrong specialist who could refer the person to the correct doctor or provide service without having the necessary comparative advantages. Imagine this process repeated countless times in order to have an intuitive vision of the possible level of inefficiency.[2]

Third, the fee-for-service system of reimbursement results in providers acting free of financial risks. For this reason, the provider will not have incentives to contain system costs. To the contrary, it is likely that the costs will increase in response to actions that benefit the provider, such as minimizing the risk of medical interventions, completely satisfying the consumer in the presence of a third party payer, and using new technologies without worrying about their cost effectiveness. However, the large copayments that characterize the private health system compensate the moral hazard problem that characterizes the fee-for-service modality.

Demand instruments such as copayments can excessively restrict access to health care services and act against the security objective that health systems ought to provide to their insured population (Ellis and McGuire 1993). This contrasts with the schemes that pass part of the risk on to the providers: per capita prospective payments, payments associated with the diagnosis, global budgets, and others.

The Public Health Sector

The public health sector covers about 70 percent of the national population, holds the major share of the country's hospital infrastructure, and in the past several years has notably strengthened its inputs and personnel. In fact, the public health sector underlies recent advances in Chile's health indicators.

The sector has serious efficiency problems, however, which are related to the traditional organization of public provision: centralization of functions; resource allocation to health facilities based on supply criteria; absence of mechanisms of accountability to its beneficiaries; use of distorted fees and internal prices; lack of financial discipline in the context of "soft" budget constraints; and bureaucratic management, with a low degree of autonomy and important rigidities regarding labor and other input decisions.

---

2. In Chile's medical culture the specialist has a high status within the profession, whereas the general medical doctor is underestimated.

Where to Go?

The public system has been actively searching for solutions to its main problems. Since the beginning of the nineties, several initiatives have been developed to reform the system of financing providers, to make more flexible management and the labor system in the sector, and to reorient the activity of FONASA toward a public insurance entity. However, the sector unions have impeded these reforms. In addition to opposing some of the changes, the unions have shifted an important part of the sector debate to other social agents.

It is possible to identify two driving forces inside the public system. One is a modernization trend, which encourages the formation of internal markets, separating the financial and production functions to generate more efficiency. FONASA's task is here visualized as "an intermediary, between consumers who demand health and suppliers who provide the services. . . . For each of these agents the insurance system adopts the role of counterpart: when facing the consumers demand, it acts as a supplier, offering alternatives—health plans with distinct coverage. When facing the providers, it acts as a purchaser of its services and, as such, it has to make good decisions regarding the purchases it makes" (Oyarzo and Galleguillos 1995).

The other driving force comes from those who view these types of changes as a threat to the public health system and a first step to its privatization. Sector unions consider modernization a threat to labor stability and to unions' ability to confront wage negotiations in a centralized manner. The discourse of the unions, and sometimes of the Medical Association, emphasizes the "scarcity of resources that the public system faces." They perceive public health as a space that must be protected from market-based resource allocation mechanisms and from privatization. This position is shared by left-wing politicians who are defending and strengthening the public health system as one of their political platforms.

The current government seems uncertain about what to do with the public health system. On the one hand, it recognizes that the massive resources transferred to the sector beginning in 1990 have not had the results expected in terms of sector productivity or population satisfaction. On the other hand, its room for political maneuvering is limited by the unions. The government recognizes their effectiveness in paralyzing the sector and the strong repercussions that such paralysis has on the daily life of the country.

Increased Public Spending and Its Results

The problem with the efficiency of public hospitals has been revealed in the context of the growth in budgetary resources. As mentioned earlier, with the objective of offering more and better health care to the people, public spending in health increased by 110 percent in real per capita terms in the 1990–96 period.

This large increase in spending was not accompanied by an improvement in the population's perception of the care provided within the public health system. Table 5-9 provides a time series of comparable public opinion results that reveal a constantly low evaluation of the performance of the government in the health sector.

The opinion surveys reflect the system's lack of response to the injection of new funds. The increase of personnel employed during the period 1989–93 was not followed by a concomitant increase in the production of services and procedures (table 5-10). Productivity has been very low. A report on this subject was discussed within the Ministry of Health toward the middle of 1994. The report advocated institutional changes to ensure the full productivity of sector resources. It was harshly rejected by the Medical Association, which argued that the report did not consider dimensions such as quality of health care and other qualitative variables.

Serious problems of efficiency exist within the management and production of public health services. The source of these problems is the dominant bureaucratic organizational model, which depends critically on the current financing system.

Table 5-9. Public Opinion Evaluation of Health Policy, 1990–97
[Ranking on a scale from 1 (very bad) to 7 (excellent)]

Year	Total population	High-income strata	Medium-income strata	Low-income strata
1990	4.0	4.4	4.1	3.7
1991	3.8	4.1	3.8	3.7
1992	3.6	3.8	3.6	3.5
1993	3.4	3.4	3.5	3.3
1994	3.8	3.8	3.7	3.9
1995	4.1	4.5	4.0	4.1
1996	3.6	3.6	3.6	3.5
1997	3.7	3.3	3.6	3.8

Source: Centro de Estudios Publicos, Opinion Surveys (several years).

Table 5-10. Public Health Sector: Personnel and Services
(index 1989 = 100)

Public health sector	1989	1993
Personnel		
Medical doctors	100.0	134.5
Nurses	100.0	122.3
Midwives	100.0	118.5
Auxiliary personnel	100.0	107.7
Services provided		
Consultations by doctors	100.0	102.7
Consultations by nurses	100.0	83.1
Consultations by midwives	100.0	105.2
Emergency consultations	100.0	124.4
Surgical procedures	100.0	94.8

Source: FONASA.

Organizational and Financial Structure

Public hospitals are financed on the basis of supply considerations. Hospital care has had two principal sources of financing since the 1980s. First, medical material and inputs are financed via a mechanism called FAP (billing for care provided). This system of cost recovery has suffered from insufficiencies relating to the cost of the services and the system of compiling information on the care effected. Second, labor costs are financed in a centralized form as long as the personnel working in the Health Services (hospitals) have the status of public employees and are ascribed to the central government administration. Their wages are predetermined according to a group of categorical variables—professional degree, experience, place of work—and are not related to the level of effort or outcomes.

The supply-oriented financing structure favors a bureaucratic organization, where procedures and rules are more important than outcomes. In this context public management is conducted in accord with a set of institutional and administrative rules. Their primary purpose is to protect the probity of public management (deterring corruption and administrative malpractice). However, these rules end up entangling the organization in a set of formal norms that have no connection with their original objective (Marcel 1993).

As currently structured, health care establishments function independently from the decisions and preferences of the consumers. As a general rule, separating the supply from the demand provokes important welfare losses because the goods and services that are consumed do not respond to the preferences and/or necessities of the population. Now then, it can be argued that the characteristics of the health service make less critical the sovereignty of demand, given that this market precisely consists of a provider looking for knowledge and information. Notwithstanding this argument, separating supply from demand favors situations of abuse of power, maltreatment, and a less satisfactory service than one where payments to providers depend on the decisions of consumers.

The organizational and financial structure in place in the public system also works against the autonomous management of health facilities. The decentralization of the Health Services is a mere formality if most financial decisions remain in the hands of central institutions. The determination of wages is centralized. In addition, the number of employees in the hospitals is controlled by the Ministry of Finance, which makes decisions about hiring and firing. Under such conditions it is not possible to achieve a supply of health care services suitable for the specifications and contingencies of each location, nor can more efficiency in the management of public health establishments be expected.

Finally, Chile lacks an undistorted price system that sends clear signals for the allocation of resources within the public health sector. This leads to economic irrationality and is a sufficient condition for the inefficient assignment of resources. Having a "soft" budget constraint in which the meaning of an operational deficit is never clear contributes to the lack of financial discipline at public hospitals.

To deal with the existing problems, a payment system was designed called PAD-PPP (associated payments for diagnosis and prospective payments for services).

The first component of the new system (PAD) establishes a payment according to the diagnosis for the patients provided inpatient care at hospital facilities. In this manner, the new system transfers resources based on outcomes and establishes adequate incentives so that the facilities provide health services in an efficient way. The system is planned based on average costs, but it is flexible. If an initial diagnosis on admission leads to another type of service, the payment is made based on the PPD; that is, a payment for the care actually received.

The PPP mechanism is also applied for less frequent services, for which there is no previously established PAD. Unlike in the present situation, the payment for care has a prospective character in the aggregate, because a global budget is established for each health care service according to the priorities of the case. In this way the PAD-PPP system introduces a mechanism to control costs.

At present this new payment system is still in the planning stages. The financing of hospital centers on the basis of the PAD-PPP mechanism requires flexibility in the system of wages and employment in the sector. In particular, the payment by diagnosis of discharge is not compatible with a headcount pre-established at the central level and with a scale of wages that does not respond to productivity considerations. Furthermore, it requires giving public hospitals a certain degree of autonomy so that the introduction of the new payment mechanisms and related incentives makes sense.

Again, the stumbling block for effective modernization of the public health service has come from workers' unions in the sector. Reforms are perceived as threats to job stability and as attempts to privatize the sector. In principle, they are neither one nor the other. The unions' resistance to changes might result in a situation that becomes so critical that even more radical changes are required.

Decentralization of Primary Care

One of the important reforms in the eighties was the transfer of administration of public primary care clinics to the municipalities. The technical supervision of these clinics remained the responsibility of the Health Services. The primary care personnel became private employees, contracted by the respective municipalities at a wage determined by market forces. The decentralization process was initiated in 1982, but it was not until the end of the decade that it was expanded to most locations in the country. At present, two Health Services, Metropolitan Central and Aysen, maintain the administration of primary care clinics. Primary care is also provided at clinics linked to several hospitals and at hospital facilities of minor complexity located in medium-size cities.

As in the case of public hospitals, the decentralization experience has been characterized by two major developments: (a) the financial shortage during the eighties and its related consequences; (b) the financial recovery during the nineties and questions concerning the productivity of the new resources.

In the Chilean case, primary health care is financed by two types of resources. Transfers from the central government to the municipalities for the exclusive financing of the health facilities are the main contribution. These transfers have operated based on historical criteria and negotiations between the different government levels. In the near future this system will be replaced by a per capita transfer: the central government will give the municipal districts an amount of funds to finance primary care in proportion to the population enrolled in municipal clinics. The per capita subsidy distinguishes between communities according to their urban-rural location and their poverty level. The communities with small populations will receive a fixed amount of funds to finance primary health care.

The second source of financing complements central support and comes from contributions that the municipality itself makes. The municipal districts call them "deficits" to signal that they cover a financial gap deriving from the insufficiency of central resources. The central government views the local contributions somewhat differently; it sees them as a reflection of local interest in the health care of the municipality's population.

Chilean municipalities cannot issue debt instruments. Therefore, deficits in municipal finance are not viable (in the sense that municipalities cannot finance excess expenditures).

The fiscal pressure of decentralization has prompted requests for larger contributions from the central government and national strikes led by unions, primary health care workers, and teachers. (Public schools also are operated by municipalities.) They seek wage increases and benefits related to job stability. The power of the unions and the success of their demands are precisely based on their centralized nature.

The concession of wage benefits in response to the unions breaks the labor relationship between municipal primary health care workers and the mayor and reduces the scope of the local administration. The new "Primary Health Care Worker Statute," which introduces clauses of national scope on wages and employment conditions of sector workers, constitutes an additional step toward re-centralizing primary health care.

One of the major criticisms of the decentralization of primary health care is that it breaks the health network. Primary care centers are the entrance door to the system. Medical doctors who work in the clinics view the separation of primary care from other care as a diminishment of their work and professional development. As a corollary, medical doctors may lose interest in working in primary care centers, leading to high turnover and personnel shortages at these facilities.

The functioning of a health network can be determined by the bureaucratic and hierarchical procedures of a centralized system. It is also possible to establish a health network through voluntary contracts between the different parties of the system, as is the case in segments of the private sector. The problem in the Chilean public sector is that the link between municipalities and the Health Services has failed to establish an efficient network, perhaps because of the disparate objectives and incentives of both types of organizations. However, such a failure is not inherent in the decentralization process.

To date there has not been a comprehensive evaluation of the municipal decentralization experience and its impact on health policy objectives. The evidence available is partial and identifies the importance of the technical health teams and the mayor as factors contributing to the different degrees of success in the municipal decentralization experience.

The great heterogeneity of the communities of the country contrasts with the standard model that is assumed in the decentralization of primary care. There are three cases of interest in this regard. First, there are communities in big urban centers; many residents in these municipal districts have alternatives for obtaining health care, either at clinics in other communities, at emergency centers of hospitals, or at private facilities under FONASA's freedom-of-choice modality. Second, the communities in small cities generally rely on low complexity hospitals that also offer primary health care services. Third, the rural communities with low population density rely on rural health posts; those facilities and their use are qualitatively different from urban clinics.

It is not clear that all communities should be treated in accordance with the standard model that supports the decentralization of primary health care centers in Chile. According to some partial evaluations, this model works the best for the first type of community—municipal districts in large urban centers (Infante 1997). Primary health care centers in small and rural municipal districts might work better in closer association with the Health Services.

Another important issue is the conflict between the central government and local governments over the financing of primary health care. Some mayors have threatened to return the primary care clinics to the administration of the Health Services. This contrasts with the central government's view of primary health care as one of the most visible and important areas of municipal administration, given primary care's impact on the local community. It is in the interest of the mayor to provide service in accordance with the objectives of national health policy: ample access, users' satisfaction, and improvement of health indicators of local population. At the same time, the municipality can see itself restricted in the administration of the clinics by insufficient financial resources and rigidities in the management of the clinics.

The "Primary Health Care Worker Statute" and the technical supervision of the local clinics by the Health Services deprive municipal management of degrees of freedom. Furthermore, municipalities will face a complicated situation if the "what," "how," and "how much" to produce health care are exogenously determined, whereas the local community holds the mayor responsible for the provision of these services.

In short, the decentralization process of primary health care is far from settled. There are important issues that need a better definition, and structural modifications may occur in the future.

Conclusion

According to Musgrove (1996), countries expect their health systems to meet four objectives: the provision of a good condition of health in the population, efficiency in attaining good health at reasonable costs, good quality health care to warrant users' satisfaction, and equity in access to health care. The reforms introduced in the Chilean health system may be evaluated on the basis of these objectives. Of course, no country in the world has fully attained these objectives.

As regards the first objective, the country had already attained advanced indicators in life expectancy, child mortality, and the other traditional health measures by the time the reforms were introduced. Life expectancy, which is the best indicator of a population's health, was close to the average achieved by developed countries. The good health of Chile's population is associated with the early expansion of the public health system and with the sanitary and educational investments in place before the reforms. In fact, the reforms were aimed at enhancing efficiency and quality in the health system rather than improving basic health indicators.

As regards the cost containment objective, it is necessary first to note that spending on health care in Chile is relatively low by international standards. However, during the nineties there was a trend to increase expenditures. The private health sector in Chile has structural characteristics that promote higher costs; among these are the lack of entry doors to the health system and a financing system for health providers based on payment per medical event. Large copayments help to reduce the problems of moral hazard and cost explosion associated with private insurance financing.

Public health systems have a better record in containing costs on account of their global budgets and the monopsonic power exerted by markets on health inputs. However, spending by the Chilean public system has more than doubled during the period 1990–96. The reasons for this trend are twofold. First, there is the necessary recovery of the operational levels that had deteriorated severely during the eighties. Second, there is the sustained pressure from the Medical Association and the workers' unions in the health sector with a view to obtain better wages.

The third objective of health services is users' satisfaction. The fast growth rate of ISAPRES in the middle-income strata indicates that this system is attractive to the population that appreciates freedom of choice. However, there are two highly problematic issues at play in the system.

First, the insurance premium for elderly people is three to five times more than for young people. This is a characteristic intrinsic to competitive health insurance, which closely relates the variables of the premium to the expected cost of health care.

Second, there is a lack of coverage for great health risks or catastrophic events. This is a well-founded criticism since it reflects a failure of the system to perform one of its main roles, insuring the population against unexpected health events. The problem is related to three factors: (i) selection means that the plans that dominate the market are those that cover the most demanded services, namely, high-frequency and low-cost events; (ii) the contingent nature of the insurance contracts together with the prohibition of premiums based on medical risk (except with regard to age and gender factors) promote coverage ceilings as a way of controlling losses in plans that have a concentration of people with high health risks; (iii) the presence of FONASA as a last resort insurance prompts many middle- and low-income people to subscribe to an ISAPRE in order to have lower cost services and then switch to the public insurance later when costs are higher.

The public system receives a definitely negative evaluation of the health care provided to the users. This reflects the operation of a bureaucratic, centralized structure financed on the basis of supply. The unresponsiveness of the public sector in matters of quality of services provided is a source of great concern, as well as the blind opposition of the workers' unions in the sector to any reform that introduces greater accountability for resources.

The fourth objective is equity in the access to health care. In this regard the public system has a health care network that covers all of the country's territory and provides short access times to the closest health care centers. The public system is insurance of last resort for people who lack an income. In turn, the private system is criticized for failing to give poor people health care of high medical cost. However, such a criticism is unfounded because public subsidies oriented to the poor are only available to those seeking medical care through public health providers. Public policy operates on the basis of financing the supply of public institutions rather than the demand of people with health needs.

Others criticize the Chilean health system because no redistribution of resources is made from high-income people to those with a low income (as in the case of a traditional health system). However, equity requires the provision of good health care to the whole population; a redistribution of income within the health system may or may not be needed. This is an instrument to attain equity, but in no way is it a necessary condition.

The overall record of the Chilean health system is mixed. It has achieved important objectives such us universal coverage and high life expectancy and low child mortality relative to other countries at a similar stage of economic development. However, there is ample room for improvement, and several reform initiatives have been advanced. The most comprehensive proposal was developed in 1996 by a team led by researchers at the Universidad de Chile.

At the core of the reform proposal is the Guaranteed Package of Health Benefits (Plan Garantizado de Beneficios de Salud, PGBS)—a basket of health interventions guaranteed by the government. In this way the PGBS becomes the new mandate in health coverage, replacing the 7 percent obligatory contribution of income to purchase health insurance. The PGBS applies to the individual health interventions. Public health interventions are covered by another plan, Plan de Salud Pública or PSP, which is financed out of general taxation. Voluntary supplement plans are allowed. These plans are privately financed and offer health interventions and related services that are not covered by the PGBS. However, the PGBS is meant to be a comprehensive plan so that the equity of the health system is not dependent on the supplement plans.

The PGBS can be offered by public or private health insurance institutions under competitive conditions. Free pricing ensures consistency between the normative design of the PGBS (what the population should have) and the availability of resources (what the population can have). The standardized nature of the PGBS introduces transparency in the insurance market. Also, it induces insurance companies to make profits by developing efficient arrangements with (public and private) health providers instead of practicing selection in the demand side.

The proposal makes the PGBS subject to community rather than individual rating. In other words, the insurance premium will not be a function of individual health risks. Competition and unregulated pricing will allow the average insurance premium to vary with aggregate conditions. In order to have consistent community rating and open enrollment, two mechanisms must be introduced. First, a second floor institution is needed to reallocate premiums among insurance companies according to the risk-related factors of their affiliates and to provide coverage for catastrophic events. Second, at the beginning existing risks must be allocated randomly among insurance companies.

Health providers are financed out of the payments that beneficiaries make to the insurance companies. Low-income beneficiaries are subsidized by the government. This way public resources to the health system are allocated by families, introducing accountability and efficiency in the provision of health services.

The reallocation of public subsidies to beneficiaries requires a structural change in the organization of public sector providers because their financing depends on the sale of health interventions to insurance companies and families. This in turn requires public organizations to manage autonomously their budget and personnel by means of a more flexible regime.

The reform needs a transition path. The crucial role of public sector providers, as well as political considerations, suggest that the change in public hospitals will be the strategic variable in the transition.

The proposed reform introduces changes that modify the most salient efficiency problems of the current health system (associated with short-run private insurance and bureaucratized public sector production); enlarges the equity of the health system by providing the beneficiaries a guaranteed package of needed health interventions; and empowers families by giving them a central role in the resource allocation process within the sector.

References

Diamond, P. 1992. "Organizing the Health Insurance Market." *Econometrica* 60: 1233–54.

Díaz C., S. Valdés, and A. Torche. 1995. "Cobertura catastrófica para los cotizantes del Sistema ISAPRE." Instituto de Economía U.C. Dic. Santiago.

Ellis, R., and T. McGuire. 1993. "Supply-side and Demand-side Cost Sharing in Health Care." *Journal of Economic Perspectives* 7 (4): 135–51.

Fischer R., P. Romaguera, and A. Mizala. 1995. "Alternativa de Solución para el tratamiento de la salud en la tercera edad en el sistema ISAPRE." Centro de Economía Aplicada, Dpto. de Ingeniería Industrial, U. Chile, Santiago.

Fuchs, V. 1996. "Economics, Values, and Health Care Reform." *American Economic Review* 86 (1): 1–24.

Fuchs, V., and M. Krarner. 1973. "Determinants of Expenditures for Physicians' Services in the United States." Occasional Paper 116, National Bureau of Economic Research, Cambridge, Mass.

Hoffmeyer, U., and T. McCarthy. 1994. *Financing Health Care*. Dordrecht, Boston, London: Kluwer Academic Publisher.

Hsiao, W. 1995. "Abnormal Economics in the Health Sector?" *Health Policy* 32: 125–39.

Infante, A. 1997. "Evaluación de la atención Primaria. Aspectos técnicos y recursos humanos." Ministerio de Salud, Santiago.

Larrañaga, 0. 1996. "Descentralización y Equidad: El caso de los servicios sociales en Chile." *Cuademos de Economía* 100 (December): 354–65.

———. 1997a. "Public and Private Social Sectors in Chile." In E. Zuckerman and E. de Kadt, eds., *The Public-Private Mix in Social Services*. Washington, D.C.: Inter-American Development Bank.

———. 1997b. "Eficiencia y equidad en el sistema de salud chileno." Serie Financiarniento del Desarrollo, no. 54. Comision Economica para America Latina (CEPAL), Santiago.

Marcel, M. 1993. "Mitos y recetas en la reforrna de la gestión pública." In E. Lahera (de)., *Como mejorar la gestión pública*. Santiago: Cieplan, Flacso, Foro 90.

Musgrove, P. 1996. "Public and Private Roles in Health: Theory and Financing Patterns." Human Development Department, World Bank, Washington, D.C.

Oyarzo, C., and S. Galleguillos. 1995. "Reforma del sistema de salud chileno: marco conceptual de la propuesta del FONASA." *Cuadernos de Economía* 95 (April).

Poterba, J. 1994. "Government Intervention in the Markets for Education and Health Care: How and Why?" Working Paper 4916, National Bureau of Economic Research, Cambridge, Mass.

Weisbrod, Burton. 1991. "The Health Care Quadrilemma: An Essay on Technological Change, Insurance, Quality of Care, and Cost-Containment." *Journal of Economic Literature* 29 (2): 523–52.

World Bank. 1993. *World Development Report 1993: Investing in Health*. New York: Oxford University Press.

6

Poverty and Income Distribution in a High-Growth Economy: Chile, 1987–95

Alberto Valdés

Chile has maintained an impressive rate of economic growth for more than a decade. Per capita income grew at about 5.8 percent per annum between 1987 and 1994. This growth was achieved in the context of a market-oriented policy framework, with relatively little direct government intervention and a very open trade regime. In this context Chile has implemented a highly targeted system of social assistance in areas such as health, education, and housing, as well as through direct income transfers. Since the reestablishment of democracy in 1990, it has pursued an explicit strategy of "growth with equity," while maintaining a market-oriented policy framework. Table 6-1 presents key economic indicators for the period 1985–95.

This chapter is based on a 1997 World Bank report prepared by a team led by Alberto Valdés and consisting of Francisco H. G. Ferreira and Indermit Gill of the World Bank, Dante Contreras and Osvaldo Larrañaga of Universidad de Chile (Santiago), Professor Ramón López of the University of Maryland, Professor Tony Shorrocks of the University of Essex (UK), and Julie A. Litchfield, London School of Economics (UK).

Table 6-1. Key Economic Indicators, 1985–95
(annual percentage change rate)

Year	GDP	Exports	Inflation	Real wages per hour	Unemployment	Savings
1985	2.4	6.9	26.4	−4.5	12.0	7.8
1986	5.7	10.1	17.4	2.0	8.8	11.5
1987	6.6	6.7	21.5	−0.2	7.9	17.3
1988	7.3	11.6	12.7	6.5	6.3	22.3
1989	9.9	16.1	21.4	1.9	5.3	23.7
1990	3.3	9.7	27.3	1.8	5.7	24.2
1991	7.3	10.7	18.7	4.9	5.3	24.1
1992	11.0	13.5	12.7	4.5	4.4	24.8
1993	6.3	4.2	12.2	3.2	4.5	23.9
1994	4.2	8.2	8.9	5.0	5.9	25.4
1995	8.5	11.4	8.2	4.1	4.7	27.6

Source: MIDEPLAN (1996).

Despite rapid economic growth and continued efforts by the government to improve social equity, a common perception in Chile is that some groups have lagged behind and income distribution has worsened. Using modern analytical and statistical techniques to examine the developments since 1987, we assess the validity of these concerns. We also try to identify plausible policy options for the government to follow in order to reduce both poverty and income inequality, while retaining the growth potential of the economy.

This chapter begins with a statistical overview of income distribution and poverty during 1987–94. This is followed by a profile of poverty and an analysis of changes in the standard of living of vulnerable groups during the same period. The question we ask is whether the reduction in poverty has been across the board, or whether some social groups have lagged behind. We then present a quantitative analysis of the evolution of poverty across regions. The chapter also explores labor market issues that are considered critical for explaining income inequality and poverty, and for evaluating policy effects. The distributional impact of tax and expenditure policies is studied, and we identify ways in which the benefits from growth can be shared more evenly. In the last section we present our main findings and policy implications.

Income Distribution and Poverty: A Statistical Overview

How have rapid economic growth and social policies affected the poverty, welfare, and distribution of income in Chile since 1987? Has poverty declined significantly? Has inequality been reduced? This section provides a quantitative analysis to answer these questions.

The Empirical Foundations for the Analysis

The analysis draws on four household survey microdata sets, *the Encuesta de Caracterización Socioeconomica Nacional* (CASEN) of 1987, 1990, 1992, and 1994.[1] In 1994 the sample covered 45,993 households. The CASEN is a nationally and regionally representative household survey carried out by MIDEPLAN (Ministerio de Planificación y Cooperación) through the Department of Economics of the University of Chile. The survey has two objectives: to generate a reliable portrait of socioeconomic conditions across the country and to monitor the incidence and effectiveness of the government's social programs. Once each survey is completed, the data are entrusted to CEPAL (United Nations Economic Commission for Latin America and the Caribbean), which makes adjustments for nonresponse, missing income values, and for under- (or over-) reporting of different income categories, using the National Accounts System as a reference.

Several additional adjustments were made to the data set for this report, which differs from earlier work based on the CASEN. Our analysis relied on household income per equivalent adult (rather than simple per capita income) as the chosen income indicator, and we reported the proportion of *individuals* (rather than households) below the poverty line. We also corrected for differences in average price levels across different regions in Chile, as well as for live-in servants. Unlike most analyses of this data, no adjustment was made to lower the poverty line in rural areas due to unmeasured prices.

Adjusted total household income is the income variable used and includes all primary incomes in cash and in-kind, monetary transfers (such as family allowance, assistance pensions, family subsidies, water subsidies,

---

1. As of August 1997, when the quantitative analysis was completed, the World Bank team did not have access to the CASEN 1996 survey data at the household level and therefore could not incorporate this data into its analysis.

and unemployment subsidies), as well as imputed rent and gifts. The income measure does not include, however, the value of transfers in-kind made to households by the government through programs in education, health, and housing. Although imputations of the value of these programs were available by quintile in MIDEPLAN (1994), the data were not available at the household level. Therefore, our measure of income per person excludes the value of these services, especially to low-income families, and thus underestimates the income of the beneficiaries of these government programs. Indirectly, poor households have also improved their living standards since general development benefits society as a whole. Access to electricity, safe drinking water, more space per person in the house, improved sewerage, increased access to telephones, and other welfare-enhancing infrastructure services have improved significantly in Chile, but are not captured by our "moneymetric" indicators.

Has Inequality Increased?

We use the following four measures of inequality: the Gini coefficient, by far the most widely known of the measures; the Theil index; the mean log deviation; and a transformation of the coefficient of variation. In table 6-2 we list the means and median monthly incomes for each year in our sample, as well as the four inequality measures. Although all four are derived by aggregating differences between incomes, they are sensitive to different parts of income distribution (for example, lower, middle, and upper).

The different measures change very little in inequality over the period. This is particularly true for the Gini coefficient and the Theil index. The mean log deviation falls monotonically over the period, while E(2) rises.

Table 6- 2. Household Incomes per Equivalent Adult, 1987–94
(1994 pesos)

Income distribution	1987	1990	1992	1994
Mean income[a]	67,232	75,007	90,797	93,981
Median[a]	36,265	42,455	50,212	53,196
Gini coefficient	0.5468	0.5322	0.5362	0.5298
Mean log deviation E(0)	0.5266	0.4945	0.4891	0.4846
Theil index E(1)	0.6053	0.5842	0.6151	0.5858
Coefficient of variation E(2)	1.3007	1.3992	1.5050	1.5634

a. Expressed in 1994 Santiago pesos, monthly income
Source: CASEN household surveys in 1987, 1990, 1992, and 1994.

The broad picture that arises from the analysis can be characterized by three observations. First, the entire distribution function has been shifting to the right, with nearly all people earning higher incomes in the same relative ranks. This phenomenon is clearly the result of economic growth. Second, the dispersion of the distribution seems to have remained broadly stable as it moved to the right over the period. If anything, there is a slight reduction in overall inequality, although there are no significant and unambiguous changes in inequality over the years. Third, to the extent that there are any discernible changes in the shape of the density function, there appears to have been a slight compression in the lower and a slight stretching in the upper tail (suggesting that inequality among the poor declined, while inequality among the very rich increased). This observation is robust for each of the income concepts used (per capita household income and household income per adult equivalent).

The finding of a stable income distribution is consistent with evidence from other countries. A recent report examining inequality measures for 108 countries concluded that, although differences in inequality across countries are substantial, distributional changes over time in any one country are very small (Deininger and Squire 1996). World Bank (1997, vol. 2, annex 1) presents distributional change undergone by some fast-growing countries in East Asia.

The Evolution of Poverty

We used three (absolute) poverty lines in computing poverty measures, all of them expressed in 1994 Santiago pesos. These were the indigence line, a lower-bound poverty line, and an upper-bound poverty line. The first two are the official measures widely used in Chile. The first is derived from the cost of a standard food basket for an average adult, and the second by doubling the indigence line to arrive at a poverty line that accounts for expenditures on shelter, clothing, and so on. The third line takes into account imputed rents as part of income.

For each poverty line three poverty measures are reported. The simplest and most common measure is the *headcount index* (the proportion of individuals with incomes below the poverty line). It does not indicate the depth of poverty of the poor, nor does it change if a person in poverty becomes poorer. A second measure is the poverty deficit index (an aggregate of the income shortfalls of the poor relative to the poverty line, divided by the population size). It reflects the depth of poverty. A family that is barely below the poverty line adds only a little to the poverty gap index, but a

Figure 6-1. Different Types of Poverty Measures for Chile, 1987–94

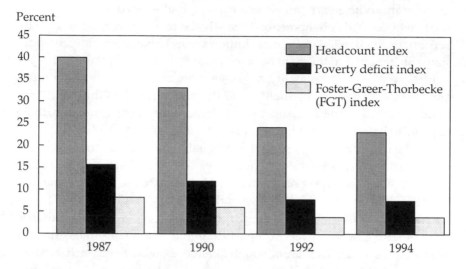

Note: The income indicator is household income per equivalent adult.
Source: World Bank (1997).

family that is extremely destitute adds a great deal. The third indicator is the Foster-Greer-Thorbecke (FGT) index, which provides a distribution-sensitive measure that gives a greater weight to larger shortfalls, and thus is more sensitive to extreme poverty.

As an illustration of the wide difference between these indicators, figure 6-1 presents the evolution of poverty in Chile from 1987 to 1994 using these three poverty indices. As expected, the three indicators reveal the same trend, namely a significant reduction in the level of poverty; however, the headcount index shows a much higher rate of poverty (almost double) than do the other two measures. As indicated by the poverty gap and FGT indexes, a significant reduction in poverty took place among the poorest of the poor between 1997 and 1982, while hardly any reduction occurred between 1992 and 1994.

Our analysis confirms that there was a sustained rise in mean income per person for all deciles during 1987–94 (table 6-3), illustrating the powerful beneficial impact of growth across the Chilean income distribution. The sustained rise in mean decile income for all deciles reveals that the growth in mean and median incomes did extend to most Chileans. Income shares

Table 6-3. Decile Mean Incomes: Household Incomes per Equivalent Adult, 1987–94

(thousands of 1994 pesos per month)

Decile	1987	1990	1992	1994
Decile 1	9.0	10.4	13.8	13.5
Decile 2	16.2	19.2	23.6	24.1
Decile 3	21.3	25.0	30.7	31.6
Decile 4	26.7	31.4	37.7	39.3
Decile 5	32.8	38.6	45.8	48.3
Decile 6	40.6	47.1	55.9	59.5
Decile 7	51.5	59.4	70.2	74.5
Decile 8	68.8	78.0	92.2	99.2
Decile 9	105.6	116.4	134.6	148.1
Decile 10	299.7	324.6	403.4	402.1

Source: World Bank (1997).

of most deciles changed little over the period (World Bank 1997, vol. 1, table 2.3). According to all three measures, both poverty and extreme poverty declined remarkably from 1987 to 1994. Poverty headcounts and poverty deficits were halved during this period. While 41 percent of the population lived in poverty in 1987, by 1994 this figure had fallen to 23 percent. The incidence of indigence fell from 13 percent in 1987 to 5 percent in 1994. The reductions were larger during the years of faster growth, from 1987 to 1992, and smallest in the years of sluggish growth, from 1992 to 1994.

The only exceptions to these sustained rises in mean incomes were registered for the top and bottom deciles in 1994. Despite growth in overall mean income since 1992, these two groups lost in absolute terms. The reason for the loss to the bottom decile was related to a cyclical deceleration in GDP growth in 1994, which brought about an increase in total unemployment from 4.8 percent to 6.5 percent in 1994. Unemployment was much higher, however, in the poorest quintile, rising from 18 percent to 22 percent (Cowan and de Gregorio 1996).

Additional evidence of the substantial reduction in poverty is derived from stochastic dominance analysis. Poverty was unambiguously lower in both 1994 and 1992 than in either 1987 or 1990. The result is independent of the specific measure used and valid for a large range of poverty lines.

Despite these achievements in reducing overall poverty, and the decline in indigence during 1987–92, indigence appears to have worsened between 1992 and 1994. The indigence headcount index rose from 4.7 percent in 1992 to 5.1 percent in 1994. This resulted directly from the income losses affecting the lowest decile, associated with the slowdown in growth (from 11.0 in 1992 to 4.2 in 1994) and an increase in unemployment (from 4.4 percent to 5.9 percent, respectively). By inference, with higher growth and lower unemployment, indigence is very likely to have declined significantly since 1994.

The Profile of Poverty

These aggregate measures of poverty reveal the overall level and intensity of poverty. In order to develop a poverty alleviation strategy, however, it is essential to discern a poverty profile that identifies the population charac-teristics most closely associated with the probability of being poor. Who are the poor? Where are they located? What are their occupations? What is the relationship of poverty to gender and age? The profile of poverty drawn in this section identifies the groups most vulnerable to persistent depriva-tion and then examines the evolution of the living standards of these groups during the 1987–94 period.

The Approach

In this report vulnerable groups were defined as those with a higher-than-average risk of being poor in 1987; headcounts of poverty were over 38 percent (over 50 percent for highly vulnerable groups). The operational definition of poverty is the same as the one applied in the previous section, except that the household rather than the individual is the unit of analysis, in order to capture relevant household characteristics. Using the CASEN survey data, households were classified into mutually exclusive vulner-able and nonvulnerable groups, and a probit regression model was esti-mated to identify the characteristics most closely correlated with poverty.

Eighteen mutually exclusive groups were identified as vulnerable in 1987, according to the economic characterization of the head of the household. A dynamic decomposition analysis was used to decompose the changes in overall poverty between intra- and inter-subgroup effects. The principal attributes of vulnerability of the head of the household included such con-ditions as gender, schooling, age (less than 35, between 35 and 64, and older), labor force status (employed, unemployed, or non-labor-force participant), economic sector (agriculture, tradable excluding agriculture, or non-tradable), and location (rural or urban).

The Evolution of Vulnerability

Based on the headcount indicator, the proportion of households belonging to vulnerable groups fell dramatically between 1987 and 1992, from 53 percent to 11.3 percent in 1992, rising slightly to 11.3 percent in 1992 (World Bank 1997, table 3.2). Similarly, the number of households that are considered highly vulnerable declined from 29 percent in 1987 to 3.7 percent in 1992 (with a small rise to 4.1 percent in 1994). The definition of vulnerability appears robust for all three poverty indicators (headcount index, poverty deficit index, and FGT index) since each indicator produces similar results.

A more disaggregated look helps us to better understand which groups improved and which groups lagged behind over the period of the report. Poverty rates across all vulnerable groups declined by 23 percentage points, and the higher the poverty during the base year, the greater the absolute reduction in the (headcount) poverty measure (table 6-4). The gains in poverty reduction are particularly notable in household subgroups headed by persons with low levels of schooling and by the unemployed, two groups that accounted for 60 percent of the population of vulnerable households in 1987. This improvement indicates the importance of economic growth as a means of reducing poverty by raising across-the-board labor incomes. On the other hand, the strong reduction in the headcount of poor urban households headed by a person older than 65 years (from 40 percent to 16 percent) suggests the importance of social policy in poverty alleviation.

In short, the reduction in poverty during 1987–94 appears to have benefited almost all vulnerable population subgroups. Of course, this does not imply that everyone was better off in 1994 than in 1987. Unemployment was still closely associated with poverty in 1994, but the share of households with unemployed household heads declined sharply between 1987 and 1994.

A closer look at the immediate factors leading to poverty reduction (using a dynamic decomposition approach) shows that around 85 percent of the reduction is explained by a decline in intra-group poverty (changes in the incidence of poverty within each group). The remaining 15 percent can be attributed to movements of the poor from high-risk to lower-risk poverty groups (variations in the relative size of the groups). The decline is particularly strong among households headed by non-labor-force participants, both male and female, and by unemployed persons. Thus, the integration of high-risk poverty groups into labor markets has been an important ingredient in the reduction of poverty.

Table 6-4. Percentage of Households Belonging to Vulnerable and Nonvulnerable Groups, 1987 and 1994

	1987		1994	
Group	Headcount index	Share	Headcount index	Share
Female household head				
1. Workers, young[a], low education[c] (*)	64	0.48	45	0.29
2. Young[a], high education[d]	32	1.17	16	1.56
3. Workers, adult[b], low education[c] (**)	44	2.69	22	3.11
4. Workers, adult[b], high education[d]	15	2.67	9	3.74
5. Non-labor-force participants, low education[c] (*)	56	5.37	35	3.78
6. Non-labor-force participants, high education[d]	32	2.73	25	2.22
Non-labor-force male participants				
7. Male, low education[c] (*)	52	3.78	31	2.66
8. Male, high education[d]	23	3.70	20	2.03
Tradable sector male workers (nonagricultural)				
9. Young[a], low education[c] (*)	64	0.94	40	0.58
10. Young[a], high education[d]	32	3.65	18	3.89
11. Adult[b], low education[c] (**)	40	3.25	22	3.02
12. Adult[b], high education[d]	16	4.53	10	4.77
Nontradable sector male workers				
13. Young[a], low education[c] (*)	61	1.94	41	1.64
14. Young[a], high education[d]	28	9.56	16	10.80
15. Adult[b], low education[c]	41	8.87	18	10.19
16. Adult[b], high education[d]	15	13.32	9	17.60
Agricultural sector male workers				
17. Young[a], low education[c] (regions VI to X) (*)	77	1.56	58	1.09
18. Adult[b], low education[c] (regions VI to X) (*)	64	4.74	42	4.44
19. Young[a], low education[c] (other regions) (*)	70	1.14	54	0.67
20. Adult[b], low education[c] (other regions) (**)	48	2.01	32	1.64
21. Young[a], high education[d] (total country) (*)	53	2.19	38	2.07
22. Adult[b], high education[d] (total country)	33	1.59	26	1.92

Table 6-4 *(continued)*

| | 1987 | | 1994 | |
	Headcount index	Share	Headcount index	Share
Group				
Male and female household heads, older than 65				
23. Urban, low education[c] (**)	40	7.90	16	8.08
24. Rural, low education[c] (*)	57	2.71	31	2.39
25. Urban and rural, high education[d]	12	3.83	4	3.55
Male and female household heads, unemployed, younger than 65				
26. Urban, low education[c] (*)	77	1.34	60	0.80
27. Rural, low education[c] (*)	94	0.32	80	0.21
28. Urban and rural, high education[d] (*)	72	2.01	55	1.27

a. A household head less than 35 years old.
b. A household head more than 35 years old.
c. A household head with less than primary school (8 years of education).
d. A household head with more than primary school.
(*) Identifies high vulnerability: group count of 50 percent or more.
(**) Identifies vulnerability group count of 38 percent (the average household headcount index of 1987).
Source: World Bank (1997).

Vulnerability is increasingly associated with locality-specific conditions, such as the general "health" of the local economy and idiosyncratic factors. Poverty in the poorer "comunas" (districts) cannot be fully explained by individual household characteristics such as levels of education, age, occupation, gender, economic sector employment, or rural or urban location. Thus, it appears that poverty is clustered in a spatially related sense, having a strong "neighborhood" or interaction effect. Household income is influenced not only by the education level of the head of households, but also by the level of education, occupation, and other variables of the related social group (family, friends, and neighbors). Identifying the poorest groups, and understanding these interrelationships, is fundamental to the design of appropriate policies for reducing poverty.

Inter-regional Distribution of Income: A Convergent Pattern

In examining the evolution of poverty since 1987 (based on the CASEN survey data with the adjustments reported earlier), we observe that pov-

Table 6-5. Poverty by Region as Measured by the Headcount Ratio, 1987–94

(percent, poverty line L)

Region	1987	1990	1992	1994	Percentage of total population
I	50.3	40.1	37.1	33.9	2.5
II	47.6	40.5	35.1	36.4	3.1
III	49.9	38.1	34.3	39.1	1.7
IV	61.9	57.3	47.3	44.7	3.7
V	47.6	46.4	34.9	32.4	10.4
VI	57.4	48.3	42.8	46.1	5.2
VII	60.2	54.4	48.3	48.3	6.3
VIII	62.6	61.2	48.3	46.2	13.1
IX	69.7	55.7	53.4	43.6	5.8
X	65.6	50.2	42.5	46.8	7.1
XI	35.1	41.3	36.1	38.7	0.6
XII	30.6	40.4	38.6	19.9	1.0
Metropolitan (Santiago)	41.0	32.9	24.7	21.6	39.5
Country	51.3	44.3	36.0	33.9	—

Source: CASEN household surveys in 1987, 1990, 1992, and 1994. Data based on headcount for individuals. See World Bank (1997, vol. 2, A table 12).

erty was reduced in 12 of the 13 regions (table 6-5). However, the rate of reduction was uneven, with Gran Santiago showing a much faster reduction in poverty than the remaining regions (48 percent compared with 25 percent). As measured by the headcount ratio, poverty reduction in Chile is largely dominated by the fall in poverty in Gran Santiago.

The dramatic reduction in the number of poor in Santiago is not matched by a reduction in poverty as measured according to the depth or intensity of poverty. Thus, in terms of reducing the absolute number of poor, Santiago has clearly been more successful. In terms of reducing both the depth and severity of poverty, the regions have done as well as Santiago.

An analysis comparing regional GDP per capita (from national accounts) with regional income (CASEN survey) during 1987–94 reveals several important issues. First, although there are clear regional disparities in both measures, these disparities are not very large. For example, the Gini coefficient for regional GDP per capita during 1987–94 is quite low, never reaching a value above 0.3, and it is even lower for per capita income, at levels of 0.14 or less (table 6-6). This means that the regional dimension is not likely to be a very important cause of the great disparities in individual or house-

Table 6-6. Per Capita Regional GDP and Income, 1987–94
(1994 US$)

Region	1987 GDP	1987 Income	1990 GDP	1990 Income	1992 GDP	1992 Income	1994 GDP	1994 Income	Annual percentage growth GDP	Annual percentage growth Income
I	3,151	1,447	3,107	1,927	3,382	1,888	3,609	1,943	1.5	4.9
II	5,101	1,452	6,218	1,827	6,823	1,704	6,966	1,820	3.6	3.7
III	2,492	1,388	2,755	1,932	3,518	2,032	3,945	1,565	6.3	3.1
IV	1,558	1,055	1,883	1,277	2,083	1,469	2,216	1,547	4.2	6.0
V	2,074	1,618	2,457	1,577	2,623	2,085	2,848	2,027	4.1	3.9
VI	2,716	1,251	2,809	1,397	3,072	1,705	3,259	1,607	2.5	4.0
VII	1,511	1,288	1,709	1,532	2,163	1,671	2,314	1,587	5.4	3.3
VIII	1,968	1,234	2,182	1,208	2,386	1,500	2,633	1,678	4.0	4.9
IX	955	1,044	1,061	1,436	1,145	1,271	1,223	1,834	4.3	10.1
X	1,328	1,138	1,565	1,695	1,623	1,772	1,819	1,720	4.8	7.2
XI	2,128	2,001	2,128	1,689	2,357	1,840	2,336	1,744	1.9	-1.7
XII	6,533	1,906	6,550	1,786	6,181	1,857	5,752	2,228	-1.3	2.5
Metropolitan	2,547	2,008	2,955	2,281	3,399	2,850	3,606	2,956	4.9	6.0
Country	2,277 (1636)	1,582	2,603 (1821)	1,808	2,918 (2,105)	2,153	3,115 (2,293)	2,237	4.3	5.3
Coefficient of variation	0.58	0.23	0.56	0.17	0.51	0.20	0.47	0.20		
Theil index	0.14	0.02	0.13	0.01	0.12	0.02	0.10	0.02		
Gini coefficient	0.29	0.13	0.28	0.10	0.26	0.10	0.25	0.09		

Note: Figures in parentheses correspond to the per capita final consumption of the households, as computed from national accounts.
Source: Income measures are from Ferreira and Litchfield (1996) based on CASEN national survey. GDP measures are from regional accounts of the Central Bank.

hold income. This is confirmed by a regional decomposition of overall inequality (World Bank 1997, vol. 1, chap. 2).

Second, the three indicators of income dispersion used (the Gini coefficient, Theil index, and coefficient of variation) indicate a lower regional variability of income than that of per capita GDP. This suggests that interregional transfers tend to smooth out the potential income variabilities due to differences in productive capacities of the regions. Regression analysis also suggests interregional convergence for GDP per capita and (although the evidence is less strong) income per capita.

Third, throughout the period there are regions that are net receivers of transfers from other regions. These are Regions 9, 10, and Gran Santiago (Region 7 was a receiver during 1987–92). As expected, the regions that generate the largest net transfers to other regions are R-2, followed by R-3 and R-12. These are regions rich in natural resources. Except for Santiago, regions that consistently were net receivers were among the poorest, such as R-9 and R-10 in the early period; in recent years they made considerable improvements. By contrast, Region 4 has remained one of the two poorest in the country, while continuing to be a source of net transfers to the rest of the country.

The allocation of public expenditures and investment by region should have influenced the evolution of income distribution across regions. After all, an important fraction of social expenditures in Chile is channeled through municipalities. This relationship could not be measured because the data on social expenditures do not include social expenditures by municipalities for the period studied.

A popular notion put forth by policymakers in Chile is that the share of public social expenditures to a region should be approximately equal to the share of the region in overall poverty. This criterion, however, does not necessarily coincide with a cost-effective allocation if the marginal cost of reducing poverty varies considerably across regions. A socially optimal criterion would allocate more social expenditures to regions where poverty can be reduced more effectively.

Labor Market and Education Policies

Key Policy Factors that Influence Poverty Reduction

In a period of rapid economic growth in Chile, successive governments' policies and programs to reduce poverty have yielded positive results. Targeted programs of social assistance have been enhanced, and an increasing share of the budget has been allocated to education. Since 1990 the real minimum wage has increased dramatically. In addition, the country has significantly readjusted its productive structure, consistently using an outward-oriented growth strategy. Taking advantage of regional growth data, we attempted to isolate the effect of key factors, including growth and output composition and policy variables (social investment, education, and minimum wage), in order to derive a quantitative measure of the importance of these variables to changes in the poverty level during 1987–94.

The modeling of the (net) effects of these policy-related variables on the reduction of poverty suggests the following:

a) Growth in labor income per capita (wages plus self-employed income per capita) has had a major impact on poverty reduction. By contrast, growth of nonlabor income (transfers, pensions, rental income, government transfers) has not had a significant impact on poverty reduction. It appears that fast overall growth has a strong poverty-reducing effect by increasing labor income, and that the trend toward a gradual increase of the share of labor in national GDP is, therefore, contributing to the alleviation of poverty.

b) Income inequality is very stable over time and in general is not very responsive to changes in most of the variables considered, including education.

c) Contrary to what is commonly believed to be true, the dynamics of growth in Chile has reduced the dependency of the economy on primary outputs (as measured by the share of agriculture, forestry, mining, and fisheries in GDP). According to our analysis, ceteris paribus, regions with a higher share of primary output have a higher incidence of poverty, after controlling for other factors that affect poverty. A higher share of primary output induced a reduction in labor income, resulting in a poverty-increasing effect. The open economy strategy has reduced the dependency of the economy on primary output during 1987–94, resulting in a positive effect on poverty reduction.

Minimun Wage

The minimum wage (in real terms) increased by about 40 percent over the period 1987 to 1994. In 1987 the minimum wage was roughly 25 percent of per capita GDP. By 1996 it had grown to 40 percent of per capita GDP, comparable to the share in the United States. The net effect of the minimum wage on poverty over the period was determined by three partial effects: (i) the direct effect, which was poverty reducing; (ii) the indirect effect through employment, which was poverty increasing; and (iii) an additional indirect effect through per capita labor income, which was also poverty increasing. As the real minimum wage increased, the effect of (i) weakened, while the effects of (ii) and (iii) strengthened.[2]

The income effect (i) raises the per capita income of those households close to the poverty line; the members of those households remain employed after the wage increase, regardless of whether the minimum wage is above or below the poverty line. The employment effect (ii) has the opposite effect: it increases poverty. Families that were originally slightly above the poverty line become poor if one or more of their members lose their employment as a consequence of the lower demand induced by the higher minimum wage. The net effect on the headcount of poverty depends on the relative strength of these two effects. If the minimum wage is low vis-à-vis the market wage, the negative employment effect could be weak because only a small proportion of the labor force is affected by the minimum wage in this case. Furthermore, at this low wage employers do not have a strong incentive to invest in unskilled-labor-saving technology. On the other hand, the enforcement of the minimum wage is easier at this very low wage, and thus the income effect could be stronger. As the real minimum wage increases, firms in the formal sector have a stronger incentive to invest in labor-saving techniques, and the income effect becomes weaker as a larger proportion of the unskilled jobs are shifted to the informal sector, where enforcement of the minimum wage is more difficult.

Thus, there is a U-shaped relationship between poverty and the real minimum wage. The turning point in Chile, when the (negative) employment effect dominates, appears to be around 1994. Given the low initial level of the minimum wage, the 40 percent increase in the minimum wage during 1987–94 is estimated to have induced a 4.4 percent reduction in poverty (out of a total of 34 percent in poverty reduction).[3]

There is virtual consensus in Chile regarding an elasticity of labor demand with respect to the average wage of –0.2. In the early 1990s about 15 percent of the labor force was directly affected by the minimum wage.

---

2. The econometric analysis of these relationships is presented in World Bank (1997, vol. 2, annex 3).

3. The possible trade-off between the direct and indirect effects was analyzed using both the headcount and intensity of poverty (FGT) numbers, with no significant difference between the two.

Hence, a 10 percent increase in the minimum wage is assumed to cause an increase in the average wage of about 1.5 percent. The effect on employment is of the order of –0.3 percent. A higher minimum wage relative to average market wage (or GDP per capita) affects an increasing fraction of the labor force, and thus has a greater impact on the average wage. For example, if 30 percent of the labor force is directly affected by the minimum wage, a 10 percent increase in the minimum wage will have an employment reduction effect of 0.6 percent instead of 0.3 percent. This implies an increase of over 10 percent in the unemployment rate, mostly affecting the lowest income households. When this occurs, the minimum wage becomes counterproductive as a tool for poverty reduction.

In general, the question is not whether the minimum wage is a poor instrument for poverty reduction, but rather at what level does it become detrimental? An analysis of the period between 1987 and 1994 indicates that the level of the minimum wage was moderate enough to be beneficial. However, over the next two years the real minimum wage continued to increase at a much faster pace than did per capita GDP, and a continuation of this trend could become counterproductive in terms of employment and earnings of the poorest groups.

Labor Markets and Income Inequality

The analysis of relevant labor market indicators such as unemployment, earnings, and job and income security yielded the following key findings.

LABOR EARNINGS. Using decile groups by household per capita income, we first examined the trends in average labor earnings per employed worker. These trends conform closely to those found for household income and income per equivalent adult. Between 1987 and 1990, average real labor earnings increased by approximately 30 percent for the poorest 10 percent of households, about 20 percent for the median class, and about 30 percent for the richest 10 percent (table 6-7). The ratio of the richest to the poorest groups rose marginally to 14.5 in 1990. Between 1990 and 1992, real earnings rose by about 16 percent. Disaggregated, however, these real earnings rose by 28 percent for the poorest group, about 13 percent for the median group, and 22 percent for the richest 10 percent. The ratio of earnings of the richest to the poorest groups fell to 13.9 in 1992. Between 1992 and 1994, earnings fell for the top and bottom quintile groups, while they rose modestly for the middle groups. The ratio of earnings of the richest to the poorest group stayed steady at about 14.

Table 6-7. Average Labor Earnings of Workers 14 to 65
Years of Age, 1987, 1990, 1992, and 1994
(1994 pesos)

Decile group	1987	1990	1992	1994
1	22,574	29,090	37,118	35,569
2	33,798	44,492	52,114	51,267
3	38,210	52,682	59,447	58,850
4	48,546	59,115	64,928	66,320
5	52,205	64,512	72,082	72,220
6	61,635	70,784	79,725	82,423
7	68,892	80,801	93,354	94,625
8	87,172	101,781	117,842	119,195
9	123,018	141,508	170,320	173,323
10	322,247	422,844	516,206	494,261
Average	99,728	124,650	144,889	142,324
Ratio of 10:1	14.3	14.5	13.9	13.9

Note: Decile groups were created using household per capita income as defined in World Bank (1997, vol. 2, annex 1).

These findings suggest that inequality remained roughly constant between 1987 and 1992, with some redistribution away from the richest 10 percent and poorest 30 percent of households and toward the middle and upper-middle classes between 1992 and 1994. It also appears that autonomous transfers prevented a decrease in household per capita income for decile groups 2 and 3, despite declines in real earnings per worker.

WAGE INEQUALITY: A WIDENING GAP? Openness to international trade and wage inequality is emerging as a controversial and important policy issue for Latin America (and the United States). New literature examines whether trade liberalization reduces or increases wage inequality in middle-income countries (such as Chile). The conventional wisdom in the past has been that openness to trade in developing countries tends to increase the demand for unskilled labor relative to skilled labor, and thus reduces wage inequality. This is supported by the evidence in East Asia. However, according to Donald Robbins (1994, 1995), the evidence from studies for Latin America and particularly for Chile suggests an increasing wage inequality.

Adrian Woods (1997) concludes that it is difficult to establish a convincing causal link between openness and wage inequality in Latin America. Influential factors in the evolution of relative wages of the skilled versus unskilled include (a) trade liberalization; (b) labor market liberalization;

(c) the entry of low-wage countries (such as China, India, and Indonesia) into world exports since the early 1980s and the 1990s; and (d) technological change (which seems to favor skilled workers). Woods (1997) presents evidence that contradicts statements by Robbins and others that wage inequality between the skilled and unskilled has widened in Chile. Although wage inequality widened for a period in the 1980s, it did not over a longer time frame.

Table 6-8 lists two measures of wage inequality calculated using hourly wages for males who are working full time (that is, at least 35 hours per week). The data show that both the Gini coefficient and the 90-10 spread measures of wage inequality rose to a high of 0.58 and 4.6, respectively in 1987–88, and have declined since to 0.45 and 3.3. Since 1970 the measures track each other closely. Both measures, especially the Gini coefficient, exhibit shorter term sensitivity; for example, the Gini coefficient drops sharply during bad economic circumstances (1975 and 1982). The year 1987 marks a break with the past in both direction and in association with the economy's health. Wage inequality begins to decrease during a period of rapid growth. By 1996 the Gini coefficient for wage inequality was the same as during the Allende years, while the 90-10 spread was only marginally higher. The period since 1987 is marked by a significant decline in earnings inequality. This change, not previously noted in the literature, suggests that the problem of wage inequality does not actually require urgent corrective measures, as many currently claim.

RATES OF RETURN TO SCHOOLING. Using a human capital earnings function developed by Jacob Mincer (1958), we examined the trends in the returns to education between 1960 and 1996. Because these functions are best estimated for those for whom work experience is well measured, returns to education are computed only for full-time male workers in Greater Santiago.

The rates of return increase from about 11 percent in 1960 to about 17 percent in 1987–88, but then decline to about 13 percent by 1996. Cyclical patterns are also similar to those for wage inequality measures. Rates of return fall during "bad" times (1975–76 and 1981–82) and rise during periods of economic prosperity.

The effectiveness of education depends on whether the high returns to education are available to workers from relatively disadvantaged households. To shed some light on this issue, we computed rates of return for workers in different earnings classes. Three main results are evident. First, rates of return to education are systematically higher for higher quantiles. In Santiago the rates of returns for males are about 10 percent for the 0.10

Table 6-8. Measures of Wage Inequality for Full-Time Male Workers, 1960–96

Measure	1960	1962	1969	1975	1980	1982	1985	1987	1990	1991	1992	1993	1994	1995	1996
Gini coefficient	0.425	0.455	0.480	0.411	0.491	0.512	0.515	0.576	0.539	0.524	0.474	0.454	0.459	0.463	0.454
90-10 percentile spread	2.1	2.5	2.9	3.1	3.3	3.9	3.3	4.6	4.2	3.6	3.8	3.4	3.3	3.2	3.3

Source: Montenegro (1996) based on Universidad de Chile (surveys for Greater Santiago) and CASEN.

quantile, about 12 percent for the 0.25 quantile, about 15 percent for the 0.75 quantile, and about 18 percent for the 0.90 quantile regressions. Second, for all quantiles, rates of return are higher for higher education levels. CASEN data indicate that the rate of return to 0–4 years of education are about 3–5 percent, rising to 5–8 percent, 8–15 percent, and 15–25 percent for groups with 5–8, 9–12, and 13+ years of schooling, respectively. Finally, rates of return are higher for higher quantile groups for levels of schooling exceeding 4 years. For example, while the 0.10 quantile regressions yield rates of return of about 4 percent for 5–8 years of schooling, the corresponding rate for the 0.90 quantile is about 6–10 percent. Similarly, the rate of return for 13 or more years of schooling is about 16 percent for the 0.10 quantile, and 26 percent for the 0.90 quantile.

Not surprisingly, workers from poor households also have low levels of education. Average schooling levels have increased by a remarkable 1.25 years in the 8 years between 1987 and 1994. Education levels have increased for all groups in every survey year, except for the poorest 10 percent of households between 1992 and 1994. Differences in schooling across groups, however, did not narrow between 1987 and 1994. For example, the 0.90-0.10 schooling spread remains more than 5 years. Average schooling levels for the bottom decile group (about 6–7 years) are a little more than one-half of the levels for the richest group (11–12 years). This implies that while the average new entrant to the labor force from the bottom one-third of households has at most some secondary education, the average labor force participant from the top one-third of households will have completed at least a few years of postsecondary education.

Unemployment and Income Inequality

Worker unemployment is an important determinant of a household's relative position in the per capita income distribution. As expected, unemployment is significantly correlated with being in a poor household. Workers in the poorest 10 percent of households are almost four times more likely to be unemployed than is the average worker. This ratio does not change significantly over the years, indicating that unemployment is always critical in determining household income. Short-term fluctuations in unemployment by decile group defy simple characterizations, however. Between 1987 and 1992, average male unemployment rates fell steadily from almost 9 percent to 4.7 percent, and then rose to about 6 percent in 1994. Female unemployment rates are higher, but they exhibit similar trends. These changes are fairly uniform across income class for men between 1987 and

1992. Between 1992 and 1994, however, male unemployment rates rose by 25 percent or more for the 1st, 4th, 5th, and 10th income decile, and rose marginally or fell for the other groups. Patterns for women are similar to those for men, although female unemployment rates for the poorest three groups rose by roughly the same proportion between 1992 and 1994.

The lower labor earnings of workers in poor households are partly due to lower levels of schooling, and partly due to lower returns on this schooling. The lower returns on years of schooling may be attributable to education-related factors or labor-market-related considerations. For any given level of schooling, the type of schooling acquired by poor segments of society may have lower returns. For example, students from poor households are more likely to enroll in (poorer quality) municipal schools at the primary and secondary levels, and in vocational-technical rather than humanistic-scientific education at the secondary level. CASEN data indicate that for all income groups, private rates of return to education are considerably higher for postsecondary education (13 or more years of schooling) than for secondary and primary education levels, and the poor are less likely to attain that level of education. The rates of return to education, for any given level of schooling, are lower for poor workers. While this can be explained by differences in education quality and type, it is also possible that this is because of labor market discrimination against job-seekers from poor households. "Discrimination" against less privileged job-seekers occurs in every country but is difficult to quantify. Anecdotal evidence for Chile appears to indicate that this may result in restricted access to high wage jobs to workers from poor households.

Job Insecurity

"Precariousness" normally refers to the uncertainty surrounding employment. The most accurate way to measure "precariousness" of employment is to estimate expected tenure on current job (that is, the stability of employment), which depends critically on the probability of losing one's job. In fact, a more meaningful proxy of the uncertainty in the labor market is the "precariousness" of earnings (that is, of a worker being without labor income and related benefits). This depends largely on how long a worker is likely to be without work (the duration of unemployment). The proxy is best estimated as the probability of finding a job in a fixed period of time, using the sample of unemployed job-seekers. In either case, because precariousness refers to the probability of a change in employment status, the relevant indicators measuring precariousness are flows, not stocks.

Using the approach suggested by Haindl (1984), the model used to address this question of precariousness is therefore a labor flows model, which converts reported data on current period stocks (for example, labor supply, employment, unemployment) into current period flows (for example, probability of exiting unemployment) and prospective indicators such as expected tenure.

An analysis of unemployment rates and duration during 1962–95 and the expected length of unemployment shows that expected job tenure declined from about 7 years in the 1960s to 3 years in the mid-1980s. Since 1987, however, expected tenure has risen 50 percent to 4.5 years and appears to be increasing (World Bank 1997, vol. 2, table 7, annex). Thus, while concerns about the "precariousness" of unemployment appear to have been well founded between 1960 and 1985, they are unwarranted since 1990.

In part, the declining trend in expected tenure before 1985 can be explained by a steady increase in first-time job-seekers, which rose from about 25,000 in 1980 to 100,000 in 1985. First-time job-seekers are more likely to change jobs than are re-entrants. With a decline in the absolute number of labor force entrants, it is likely that expected tenure will continue to increase. Finally, shorter term fluctuations in expected tenure are explained by cyclical fluctuations in labor demand. For example, expected tenure fell during the recession years of 1975–76 and 1982–83. Years of economic prosperity are associated with increases in expected tenure, and this basic relationship has not changed over the years.

When accurately measured, therefore, "precariousness" of employment does not appear to be increasing. While it is legitimate that workers, policymakers, and nongovernmental organizations are concerned about job permanency, these findings provide a compelling argument that changes in labor legislation to reduce involuntary turnover may not be necessary.

If job changes occur frequently, but workers do not spend long periods unemployed, employment can be classified as "precarious," but labor earnings may be quite stable. To determine if Chilean workers have experienced increases in instability of earnings, we analyzed the changes in the duration of expected unemployment and the probability of exiting unemployment (table 6-9). We found that unemployment rates rose from 5 percent in 1962 to about 16 percent in 1974–75, and peaked at about 22 percent in 1982–83. Since then unemployment rates have fallen sharply to less than 7 percent. The duration of unemployment rose from less than 3 months to about 10 months in the two decades since 1962, and has since fallen to below 3 months. The probability of finding a job is perhaps the best indicator of the likelihood that a person will have or not have labor earnings. The

Table 6-9. Estimates of Unemployment Rates and Duration, 1962–95

Year	Rate %	Probability of finding job in				Expected length (months)
		1 mo. %	3 mos. %	6 mos. %	1 yr. %	
1962	5.1	26.7	60.6	84.4	97.6	2.7
1969	6.2	20.1	48.9	73.9	93.2	4.0
1975	16.1	9.6	26.2	45.5	70.3	9.4
1980	11.8	16.7	42.2	66.6	88.9	5.0
1982	22.1	8.9	24.5	43.0	67.5	10.2
1985	16.4	12.7	33.6	55.9	80.5	6.8
1987	12.2	15.6	39.8	63.8	86.9	5.4
1988	10.9	19.8	48.4	73.4	92.9	4.0
1989	9.1	21.3	51.3	76.2	94.4	3.7
1990	9.6	23.1	54.6	79.4	95.7	3.3
1991	7.4	23.4	55.0	79.8	95.9	3.3
1992	6.0	25.0	57.9	82.3	96.9	3.0
1993	6.3	26.8	60.9	84.7	97.7	2.7
1994	6.8	26.2	59.8	83.8	97.4	2.8
1995	6.8	26.1	59.7	83.8	97.4	2.8

Note: The unemployment rate is averaged for March, June, September, and December. It is calculated using Haindl's labor flow model.

Source: Haindl, Gill, and Sapelli (1997); calculated using Universidad de Chile surveys for Greater Santiago.

probability of finding a job in 3 months or less was about 60 percent in 1962, falling to about 30 percent in 1982–83, and rising to about 60 percent again in 1993. The probability of a worker joining the ranks of the long-term unemployed (defined as being unemployed for more than a year) was negligible in 1962, rose significantly in the 1970s and early 1980s, but declined to almost zero by 1995.

Between 1989 and 1995, expected job security increased, unemployment rates and the duration of unemployment fell significantly, and long-term unemployment became practically nonexistent. The data flatly contradict the proposition that employment and labor earnings became increasingly uncertain during the past decade.

Labor Policy Implications

Aside from the obvious implications of these findings—that present labor policies are successful to the extent that they have yielded positive results—these policy recommendations based on labor market analysis can be made.

a) Increasing the cost to employers of dismissals would likely be counterproductive. In the presence of means-tested income transfers, a system of mandated severance payments, and the low level short duration
   of unemployment, an unemployment compensation system may not
   be needed in Chile.
b) The usefulness of further increases in minimum wages in reducing
   poverty or income inequality is diminishing rapidly.
c) Improvements in the *quality* of education appear to be twice as effective as improvements in *access* in reducing the gap between the poor
   and the nonpoor, and the returns to improvements in education quality are largely obtained at low levels of schooling (0–8 years).
d) Trends in wage inequality and returns to education may appear at
   first blush to justify higher levels of schooling in order to reduce inequality. However, further improvements in access to schooling by
   the poor will have relatively modest effects on earnings inequality,
   and more important, only at grade 9 and above.
e) International experience suggests that public training programs do
   not have a significant effect on earnings inequality of employed workers. However, well-targeted training programs and job search assistance may help some unemployed workers find jobs. The results show
   that while these programs are always costly, their impact differs greatly
   from country to country. Chile's training programs appear to be well
   run, and some of the programs have been evaluated. Both from an
   equity and an efficiency point of view, these training programs should
   be systematically evaluated (using control groups), and such programs
   should be tightly targeted to those among the poor who are found to
   benefit the most.

Social Policies in Chile: A Distributional Analysis

Expenditures on Social Programs

Chile regularly reports two social expenditure figures: gross expenditures
(the total amount spent in public programs) and net (or fiscal) social expenditures (which exclude contributions and copayments from beneficiaries). The latter is a more reliable guide to social benefits from public funds,
since in areas such as health, net expenditures account for less than half of
gross expenditures. Overall, social security is the biggest component accounting for 43 percent of total gross social spending in 1995. The balance

Table 6-10. Incidence of Social Expenditures by Household Income Quintiles, 1992

	Household income quintile					
Expenditure category	Q1	Q2	Q3	Q4	Q5	Q1 + Q2
Households	20	20	20	20	20	40
Individuals	24	22	20	18	16	46
Money income	5	9	12	18	55	14
Social security	4	9	15	25	47	13
Education	27	23	19	16	15	50
Primary	35	27	18	13	7	62
Secondary	24	26	22	17	11	50
Tertiary	9	12	17	24	38	21
Health	32	26	21	15	6	58
Housing	20	18	19	23	19	38
Cash benefits	33	24	18	13	12	57
Total social expenditure	16	16	17	21	30	32
Total excluding social security	29	24	19	16	16	53

Source: Larrañaga (1994).

consists of 22 percent for education, 18 percent for health, 8 percent for housing, and 9 percent for other programs (of gross social expenditures).

It is questionable whether all of the social security payments should be classified as social expenditures. Some pension payments, for example, have objectives that differ from those of other social programs, and their inclusion in this category could lead to a distorted assessment of the size and distributional impact of social expenditures. For this reason, we recommend reexamining the composition of social security expenditures as reported in the Public Finance Statistics, with the purpose of limiting the inclusion of pension payments in social security to those clearly identifiable with social objectives.

Through time, spending on education has been a relatively constant proportion of both GDP and total social expenditure. The share of expenditures on health and housing has increased in the fiscal budget, offsetting the decline in expenditures on employment programs that were phased out in the late 1980s.

Targeting of Social Expenditures

Although tabulations of the imputations for social expenditures in the form of transfers-in-kind are available by income quintiles through MIDEPLAN, it was not possible to obtain these data at the household level. As a consequence, we reluctantly confined our analysis to published data on per-capita household income quintiles. The cost of the provision of social services was used to estimate the value of benefits received by households. This method does not accurately reflect the impact of those benefits on living standards of Chilean households.

A crude index of targeting was obtained by comparing the expenditure share of the poorest two quintiles with the corresponding population share (table 6-10). On this basis, primary education, health care, and cash benefits are reasonably well targeted, although not as much as expected given the prevalence of means-tested benefits in Chile. (For example, 25 percent of cash transfers are received by households in the top two quintiles.) Other categories of social expenditures are not well targeted. Social housing is one such category, where consideration might be given to tightening the eligibility criteria to improve targeting performance.

This being said, there is evidence that the degree of targeting has in fact improved over the years. A report by A. H. Petrei (quoted in Tanzi 1996) suggests that the lowest quintile's share of total social expenditure rose from 15 percent in 1980 to 19 percent in 1990. Nevertheless, our analysis does suggest that social expenditures might be better targeted, in particular by ensuring that the allocation of social transfers be made more directly in proportion to the unmet needs of households rather than on the basis of family size alone.

A Simulation of the Tax and Benefits Incidence in 1990

To further explore the distributional impact of government revenue and expenditures, we computed simulation estimates of the marginal change in the value of the Gini index of inequality following changes in taxes and social expenditures (table 6-11). The results suggest that total social expenditure (excluding pensions) has a substantial redistributive impact, reducing the Gini coefficient by 53 percent, most of which is accounted for by elementary and secondary education followed by primary health care. The results of this exercise also confirmed that progressive income tax and regressive VAT (value added tax) payments combine to yield a tax structure that has no overall effect on inequality.

A second simulation was estimated in a different way by expressing tax payments and benefits receipts of households in each income quintile as a percentage of their autonomous or primary income. For example, social programs (education, health, and housing) were estimated to add 72 percent to primary income, or 70 percent after tax. Of the individual compo-

Table 6-11. Incidence of Tax and Social Expenditure by Quintile of Household Income, 1990

Expenditure category	Average monthly amount (pesos)	Q1	Q2	Q3	Q4	Q5	Q1 + Q2	Total	Per peso
Households		20	20	20	20	20	40		
Individuals		23	22	20	18	16	45		
Autonomous income	132,788	4	9	13	19	56	12	0.000	
Money income	134,685	4	9	13	19	55	13	−0.010	
Total tax	19,839	4	9	13	19	56	12	0.000	0.0
VAT	17,729	4	10	14	21	50	14	0.006	−0.1
Income tax	2,109	0	0	0	1	99	0	−0.005	0.8
Total social expenditure	9,776	36	28	20	12	4	64	−0.053	1.6
Cash benefits	1,897	36	25	19	12	7	61	−0.010	1.6
Noncash benefits	7,879	36	28	20	12	3	65	−0.044	1.6
Cash benefits									
Family allowance	813	22	26	21	18	14	47	−0.003	1.2
PASIS	763	45	22	19	10	3	68	−0.005	1.8
SUF	259	51	29	14	5	2	80	−0.002	2.1
Unemployment benefit	62	57	28	8	5	2	86	−0.000	2.2
Education benefits	5,180	34	27	19	13	8	61	−0.027	1.5
Preschool	433	28	29	20	14	10	56	−0.002	1.4
Elementary	2,928	36	27	18	13	7	63	−0.016	1.6
Secondary	1,061	24	26	22	17	10	51	−0.005	1.3
University	166	23	16	22	20	20	39	−0.001	1.0
PAE school meal program	592	52	27	13	5	2	80	−0.004	2.1
Net health benefits	1,857	50	35	21	6	−12	84	−0.015	2.3
Primary health care	3,146	28	25	22	17	9	52	−0.015	1.4
Maternity benefit	235	2	5	11	20	63	7	0.000	−0.2
Preventative care	304	5	13	17	24	41	18	−0.000	0.3
PNAC nutrition program	384	38	31	18	10	4	69	−0.002	1.8
FONASA contributions	−2,213	5	13	20	26	36	18	0.003	0.4
Housing benefits	842	21	23	24	20	13	44	−0.003	1.2
Housing subsidies	532	16	20	23	23	17	36	−0.002	0.9
Social housing	237	29	28	23	14	5	58	−0.001	1.6
Other housing benefits	73	27	28	27	14	4	55	−0.000	1.5

Source: World Bank calculations based on MIDEPLAN (1993) and Schkolnik (1993).

nents, education makes the largest contribution to income and has a marginal equalizing impact (as represented by a 35-point change in the Gini coefficient index) greater than the combined effect of both cash transfers and taxation. The heavy reliance on tax revenue from VAT, and the regressive nature of this tax considering the large proportion of income paid in indirect taxes by the lowest income quintile, makes the VAT an obvious candidate for attention. This analysis abstracts from some important complications. An in-depth study of taxes, not only their incidence but also collection costs, degree of distortions, and impact on savings, would be useful.

The poverty incidence analysis presented in our report suggests that modest modifications of tax and expenditure programs can achieve a greater degree of targeting and a reduction in inequality. This reduction can be achieved by using the higher expected income tax revenues (from overall growth and by reducing important tax loopholes) to reduce the uniform rate of VAT, to exempt food purchases from VAT, or to increase expenditures on cash subsidies and other well-targeted social programs.

The Main Findings and Policy Implications

What We Have Confirmed

First, the report has confirmed that even within a short period of time (1987–94), there was a significant decline in poverty. The report confirms that high economic growth is strongly and positively correlated with declining poverty. During the period 1992 to 1994 when economic growth fell, there was also a deceleration in the rate at which poverty declined.

Second, for the poorest decile group, the slowdown in growth from 11 percent in 1992 to 4 percent in 1994, and the accompanying rise in unemployment from 4.5 percent to 6 percent, actually increased this group's poverty slightly. More recently, the reduction in unemployment to rates around 4.5 percent in 1995 is likely to have reduced poverty for this group.

Third, income inequality in Chile is high by international standards. However, sustained high growth has resulted in a significant reduction in poverty despite this high level of inequality. Chile's success in reducing headcount poverty during 1987–94 rivals the performance of countries such as Korea, Indonesia, and China; it should be noted, however, that these other countries are believed to have experienced increases in inequality in the process of high economic growth.

Fourth, the reduction in poverty during 1987–94 has benefited almost all groups classified as vulnerable at the beginning of the period. While growth obviously helped those among the poor who could work, poverty reduction policies benefited even nonworkers: for example, old, poorly educated, male and female household heads in both rural and urban areas experienced significant declines in the probability of being poor.

Fifth, education is an important determinant of labor earnings and hence of household income. Differences in educational attainment account for almost one-third of overall income inequality and are by far the largest single explanatory factor.

The report confirms that the income tax is progressive, and the VAT is regressive. The combined result is a tax structure that is largely inequality-neutral. On the other hand, if public spending on pensions is excluded, total social expenditure has a substantial redistributive impact, most of which is accounted for by basic education and health care.

Overall, Chile's policy in recent years of growth with equity has been effective in reducing poverty without exacerbating income inequality. As with virtually any program, there is scope for improvement at the margin; this report attempts to draw out options for consideration by Chilean policymakers.

What We Have Refuted

First, contrary to a popular perception, income inequality did not increase during 1987–94; in fact, there is a slight improvement in the income distribution evidenced by a small decline in the Gini coefficient from 0.55 to 0.53.

Second, inequality in labor earnings declined considerably in the past decade. While the Gini coefficient for labor earnings in Gran Santiago between 1960 and 1987 rose from 0.43 to 0.58, it then fell steadily to 0.46 in 1996.

Third, refuting growing concerns about precariousness of employment and earnings, the report finds that job and income security have increased substantially since 1987. Average expected tenure on a job rose from 47 to 55 months between 1987 and 1995, and the average duration of unemployment declined from 5.5 to 2.8 months.

Fourth, allaying concerns that rapid growth has exacerbated regional income disparities, the analysis shows a convergent pattern. All indicators of inter-regional dispersion of income show a reduction between 1987 and 1994: real per capita income of the poorest region (region IX) grew by 10 percent, which is twice the national average for the period. It is reassuring to note that reductions in poverty have been shared by all regions (except region XI, which has only 0.6 percent of the country's population), and these gains have not been restricted to Gran Santiago. While Santiago did better in reducing *headcount* poverty ratios, other regions matched its performance if indicators that measure the depth of poverty are used instead.

Finally, although educational attainment of all income groups increased between 1987 and 1994, the difference in years of schooling between the richest and poorest groups increased. While the years of schooling for the poorest 20 percent increased by 0.8 years, the schooling of the richest 20 percent increased by 1.3 years.

Limitations of Our Statistical Analysis

Besides labor earnings and other income (including imputed rents of owner-occupied dwellings), measures of household income in this report include monetary transfers such as means-tested old age, disability, and family allowances, and other cash subsidies. Omitted from our income measures are welfare-enhancing improvements such as better access, lower prices, and higher quality of public utilities, which are believed to have improved more for poor than for nonpoor households.

More importantly, this income measure does not include the value of government transfers in kind, through public housing, health, and education programs, which together were 6.5 percent of GDP and 30 percent of total government expenditures in 1994. Nonavailability of household level data for all four survey years for these transfers made this adjustment impossible. Since the incidence of public spending on these programs is regarded as progressive, this results in a greater underestimation of the real income of poor households than of the nonpoor.[4]

The findings discussed above, and their policy implications, must be considered with this caveat in mind: our estimates probably overstate the level of poverty in Chile and understate its reduction over the period examined. In order to achieve the goal of "supertargeting" of public spending, policymakers will need to correct for this shortcoming in data collection.

---

4. World Bank (1997, vol. 2, annex 1) does report some of the imputations for public education and health services by household quintiles made by MIDEPLAN.

Implications for Labor Policies

The labor market has served Chile's poor well in recent years. Labor earnings have contributed more to poverty reduction than has nonlabor income (mainly transfers). While household inequality measures have not shown an improvement, inequality in labor earnings has fallen significantly since 1987. These developments may not justify inaction, but they do call for restraint in changing labor market policies.

Labor legislation that would make dismissals more costly for employers is likely to be counterproductive and could, as in other countries, increase unemployment.

An unemployment insurance system is largely unnecessary given existing severance benefit legislation, the low duration of unemployment, and the existence of means-tested transfers. Steps to introduce an unemployment insurance system should be carefully evaluated by policymakers, keeping in mind the distortions such a system can create.

While the minimum wage could be increased, further increases in the ratio of the minimum wage to per capita income are likely to result in greater unemployment and could actually worsen poverty.

Implications for Education and Training Policies

Compared with measurement of the effects of improved access to schooling (reflected in years of schooling), the benefits of improved quality of schooling are difficult to measure. Our estimates indicate, however, that increasing access to primary and secondary education yields smaller increases in earnings relative to improvements in education quality at these levels and increased access to higher education. But even access to higher education by the poor is best facilitated by raising the quality of their primary and secondary education. These findings suggest that efforts to improve education quality in municipal and private subsidized primary and secondary schools would help reduce poverty and inequality. Combined with institutional measures to improve the quality of instruction, reducing public spending on tertiary education (62 percent of which goes to the richest one-third of individuals) and allocating it to quality-enhancing initiatives at lower levels could be an effective medium-term strategy for reducing inequality of education, and hence of earnings.

The socioeconomic status of vocational-technical students is considerably lower than that of students enrolling in humanistic-scientific education programs, and secondary vocational education has lower economic returns than general education because it is more expensive. Until improvements in primary education quality for the poor have been achieved, however, measures to increase the relevance and quality of secondary vocational schools are likely to be equity enhancing.

International experience suggests that these training programs, if they are designed well, can help carefully selected groups find jobs, but they are not likely to reduce earnings inequality of employed workers. Because these programs are always expensive, Chile's training programs should be scientifically evaluated (with a control group).

Implications for Tax and Social Expenditure Policies

Introducing dual VAT rates or exemptions for goods comprising relatively large shares of the budget of poor households will raise administrative costs. Therefore, further study of the tax system is warranted, despite the regressivity of the current VAT system, if looked at in isolation.

Despite the payoff in terms of inequality reduction that a greater reliance on income taxes would yield, the current strategy of closing loopholes has the advantage of being equity enhancing and increasing tax collection efficiency.[5]

To better monitor the incidence of social spending as a whole, policymakers should reexamine the classification of what constitutes social spending. Spending on items such as pensions for public servants, for the military, and for police should not be lumped with items clearly identified with social policy objectives.

Chile's past successes in improving the efficiency of targeting notwithstanding, there is considerable scope for further improvements. They could be achieved in two ways: by allocating a greater fraction of social spending to programs that have had good targeting records (for example, primary education and health, and cash benefits, where the poorest 40 percent receive 60 percent of expenditures) and by improving targeting efficiency of programs, such as housing subsidies, which have been essentially untargeted.

---

5. The broader issue of the effect of a possible tax reform on income distribution was beyond the scope of this study. For a recent analysis on the subject for Chile, see Engel, Galetovic, and Raddatz (1997).

Despite extensive individual and household-level controls, living in poor comunas (districts) remains an important factor in accounting for the likelihood of being poor. Strong location or "neighborhood effects" on poverty deserve further study, because they expand the set of potential measures to deal with residual or hard-core poverty.

Conclusion

The debate on poverty, welfare, and income distribution in Chile is lively and complex. It is lively because it touches on sensitive issues of equity with implications for efficiency and overall growth. The debate is complex because it is about welfare and human development. Poverty and equity are usually thought of simply in terms of income or wealth. Welfare and human development are much broader concepts, which try to capture the well-being of a household, individual, or the population.

The debate is hard to resolve because poverty and inequality are difficult to measure and because of widely differing concepts of poverty, the reliability of data, and methodological complications. As a result, misconceptions of poverty and inequality are common. There is a widespread perception, for example, that reductions in poverty and inequality are the same thing. But a country can make remarkable progress—as Chile has—in reducing poverty, while at the same time making little or no improvements with regard to the distribution of income as usually measured.

Income distribution, as measured by the Gini coefficient and variants of this coefficient, changes very slowly (Deininger and Squire 1986). Thus, the success or failure of Chile's social policy should not be measured exclusively in terms of income distribution.

The priority is poverty reduction. The government contributes directly to reducing the handicap of being poor by raising the quality of education for the poor; providing medical care to poor households; improving inadequate housing and sanitation (potable water, sewerage); and instituting cash transfers to the elderly.

Poverty and income distribution are part of a broader concept of social equity. Social equity is the birthright of those children born into poor households and includes equality of opportunity. Poor children deserve the opportunity to escape the poverty their parents suffer.

Can Chile do a better job than it is doing now with respect to income distribution, continue doing as well as it has on poverty alleviation, and not seriously compromise the growth potential of the economy? The distribution of income today is the product of the distribution of endowments and the pattern of demand, and thus largely the product of past history. It is not something a government can "determine." Recognizing that income distribution is fundamentally influenced by market forces, policymakers must ask: what plausible and feasible policy alternatives can the government offer to change the final distribution per se? We hope that this study sheds light on this complex question.

References

CEPAL (United Nations Economic Commission for Latin America and the Caribbean). 1995. "La Medición de los Ingresos en la Perspectiva de los Estudios de Pobreza: El Caso de la Encuesta CASEN de Chile: 1987–1994." CEPAL Working Paper LC/R, 1604, Santiago.

Consejo Nacional para la Superacion de la Pobreza. 1966. "La Pobreza en Chile— Un Desafio de Equidad e Integracion Social." Santiago.

Cowan, Kevin, and J. de Gregorio. 1996. "Distribución y Pobreza en Chile: Estamos mal? Ha habido progresos? Hemos retrocedido?" Ministerio de Hacienda, Santiago.

Deininger, Klaus, and Lynn Squire. 1996. "A New Data Set Measuring Income Inequality." *The World Bank Economic Review* 10: 565–91.

Engel, Eduardo, Alexander Galetovic, and Claudio Raddatz. 1997. "Taxes and Income Distribution in Chile: Some Unpleasant Redistributive Arithmetic." Documentos de Trabajo No. 41, Serie Economia, Centro de Economia Aplicada, Facaultad de Ciencias Fisicas y Matematicas. Universidad de Chile, Santiago.

Ferreira, F. H. G., and J. A. Litchfield. 1996. "Growing Apart: Inequality and Poverty Trends in Brazil in the 1980s." LSE STICERD DARP Discussion Paper 23. London.

Haindl, Erik. 1984. "Un Modelo para la Determinación de Flujos y Parametros Dinamicos en el Mercado de Trabajo." *Encuentro Anual de Economistas*. Santiago.

Haindl, Erik, Indermit Gill, and Claudio Sapelli. 1997. "Is Employment in Chile Becoming More Precarious? Evidence from a Labor Flows Model." World Bank, Latin America and the Caribbean Region, Washington, D.C.

Larrañaga, Osvaldo. 1994. "Pobreza, Crecimiento y Desigualdad: Chile, 1987–92." *Revista de Analisis Economico* 9 (2): 69–92.

MIDEPLAN. 1993. "Programas Sociales: Su Impacto en los Hogares Chilenos." CASEN 1990. Minesterio de Planificación y Cooperación, Santiago.

———. 1996. "Balance de Seis Años de las Politicas Sociales: 1990–96." Santiago.

Mincer, Jacob. 1958. "Investment in Human Capital and Personal Income Distribution." *Journal of Political Economy* 66 (August): 281–302.

Montenegro, Claudio. 1996. "The Structure of Wages in Chile, 1960–1993: An Application of Quantile Regressions." Inter-American Development Bank, Washington, D.C.

Robbins, Donald. 1994. "Relative Wage Structure in Chile, 1957–1992: Changes in the Structure of Demand for Schooling." Estudios de Economia, Universidad de Chile, Santiago.

————. 1995. "Trade, Trade Liberalization, and Inequality in Latin America and East Asia: Synthesis of Seven Country Studies." Harvard Institute for International Development, Cambridge, Mass.

Schkolnik, Mariana. 1993. "Estudio de Incidencia Presupuestaria: El Caso de Chile." División de Desarrollo Economico, CEPAL, Santiago.

Tanzi, Vito. 1996. "Fiscal Policy and Income Distribution." Presented to the Inter-national Development Bank Workshop on Income Distribution, Santiago, Chile.

Woods, Adrian. 1997. "Openness and Wage Inequality in Developing Countries: The Latin American Challenge to East Asian Conventional Wisdom." *The World Bank Economic Review* 11 (1, January).

World Bank. 1997. "Poverty and Income Distribution in High-Growth Economy: Chile 1987–95." Report No. 16377 CH, Chile Country Department, Washington, D.C.

Part III

Governance

7

Effectiveness of the State and Development Lessons from the Chilean Experience

Mario Marcel

The effectiveness of the state can be understood as the capability of public institutions to deliver the public goods and services sought by its citizens. From that standpoint, state effectiveness is a primary determinant of the outcome of public policies in areas as diverse as macroeconomic policy coordination, the struggle against poverty, education, and regulation of natural monopolies.

This chapter draws heavily on the author's experience as Director of Budget in the Chilean Ministry of Finance, and as a professor in the Public Management course of the Graduate Program in Public Policy, Industrial Engineering Department, University of Chile. The author is grateful to Tomás Campero, Carmen Celedón, Nelson Guzmán, Roberto Jiménez, Carlos Pardo, and Luis Zaviezo for their inspiring support over the years. The support of Carolina Tohá in the preparation of this essay is gratefully acknowledged, as well as contributions from Rodolfo Sepúlveda, Marianela Armijo, Antonia Silva, and Javier Game. Translation support was provided by the Inter-American Development Bank staff. Comments from David Shand and Edgardo Boeninger on a previous version were particularly enlightening. The views expressed by the author in this chapter are, of course, his own.

265

Even first-rate policies will be stymied on the drawing board if a country's public institutions are unable to rise to their tasks. Countries, as we know, do not operate on the strength of good intentions. By the same token, a country whose public policies have helped to propel economic growth and improve social conditions necessarily had state institutions equipped to administer and enforce those policies.

According to recent studies, an effective state can by itself spur growth and investment: in international comparisons the relation between the two has been shown to be statistically robust even after indicators of the quality of policies are factored out.

In the past ten years, Chile achieved remarkable growth rates and made impressive gains in stability and poverty reduction. How much of the credit for this success should go to the state? If, to a large extent, the advances are the fruit of a quarter-century of deep-seated structural reforms, how much did effective state institutions do to move the reform programs forward?

Rather surprisingly, these questions have rarely been raised. In examinations of Chile's track record, it is taken as a given that able policymakers have worked with a well-oiled implementation apparatus at hand. Anyone who has worked inside a public institution, either in Chile or anywhere else, knows that such an assumption is dubious at best.

There is growing recognition in recent years of the crucial part that institutions, regulations, and a state's organizational culture play in a nation's progress. This idea has been brought firmly into the mainstream of economic development thinking with the publication of the *World Development Report 1997*, which is devoted to the question of the effectiveness of the state. According to the foreword to the report,

> the determining factor behind these contrasting developments is the effectiveness of the state. An effective state is vital for the provision of the goods and services—and the rules and institutions—that allow markets to flourish and people to lead healthier, happier lives. Without it, sustainable development, both economic and social, is impossible. Many said the same thing fifty years ago, but then they tended to mean that development had to be state-provided. The message of experience since then is rather different: that the state is central to economic and social development, not as a direct provider of growth but as a partner, catalyst, and facilitator (World Bank 1997, 1).

A review of Chile's experience on this front is thus both timely and essential for an understanding of the decisive changes in the country's development strategy and what they have meant for its economic and social performance over the past decade. The examination of Chile's successes and missteps along the way, as well as its pending challenges, can provide useful lessons for Chile and for other countries that are making their way down the rough road of reforms.

This chapter will examine the effectiveness of Chile's public sector. The next two sections follow the World Bank's methodology to examine the relationship between the state's role and its capability, as well as the factors that determine that capability. Such factors have been grouped into four dimensions of public sector operations: institutional structure, human-resources management, financial management, and control systems. The chapter reviews some of the Frei government's initiatives for the modernization of public sector management. The last section discusses lessons that can be drawn from this experience that might prove useful to other developing countries. To that same end it examines the World Bank's analytical approach to see if it holds up in a fast-growth setting like the one in Chile in recent years.

In keeping with this approach, the chapter confines itself to public policies that had an impact on state roles or capabilities. The focus is on the historical, institutional, cultural, and legal factors that have determined the effectiveness of the state in these different spheres.

The Effectiveness of the State in Chile: A Preliminary Appraisal

International Comparisons of State Effectiveness

It is no easy task to assess the effectiveness of the state in Chile, or indeed in any country. The very concept of "effectiveness" suggests a standard of comparison given by the state's roles and objectives and the tasks entrusted to it; but these mandates, as we know, are far from direct or precise. In every country there is dissatisfaction, in one way or another, with the workings of government, but the source of such dissatisfaction varies widely and may, in fact, be the opposite in any two countries at any given time. In one country the public may be weary of cumbersome state regulations; in another the citizenry may be entreating the government to restrain corruption and discretionality. Echoing the diversity of views of the state from diverse groups are the differing—and perhaps contradictory—views that individuals may hold of the state, from their standpoints as either taxpayers, subjects, or clients.[1]

Against such a wide arrangement of possibilities, this chapter proposes only to offer some indicators of the effectiveness of the state in Chile as compared with the situation in other countries.

COMPETITIVENESS STUDIES. According to recent studies, the Chilean state has played a pivotal role in making the country globally competitive. The *World Competitiveness Report 1996* ranks Chile in fifth place among 45 countries for "government" (IMD International 1996).[2] This was Chile's highest ranking; it ranked ninth for "management" and thirteenth for "overall competitiveness." Allowing for the limitations of this type of analysis, it would appear that the state's performance has helped, and definitely not hindered, Chile's competitive standing.[3]

Table 7-1 shows some of the factors that would account for Chile's strong showing vis-à-vis its competitors. Preeminent on the assets side are macroeconomic and institutional factors: few government controls and infrequent state interference in business activity; dependable fiscal and monetary policies that are flexible enough to adapt to changing circumstances, and openness in public sector contracting. The country's macroeconomic strengths fall mainly in the area of public finance because of factors such as government consumption expenditure, balanced budgets, and government employment.

On the liabilities side are sluggish improvements in the standard of living and in the material conditions that are part of development: education, training, health, and human development.[4] They affect the resources the state is able to mobilize as well as the content of public policies.

---

1. For an examination of the different relationships between the state and the citizenry, see Marcel and Tohá (1997, part II.1).

2. Twenty-five of the 45 countries examined are industrialized OECD member countries. Of the other 20, 7 are in Southeast Asia and 5 in Latin America (Argentina, Brazil, Chile, Colombia, and Venezuela).

3. The World Economic Forum's *Global Competitiveness Report* came out with similar findings for 1996: overall, Chile ranked 18th among 49 countries, but 4th for government and 11th for management. The picture was less bright for infrastructure and civil institutions, which earned it 27th and 32nd place, respectively.

4. Most of these variables are measured in absolute terms and thus reflect differences in the economic capability of states and countries. For instance, public expenditure on education is measured in absolute terms (outlays per student), which means that industrialized nations take all the top positions in the ranking.

Table 7-1. Chile: Government Competitiveness

Criteria	Chile's ranking among 45 countries
Employee's social security contribution	1
Government employment	2
Price controls[a]	2
Capital and property tax revenues	2
Government subsidies	3
Antitrust laws and fair competition[a]	3
Central Bank[b]	3
Central government budget surplus/deficit	4
Government final consumption expenditure	6
Environment laws and regulations[a]	6
Flexibility of hiring and firing practices[a]	6
Openness of public sector contracts[a]	7
Flexibility of economic policies[a]	7
Fiscal policy[a]	7
Transparency of government[a]	8
Quality of the political system[a]	9
Bureaucratic interference[a]	12
Overall tax burden	14
Regulation of financial institutions[b]	15
Personal income tax	16
Employer's social security contribution	16
Improper practices (bribery and corruption)[a]	20
Distortions from personal taxes[a]	21
Protection of intellectual property[a, b]	22
Confidence in justice[a]	23
Confidence on personal and property protection[a]	23
Basic research[a, b]	25
Educational system[a, b]	25
Availability of skilled labor[a,b]	26
Human development[b]	27
Secondary school enrollment[b]	29
Central government foreign debt	30
Total reserves	30
Administrative decentralization[a]	30
Higher education enrollment[b]	31
Teaching of science at schools[a, b]	33
Density of road network[b]	37
Population per physician[b]	37
Public expenditure on education (US$ per student)[b]	38
MEMORANDUM	
Government	5
Management	9
People	23
Overall competitiveness	13

a. From surveys.
b. Classified in factors different from government.
Source: IMD International (1996).

Midway between assets and liabilities depicted in the competitiveness reviews are factors associated with Chile's tax system. They also tie in to essential roles of the state, such as the administration of justice and personal and property protection. Some of these factors are distorted, in our view, by the indicators used in the *Global Competitiveness Report* (World Economic Forum 1996).[5]

In sum, the comparatively strong position of the Chilean state owes much to its capability to correct longstanding government distortions in the operation of the economy, on the macro and micro sides alike. Chile has yet to develop capabilities on a par with the more industrialized nations for the delivery of essential social services and certain public functions—among them the safeguarding of law and order—that are traditionally the province of government.

Competitiveness rankings of this type have major limitations, however. For one thing, they are posited upon an *a priori* concept of what the state should be—in this case, an eminently economic notion. And they typically look at questions of government and social services delivery in absolute terms, thereby leaving no room for considering the countries' *relative* efforts or their efficiency in applying the resources at their disposal.

Given these drawbacks, it would be useful to review some specific evidence on the effectiveness of the state in Chile.

PUBLIC FINANCES. After painful fiscal adjustments in the 1980s, the country enjoyed 11 years of stable budgetary surpluses and rising public saving. These gains were achieved despite intermittent external shocks, a thoroughgoing restructuring of the public sector, and sharp shifts in priorities for the allocation of public monies.

In the 1980s, exogenous, cyclical, and structural factors had a particularly pronounced effect on the treasury, as the Chilean state wrestled with a broadening fiscal deficit. In less than a decade the country managed to close

---

5. On the question of corporate taxes, for instance, Chile is ranked near the bottom, even though its 15 percent tax rate is one of the lowest in the world. The apparent explanation is that the indicator used for the ranking is the ratio of aggregate business tax receipts to GDP. But including the proceeds of the extremely high average levies paid by the state-owned copper and petroleum enterprises skews Chile's ratio. Since those taxes exist solely as a ready means of transferring the companies' surpluses into the treasury, they have scant impact on the country's competitiveness, which will depend instead on taxes on corporate earnings in the private sector.

a budget gap on the order of 10 percent of GDP. Government spending felt the brunt of the adjustment.

Since 1990 fiscal accounts have been in the black, with surpluses fluctuating around 1.5 percent of GDP and a doubling of the public saving to GDP ratio, from 2.5 percent in 1990 to 5.6 percent in 1996 (table 7-2). Thanks to this steady surplus, the public debt was pushed down from 43 percent of GDP to less than 16 percent over that same interval. The country's fiscal policy has remained stable, and somewhat contractionary, through these years of varying growth rates and changing terms of trade.[6]

Though balanced budgets and rising savings clearly go some way to explain Chile's healthy public finances in the 1990s, they do no tell the whole story: against this backdrop the state was able to attend to the most pressing needs of the Chilean people. Central government spending on education and health climbed by 13 percent per annum, in real terms, between 1990 and 1996. Infrastructure expenditure rose at twice that rate, tackling many of the deficiencies inherited from the 1980s. Helping to fuel these increases was the 1990 tax reform, which provided the government with badly needed resources to step up its action in the social sectors.

The government has raised these resources at a limited cost to the taxpayer. Chile has a moderate tax burden of 17 percent of GDP (table 7-2) and a simple tax system consisting of a handful of broad-based taxes. The two centerpieces of the system are a comprehensive value-added tax (VAT), which brings in close to half of all revenues in local currency, and an income tax that is increasingly geared toward taxing consumption and spurring corporate saving. In surveys conducted after the 1990 tax reform, a clear majority of Chilean taxpayers agreed to the statement that the tax system is fundamentally a fair one, that their taxes do go to help the neediest, and that tax evasion is a serious crime.[7] Thanks to the uncomplicated tax system in place, the quality of compliance monitoring systems, and taxpayers' inclination to honor their obligations, Chile's tax evasion rates are relatively low—nearly 18 percent for the VAT.[8]

---

6. For an analysis of fiscal policy in these years, see Marcel (1997b).

7. Findings of surveys commissioned by Chile's Internal Revenue Service in 1992, cited in Marcel (1997a).

8. Internal Revenue Service estimates. These figures obviously denote only tax evasion, not tax avoidance, whereby taxpayers take advantage of loopholes in the system. Both evasion and avoidance are probably higher for income taxes.

Table 7-2. Public Finances in Chile, 1987–97

Fiscal account	Public spending by central government as percentage of GDP										
	1987	1988	1989	1990	1991	1992	1993	1994	1995	1996	1997[a]
Current expenditure	22.2	20.0	18.2	18.1	18.6	17.5	17.7	17.2	16.2	16.8	17.0
Public investment[b]	2.7	3.2	2.7	2.3	2.5	2.8	3.1	3.3	3.0	3.4	3.6
Total expenditure[c]	25.5	23.9	21.7	21.0	21.8	21.2	21.5	21.1	19.7	20.7	21.2
Tax burden[d]	18.1	15.5	14.8	14.5	16.7	16.9	17.6	17.1	16.5	17.6	17.2
Current surplus/deficit[e]	3.0	2.3	3.0	2.5	3.7	4.9	4.8	4.8	5.3	5.6	5.2
Overall surplus/deficit[e]	1.9	1.0	1.4	0.8	1.5	2.2	1.9	1.7	2.5	2.2	1.6

a. Estimated.
b. Real investment plus capital transfers.
c. Also including financial investment.
d. Net tax revenue different from public copper companies.
e. Excludes net deposits into the Copper Stabilization Fund.
Source: Estadísticas de las Finanzas Públicas 1987–1996 and Dirección de Presupuestos.

THE PUBLIC SERVICE. Chile's central government in 1997 had some 255,000 public servants on the payroll; just over 40 percent of them were employed by the armed forces and the police. A further 155,000 worked for the municipalities, either in municipal government offices or in the education or health services, which have been handed over to the municipalities. Taken together, the central and municipal governments accounted for just under 410,000 direct jobs, or 8.1 percent of total employment in the country. If defense and the police are factored out, government accounted for only 5.9 percent of jobs in the economy.

These figures compare favorably with those reported for countries at a similar or higher stage of development. If we consider central government and municipal employees, we can see that government jobs account for a smaller share of total employment in Chile than in regions at similar stages of development and in the industrialized nations. This is true regardless of the yardstick used in the measurement—government jobs as compared to total population, the workforce, or total employment (table 7-3).

This moderate share of the public service in Chile's labor market is the fruit of sweeping adjustments during the military regime and of the prudent policies followed by democratic governments in recent years.

INSTITUTIONAL EFFECTIVENESS. The relatively modest size of the Chilean public service has not hindered the state's ability to mobilize huge volumes of resources: although the public sector employs less than 6 percent of the

Table 7-3. Public Employment in Chile: International Comparisions

Country or region	Government jobs as a percentage of		
	Population	Labor force	Employ- ment total
Africa	2.0	5.0	6.6
Asia	2.6	5.6	6.3
Eastern Europe	6.9	14.3	16.0
Latin America and the Caribbean	3.0	7.6	8.9
Middle East and North Africa	3.9	14.2	17.5
OECD countries	7.7	15.6	17.2
Chile	2.1	5.4	5.8

Note: For Chile, 1996; for other regions, early 1990s.

Sources: Chile, Instituto Nacional de Estadísticas and Dirección de Presupuestos; other regions, Schiavo-Campo, de Tommaso, and Mukherjee (1997).

nation's economically active population, it manages resources equivalent to some 23 percent of GDP. By way of comparison, public bureaucracies in industrialized countries have nearly tripled the number of civil servants on the payroll for every active member of the workforce, but they handle only twice the relative amount of resources. Chile also fares well in comparisons with Latin America overall: it sits below the regional average in terms of employment, but above the average for government spending as a percentage of GDP.

The ability to mobilize large amounts of resources, however, does not necessarily reflect differences in public sector productivity from one country or region to another. For one thing, the methodology would need substantial refinements.[9] On the other hand, an analysis centering on public spending levels reveals little about the outcome of public policies. A more illuminating exercise would be to compare the standards a country has managed to achieve in its delivery of basic public services with the resources available to the government.

Figure 7-1 compares the ratio of the UNDP Human Development Index to general government per-capita spending in selected industrialized and developing countries. Chile comes through with a high ratio, even though its per-capita government spending figure is relatively low compared with the more developed countries. More important, Chile lies above the line depicting the statistical relation between the two variables for the countries portrayed, meaning that it has above-average capacity to marshal and deploy public monies to raise social standards.

This assertion is supported by direct measures of effectiveness of the Chilean state compared with other countries. According to the yardsticks used by Business International, which Mauro (1995) groups under the heading of bureaucratic efficiency, Chile stands 18th among the 68 countries examined, surpassed only by a number of industrialized nations (table 7-4).[10]

---

9. The figures cited here are no more than a first proxy to a comparative analysis of productivity. For one thing, expenditure figures include payroll costs—which when divided by employment levels yield only mean public sector remuneration—and public debt service—which has nothing to do with the current supply of public goods or services and hence requires no personnel.

10. Mauro (1995) examines the rankings awarded by Business International analysts for countries surveyed for selected variables including efficiency of the justice system, red tape, and corruption. Rankings are for the period 1980–83.

Figure 7-1. Human Development and Public Expenditure: International Comparisons

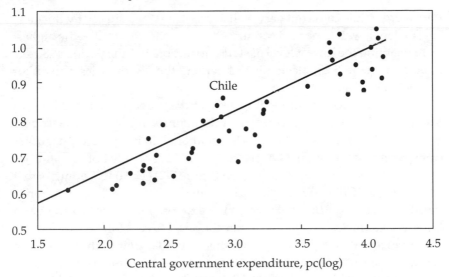

UNDP Human Development Index

Central government expenditure, pc(log)

Source: United Nations Development Programme, International Monetary Fund.

Even with limited resources at their disposal, Chile's public institutions can tackle problems and run effective public programs. Nowhere is this capability more in evidence than in health services, one of the most complex of the social sectors. Comparative studies by the World Bank show

Table 7-4. Comparative Indicators of Bureaucratic Efficiency in Chile

Indicator	Average score for 1980–83 (maximum 10)	Ranking among 68 countries
Efficiency of the judiciary system	7.25	28
Red tape (absence of)	9.25	8
Corruption (absence of)	9.25	15
Political stability	6.46	55
Bureaucratic efficiency	8.58	18

Note: Based on assessments in standard questionnaires filled by analysts in each country.
Source: Mauro (1995, appendix 3) quoting figures from Business International.

that Chile's basic health indicators—infant mortality, malnutrition, life expectancy—are among the highest in the developing world, although Chile's share of health spending in GDP is substantially lower.

INTEGRITY. Chile came out very well in an early-1980s survey by Business International, which marked countries on a scale from 0 to 10—the highest score denoting the lowest level of state corruption. For the period 1980–83, Chile averaged a 9.25, placing it 15th among the 68 countries ranked for this factor.[11]

Although the world competitiveness studies cited earlier yielded less remarkable rankings on corruption for the country, recent analyses appear to confirm the findings of Business International. In its specialized studies Transparency International has ranked Chile 14th on a list of 41 countries according to its low level of corruption (figure 7-2). The only countries that do better than Chile are certain industrialized nations. Chile even ranks ahead of such countries as France, Hong Kong, and Spain, all the Latin American countries, and all the Asian countries except Singapore.[12]

It appears that most Chileans share this favorable view of the integrity of public services. According to a recent survey on government-service quality commissioned by the Budget Directorate of the Ministry of Finance, close to 72 percent of the respondents believed Chilean public servants were honest.[13] A separate survey conducted simultaneously in 18 Latin American countries and Spain shows Chile's public service to be among the most trusted in the region.[14]

INSTITUTIONAL STABILITY. On the matter of stability of public institutions, Chile's showing in the early 1980s was less impressive, according to the studies cited by Mauro (1995).[15] At the time of those assessments, a de facto

---

11. Mauro (1995, appendix 3).

12. The Latin American countries surveyed and their rankings were Argentina (24th), Colombia (31st), Mexico (32nd), Brazil (37th), and Venezuela (38th).

13. TIME FORO (1996).

14. Corporación de Estudios de Opinión Publica Latinoamericana (1996). Thirty-eight percent of Chileans interviewed claimed to have "a lot of confidence" or "some confidence" in the government. On average, positive responses were elicited from 25 percent of respondents in the 11 Latin American countries overall; in Central America the percentage was 31 percent. Chile's 38 percent positive response rate was surpassed only by Nicaragua (39 percent) and Spain (41 percent).

15. Chile's average score for "stable institutions," on a scale of 0 to 10, was 6.46 for the 1980–83 period, placing it 55th among 68 countries.

Figure 7-2. Transparency International Corruption Indices

Corruption index (1 = high corruption, 10 = low corruption)

Source: Transparency International.

regime was being challenged by a citizenry that had begun to mobilize to restore democracy.

Democracy did return in 1990, and none of the authoritarian advocates' predictions of instability proved correct. Institutional stability and broad-based political consensus-building have been leitmotifs of the two democratic administrations that have presided over Chile's political transition since the early 1990s. Cabinets have remained relatively stable, and no major political crisis has surfaced. Political consultation has led to key pieces of legislation.

Nevertheless, these positive moves have not been enough to shore up Chileans' confidence in the democratic system. After a history of strong activism, many Chileans today have withdrawn from politics altogether. Few young people bother to register to vote, and most citizens are indifferent to political parties. When Chileans are asked about the credibility of public institutions, they rank the three branches of government—the executive, the Congress, and the judiciary—at the bottom of the scale, amply surpassed by the Catholic Church and the media.[16]

Although many reasons could be ventured to explain this skepticism, the one that stands out is Chileans' mistrust, not just of institutions but of their fellow citizens, as revealed by the surveys mentioned above. We must leave to others an exploration of the reasons for this general distrust in Chilean society, and what effect it has on Chileans' quality of living.[17] Suffice it to say that the disillusionment with politics and institutions almost certainly is part of a more widespread phenomenon in the country.

At the end of the day, however, it would appear that Chileans still have more faith in their institutions than do other Latin Americans. For one thing, they profess greater confidence in the legislature.

In sum, the evidence at hand appears to corroborate the impression of a fairly effective Chilean state, particularly when compared with countries at similar stages of development. This effectiveness is reflected in the country's macroeconomic performance, the state's ability to deliver basic services to the population despite its limited resources, and the integrity and predictability of its operation.

Three caveats caution us against too rosy an appraisal of Chile's standing, however. The first is the country's weak showing on the essential role

---

16. Centro de Estudios de la Realidad Contemporánea (1997).

17. These questions have been addressed recently by Moulian (1997) and Campero (1997).

of the state in safeguarding law and order—a function *sine qua non* for the rule of law, for the stability of national institutions, and for the confidence of the people in those institutions. The relative weakness of the judiciary in Chile, for instance, indicates that there is considerable work to be done to bolster key public functions.

A second caveat is the apparent contradiction between the opinions elicited in competitiveness surveys and the views expressed by Chileans when questioned about their confidence in the country's institutions. This contradiction points up the problem with looking at questions of effectiveness of the state and its institutions from a preeminently economic standpoint, as though the state's sole role was to foster private businesses instead of serving the common good.

The third reason for caution is that international comparisons overlook the issues related to the *quality* of state action, particularly in the social sectors. We need hardly be reminded that the quality of service in the public sector has been key to the reforms tackled by several countries in recent years.[18] The lack of quality indicators in these studies serves as a reminder that they do not tell the whole story.

State Effectiveness, Roles, and Institutions

More and more studies are highlighting the critical role of institutions in determining a state's effectiveness and, by extension, investment levels and economic growth. This marks a clear departure from past approaches, which focused solely on government policies and how they were implemented.

Drawing on specially commissioned studies and surveys, the World Bank (1997) delivers convincing evidence of the importance of institutions as determinants of state effectiveness and economic development. The Bank then suggests a two-step approach to translate these views into a concrete agenda for change.

The first step is to match the role of the state with its actual capabilities. Theoretically, this could mean either broadening or reducing the state's functions, depending on the sign of the gap between role and capability, but most of the policy examples discussed in the *World Development Report 1997* fall into the second category. The states in question are performing too many roles without having the required capabilities, and they

---

18. For a review of some of these experiences, see the articles included in Dirección de Presupuestos (1997b).

will need to trim or do away with a number of them. By privatizing public enterprises, phasing out costly production-development programs, freeing up markets, and streamlining their complicated regulatory apparatus, states could focus their capabilities, and public monies, on truly core roles or functions inherent to the state, such as the administration of justice, the protection of property, the delivery of basic social services, and macroeconomic management.

The second step in building effective states is to reinvigorate state capability by decentralizing functions and responsibilities, contracting out to the private sector, establishing a professional bureaucracy, creating institutional checks and balances, and devising mechanisms for input and feedback from the public, in order to give the community a voice in public decisions.

The World Bank (1997) offers this two-step approach as an agenda for countries held back by state inefficiency, corruption, or patronage. From this standpoint, an effective state is one that has managed both to build capability and to bow out of roles it is not equipped to perform.

To see whether the Chilean experience can be fitted into this framework, we ask four key questions. What has Chile done to match the state's role to its capabilities? What are those capabilities, and how did they develop? How much of the capabilities built up by the state can be attributed to its having stepped back from more complicated or controversial roles? Given its present capabilities, which, if any, new roles and tasks can Chile take on?

Role and Functions of the State

Transformation of State Functions, 1970–96

The state that existed in Chile in the early 1970s was unquestionably interventionist and entrepreneurial, with a tradition built up over at least 30 years.[19] Table 7-5 summarizes some of the functions performed by the state at that time. As can be seen, it played an active role in the provision not only of conventional public goods or social services, but also of public infrastructure, housing, public utilities, and in fostering industrial develop-

---

19. For a good analysis of Chile's economic structure at the end of the 1960s, see Ffrench-Davis (1973).

Table 7-5. Evolution of State Functions in Chile from Late 1960s to Mid-1990s

Functions of the state	Late 1960s	Reforms under the military regime	Democratic reforms	Current role of the state
Public goods				
Defense	Defense expenditures subject to civilian rules and priorities.	Defense expenditures increased and protected. Development of public defense industry. Social insurance for militaries protected from reforms.		Delivery. Limited defense industry.
Law and order	Police under control of civilian authorities. Independent judiciary.	Police militarized.	Major reforms in Supreme Court, criminal justice, domestic relations courts, and management.	Delivery, except for specific arbitration mechanisms in commercial disputes.
Property rights	Guaranteed by the Constitution.	Constitutional protection strengthened.	Intellectual property legislation.	Enforcement and regulation.
Macroeconomic management	Fiscal and monetary policy closely tied. Prices, exchange rate, and interest rates under direct controls.	Central Bank autonomized. Elimination of price, exchange rate, and interest rate controls. Trade liberalization.	Restriction to short-term capital flows.	Delivery. Fiscal and monetary policy constitutionally separated.

(Table continues on the following page.)

Table 7-5 *(continued)*

Functions of the state	Late 1960s	Reforms under the military regime	Democratic reforms	Current role of the state
Social programs Primary health	Child nutrition and school meals programs. Primary health provided by central services.	Transferred to municipalities. Child nutrition programs strengthened.	Labor relations in health regulated under decentralized scheme. School nutrition and health programs widened.	Delivery through municipalities.
Education	Open access to primary and secondary education in public schools. Universal coverage in primary education. Free higher education.	Transferred to municipalities and private providers on the basis of fee-for-service financing. Tuition fees in universities and student loans.	Increase in public funding. Programs for improving quality of education. Teachers' pay and conditions regulated and centralized. Systemic reforms under way. University loans reformed and targeted grants created.	Financing, partial delivery by municipalities and autonomous universities; oversight and regulation in higher education.

Housing programs	Subsidies to middle class through interest rates. Direct housing provision to the poor. Active role of the state in major urban developments.	Housing associations terminated. Replaced by subsidy programs. Land use deregulated.	Increase and diversification of social housing programs and subsidies. Regulation of land use partly reinstated.	Financing. Delivery for targeted programs. Production in private sector. Regulation of land use by municipalities.
Antipoverty programs		Emergency employment programs during crises. Monetary subsidies for children, the handicapped, and the elderly.	New programs created for vulnerable groups: unemployed youths, single mothers, handicapped, indigenous, etc.	Financing of subsidies. Delivery of social programs through nongovernmental organizations and private companies.
Infrastructure and transportation	Active role in road building. Urban planning and development. Rail and bus services provided. Regulation of urban transportation.	Urban transportation deregulated. Public buses eliminated. Investment partly decentralized to regions.	Reregulation of urban transportation. Concessions system for major infrastructure projects. Decentralization deepened. Base for privatization of railways and ports approved.	Delivery through central and regional governments and concessions to private sector. Private production. Regulation of urban transportation and ports.

Source: Compiled by the author.

ment. Those functions were performed under a wide variety of arrangements, which included direct provision of many public goods, entrepreneurial involvement through state-owned enterprises, price setting, protection of domestic industry, and safeguarding of economic, social, and labor rights. Only in a few areas, such as environmental protection, poverty alleviation,[20] and protection of consumers and small stockholders—areas that reflect more recent developments in public policy—was there little sign of state involvement.

Despite its strong involvement in entrepreneurial activities, the Chilean state of the early 1970s was active in the social sphere. By then the important reforms of the 1920s had established a strong public commitment to education, health, social security, housing and workers' protection. With central government expenditures accounting for 31 percent of GDP at the end of the 1960s, at least 60 percent of the total was already being earmarked for social functions.[21] These funds were administered by public agencies with a strong institutional record, which provided cumulative experience and know-how for the design of new programs and policies.

Following the 1973 coup d'état, the Chilean economy began a process of deep restructuring. After a painful macroeconomic adjustment and the rationalization of key public functions, the military regime pushed through structural reforms that changed the role of the state in the economy and in society, as well as the mechanisms for exercising that role.[22]

Table 7-5 also depicts the main reforms that affected the public sector in the period 1973–89. These reforms deregulated the goods and capital markets and opened up the economy to international competition. With the

---

20. Antipoverty programs are taken here to mean actions or subsidies specifically designed to reach the poorest families; they are thus distinct from the broad-coverage social benefits. Most social programs before the 1970s lacked specific targeting mechanisms. This does not mean, of course, that the incidence of some existing social programs might not have been greater among the lower-income groups.

21. For an account of the historical evolution of social policies in Chile, see Arellano (1985, 19–57). An overview of the role of these policies in the country's political and institutional development can be found in Vial (1997).

22. The rationalization of functions refers to the return of nationalized companies to private ownership, the tax reform of 1974, the standardization of the labor and pay systems for government employees, and the unification of the rules governing financial management in the public sector. The latter two reforms are analyzed in greater depth in the next section.

abandonment of the import-substitution strategy of development came sweeping changes in the role of the state in fostering production, greatly broadening the role of markets in the allocation of resources in the economy.[23] This did not mean, however, that the state ceased all involvement in industrial promotion. As can be seen from table 7-5, new programs aimed at promoting exports or at facilitating access to credit took an important part in state action from the late 1970s onward.

The predominant role of the markets, coupled with the emergence of the private sector as an engine of development, was reinforced by the large-scale privatization of state-owned enterprises throughout the military period. These privatizations began with the devolution, transfer, or sale of hundreds of companies and agricultural estates nationalized during the Allende administration. In the second half of the 1980s, privatizations were extended to traditional public sector enterprises associated with activities previously defined as strategic or associated with public utilities. In some cases the privatization process spelled a complete break with all state activity in the sector (as in steelworks and sugar refining); in other cases direct entrepreneurial activity was replaced by a regulatory and indicative planning role (as in power generation and telecommunications). Thus, the 530 enterprises held by the public sector at the end of 1973, covering virtually all areas of economic activity, had by 1990 been pared to 41, most of them in copper and oil extraction, water and sewage, and residual areas of transportation and power generation.[24]

The reforms implemented by the military regime included changes in the way certain public goods or services were provided; the state, however, did not relinquish its responsibilities altogether. In the case of education, for example, direct administration of primary and secondary schools by the Ministry of Education was replaced by the funding of educational services using grants per student, paid either to public schools—devolved to municipalities—or to private schools that gradually flourished under this system. In the case of social security, neither the pension reform of 1980 nor the creation of the ISAPRE system a few years later changed the mandatory nature of social insurance; the state retained an oversight role, but it transferred to the private sector the administration of the systems. Not all

---

23. These reforms are described in Foxley (1982), Edwards and Cox-Edwards (1991), and Larraín (1991).

24. For an analysis of the processes by which public enterprises were privatized in Chile, see Hachette and Lüders (1992), Marcel (1989), and Saez (1993).

these changes, however, involved transferring responsibilities to the private sector. With regard to primary health care, public hospitals, and investment in social infrastructure, the aim of the reforms was decentralization within the public sector.[25]

Under the military regime, the state also expanded its intervention to some emerging areas. For example, during the economic crises of the mid-1970s and early 1980s, it spearheaded emergency employment programs and cash allowances for those unemployed or in extreme poverty. In addition, antitrust legislation was enacted, and, after the financial crisis of 1983, regulation of the financial system was strengthened.

However, not all of the reforms implemented during this period bore the same liberalizing stamp, nor did they achieve the same degree of success. In defense, for instance, institutional criteria carried the day, and egregious exceptions were made to the streamlining of the financial administration systems, the pension reform, and the transfer of productive activities to the private sector.[26] Similarly, some of the most ambitious exercises in deregulation (as in the case of the financial sector) had to be reversed later because of their damaging consequences.

Despite the impressive breadth and depth of most reforms carried out by the military regime, by the end of the 1980s they still had not earned significant public support. This was not only because of their evident lack of democratic legitimacy and the country's statist tradition, but also because of the deterioration in the quality of many of the services provided. This was particularly evident in the social services transferred to the municipalities, which were hit by a substantial reduction in state funding during the 1980s.

The democratic administrations that succeeded the military regime after 1990 shouldered these difficulties while upholding the basic elements of a market economy. Some of the governments pushed reforms aimed directly at broadening the sphere of action of the markets. Private concessions, combined with a hefty increase in public investment, proved instrumental in rehabilitating much of the country's public infrastructure, which had dete-

---

25. For a review of the main reforms enacted by the military regime in the social field, see Castañeda (1989) and Larroulet (1991). The reform of social security in Chile is fully documented in Diamond (1994), Uthoff (1995), and Marcel and Arenas (1991).

26. For example, national security considerations were adduced to justify the formation of a consortium of military armaments and equipment manufacturers. It has incurred systematic losses.

riorated badly after nearly 20 years of neglect. Privatizations since 1990 have sought to stimulate competition in heavily concentrated sectors, like electricity, or to mobilize fresh resources for investment, while at the same time improving competitive bidding procedures.[27] Legislation was passed in 1997 to allow private involvement in the water and sewage sector and private management of the state-owned ports.

In some cases the reforms by the democratic administrations improved the regulatory systems in particularly sensitive areas, such as collective wage bargaining, urban transportation, regulation of conflicts of interest, environmental protection, and consumer protection. At the same time, a large amount of public money was spent to restore operating capacity in essential social services, such as education and health, pay the social debt caused by the sharp deterioration in social benefits during the 1980s, and sustain a broad range of new antipoverty programs.[28] Initiatives in the social sphere have broadened social protection. One example is the unemployment insurance scheme under discussion in the Chilean Congress in 1997.[29] A major reform of the judiciary system will also improve social well-being, access to justice for the poorest, and the protection of citizens' rights. By incorporating principles of social equity and justice into the operation of Chile's economy and society, these kinds of initiatives have been instrumental in building a development strategy that enjoys greater legitimacy and public acceptance.

However, the democratic administrations encountered strong corporate resistance to reforms to lower the costs of the pension funds, enhance the transparency and coverage of private health insurance, and improve regulation of the power sector. In other cases these same corporate pressures have triggered backsliding in the privatization and decentralization processes. An example of this is the recentralization of labor relations in education.

---

27. Since 1990 five companies have been privatized, the minority holdings have been divested from two others, the money-losing coal company has been scaled back to a minimum, and possibilities of joint ventures with the private sector have opened up in CODELCO's copper deposits. After privatization of the northern railroad company, freight haulage was transferred to the private sector. A similar process is anticipated for passenger transport in the south central region.

28. For a review of the social policies implemented since 1990, see Raczynski (1997, 92–125).

29. A short description of the proposed system, which is based on the principles of individual capital formation, can be found in World Bank (1997, 58). A scheme with similar features has been discussed in Argentina.

Assessing the Reforms

A comparison of the last two columns in table 7-5 provides us with a more comprehensive scorecard on the consequences of reforms affecting the role of the state in the economy. Only in a very few cases did the state completely end the functions it was performing at the close of the 1960s. Usually the reforms altered the mechanisms by which the state fulfilled those functions. At the same time the state gradually assumed new functions arising out of the development process that the country was pursuing.

Indeed, the only areas in which the state actually relinquished its earlier role are in the deregulation of the goods and financial services markets, the opening up of trade, the privatization of public enterprises operating in competitive markets, and the redistribution of assets. In the provision of public goods, the only significant change was in the institutional structure underlying state action—for example, when the Central Bank was made autonomous. In the social sphere and in the provision of infrastructure, the state's involvement tended to become more intensive, especially after the end of the military regime, while the direct provision of public utilities was replaced by regulatory systems geared to optimizing the relationship between supply, quality, and pricing of such services by private companies. Industrial policy has taken the form of government programs designed to gradually raise the productivity of domestic companies, particularly small and medium-size ones.

Despite the radical nature of the social security reforms implemented in Chile, the state has retained basic responsibilities in guaranteeing the operational and financial soundness of the system and the minimum benefits granted by law. Under the democratic administrations, in fact, major efforts have been mounted to increase the real value of minimum pensions. In this respect, it is inaccurate to speak of Chile's welfare state being dismantled, since all its basic components at the end of the 1960s still exist and in some cases have even expanded.[30]

One of the foremost instances of permanent expansion of state activity is the antipoverty programs. A genuine network of protection is developing

---

30. These components include a universal and mandatory system of old-age, disability, and survivor pensions; mandatory health insurance; an occupational health system; and a free, universal school system. Among the components that have been added are maternal allowance, the system of severance compensation for domestic employees, and, when approved, the new unemployment insurance scheme.

that provides low-income families and vulnerable groups with state grants and support. This network is steadily evolving from pure compensation and assistance under the military regime to enabling programs under the democratic administrations. Moreover, new state functions are making their appearance in the areas of environmental protection, consumer rights, and regulation of the capital market.

The least popular changes during the military regime were not those that most radically transformed the state's role in the economy (such as deregulation of financial markets, the opening up of trade, or the privatization of companies), but those that altered the means by which public goods or services were provided (such as the reforms to social security and the delivery of social services). Not surprisingly, popular discontent was directed at areas where the state retained responsibilities, particularly responsibilities that fell within the conventional functions of government. The reforms that changed the means of providing services were especially bedeviled by design and implementation errors, as well as by the fiscal constraints of the 1980s.

Be this as it may, by the end of the 1980s, state withdrawal had surpassed the limits that most Chileans would approve, and they threw their support behind a political coalition representing not only the restoration of democracy but a greater commitment to justice and social equity through state action. This support enabled the coalition to remain in power for two successive terms and to increase state funding by increases in taxation, which were initially resisted by the business community and the political opposition.

Table 7-6 illustrates the effect of these changes on public finances. Expenditures on the nonfinancial public sector (excluding municipalities) as a share of GDP experienced a reduction in the past 25 years that is more moderate than might have been expected. At the same time municipalities—not included in the table—doubled their share of GDP between 1980 and the mid-1990s to nearly 4 percent. If the latter were brought into the

Table 7-6. Public Expenditure as a Percentage of GDP, 1969, 1996

Public expenditure	1969	1996
Current expenditure	26.7	24.5
Capital expenditure	11.4	6.3
Total expenditure	38.1	30.8

Note: Central government and public enterprises. Municipalities not included.
Source: Author's own estimates based on data from Dirección de Presupuestos.

picture, the overall reduction in the relative size of the consolidated public sector would be even smaller.

The Cycle of Reforms and State Functions

Some have argued that state withdrawal from nonessential functions is justified because it allows limited state resources and capabilities to be targeted to those functions for which there is no substitute for the state. In their view these reforms strengthen the state in its essential functions rather than weaken it. Can the Chilean experience be seen as empirical proof of the validity of a "retreat in order to advance" approach? At least three features cast doubt on such an interpretation.

First, it is questionable to argue that the state's withdrawal from certain state functions freed up public resources for higher priority areas. Indeed, an analysis of the actual role that institutions played in the state's intervention in production and in the redistribution of wealth in Chile in the late 1960s reveals that these cases did not necessarily involve sectors with low institutional capabilities. On the contrary, the public institutions and enterprises that spearheaded state expansion had a sizable cadre of professionals and technicians who not only represented a large proportion of the country's skilled workers but also succeeded in shielding these institutions from the pervasive political interference that marked the experience of other countries and of other parts of the Chilean state. Institutional downsizing or straight privatization led to the transfer of most of these professionals and technicians to the private sector, rather than to their reassignment elsewhere in the public sector.

The majority of privatizations during the 1980s involved companies with little indebtedness after large-scale internal restructuring. There is pervasive evidence that the privatization of these companies generated a capital loss to the state, either because they were sold below their economic value to the state, or because the proceeds helped finance the public sector's current account.[31]

---

31. In Marcel (1989) it is estimated that the undervaluation of the companies privatized between 1985 and 1988 was somewhere between 40 percent and 60 percent of their economic value to the Treasury. Hachette and Lüders (1992) dispute these estimates on the basis of a different set of parameters. Saez (1993) offers arguments for refuting the values that Hachette and Lüders assign to the variable that accounts for most of the discrepancies, and thus he tends to corroborate the estimates in Marcel's study.

In other words, the state's withdrawal from its corporate functions in Chile, though justifiable from the standpoint of overall economic efficiency, entailed a loss of human and financial resources for the public sector, rather than their reallocation to other government functions.

Secondly, it is doubtful whether in some areas the restructuring of state functions produced more effective action. This is particularly true with respect to the regulation of natural monopolies and of private insurance, for two different reasons. In the case of regulation, the effectiveness of the systems used was limited by the low capacity and autonomy of the regulatory agencies, the lack of competition in the markets due to the industry's vertical and horizontal integration, and the limited institutional clout exerted by the users of public utilities. These factors, arising from the institutional structure created under the military regime and the privatization mechanisms applied, resulted in processes resembling the capture of regulators as depicted in the literature on the subject. These processes only recently have attracted the attention of the government authorities.[32]

For their part, the private pension and health systems, which suffer from design flaws that raise their administrative costs and restrict market mechanisms, have resisted reforms to correct these distortions. This resistance, based on arguments and lobbying methods typical of corporate interests, has prevented the state from performing its oversight responsibilities and has limited the effectiveness of its actions.

In theory, the shift in state functions from producer to regulator appears justified. In practice, political, administrative, and institutional factors have prevented the benefits of that shift from being fully realized.

Thirdly, in the Chilean experience the state's withdrawal from some functions and its heightened role in others is not part of one and the same process, but a consequence of the deep political transition that the country underwent at the beginning of the 1990s. Indeed, it seems clear that in the late 1980s the state's withdrawal from some functions and the changes in the delivery systems of others went far beyond an attempt to increase the effectiveness of the state. Those reforms, accompanied by severe cuts in public spending that seriously affected the state's most basic functions, were followed by across-the-board reductions in tax rates. It seems obvious that the purpose of the military regime was to continue to downsize the state as far as it could.

---

32. For an evaluation of the effectiveness of these regulatory systems, see Bitrán and Saavedra (1993). The case of the power sector is dealt with at length in Blanloth (1993).

The first democratic administration partially reversed this process. It restored the operational capacity in social services; raised the value of pensions, social subsidies, and minimum wages; and set in motion important social investment and infrastructure programs. Starting in 1994, this process soon extended to the modernization of key sectors and a priority commitment to education.

These initiatives to some extent constitute a reversal of the course embraced by the military regime in the second half of the 1980s. But it took a change in the political regime, two center-left governments, strong fiscal discipline, and three tax reforms to transform state functions—a far cry from the "retreat in order to advance" strategy.

Development of the State's Capabilities

When it comes to evaluating the development of the state's capabilities, it seems useful to distinguish four basic subsystems within the public management system: organizational structure, human resource management, financial management, and control systems. This section analyzes the elements that make up each of these four systems in the Chilean state, their origins, and their effects on the development of the public sector's institutional capabilities. It also reviews current initiatives to modernize public sector management.

Organizational Structure

INTERNAL ORGANIZATION OF THE PUBLIC SECTOR. The organizational structure of Chile's public sector is governed by Law No. 18,575, General Basis of State Administration. This 1986 law establishes a fundamental distinction between ministries and the so-called decentralized public services. The ministries collaborate with the president of the republic in the top-level administration of the state, acting for this purpose as a single legal entity. Public services are responsible for meeting the basic needs of the citizenry, to which end they are endowed with their own legal personality and administrative autonomy, within the common framework applicable to all public institutions. Whereas the ministries have essentially political functions, the decentralized services have executive functions, and different administrative powers are associated with each of these roles.

Divisionalization is the transfer of executive functions to public agencies, which are given greater autonomy and flexibility in order to perform these functions adequately. Divisionalization has been an integral part of reform in a number of developed countries in recent y ırs. It is embodied in the organizational structure of the Chilean public sector that was established in the mid-1980s, and it has had a long-standing basis in the evolution of the country's public institutions for several decades.

Indeed, the origin of the decentralized public agencies springs from an organizational mold shaped by the expansion of the Chilean state during the first half of this century. During that time, the state expanded and significantly diversified its executive functions, but the traditional ministries and public institutions were ill prepared to assume them because of the rigidity of management and a lack of qualified personnel. In the face of these difficulties, the emerging executive functions of the state were systematically entrusted to "decentralized" or "autonomous" institutions, the legal existence of which rested on waivers written into the legislation and which were exempt from many conventional procedures and controls. In some cases, special laws were passed to create new institutions whose powers and autonomy went beyond even what was permitted by such waivers.[33]

Unlike the marginal role that organizational responses of this kind customarily play in other countries and despite the criticisms of many Chilean administrative experts, who characterized this process as "inorganic expansion" of the public sector,[34] the "decentralized service" ended up as Chile's dominant form of public organization for performing executive functions. It was ultimately recognized as such by the legislation enacted during the military regime. This process not only predated what would later become a dominant trend in institutional modernization in other countries, but it gave the organizational culture of these institutions a strong professional basis, thereby shielding the state's principal executive functions from the kind of politicization, patronage, and red tape that crept into other areas of Chile's public sector.

DECENTRALIZATION. The history of Chilean political and institutional life reflects a strong centralist tradition. From its inception as a republic in the early nineteenth century, the Chilean state was characterized by a strong presidential regime in which the provincial authorities generally acted as

---

33. A case in point is the Corporación de Fomento de la Producción, created in the 1930s.

34. For a critique of this process from the standpoint of administrative law, see Urzúa and García (1971).

delegates of the central government. Nevertheless, over the past 20 years, major processes of decentralization have been undertaken, significantly changing the structure and operation of the public sector. These processes have had a political impact. For the first time all the municipalities in the country have mayors and municipal councils elected by local citizens; regional governments have been established with their own bodies, powers, and participation arrangements.

The municipalities and regional governments are endowed with specific responsibilities and powers in the areas of administration, delivery of social services, and investment in infrastructure. Most of these functions have been transferred from the central government, which has thus narrowed its scope of activity.[35] This transfer of responsibilities has gone hand in hand with the transfer of considerable resources, varying from taxes and fees exclusively earmarked for municipalities to conditional transfers from the central government. Altogether, these resources represent some 5 percent of GDP, which is the equivalent of one-fifth of general government resources.

Although these figures show only a modest degree of decentralization, even by Latin American standards, the situation in Chile is noteworthy for the speed of implementation, for the connection between the political and institutional processes and the fiscal processes, and for the development of innovative mechanisms to transfer resources and responsibilities.[36] The following paragraphs review the most prominent aspects of municipalization and regionalization, their impact on the organizational structure of the public sector, and their effects on the development of capacities within the state.

The regionalization process began in 1974 with a change in the political division of the country, which was divided into 13 regions, replacing the previous province-based system. In addition, an institutional structure to support regional administration was established in order to help ensure more decentralized management.[37]

---

35. Some functions, such as education and health, "share responsibility" between the central and municipal governments. Practically speaking, this means that the central government is required to establish specific systems for financing and oversight. In the case of the regional governments, it could be argued that all their functions are in some way shared, since they lack the political and institutional autonomy of the municipalities.

36. For a comparison of decentralization experiences in seven Latin American countries, see CEPAL/GTZ (1996).

37. For a review of the Chilean experience with regionalization, see Serrano (1996) and Gatica and Marcel (1997).

The primary impact of the regionalization process carried out from 1975 to 1989 was to give the regions power to allocate public resources to specific investment projects. To this end, the National Regional Development Fund (FNDR) was created in 1975. It provided financing for investments in local infrastructure through a system of decentralized project identification and selection. FNDR resources are distributed to the regions annually, based on a compensation system. Until 1991 they were allocated to specific projects by Regional Councils of businesspeople and representatives of the recognized organizations of civil society.[38]

After its establishment in 1975, the FNDR grew rapidly until 1979, when it represented approximately 2 percent of fiscal spending during the period. This upward trend was reversed in 1980, and funding plummeted during the 1982–83 crisis. The FNDR began to recover again in 1985 thanks to a loan from the Inter-American Development Bank, which not only tripled FNDR spending in one year, but helped develop its operating mechanisms by establishing stricter eligibility criteria for projects. Subsequently, the fund continued to grow, achieving a cumulative real growth rate of 80 percent between 1986 and 1991.

The purpose of the regionalization process from 1975 to 1989 was to modernize the structure of government by decentralizing decisionmaking authority with the proper technical support, as well as to reconcile geopolitical objectives with the needs of an authoritarian regime. To some extent this was the natural result of the planning processes devised during the 1960s, whose purposes and methods the military strongly shared.

It should come as no surprise that with the return to democracy, the geopolitical and corporatist aspects of regionalization weakened, and in their place a strong demand emerged for greater participation by the regions in public decisionmaking. The result was a new series of reforms. In 1991 a constitutional reform was enacted, establishing regional governments as a new institutional device in the country. The regional governments were granted authority in the area of finance, particularly in the allocation of public investment resources, and they were given their own governing bodies and the administrative structure of a decentralized public service.

The 1991 reform introduced mechanisms to transfer more decisionmaking power from the central to the regional level, following the positive experi-

---

38. The basic idea behind the FNDR was to ensure that a significant portion of public investment would be allocated annually under this system. In practice, this never happened because the economic authorities rejected the introduction of rigidities in public finance.

ence of the FNDR. To this end, new formulas for the allocation of resources to investment projects were devised. With the increase in resources mobilized by the FNDR and other supplementary systems, regionally allocated public investment grew at an average annual rate of 21.4 percent from 1990 to 1997, increasing its share of total public investment from 13.7 percent to 26.6 percent during that period.[39]

In the late 1970s reforms had been undertaken by the military regime to expand the powers of municipalities. Certain conventional functions in connection with administration and development of urban areas were institutionalized, and social functions were significantly expanded. The municipalities shared responsibilities with the central government in the provision of education, health, culture, recreation, sports, job search, housing, and social welfare services.[40]

Along with the transfer of responsibilities to the local level, changes in the financial and administrative framework of municipalities were instituted to provide them with the autonomy and tools necessary to undertake those responsibilities. Through the Municipal Revenues Act, the municipal reforms established a special financing system. A set of tax revenues was exclusively earmarked for local use: the property tax, vehicle tax (driver's license fee), and fees on productive and commercial activities (patents). In addition, the Joint Municipal Fund established a system for redistribution of these resources to compensate municipalities with a small tax base. Lastly, charges were established for certain municipal services (residential refuse collection, for example). The reforms of the late 1970s substantially broadened the administrative and financial independence of the municipalities by giving them autonomous management of their budgets within a common framework of regulations on public sector financial administration.

The most radical reforms during the period transferred to the municipalities the administration of public schools and primary health care centers, a process that continued throughout the 1980s. This transfer was accompanied by a financing system consisting of grants from the central government based on the services provided by the establishments, and the deregulation of contractual arrangements for the respective staff.[41]

---

39. For a description of the reforms instituted in 1991, see Martner (1993).

40. For an analysis of the municipalization process in Chile, see Espinoza and Marcel (1994).

41. On the transfer of education and primary health care services to the municipalities, see Carciofi, Centrángolo, and Larrañaga (1996, pt. III).

Municipal authority in the social sphere was also expanded to aid families in extreme poverty, an area that required special attention during the serious economic crisis of 1982–83. During this period, municipalities thus assumed responsibility for the allocation of monetary transfers to poor families and the management of emergency employment programs. Specific instruments were established to support this function, such as the "socioeconomic identification card" (CAS card) used to identify the beneficiaries of those programs.[42]

The implementation of these reforms continued throughout the 1980s. The reforms faced not only economic, administrative, and political obstacles, but also the more apparent biases of decentralization under the military regime.

These difficulties were especially clear in the transfer of education and primary health care to the municipalities. The main problems encountered were financial. The financing system was initially designed to cover the operating costs of the schools and health clinics transferred to the municipalities based on standard costs per student in attendance (for education) or per service rendered (health care). However, during the 1982–83 crisis, the government eliminated the indexing system for the subsidies, which then fell in real terms during the decade. The municipalities responded to this situation by reducing the salaries of the transferred staff. Toward the end of the period, these factors, compounded by a perception of deteriorating quality in the services transferred to the community, led to a profound questioning of the municipalization process, whose future was now uncertain.

Finally, during the implementation of the municipal reforms in the 1980s, the weight of political factors in the operation of the system became especially evident. Mayors, invested with sweeping powers, were appointed by the president. Although the president imposed a high degree of financial discipline, operation of the municipalities began to depend almost exclusively on the mayors' preferences and interests and the central government's policies, leaving little room for local initiative. The internal management of the municipalities and transferred services was characterized by arbitrariness, especially in personnel management. Although one of the purposes of reform was to lessen politicization of the municipalities, by the end of military rule, the municipalities had directly assumed political control and propaganda duties. Pure and simple authoritarianism re-

---

42. For a description of the CAS card and its use by municipalities in the selection of beneficiaries of social programs, see Raczynski (1991).

placed the initial plan to install a local administration with technical support and a system of participation without democracy.

The new government that took office in March 1990 therefore faced considerable challenges. While decentralization rapidly became a political priority, the municipal model inherited from the military regime needed to be changed. This led to a series of reforms launched in 1991.

The main reforms during this period have been political. The Constitutional Reform of 1991 established the democratic election for mayors and created elected municipal councils as a check to their power. In recent years, initiatives have been undertaken to improve the capabilities of municipalities, especially in those areas badly hit by the fiscal adjustments of the 1980s.

Summing up, it is clear that the decentralization process in Chile has taken a major step forward, especially considering the weight of centralism in the political and institutional history of the country. The regionalization and municipalization processes implemented under the military regime reflected different approaches to organization of the state: regionalization was designed to achieve harmonious development of the country, while municipalization was intended to incorporate the logic of the market into the delivery of social services.

In the early 1990s, however, the two processes were called into question, from both a political and economic perspective. The political reforms undertaken by the democratic governments and the substantial increase in transfers from the central government not only salvaged the decentralization process, but also gave it a different meaning. Thus, the election of mayors and municipal and regional officials contributed to democratization of state institutions and at the same time made the decentralization process itself more coherent.

Indeed, decentralization contributes to more efficient allocation of public resources the more it adapts the supply of resources to the preferences of communities. Accordingly, it is important, first of all, for the functions of subnational governments to be associated with the provision of public services and goods for which there are effectively different preferences. Secondly, institutional mechanisms must be in place to enable the community to convey its preferences to the regional and local authorities, which in turn must have the authority necessary to provide the proper quantity and quality of such services.[43] With regard to the first condition, the functions of the

---

43. For a discussion of the conceptual basis for this system, see Espinoza and Marcel (1994, 45–50).

local and regional governments are properly adjusted to what could be described as an efficient structure.[44] Democratization of the election of local authorities and the establishment of regional governments represent a step toward fulfillment of the second condition, but much remains to be done to design accountability mechanisms besides those of election by popular vote. More flexibility and better management of the municipalities and regional governments are needed.

Human Resources

PUBLIC EMPLOYMENT. About 410,000 persons are employed in government as a whole, which is 8.1 percent of total employment in the country. If we exclude members of the armed forces and the police, the proportion is reduced to 5.9 percent. These figures compare favorably with other countries at the same or higher levels of development, which we interpret as a sign of efficiency.

Public employment in Chile today reflects the adjustments made in the public sector after the military coup of 1973. It is estimated that about 90,000 persons lost their jobs in the central government between 1973 and 1976, a contraction of 30 percent in the 1973 work force. Starting in 1977 the pace of this adjustment slowed, though another 45,000 positions were eliminated between 1976 and 1980. The number of public employees leveled off in the 1980s.

Since 1990 employment in the public sector has increased moderately as operations have recovered in some social services. Between 1990 and 1996 the number of civilian employees of the central government underwent a net increase of 12,000, or 1.6 percent a year (table 7-7). More than 90 percent of the employees filled staff shortages at public hospitals and prisons.

Containment of the growth of public employment in the 1990s has been particularly remarkable when it is considered that it has taken place in a setting of sustained growth of economic activity and aggregate employment and of strong reactivation of government activity in the social sphere and infrastructure. Employment in the central government grew below aggregate employment, but it has done so despite the concurrent growth of the volume of resources channeled by government in the same period. Thus, the central government's expenditure per employee, excluding salaries and

---

44. For a thorough analysis of the functional and financial structure of subnational governments in Chile, see World Bank (1994).

Table 7-7. Employment and Productivity in Central Government, 1990–97

Year	Employment (annual percentage change)	Productivity (expenditure other than payroll and debt service/total staffing. millions $1997)
1990	3.8	27.2
1991	3.0	28.4
1992	2.3	31.4
1993	1.1	33.1
1994	1.8	34.2
1995	1.1	35.5
1996	0.6	38.8
1997[a]	0.7	43.1

a. Estimated.
Source: Vial (1997).

public debt service, rose from $27.2 million in 1990 to $38.8 million in 1996— a 43 percent increase (table 7-7). This accounts for a major increase in the productivity of the public sector.

REMUNERATIONS. The current system of remunerations in the public service consists of a set of wide-ranging salary scales. These scales resulted from the unification of the pay systems in effect until 1974 into the Unified Scale of Remunerations (EUR). This was one of the primary components of the administrative reforms carried out in the early stages of the military regime. Although it never became universal, and its scope narrowed over time,[45] the principle of determination of public sector wages on the basis of centrally administered pay scales has remained valid until today. This means, however, that each grade carries a specific wage that is not greatly affected by the duties of the workers employed in it, their working conditions or, even less, their performance.

Salaries in the Chilean public sector have fluctuated greatly over time (figure 7-3). After a rapid rise in the early seventies, salaries plummeted in 1973–75, a 55 percent decline from their peak level in 1972. During the re-

---

45. The groups now excluded from the EUR include the armed forces and police, physicians, the staff of regulatory agencies, and municipal employees. In each of these sectors are scales similar to the EUR.

Figure 7-3. Central Government Wages Compared with General Wages Index, 1970–97

Index 1970 = 100

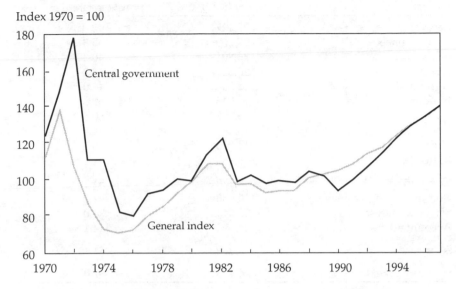

Source: Dirección de Presupuestos.

mainder of the 1970s, they partly recovered from this loss only to drop farther between 1982 and 1987. A sustained recovery in the 1990s raised the wages of public employees a cumulative 50 percent.[46]

Public sector wages have largely followed the pattern of change in public finances. The steep reductions in pay of 1973–76 and 1982–87 were associated with severe fiscal retrenchments. In other words, public wages were one of the principal variables employed in fiscal adjustments. Similarly, the recovery of the 1990s was made possible by the sustained rise in fiscal revenue during this period.

---

46. These figures convey nothing of the effect on remunerations of reclassifications of personnel to higher grades or of increases in pay supplements and bonuses, both of which have played an active part in the wage policies of the democratic administrations. If these factors are added to the general pay increases, public sector remunerations between 1990 and 1997 increased by an average of 75 percent in real terms.

Table 7-8. Public versus Private Salaries

Position	Average annual salary (US$)[a]	Salary as a percentage of private sector salary
Lawyer	27,127	40.0
Civil engineer	27,260	35.8
Economist	26,801	40.3
Auditor	20,822	40.3
Agronomist	22,230	42.0
Builder	21,046	59.8
Physician	26,097	60.8
Counsellor	16,587	84.8
Nurse	14,006	78.1
Educator	16,285	141.2
Computing clerk	8,170	51.2
Computer programmer	10,086	62.2
Systems analyst	23,543	74.0
Accountant	22,001	114.1
Secretary	8,369	81.1
Service worker	4,423	67.0

a. Average annual salary in civil central government, projected from actual salary paid in June 1996.

Source: Dirección de Presupuestos, Deloitte, Haskins & Sell, and Price Waterhouse.

In the long term, changes in public sector wages have largely paralleled those of the economy as a whole (figure 7-3). Does this mean that the public sector can compete with the private sector for qualified staff? Not necessarily, according to table 7-8. As can be seen, the public sector is reasonably competitive at the level of low-skilled personnel, such as systems analysts and secretarial and service personnel, and professionals employed in the social sectors, such as nurses, social workers, and educators.[47] On the other hand, professionals in highest demand in the market, such as engineers, lawyers, auditors, economists, architects, and agronomists, earn more than twice as much in the private sector than in the public sector. Every indication is that this gap is even wider for staff at the managerial level.

These differences are largely accounted for by the variation in pay increases in the public sector during the 1990s from one personnel sector and

47. Table 7-8 refers only to educators employed in the central administration and not to schoolteachers, who are employed by the municipal governments at lower remunerations.

category to another. The greatest increases have been awarded to workers earning the lowest salaries and those employed in sectors that suffered the most in the adjustments of the previous decade. For example, four groups of workers have seen their pay increase more than 100 percent in real terms. These are the workers in health services, the judiciary, and in the educational and health establishments transferred to the municipal governments. Similarly, among the civilian personnel of the central administration from 1990 to 1996 the largest increases went to the lowest skilled workers—clerical and auxiliary personnel—and within each category chiefly to the poorest 20 percent of wage earners.

CAREER DEVELOPMENT. Most public sector workers are employed under special statutes on job selection, promotion, and termination. These statutes operate on the principle of adherence, meaning that the employment relation does not stem from an individual contract but from the law itself. The main features of these statutes date back at least to the early 1930s.

In general, the statutes applicable to civilian personnel provide for two types of employee: permanent and on temporary contract. Only permanent employees are tenure based, whereas the contracts of employees of the second type can be terminated at any time. These contracts cannot extend beyond the end of the calendar year, although they can be renewed. The rules of the public sector also allow hiring fee-based consultants and in exceptional cases employees on private contracts. Table 7-9 shows that about two-thirds of the civilian personnel of the central administration are per-

Table 7-9. Central Government Employment Tenure Composition, 1996

Employment category	Number of employees/positions	Percent
Available tenured positions[a]	101,494	
Staffing cap[b]	133,701	
Actual staffing level[c]	131,451	100.0
Tenured	90,048	68.5
Fixed-term contracts	38,474	29.3
Consultants	311	0.2
Other[d]	2,618	2.0

a. As determined in the statute of each ministry or agency.
b. As determined in the annual budget.
c. As of June 1996.
d. Security guards, temporary workers, and other employees under private contracts.
Source: Dirección de Presupuestos.

manent, 31 percent are on temporary contract, and the remaining 2.5 percent are employed either as consultants or under private contracts.

In the Chilean public sector, the career of an employee develops within each public institution. No provisions exist for horizontal movements in the public service. While all institutions are governed by the same employment statute, each must conduct its own personnel management. Chile has no centralized recruitment, promotion, or training systems, like those that typically exist in countries with a classical civil service.

Career development comes from promotions to vacant posts within the organization. Vacancies are filled by automatic promotion of the employee in the top step of the next lower grade in the case of career posts, by competition if there are no employees with the required qualifications in the lower grades, or by decision of the head of the service or the president in cases of politically appointed posts.

While they establish a system of utmost simplicity in operation, these rules carry negative consequences for the functioning of the public services. In the first place, only in exceptional cases is there real competition for vacant public posts, and even in such cases competition is confined to a handful of employees in the grade just below the grade of the vacancy. Secondly, there is only a generic connection between post and duties. Thus, when a position becomes vacant, it is rarely filled by someone who will work in the same office and location. This is because the legal template of posts in each organization is conceived more as a mechanism for pay increases than as a means of matching a suitable person to the needs of the service. Thirdly, since promotions of permanent personnel depend on the occurrence of vacancies at the higher grades and there is no horizontal mobility in the public administration, professional and pecuniary advancement relies not on the employee's performance but on other employees' decisions to withdraw from the service.

These problems are accentuated by the fact that most of these rules, as well as job tenure, were suspended during the military regime. It made heavy use of its discretionary power, leaving the system with political distortions and arbitrary situations that were profoundly resented by public servants.

MOTIVATION AND *ESPRIT DE CORPS*. The far-reaching restructuring process and government cutbacks took their toll on Chile's public sector, which suffered massive layoffs and severe erosion of salary levels throughout the 1970s and 1980s. To this was added the widespread discretionary use of special powers and the systematic discrediting of the public service during the military regime. Despite limitations common to many developing countries, the civil service contained many elements typical of the civil service structures that arose under the bureaucratic model. Although the most egregious effects of the authoritarian period have been corrected by the democratic governments, it is worth asking to what extent this series of processes has sapped the motivation and *esprit de corps* of Chile's public servants.

A recent study on the public sector's organizational climate commissioned by the Budget Directorate of the Ministry of Finance (DESUC 1997) provides insight into this question. The study reveals a very high degree of dissatisfaction among civil servants with respect to both wages and opportunities for career advancement. Despite the evidence of rising civil service salaries during the 1990s, more than 60 percent of the officials surveyed reported that their economic situation had improved little or not at all. Respondents were equally pessimistic concerning career prospects in the civil service. Seventy-one percent said they disagreed with the statement that officials in their department who make the greatest effort are most likely to receive a promotion.

Apparently, Chile's civil servants are very dissatisfied. Yet staff turnover has been low. As table 7-10 shows, only 4 percent of the central government's employees have left the public service on a voluntary basis. This is corroborated by other findings that indicate that close to 70 percent of public officials have neither sought nor accepted other employment in two years, even though many of them were offered a job by other employers and unemployment remained low.

How can this apparent paradox be explained? A worker's motivation is not solely dependent on remuneration or prospects for advancement; other

Table 7-10. Voluntary Withdrawals from Central Government, 1995–96

| Position | *Withdrawals as a percentage of total staffing* | | | |
	Unified Salary Scale	*Regulatory bodies*	*Judiciary and legislature*	*Total*
Managers	5.7	11.6	0.9	5.5
Professionals	6.2	6.4	1.0	6.1
Technicians	2.2	6.9	0.0	2.3
Administrators	3.4	5.0	0.8	3.3
Service workers	3.4	9.0	2.9	3.6
Total	3.9	6.8	0.9	4.0

Source: Dirección de Presupuestos.

factors also affect job satisfaction. Particularly important in this regard are the job content and working conditions.

Working conditions are especially important to Chilean public employees. For example, the above-mentioned study on the organizational climate in Chile's public sector found that most civil servants have a positive perception of the opportunities for professional development afforded by their government: some 80 percent of those surveyed felt that they had made progress in their professions while working in the public sector. The study shows that most view their jobs as interesting and only moderately demanding or stressful, with reasonable working hours.

The situation of Chilean public employees in this respect can be summarized in terms of three fundamental indicators. First, on job satisfaction, only 15 percent of those surveyed indicated dissatisfaction with their work. Second, on commitment to the service, some 61 percent of respondents indicated a desire to remain in the public service in the future. Third, on dedication, only 9 percent reported a lack of commitment to their jobs.

These positive views contrast sharply with the answer of the same officials when asked how other Chileans perceive them. Most felt that their countrymen view civil servants as inefficient, lacking in dedication to their jobs, not especially corrupt but not overly honest either, and neither total failures nor outstanding successes in their work.

The result is that officials tend to be critical of the system in which they operate (table 7-11). There is a stark contrast between what they identify as the aspects most valued by the civil service at present (punctuality and adherence to rules) and those values that ought to be most prized (efficiency and initiative). When asked to indicate the main problems in government service, officials were critical of senior authorities (for inappropriate hiring practices and political influence) and their fellow civil servants (for abuse of power and absenteeism during working hours).

In short, government officials see their work as useful and interesting, but they feel that little value is placed on their work by the public, which views them as mediocre. All of this results in a critical view of the system and a sense of dissatisfaction with the state of affairs. This attitude is being increasingly expressed through greater union militancy and a rise in the frequency of strikes and other forms of labor unrest.

Since a significant proportion of its officials (43 percent) entered the public sector only in the past ten years, it is clear that Chile cannot continue to rely on the traditional values and motives that have inspired its civil servants. There is an urgent need to build a strategic alliance between government authorities and civil servants in order to improve the economic welfare

Table 7-11. Values and Priorities in the Public Sector
(percent)

Issues	What is more valued?	What should be valued?
Punctuality	35.2	12.7
Rule compliance	20.2	6.3
Loyalty	9.7	12.5
Efficiency	12.4	28.7
Initiative	4.4	16.4
Effort	1.4	7.3
Dedication	2.6	3.0
Experience	5.4	10.6

Source: Departmento de Sociologiá, Pontificia Universidad Católica de Chile (DESUC), "Situación Organizacional de la Administración Pública Chilena," study commissioned by the Ministry of Finance.

and working conditions of public employees, while at the same time increasing the effectiveness of the state. There are reasons for optimism in this regard. Surveys conducted to date indicate a willingness on the part of officials to modernize their institutions. The surveys also show significantly higher job satisfaction among those who are already undertaking such renewal.

Financial Management

The size of budget deficits in many countries, coupled with the political difficulty of bringing them under control, have led to a growing stream of studies seeking to explain the effectiveness of fiscal policy from an institutional perspective.[48]

If countries, in fact, differ significantly in their budgetary institutions and practices, and if such differences to a large extent determine the influence of the various pressure groups and economic authorities over the formulation of budgets, we should perhaps turn to such differences in seeking an explanation of why the fiscal performance of some countries is better than that of others. A study of the relationships between these practices may help identify "correct" budgetary institutions that are able to ensure solid fiscal performance.

Milesi-Ferretti (1996) divides studies of the influence of budgetary institutions on fiscal policy into two main categories. On one side are those that

---

48. This section is based on Marcel (1997d).

concentrate on fiscal regulations (for example, a constitutional provision requiring a balanced budget or the "convergence criteria" in the Maastricht Treaty of the European Union). These studies emphasize how fiscal regulations can help eliminate systematic bias in efforts to achieve balanced budgets and focus budget discussions on the desired results in terms of fiscal policies.

On the other side are studies that concentrate on budget procedures and how such procedures assign greater initiative and control to actors who represent the interests of the community as a whole, compared with those who advocate particular interests in each of the stages that a budget must pass. These studies seek to identify at each stage in the process those institutions and practices that assign priority to the economic authority or the various ministries, parliamentarians, pressure groups, or government agencies. Comprehensive analysis of these institutions would reveal whether a country's budget system should be classified as "hierarchical" (the Ministry of Finance takes precedence over the sectoral ministries in the formulation and execution of the budget, and the executive branch rather than the legislature has the last word in the approval process) or "collegiate" (the sectoral ministries, parliamentary bodies, and government agencies take the lead during preparation, approval, and execution of the budget, respectively).[49] In principle, *hierarchical* systems should result in better fiscal performance than *collegiate* systems.

From these studies it is possible to draw clear conclusions regarding policies. To obtain good fiscal performance, it is not enough to have a competent economic authority with the capacity to analyze and define policies. Adequate institutions are also essential. These institutions must ensure the preeminence of the Ministry of Finance and the executive branch during the budget-making process, or otherwise impose a priori restrictions on that process. While the corresponding reforms are not easy to carry out, the effort is well worth it since the goal is one of the most valued in contemporary economies: powerful and stable means for controlling budget deficits.

CHILE'S BUDGETARY INSTITUTIONS. Chile is a country that has suffered the social and economic consequences of fiscal imbalances. These imbalances, which resulted originally from the sensitivity of public finances to fluctuations in the country's terms of trade and the rigidity of its spending commitments, have been responsible for the past volatility of the country's

---

49. Alesina and others (1995, 5–8).

economy and, in particular, for the inflation that characterized the Chilean economy until the mid-1980s.

Although Chile's terms of trade continue to affect public finances because of the importance of copper earnings to government revenues, and although spending rigidities persist owing to the effects of statutory provisions governing wages, pensions, and debt service, the country's public finances have recorded highly satisfactory results in recent years. As indicated earlier, Chile is coming up on 11 straight years of fiscal surpluses and enjoys a level of public savings that has been steadily rising over time. During the 1990s fiscal discipline was an obstacle neither to the recovery of the lost ground in wages, pensions, and social subsidies, nor to expansion of the government's actions in the social sectors. It also did not impede vigorous steps to build basic infrastructure.

Much of this positive fiscal performance has taken place under democratic rule. Notwithstanding dire predictions at the time, the restoration of democracy in Chile, far from undermining fiscal discipline, actually strengthened it, not only during the budgetary process but with respect to initiatives affecting long-term fiscal commitments and revenues.[50] It is worth examining the role played by budgetary institutions in this process.

At various times public finances and the national budget have become an area of confrontation between opposing political forces or branches of government in Chile. Such confrontations even prompted a civil war at the end of the nineteenth century. The political crisis during the government of Salvador Allende was in part reflected in conflicts arising from the approval of deficit budgets.

For this reason, the Chilean system has gradually furnished the executive branch with greater powers over economic matters and management of the state's finances. The current institutional arrangements derive from the Constitution of 1980 and the State Financial Administration Act of 1975.

Chile's national budget is broadly inclusive, covering the various agencies and ministries of the central administration, the judiciary, and the Con-

---

50. One example of this is the tax reform introduced in 1990. Its objective was to finance major increases in social spending, none of which was allowed to go forward until the reform program had been approved. More recently, the government announced ambitious educational reforms that would require an increase of over 30 percent in the government's school subsidies. Approval of these reforms was made conditional upon retaining the VAT rate at existing levels rather than lowering it by one percentage point beginning in 1998, in accordance with legislation approved in 1993.

gress. Not included are the country's municipalities, government enterprises, state-run universities, and a part of defense expenditures. The Chilean budget is also comprehensive in terms of the transactions covered: all fiscal revenues and expenditures are included.[51]

It takes a relatively short time to prepare the budget in Chile compared with the process in other countries. Deadlines are mandated by law and thus compulsory. This requires a highly centralized system of administration, particularly within the Ministry of Finance.

The budgetary powers of Chile's Congress are limited to reducing items of expenditure proposed by the administration. Members of Congress are prohibited from altering the calculation of revenues, increasing expenditures, or reallocating resources between programs. This differs from the previous institutional organization in which parliamentarians were permitted to increase expenditures, provided they specified a source for financing such increases.[52]

In contrast to the limited powers of the National Congress, the Chilean budget is relatively detailed. It includes more than 4,000 items plus approximately 1,000 special clauses. However, the current institutional framework has built-in flexibility through provisions that allow the Ministry of Finance to adjust budget allocations during the year. An important feature of this flexibility is the inclusion in the budget of a central reserve to cover the fiscal cost of laws passed during the course of the year, as well as contingencies.

As a counterweight to the high degree of centralization of the country's financial administration, the execution of its national budget is highly decentralized, particularly in the management of revenue accounts and government accounting in general. Thus, cash funds are transferred by the Ministry of Finance to the responsible public institutions in the form of monthly disbursements based on a cash allocation schedule drawn up at the start of the year. These resources are deposited in bank accounts for

---

51. The budget approval process may not alter certain expenditures laid down in law. For example, it cannot change welfare benefits, the wage bill for the permanent personnel of the public administration, or expenditures that result from contractual commitments such as servicing of the national debt.

52. This led to a plethora of special laws, most of which ran counter to the wishes of the administration. The Constitution of 1980 not only restricts congressional powers in this area, but also expressly prohibits allocation of taxes for specific purposes, thus ensuring centralized financial management.

each institution, which may then draw on the funds in accordance with the provisions of the budget. The use of these resources must be reported monthly to the Comptroller General and to the Budget Directorate.

Given these arrangements, the institutional framework responsible for formulating and executing Chile's budget can be categorized as markedly hierarchical. This is confirmed in the study by Alesina and others (1995) in which Chile is included among those countries whose budgetary institutions enjoy the most clearly established lines of authority and responsibility in Latin America. Chile, along with Jamaica, is at one extreme in the distribution of 20 countries in Latin America and the Caribbean based on the degree of hierarchy in its budgetary process and public-sector primary deficit.

FLAWS IN THE BUDGETARY SYSTEM. Chile's budgetary system is not flawless, however. At least two problems are worth noting. First, Chile's financial management system, despite all of its successes, remains a traditional system based on controlling expenditure of liquid resources. Therefore, it cannot assess either the results of the application of public funds, or the true economic cost incurred to obtain these results. In other words, this is a system that is effective in controlling overall fiscal aggregates and monitoring their composition, but not in facilitating or promoting efficient management of public institutions.

In the past few years many countries have tried to transform their budgets into instruments for promoting more effective and efficient management in the public sector. These reforms include the use of indicators and targets for budget management, evaluation of government programs, application of commercial accounting in public sector agencies, allocation of resources based on management contracts, developing multi-year budgeting exercises, and so forth. Some of these reforms have already been taken up with the public-sector modernization agenda adopted by the current government in Chile, but much remains to be done.

Second, the hierarchical structure of the public-sector financial system has yet to be fully accepted by the different actors in the budgetary process. Ever since the country's democratic institutions were fully restored and began applying the financial regulations created under the military regime, Chile's parliamentarians have complained about the limited role assigned to them in the budget approval process. They have sought means to apply greater pressure on the executive than is permitted under those regulations. For their part, the sectoral ministries resent the degree of discretion that the Ministry of Finance enjoys in drawing up the budget, as well as the controls and authorizations required during its implementation phase.

These problems are to some extent representative of the natural limitations of a hierarchically organized budgetary system. The fact that this system concentrates responsibility for conducting the state's financial affairs in the executive—specifically, within the administration's economic authority—does not protect that authority from the pressures and influence of the other powerful actors. To ensure success, these other actors must value fiscal discipline and share a common goal of ensuring efficient use of public resources.

Chile's experience suggests that fiscal governance can be reinforced through two types of initiatives that are less onerous from a political point of view.[53] The first is to develop instruments that can be used to promote common awareness of the importance of fiscal discipline (for example, establishing stabilization funds, developing fiscal policy indicators and medium-term financial projections, and setting budget ceilings based on *a priori* grounds). The second type of initiative would establish within the hierarchy of institutions responsible for budget decisions a mechanism enabling the legislature to participate in the evaluation of the merits, efficiency, and results of the programs that make up the budget.

Control and Oversight

EXTERNAL CONTROL. External monitoring of public administration in Chile is the responsibility of the Comptroller General of the Republic. This is a politically autonomous body whose mandate includes the legal control of administrative acts, oversight of the use of public funds, and financial accounting. These duties are carried out under a system that relies primarily on ex ante supervision, auditing, and drafting of legal opinions at the request of those affected by administrative decisions. The Comptroller General's Office has jurisdiction over the institutions of the executive branch, municipalities, and government enterprises established under special statutes. In addition, the Comptroller General is empowered to conduct audits and inspections of any institution that receives public resources.

The Comptroller General's Office is politically and administratively independent from the executive branch. The Comptroller General is appointed by the Senate upon a proposal by the president and may be removed from office only for gross abandonment of duty. Under the Chilean scheme of

---

53. For a detailed examination of these proposals, see Marcel (1997d).

comprehensive rules in the public sector, the Comptroller General's Office is subject to the same standards governing administration of human and financial resources that apply to all other public institutions. Thus, it is staffed by career civil servants whose salaries are determined in accordance with the laws applicable to all public regulatory bodies. These salaries, combined with special benefits, ensure that personnel in this office receive higher pay than do civil servants in other branches of Chile's civil service.

The legal regime, powers, and instruments entrusted to the Comptroller General have undergone little change since its creation in the 1930s as the result of a complete transformation of the Court of Accounts. Taken together, these regulations provide a consistent and powerful set of tools enabling the Comptroller General's Office to impose its authority on Chile's public sector. Its decisions are widely feared and duly respected, with many institutions opting to consult with it before engaging in activities that might prove controversial. The powers and independence of its officials have earned the Comptroller General in Chile public confidence and broad respect within Latin America.

It must be acknowledged, however, that a system of controls that relies on ex-ante approvals by the Comptroller General's Office introduces enormous rigidity and slows down the operation of public institutions. Moreover, the ability of the Comptroller General to prevent administrative irregularities or outright fraud depends more on the institution's deterrent powers than on its capacity for detecting such acts. By the same token, inspections carried out by the Auditor General's staff often become bogged down in irrelevant administrative detail, limiting their effectiveness in identifying real problems. To this must be added the fact that during the military regime, the Comptroller General's Office operated under the subtle tutelage of the government.

All of these events took place within a public administration that has been doing everything possible to introduce flexibility into its day-to-day management operations. Either because of this effort or the particular way in which the decentralized institutions of Chile's public sector developed, many processes that are highly centralized in other countries have been left to the discretion of individual institutions in Chile. Among the more conspicuous examples are the aforementioned management of fiscal accounts, personnel recruitment and training, and government procurement. As a result of this combination of factors, public administration in Chile depends to a much larger extent on the ethics and dedication of its officials than is otherwise common in countries with a similar level of development and with similar legal traditions.

Clearly, these factors impose limits on the Comptroller General's oversight capabilities, and its current authorities have sought the necessary powers and resources to strengthen its capacity.[54] Meanwhile, the government, concerned about the recent detection of improprieties, introduced a number of legal changes designed to combat corruption in the public service. These reforms include regulations penalizing influence peddling and establishing access to information rights. By 1997 little progress had been made in either area.

It would be fair to note that the absence of progress is attributable to a lack of clarity among the respective authorities concerning the characteristics of a modern system for independent controls and monitoring of public administration in Chile. While the existing systems cannot be said to be in crisis yet, progress is clearly needed.

CITIZEN OVERSIGHT AND ACCOUNTABILITY. The state is the political expression of organized society and the means *par excellence* for implementing collective decisions. Yet the state also has certain powers that allow it to affect the well-being of individual citizens. Throughout history this fundamental relationship between the state and its citizens has led many countries to introduce reforms aimed at ensuring the legality of government actions and reducing the discretionary powers of public officials. The bureaucratic model of government is to a large extent the embodiment of this approach. The reforms introduced more recently in various countries have strengthened the relationship between institutions managing public services and the people they serve, casting the latter as "clients" and establishing systems of consultation, choice, and compensation modeled on market mechanisms. In view of this, we might well ask: to what extent is the organizational and institutional structure of the Chilean state accountable to its citizens?

The answer to this question is relatively simple: public institutions in Chile are subject to no other means of accountability than those inherent in its democratic institutions (the executive branch and Congress made up of legislators elected by the people, the Chamber of Deputies with its oversight powers, and the general legal accountability of authorities for their public acts), and the need to comply with existing laws and regulations. The country's institutional framework does not include any special provisions for holding government bodies accountable, such as specialized administrative tribunals, ombudsmen, or participatory action groups. Only a

---

54. For a review of some of these proposals, see Contraloría General de la República (1995).

handful of Chile's public sector institutions have systems to process complaints from the public.

This situation is probably caused by two factors. First, the Chilean state has a long history of top-down, authoritarian government. Its network of technically advanced, autonomous public agencies, while useful for purposes of improving the effectiveness of the state in fulfilling its administrative functions, likely helped generate a degree of paternalism in the relationship between these institutions and their users. These tendencies can only have been exacerbated during the military regime.

Second, the country has had a characteristically weak civil society. Notable for their absence, community groups have been highly vulnerable and often manipulated by the political parties. Citizens make few demands on the state and its institutions. In fact, people generally adopt a conformist attitude when dealing with the bureaucracy.

This situation, however, appears to be ripe for change. The development of markets is helping Chileans view themselves as consumers with rights of their own. Half of the public sector's tax proceeds comes from the VAT. This is strengthening citizens' perception of themselves as taxpayers with the right to demand that the state make efficient use of their contributions.

It is doubtful that the current political system will be able to meet the new demands on the state deriving from these changes. The Chilean state covers too wide a range of functions to be able to keep track of the countless relationships that develop between a state and its citizens.

Although small advances have been made in promoting greater accountability of public institutions under the democratic governments, the progress has been limited to isolated cases that do not form part of an overall policy. Thus, developing institutional mechanisms for strengthening the relationship and bringing the state closer to its citizens constitute important challenges still ahead.

Modernization of Public Sector Management under the Democratic Governments

At the start of the first democratic government following the military regime, there was no clear consensus on the urgency, objectives, and instruments needed to modernize the state. The authorities who took office in March of 1990 had had little hands-on experience in government and assumed that the structural changes introduced during the period of military rule had taken root within the various public institutions. Although this notion soon proved to be wrong, the first democratic government nevertheless concentrated its efforts on purely institutional reforms (including reforming district and regional administrations) and revamping the legal system (such as proposals for establishing administrative tribunals). While the first reforms represented an important advance in the decentralization process, the second set of proposals did not got through the legislature.

At the same time, the authorities were becoming increasingly aware of problems with public sector management. The Ministry of Finance became particularly concerned about difficulties in implementing public programs and the absence of results in institutions and sectors receiving major infusions of resources.

In view of these problems and the urgent need for specific experimental projects to help guide future policies, a pilot program was launched at the start of 1993 to help modernize management in the public sector. The program was based on the idea that public services (rather than institutions of the central government) would define successes and failures in public sector management and that those services had ample room, despite legal and regulatory restrictions, to carry out initiatives aimed at improving management. Based on these principles, the core objective of the program was the development of strategic planning. With the participation of senior managers, officials, clients, and supporters, this exercise would define each institution's mission, including its primary management objectives, clients, and principal products. Based on this analysis, specific projects would then be developed to improve management and to organize a management information system. Such a system provides indicators for effective internal and external monitoring of the institution's operations, and it establishes goals and specific management targets. These goals and targets could then be incorporated into performance contracts specifying incentives and awards for good management.

Members of the second democratic government were inspired by initiatives such as the pilot program and began to develop policies with a larger scope. They rejected the idea of a comprehensive administrative reform process in favor of smaller viable initiatives that could be carried out without major changes to the legal framework, in areas where incentives, demand, and the leadership of key institutions would play a central role. The ultimate aim of this process was to develop a new organizational culture that would be performance driven and based on satisfying users' requirements.

In line with this philosophy, the Frei government established a joint ministerial committee made up of officials from the Ministry of the Interior, the Ministry of Finance, and the General Secretariat of the Presidency. Its fundamental task would be to promote, coordinate, and plan new initiatives to be carried out within the public services.

In mid-1994 modernization agreements were reached between the central government, in the person of the president, and 43 public services. These agreements were drawn up by the public services in question, covering the widest possible range of fields and representing various levels of complexity and difficulty. When progress under these agreements was assessed at the beginning of 1995, they were found to be 80 percent completed.

Meanwhile, the Budget Directorate of the Ministry of Finance had begun a more broadly representative project aimed at developing performance indicators that could be incorporated into the budgetary process. As part of this effort during the preparation of the budget for 1995, public services were asked to be ready to identify their performance indicators and targets for the year.

Replies to this request were received from 26 public services, for which 107 performance indicators were selected. This information was included in the data attached to the draft budget for 1995, and it was welcomed by the National Congress and the press. The scope of this initiative continued to expand and diversify. By 1996 it included a total of 67 institutions with 291 indicators for that year.[55]

The increased attention to results and performance soon shifted to public sector pay where the priorities of the Aylwin administration had focused on making up the ground that was lost during the 1980s. The achievement of these goals, and the fact that improved pay levels actually had little impact on performance by civil servants, led the new government to revise its policy on wages and to link salary levels closely to public sector performance.

The government not only reaffirmed its aim of linking pay raises to gains in average productivity levels and future inflation, but also developed specific instruments for linking pay, responsibility, and performance. To this end, in 1994 the government began applying performance-based pay schemes to schoolteachers in the state-funded educational system, municipal health care services, the customs service, the health services in general, and the judiciary. By the end of 1997, it was agreed to extend these schemes to all personnel in the remaining institutions of the central government beginning in 1999. Thus, as salary levels in the public sector have grown in

---

55. For an assessment of recent experience in developing performance indicators for Chile's public sector, see Marcel (1997c).

real terms, they have been linked to the performance of public servants. By mid-1997, some 220,000 public employees were covered by performance-based wage systems of this sort.

Skills improvement also has occupied an important position in the program to modernize public administration in Chile. Between 1990 and 1996, investment in civil service training programs quadrupled. In addition, a program aimed at modernizing the entire public sector training system was launched in 1995.

At the end of 1996, new activities were identified to ensure continuing progress in public sector management. First, all public services were required to prepare an annual performance report indicating the degree to which they had met their budget, program, and management targets for the preceding year. Second, the Executive, in an agreement with the National Congress, decided to conduct a systematic evaluation of Chile's public programs. The evaluation could be extended over four years to include all social, productive, and institutional development programs managed by institutions of the central government. Third, a new round of modernization agreements was launched; despite demands for higher quality and project requirements, it has succeeded in engaging all of the services in the central government's public administration.

Thus, the program to modernize the public service in Chile has experienced rapid and dynamic progress, resulting in numerous initiatives that have been carried out since 1995 under a program coordinated by the Joint Ministerial Committee for Modernization of Public Administration.

Lessons and Challenges from the Chilean Experience

The indicators we have gathered confirm the view that the effectiveness of Chile's public sector can be positively compared with that of countries with similar or even higher levels of development. However, the process that generated such results looks substantially different from a "big bang" unleashed by liberalizing economic policies aimed at retrenching the state from ineffective activities toward core functions.

Chile's military government rolled back the frontiers of the state, particularly by eliminating controls over prices, foreign trade, and the financial sector. Asset redistribution, which attracted so much attention during the 1960s and early 1970s, was also cut out from the public agenda. The entrepreneurial activity of the state was curtailed in successive waves of privatization. But the functions of the state, except in a few areas, changed much less than did the means of performing them.

Changing public sector instruments and policies was much more of an interactive than a one-way process. New policies were facilitated by the existing capabilities of the state, which were modified in turn. The reasons for this phenomenon can be readily understood as we analyze four landmarks in the development of the state's capabilities.

The first landmark is the basic framework of government in Chile since the 1930s: "decentralized services" for the fulfillment of executive functions, a comprehensive labor statute with features characteristic of a professional civil service, the hierarchical structures of public financial management, and a powerful Comptroller General.

The second landmark is the military regime's administrative reforms. These include "regionalization" as a device for strengthening economic planning, decentralized public services, the unified scale of public salaries, and the strengthening of the powers of the executive through the financial management bill and the 1980 Constitution. These reforms took place mostly in the early stages of the military government and can hardly be associated with its liberalizing program.

The third landmark is the toll on public management taken by the harsh fiscal adjustments of the mid-1970s and most of the 1980s as well as by the weight of authoritarian rule during the military regime. The public sector was deprived of the resources needed to deliver its most basic services, and systematic political interference hampered its internal functioning. Furthermore, the morale of public servants was seriously damaged. Had it not been for the strength of Chile's public institutions, and the social capital accumulated within them, such factors might have had a devastating impact on the state's effectiveness.

A last landmark is the recovery of the state's capabilities during the democratic governments of the 1990s. These governments provided the public sector with the resources needed not only to recover its operational capacity, but also to legitimize some of the policies and institutions left by the military regime. In addition, new functions were developed, particularly those related to social programs, infrastructure development, environmental protection, and competitive markets.

As we can see, developments affecting the functions and capabilities of the Chilean state were far from linear and cannot be easily adapted to schemes such as the one proposed by the *World Development Report 1997*. Adapting role to capabilities cannot be more than a state-shrinking exercise unless (a) democratic institutions allow the people to voice their views on the role of the state and provide checks and balances for major decisions affecting it; (b) the public sector is given the resources needed to perform its remaining functions; and (c) public sector institutions are adapted to the needs of a more open and competitive environment. If such conditions are not present, the criticism of public inefficiency that necessarily comes with deregulation and privatization is not constructive. It easily becomes a generalized attack on all public functions, and the run down of public sector capabilities would easily become a self-fulfilling prophecy.

In the Chilean case, nothing less than a change in the political regime and in the government was needed to stop what looked like an unyielding retrenchment of the state. Only then could some political sustainability be gained for the reforms developed in the 1980s. There was no automatic relation between the retrenchment of the state in certain areas and its strengthening in others; neither was there an automatic relation between the change in the functions of the state and the development of its capabilities.

However, the retrenchment of the state during the military government did not have a neutral effect on its later recovery. A radical experience like Chile's may damage the remaining capabilities of the state in a number of practical ways. This is particularly true of the privatization process. The industrial organization generated by the privatization of electricity precluded further competition and weakened the regulatory capability of the state. Privatization also carried heavy capital losses for the state, reducing its net worth by some US$1 billion. Indeed, such outcomes are avoidable. What generated them was not privatization itself but the political pressure to privatize at all costs and the contempt with which the public sector was regarded by the economists and the authorities of the military regime. In sharp contrast with the above, the privatization of the electricity company that remained in the hands of the state took nearly six years to complete.[56] When it was finally achieved, the government obtained a price that was higher than the sum of the electricity companies privatized under the military regime.

Effective public institutions are not created by a pure act of political goodwill, but by the accumulation of experience and capabilities over long periods. When policymakers allow these processes to develop and when they

---

56. We are referring to Colbun-Machicura, responsible for some 15 percent of electricity generation in the central system. Half of the company was sold to a strategic investor through a carefully drafted public process. The main purpose of the government in this privatization was to attract new competitors to the Chilean electricity system. The main participants were banned from participating in the bid. In order to make the company more attractive to investors, a whole development program for building three new power centers plus a distribution line was studied and devised.

furnish public institutions with the tools needed for effective management, such institutions are able to withstand even the darkest times.

The Chilean experience draws attention to the importance of building upon previous experience and existing institutions in the development of the state's capabilities. The military government did just that in the area in which it recorded its most noted achievement in social policy (child nutrition programs). In other cases the weakening of public institutions, either because of the withdrawal of resources or because of the exercise of discretionary powers, pushed cherished reforms to the brink of collapse. Had it not been for the incoming democratic authorities' commitment to stability, the story of these reforms could have easily ended in a policy reversal that cost the country very dearly.

The institutional capability to withstand difficult times and survive U-turns in public policy is not unlimited. Indeed, the Chilean experience provides plenty of examples of the cost of policy changes. Consider attempts to correct features of the new pension and health insurance systems. When the political tide had abandoned the creators of the system and new authorities were in charge, corporate interests had already become sufficiently entrenched to block any reform, regardless of whether it helped to ensure long-run sustainability. This calls into question the very future of these systems. The same can be said of recent developments in the electricity sector. The economic and political power of the conglomerate built around the vertical integration of this sector was so overwhelming that when the sector became more vulnerable than expected, the regulatory bodies were unable to rise to their duties, and a complete restructuring of the regulation system had to be studied.

If reforms that modify the functions of the state are so risky, are they worthwhile? To answer this question, we have to go back to the essentials of such reforms. In any democratic country the functions undertaken by the state are not the result of the pure will of the authorities; they also reflect choices and mandates from the population. In many cases such choices do not relate to the specific means employed but to policy objectives shared by a majority. From this point of view, objectives will change only slowly, and it is more likely that new objectives will be added to, rather than replace, existing ones. But the means for achieving these objectives can indeed change rapidly as old tools prove ineffective to achieve the stated purposes of policies. The management of public enterprises is a good example. Except during the Unidad Popular government of the early 1970s, reforms in the management of public enterprises were seen as a means of fostering industrial development, solving market failures, or redistributing income. Privatization could thus be understood not as a recognition of the limited capabilities of public enterprises themselves, but of their ineffectiveness in achieving the corresponding policy aims. If the reforms had been viewed from this standpoint, the privatization process might have followed, as in other countries, a path that ensured competition and effective regulation where needed, and protected the public sector's worth.

Despite the Chilean state's achievements, there is not much room for complacency about the current situation. This is not only because of failures and weaknesses like the ones identified in human resources management, the relationship between budgeting and public management and control systems, but also because the development of the country creates new demands upon the state.

This brings us to a final question: if a country is able to develop its state's capabilities, should it also develop new functions? We believe the answer is yes—not because of a notion of an ever-expanding government, but because the economic and social development associated with the right policies and institutions brings in more complex structures that usually demand new commitments by the state.

As in the past, development is associated with urbanization and new public services. Today a more complex society entails new social groups that in one way or another demand attention from the state. However, public institutions are not always well equipped to deal with such challenges. Changing the delivery of public services is more than a means of saving public monies. It is a way to gain flexibility to face the new needs that arise with economic and social change.

In order to address these needs, the state must remember its essential role—serving the public. The broad interests of the population must be preserved in decisions concerning policy and delivery systems design. This is particularly true in Chile, a country that apparently owes so much to policymakers. A state closed to society might well survive and flourish under the capabilities of its technocrats and policymakers as long as it presides over a closed and simple economy or a weak civil society, but it would hardly survive the tests posed by a fast-moving global environment.

The main challenge for the state in Chile is to deal with the complexities of an open economy and a more active civil society while completing the bureaucratic revolution that developed countries experienced decades ago. This would be an insurmountable task if the citizen's perspective is not brought into the picture. The state's accountability to citizens must be strengthened as part of the institutional checks and balances that make a democratic and pluralistic nation. Only then will Chile be able to reconcile modernization with tradition and stability with flexibility.

References

Aghón, G. 1996. "Descentralización Fiscal En América Latina: Un Análisis Comparativo." In *Descentralización Fiscal En América Latina: Balance y Principales Desafíos*. CEPAL/GTZ, Santiago.

Alesina, A., and others. 1995. "Budget Institutions and Fiscal Performance in Latin America." Inter-American Development Bank, Washington, D.C.

Arellano, J. P. 1985. *Políticas Sociales y Desarrollo. Chile 1924–1984*. Santiago: CIEPLAN.

Bitran, E., and E. Saavedra. 1993. "Algunas Reflexiones en Torno al Rol Regulador y Empresarial del Estado." In O. Muñoz, ed., *Despues de las Privatizaciones. Hacia el Estado Regulador*. Santiago: CIEPLAN.

Blanloth, V. 1993. "La Regulación del Sector Eléctrico: la Experiencia Chilena." In O. Muñoz, ed., *Despues de las Privatizaciones. Hacia el Estado Regulador*. Santiago: CIEPLAN.

Campero, G. 1997. "Mas allá del Individualismo: la Buena Sociedad y la Participación." CIEPLAN, Santiago.

Carciofi, R., O. Centrángolo, and O. Larrañaga. 1996. *Desafíos de la Descentralización. Educación y Salud en Argentina y Chile*. Santiago: United Nations, CEPAL.

Castañeda, T. 1989. *Para Combatir la Pobreza: Política Social y Descentralización en Chile Durante los '80*. Santiago: Centro de Estudios Públicos.

Centro de Estudios de la Realidad Contemporánea (CERC). 1997. *Barómetro CERC*.

CEPAL/GTZ. 1996. *Descentralización Fiscal en América Latina: Balance y Principales Desafíos*. Santiago: Proyecto Regional de Descentralización Fiscal.

Contraloría General de la República. 1995. *¿Qué Contraloría General de la República Necesita en Chile de Hoy y del Futuro?* Proceedings from a seminar held by the Comptroller General. Santiago.

Corporación de Estudios de Opinión Pública Latinoamericana. 1996. *Latinbarómetro 1996*. Presented to the VI Ibero-American Summit of Heads of State. Santiago.

DESUC. 1997. "Clima Organizacional en la Administración Pública." Commissioned by Dirección de Presupuestos, Santiago.

Diamond, P. 1994. "Privatization of Social Security: Lessons from Chile." *Revista de Análisis Económico* 9: 1 (June).

Dirección de Presupuestos. 1997a. *Estadísticas de las Finanzas Públicas, 1987–1996*. Santiago.

————. 1997b. *Calidad de Servicio y Atención al Usuario en el Sector Público*. Santiago: Ediciones Dolmen.

Edwards, S., and A. Cox-Edwards. 1991. *Monetarism and Liberalization: The Chilean Experiment*. University of Chicago Press.

Espinoza, J., and M. Marcel. 1994: "Descentralización Fiscal: El Caso de Chile." CEPAL, Serie Política Fiscal, No. 57, Proyecto Regional de Descentralización Fiscal, CEPAL/GTZ. Santiago.

Ffrench-Davis, R. 1973. *Políticas Económicas en Chile, 1952–1970*. Santiago: CEPLAN, Ediciones Nueva Universidad.

Foxley, A. 1982. *Experimentos Neoliberales en América Latina*, special issue of Colección Estudios CIEPLAN No. 7. Santiago.

Gatica, J., and M. Marcel. 1997. "Economía Regional y Descentralización." CIEPLAN, Santiago.

Hachette, D., and R. Lüders. 1992. *La Privatización en Chile*. Santiago: Centro Internacional para el Desarrollo Económico.

Hausman, R., and M. Gavin. 1995. "Hacia una Economía Menos Volátil," segunda parte de *Progreso Económico y Social en América Latina. Informe 1995*. Washington, D.C.: Inter-American Development Bank.

IMD International. 1996. *World Competitiveness Report, 1996*. Lausanne.

Inter-American Development Bank. 1997. *Latin America after a Decade of Reforms*. Economic and Social Progress in Latin America, 1997 Report. Washington, D.C.

Larraín, F. 1991. "Public Sector Behavior in a Highly Indebted Country: The Contrasting Chilean Experience." In F. Larraín and M. Selowsky, eds., *The Public Sector and the Latin American Crisis*, International Center for Economic Growth, San Francisco: ICS Press.

Larroulet, C. 1991. *Soluciones Privadas para Problemas Públicos*. Instituto Libertad y desarrollo, Santiago.

Marcel, M. 1989. "Privatización y Finanzas Públicas: el caso de Chile, 1985–88." Colección Estudios CIEPLAN No. 26. Santiago.

————. 1997a. "Políticas Públicas en Democracia: el Caso de la Reforma Tributaria de 1990 en Chile." Colección Estudios CIEPLAN No. 45. Santiago.

————. 1997b. "Indicadores para la Medición de la Política Fiscal Macroeconómica: una Aplicación para Chile." CEPAL, Santiago.

————. 1997c. "Modernización del Estado e Indicadores de Desempeño en el Sector Público: la Experiencia Chilena." Departamento de Ingeniería Industrial de la Universidad de Chile, Santiago.

————. 1997d. "Los Caminos de la Gobernabilidad Fiscal en América Latina. Reflexiones a Partir de la Experiencia Chilena." In *Pensamiento Iberoamericano*, Madrid.

Marcel, M., and A. Arenas. 1991. "Reformas a la Seguridad Social en Chile." Serie de Monografías No. 5. Inter-American Development Bank, Washington, D.C.

Marcel, M., and and C. Tohá. 1997. "Reforma del estado y de la gestión Pública." CIEPLAN, Santiago.

Martner, G. D. 1993. *Descentralización y Modernización del Estado en la Transición*. Santiago: LOM Ediciones.

Mauro, P. 1995. "Corruption and Growth." *The Quarterly Journal of Economics*, vol. CX, no. 3, August.

Milesi-Ferretti, G.M. 1996. "Fiscal Rules and the Budget Process." IMF Working Paper no. 60, Washington, D.C.

Moulian, T. 1997. *Chile Actual. Anatomía de un Mito*. Santiago: LOM Ediciones-Universidad Arcis.

Premchand, A. 1993. *Public Expenditure Management*. Washington, D.C.: International Monetary Fund.

Raczynski, D. 1991. "La Ficha CAS y la Focalización de Programas Sociales." Notas Técnicas no. 141. CIEPLAN, Santiago.

———. 1997. "Social Policies in Chile. Origin and Transformations." Paper presented at the seminar on Social Policies for the Urban Poor in Latin America: Welfare Reform in a Democratic Context. Hellen Kellogg Institute for International Studies, University of Notre Dame.

Saez, R.E. 1993. "Las Privatizaciones de Empresas en Chile." In O. Muñoz, ed., *Despues de las Privatizaciones. Hacia el Estado Regulador*. Santiago: CIEPLAN.

Schiavo-Campo, S., G. de Tommaso, and A. Mukherjee. 1997. "An International Statistical Survey of Government Employment and Wages." Policy Research Working Paper 1806. World Bank, Policy Research Department, Washington, D.C.

Serrano, C. 1996. "Gobierno Regional e Inversión Pública Descentralizada." Colección Estudios CIEPLAN, no. 42, Santiago.

TIME FORO. 1996. "Estudio Calidad de Atención en los Servicios Públicos." Commissioned by Dirección de Presupuestos, Santiago.

Urzúa, G., and A. M. García. 1971. *Diagnóstico de la Burocracia Chilena, 1818–1969*. Santiago: Editorial Jurídica de Chile.

Uthoff, A. 1995. *Reformas a los Sistemas de Pensiones en América Latina y el Caribe*. Santiago: United Nations, CEPAL, Proyecto Regional.

Vial, G. 1996. *Historia de Chile, 1891–1973*. Vols. III and IV. Santiago: Zig-Zag.

Vial, J. 1997. "Aspectos Macroeconómicos del Proyecto de Ley de Presupuestos del Sector Público del anño 1998." Dirección de Presupuestos, Santiago.

World Bank. 1994. *Chile Finanzas de los Gobiernos Subnacionales*. Washington, D.C.

———. 1997. *World Development Report 1997: The State in a Changing World*. New York: Oxford University Press.

World Economic Forum. 1996. *The Global Competitiveness Report, 1996*. Lausanne.

8

Privatizing and Regulating Chile's Utilities, 1974–2000: Successes, Failures, and Outstanding Challenges

Eduardo Bitrán
Antonio Estache
José Luis Guasch
Pablo Serra

Chile has been at the forefront of privatization efforts in Latin America in terms of timing and scope of the program. It included the privatization of a large segment of public services and infrastructure, such as telecommunications, electricity and gas, and significant components, but not all yet, of water and sanitation and transport. Privatization has substantially improved efficiency and coverage rates.

Chile's regulation of its privatized infrastructure services has received less attention, but it certainly is just as relevant to countries considering following its lead. Privatization alone, without proper regulation, does not ensure internal efficiency and pricing at efficiency levels. This chapter discusses the interactions between the privatization strategy and the regulatory framework introduced to maximize and distribute the gains from private sector participation. Unfortunately, this is an area viewed as of second order importance in many countries ("let's privatize first and deal with regulation later"), and yet it is critical to the long-term sustainability of the gains from privatization.

In spite of its impressive accomplishments, Chile has not fully succeeded in distributing the efficiency gains fairly between investors and users. As a result, the country may be facing one of its most demanding policy challenges as it prepares for a new round of infrastructure privatization in the water and ports sectors. The chapter reviews the weakness of Chile's competition policies, its limited capacity to regulate effectively, the problematic regulatory framework in interconnection and access issues, and the enormous influence of the privatized utilities in the rate-setting process. All of these shortcomings are preventing further efficiency gains and the sharing with consumers of many of the gains already achieved. Indeed, the prices in many regulated utilities are not as low as they could or should be. In fact, drastic price cuts have been seen only where competition has been sustained.

The chapter concludes with an overview of actions still needed. The institutional rules under which regulation is enforced need to be redesigned, and interconnection and access issues must be addressed. There should be more reliance on incentive-based regulatory schemes and less on cost plus models based on benchmarks. Finally, an overhaul of the objectives of competition policy and its interplay and complementary jurisdiction with regulation is warranted.

Introduction

In November 1997 Chile's Congress cleared the way for a new round of infrastructure privatization by approving a new regulatory framework for the water utilities.[1] One of the government's purposes was to ease the financing of investment needs of about US$2.5 billion over the next five years, mainly in wastewater treatment plants.[2] This was done by relaxing the restrictions on the sale of shares in 11 regional firms. Previous legislation limited to 49 percent the number of shares that could be sold. The state's participation can decline inasmuch as it does not decide to contribute to

---

1. The plan included the restructuring and the privatization of ports.

2. Many of these companies have little debt, and hence could easily borrow. In fact, with the recent tariff increases, the firms could finance a fair share of the investment requirements out of retained earnings, at least for the next few years.

requested increases in capital. However, as long as the state owns more than 10 percent of the shares, it has veto power. The sale of the public assets started in 1998, and the transfer of the management of the sector into private hands should follow in 1999. The new law allows the government to sell up to 65 percent of each water company or raise private capital through capital increases. More importantly, the new law strengthens the regulatory structure of the sector.[3]

In this context, it seems appropriate to review the main lessons of the previous privatization experiences in Chile. The successes achieved through the divestiture of electricity and telecoms have recently enjoyed mixed reviews in Chile, as evidenced by the intensive political marketing that was required to obtain congressional support for the privatization of these water companies. The electricity and telecoms regulators have not yet been able to ensure a fair distribution between suppliers and consumers of the impressive efficiency gains achieved under private ownership. Very few of the gains have been translated into price cuts to consumers because the private companies have the upper hand in dealings with their sector-specific regulators. This is partially explained by the sheer economic size of the private utility companies.[4] It is also a consequence of the decision to allow a strong concentration of shares in the hands of a few investors as part of the initial privatization strategy—followed later by an attempt to rely more systematically on popular capitalism through a wider diffusion of ownership in new privatizations. Jointly, these two facts have given the utilities political leverage that is difficult to match for regulators who lack political independence and have limited administrative capacity.

During the political debates concerning the law adopted in 1997, it was obvious that many members of Congress feared that the water companies could be taken over by some of the same players who control the utilities privatized a decade ago. Many members of Congress were also concerned about the institutional weaknesses the regulators have demonstrated. To minimize this risk, the new owners of the water companies will not be allowed to hold electricity or phone service in the area in which they deliver

---

3. Before the 1997 law, the state could sell 100 percent of the two largest firms (EMOS and ESVAL), accounting for 54 percent of the state customers. The regional companies could have been privatized also through selling assets and licenses, as happened in Valdivia. Thus, the main purpose of the 1997 law was to strengthen the regulating framework.

4. Four of the ten companies with the highest profits are either public utilities or holdings controlling public utilities.

water services. The stimulation of effective competition whenever possible—including by comparison benchmarking—is likely to be the focus of this new round of privatization in Chile. While the goal is simple enough, its implementation will be challenging. Some of the arrangements made under the previous waves of privatization will require fine-tuning, and habits are hard to change, in particular when the stakes are as high as they are for the current owners of the utilities. Fine-tuning, however, is critical to the success of this new wave of privatization and to the long-term sustainability of the impressive successes already achieved.

The Privatization Process

When casual observers talk about Chile's' experience with privatization, they often forget that this new wave of privatization is really the tail end of a wave of privatization started in early 1994.[5] This wave followed two other waves that influenced the new role of the state in the delivery of infrastructure services. The first wave set up the initial conditions for the privatization of utilities.

The First Privatization Wave, 1974–78

Between 1974 and 1978 more than 550 companies were privatized as part of the neo-liberal revolution carried out under the military regime of General Pinochet. This revolution aimed at a major structural and institutional change that would open up the economy, reduce state participation in productive activities, and eliminate domestic and international price controls.[6] The transitional adjustment process demanded stabilizing the economy and very restrictive fiscal policies. That first wave did not include utility companies.

To maximize revenue from privatization—a key objective of the first wave—the government offered controlling packages to investors and provided credit (often through auctions) to investors to ease the constraints

---

5. Since early 1994, this privatization wave has seen the transfer of ownership to private investors of El Abra, Valdivia, and Litoral Central and even some electricity companies (Edlenor, Colbun, Electrica Tocopilla, Empemar), Radio Nacional, Transconteiner, Minsal, and the remainder of Lan Chile.

6. Luders (1991, 1–19).

imposed by the underdeveloped Chilean capital mark⌐t.[7] The resulting industrial structure included large, highly indebted congꞁomerates that controlled enterprises in multiple sectors. Some argue these conglomerates aggravated the financial crisis of the early 1980s. The government intervened in many companies privatized in that wave and overhauled the banking sector to ensure the development of sustainable long-term capital markets. A second wave of privatization, which would include the main utilities, followed.

The Second Privatization Wave, 1984–90

The second wave of privatization began in 1984 with the "reprivatization" of many of the "intervened" firms of the first wave (most in the finance sector) and continued between 1985 and 1990 with the sale of about 30 infrastructure companies, including Endesa (in electricity) and Entel and CTC (in telecoms). The political context was challenging. The failures of the first wave left many concerned about the highly leveraged conglomerates and the need to develop a long-term borrowing capacity for investment requiring slow amortization rates. These concerns were particularly important for the success of the privatization of utilities, which were viewed by the large public as fairly efficient since their restructuring and deregulation between 1974 and 1979.

To obtain the required political support, this second wave of divestiture needed objectives quite different from those of the first wave. Increasing the distribution of ownership was now the main goal rather than maximizing revenue or simply returning the economy from the state to the market. This required first the transformation of these utilities into public companies. Their shares would have to be tradable, and these companies would be subject to standard commercial auditing procedures. The sale of shares would generally be gradual. The percentage of private owners of CTC increased slowly from 11 percent in December 1986 to 86 percent three years later. For Endesa, the increase during the same period was from 30 percent to 72 percent. Institutional investors (such as pension funds) would eventually account for about 25 percent of the total stocks of privatized utilities, providing a good long-term commitment to the financing of the sector. Usually workers of the privatized company received between 5 and 10

---

7. There were cases in which the government simply returned the assets to their previous owners.

percent of the shares to ensure their political support. In the case of the electricity and telecommunication companies, a few former civil servants would acquire a large percentage of those shares.

Significant efforts were made to deconcentrate ownership. Popular capitalism was implemented in the reprivatization of the financial sector. Shares of banks and other financial institutions were offered to the general public at very attractive conditions, but with limits on the number of shares each person could buy. The incentives included tax credits, which in some cases had a present value exceeding the price of the share, and soft credits for paying the shares or a 30 percent discount for those paying up-front. Labor-friendly capitalism was implemented in the privatization of infrastructure companies and traditional public enterprises—that is, enterprises created by the state itself. (Nontraditional public enterprises were those nationalized during the socialist government in power from 1970 to 1973.) Workers of enterprises being privatized and public employees could use their accumulated severance payments in order to buy shares. Soft credits were available for those employees willing to buy more shares.

The Third Privatization Wave, 1994–

The third privatization wave in Chile started around 1994 and continued throughout the decade. Its objectives (to improve regulation and competition) have differed from the objectives of the first wave (revenue generation and a change of ownership) and second wave (distribution of property). Water companies, ports, roads, railways, and aviation have been the main targets of the third wave, along with residual companies in the energy sector.

Not surprisingly, the objectives of the third wave proved to be the hardest to achieve, primarily for political reasons. On the institutional side, they necessitated a broad revisiting of the regulatory framework on issues such as autonomy, the composition of regulatory commissions, administrative procedures, and the interface of regulatory policies and competition policies.

Overall, privatization has significantly improved the performance of the privatized utilities.[8] In electricity coverage rates have reached 97 per-

---

8. A more analytical assessment of the welfare gains of utilities deregulation and privatization is provided by Galal and others (1994) and Hachette and Luders (1993) and summarized in a critical survey by Paredes (1995).

cent. The annual growth rate of demand averaged about 8 percent between 1986 and 1997.[9] The largest distribution company managed to cut energy losses to a third of its historical levels (to less than 8 percent in recent years), and it doubled the number of clients per worker (from fewer than 300 at the end of the 1980s to almost 600 by 1997). Similarly, the number of gigawatt hours (GWh) of output generated per worker went up from fewer than 5 to almost 8.

Similar performance improvements have been achieved in telecoms. In 1987, the year before the government privatized the main local phone company, the number of telephone lines was 581,000. It rose to almost 3,700,000 in 1997, reflecting a penetration rate of about 30 percent, the highest in Latin America. Outgoing international traffic, which in 1987 amounted to approximately 21 million minutes, in 1996 exceeded 175 million minutes, while the mobile telephone system, which started operations in 1988, could claim more than 340,000 subscribers by the end of 1996. The local phone network, which was 37 percent digital in 1987, has been fully digital since 1993. The privatization of telecom firms also led to substantial improvements in their internal efficiency, as exemplified by the number of phone lines per worker, which rose from 74 to 235 between 1987 and 1995. More than 70 percent of the required investments in electricity and telecoms have been made by private operators.

The Keys to Success

Privately owned utilities' willingness to make significant investments can be explained by many of the macroeconomic reforms, including the relaxation of the financial constraints faced by public enterprises, the isolation of public services from political pressures, and rapid economic growth—averaging about 7 percent between 1986 and 1997. Another key factor was probably the explicit regulatory framework embedded in legislation that encourages such efficiencies. The embodiment of the regulatory framework into a law provides for the credible commitment and stability of the regime, an essential ingredient to secure investors' confidence and thus optimal levels of investment. As Guasch and Spiller (forthcoming) point out, Chile's new regulatory system included detailed regulations for tariff setting and for settling disputes between the regulators and the utilities, with the judiciary as final arbiter. Very specific legislation was used to restrain

---

9. The growth rate was almost 9 percent between 1990 and 1996.

administrative discretion.[10] The telecommunications law even stipulates the type of regression to be used in estimating a fair rate of return to the "efficient" firm (box 8-1). This experience also shows how difficult it is to write a comprehensive law in a sector characterized by technological change. Indeed, the telecommunications law was changed several times prior to privatization, and prior to the advent of democracy.

Chile's electoral system promotes party fragmentation, regionalization, and legislative independence. The number of parties in the legislature has traditionally exceeded three, so enacting laws with the degree of specificity presented in box 8-1 is a great political achievement. It is not surprising, however, that such legislative action was undertaken during periods of unified government. During the Pinochet regime the president had control over legislation, making it *de facto* a unified government. While the choice of specific legislation embodying the regulatory framework is an option for countries with fragmented legislatures, it is not usually very feasible because of the difficulties in reaching consensus.

Chile's clear rules of the game were initially credible because of the country's long tradition of judicial independence in these matters. Over time, however, the limited institutional capacity and independence of regulators and the Chilean judicial system's limited understanding of regulatory issues became a source of political concern and disappointment. These problems were reflected in the intensity of the debates required to obtain the endorsement of the regulatory reforms and privatizations that started in 1998.

Chile's success had additional key ingredients. First, there was a pattern of denying exclusivity rights to any operator and a policy of free entry into any segment of the utilities sector. Second, the regulatory framework was in place at the time of privatizations. Many countries make the mistake, with dire consequences, of postponing the implementation of the regulatory framework until after privatization. Third, Chile shaped (almost correctly) market structure before privatization. Fourth, Chile limited regulation to the essential segments of operations that still included natural monopolies. Fifth, Chile eliminated cross-subsidies and rebalanced rates prior to privatizations. This facilitated efficient new entry and pricing. Sixth, success was promoted by innovative use of benchmark regulation through the "efficient" firm comparator. Seventh, universal service was provided

---

10. See Spiller and Viana (1992) for a discussion of Chile's electricity regulatory reforms, and Galal (1994) for a discussion of Chile's telecommunications regulation.

Box 8-1. Price-Setting Procedures in Chile's Telecommunications Law

1. Demand is first estimated for each service/zone/firm bundle.
2. The efficient firm is defined as one that starts from scratch and uses only the assets necessary to provide that service.
3. For each service, the incremental cost of development is calculated. This is nothing but the long-run marginal cost (LRMC), provided no investment plans are considered. The law stipulates that regulated companies have a minimum of five years of investment plans. These plans are prepared by the companies and presented to SUBTEL on the basis of a detailed outline defined in Law No. 18,168 (Article 301) under the heading "Technical and Economic Basis."
4. Revenue for each service is estimated so that the net present value of providing the service is equal to zero. This revenue is the incremental cost of development.
5. After the incremental cost of development is calculated, the long-run average cost (LRAC) is found. Full coverage of cost is attained by increasing efficient tariffs in a least distorting fashion.
6. The fair rate of return (ROR) is defined as the sum of the rate of return on the risk free assets and the risk premium of the activity, weighted by the systematic risk of the industry. That is, $R_i = R_f + b_i (R_p - R_f)$, where R_i is the ROR on revalued capital for firm i, R_f is the ROR on risk free assets, b_i is the firm i's systematic risk, and R_p is the ROR on a diversified portfolio.
7. Since tariffs are calculated every five years, the law allows firms to adjust tariffs every two months, using the inflation index of each service and the Divisia index.
8. Disputes between the companies and regulators are settled by a committee of three experts; one is nominated by each party, and the third by mutual agreement.

Source: Galal (1994).

---

through competitive auctions or minimum government subsidies to provide service to the poorest families. Finally, special provisions and prices enabled workers to acquire shares in the privatized companies, enhancing political support.

The Need for Fine-tuning in the Regulation of Utilities

Without a doubt, gains have been secured: significant cost reductions, increased efficiency and coverage, and increased competition in the nonregulated segments of the utilities, with corresponding decreases in prices in those segments. However, signs of deficiencies have also appeared: above normal rates of return, particularly in the regulated segments of the sectors (four of the ten firms with the highest rates of return in Chile are utilities); prices above their competitive adjusted levels, particularly in the regulated segments; unnecessary entry delays with a large associated welfare loss; years of lawsuits related to interconnection to the networks (a result of the failure of the regulatory framework to address network access terms and rights); lengthy and costly resolution of conflicts and the unpredictable, high turnover of regulators to the private sector, with potential capture implications; extensive use of courts to resolve disputes; limited sharing of the gains with the consumers; and confusing overlapping jurisdictions of agencies (regulatory, antitrust, and National Economic Prosecutor's Office).

The heated debate in Congress was understandable. Santiago's severe drought in 1996 led to water rationing during the summer as a result of insufficient incentives to water companies for appropriate investment. The existing private water companies failed to develop contingency plans to cope with severe drought episodes. Areas under the responsibility of private water companies were the hardest hit. The public outcry probably reflected the frustration of consumers with the price of electricity and telephone service. Indeed, the difficulties encountered in Congress may reflect the uneven distribution in the economy of privatization gains. While the population has generally benefited from coverage expansion and improvements in service quality as a result of privatization so far, the impressive efficiency gains have not necessarily translated into lower charges, even after two rate reviews.

Drastic price reductions have occurred only where competition has emerged. Regulated local phone rates have risen by about 35 percent since privatization, whereas deregulated prices on long-distance phone calls have fallen by over 70 percent. In 1996 the price of 1 minute for a national long-distance call in Chile was even lower than in the United Kingdom. Electricity distribution prices, for their part, do not reflect the enormous reduction in distribution losses and increases in productivity achieved since privatization. The price of electricity for residential customers increased from US¢8.05 per kilowatt hour (KWh) in 1988 to US¢13.13 per KWh in 1995 (table 8-1).

Overall, this situation has led to significant increases in the profits of regulated firms in electricity distribution and local basic telephone services, with regulated segments reporting much higher rates of return on equity

Table 8-1. Annual Rate of Return on Equity for Chilean Firms, 1995–97, and Users' Prices in Selected Years

Utility	Rate of return (percent)	
Electricity distribution (regulated)	30	
Electricity generation (competitive)	12	
Basic telephony (regulated)	18	
Long distance (competitive)	6.5	
	1988	*1997*
Electricity distribution price (KWh) (in current U.S.¢)	9.44	12.0
Average household's telephone bill (in constant Ch$ of June 1998)	7,773	11,403

Note: Latest comparable data available.
Source: National Statistical Institute.

(ROE) than unregulated segments in the same industry. This difference is even more striking when one considers that there are fewer risks in the regulated segments since they are natural monopolies and often can pass cost increases to users. In the electricity sector, the average ROE among regulated distribution companies was 30 percent in the 1995–97 period; for (largely) unregulated generating companies, the figure was 12 percent. In the same period the ROE in the largest basic phone service company was 18 percent, while for the largest long-distance carrier it was 6.5 percent (table 8-1). To understand these developments, it is necessary to understand how regulation was designed, introduced, and implemented in each sector.

Institutions in the Regulation of Utilities in Chile

Legislative Focus on Efficiency

The legislation introduced in the early 1980s encouraged efficiency by defining rate-setting schemes based mainly on marginal-cost pricing. The "simulated efficient enterprises" served as benchmarks against which the real companies were compared. The regulatory framework takes account of the fact that current natural monopoly conditions can disappear. Even in price-regulated sectors, licenses are nonexclusive. Equal access and inter-connection requirements are essential for promoting competition in net-work utilities. The regulatory framework also eliminates cross-subsidies to ease the introduction of competition in regulated industries.

Within this framework, prices are set in such a way that an efficient firm can attain the pre-established rate of return. To correct the main problems of the traditional rate-of-return approach, benchmark price setting dis-tinctly separates prices from firms' actual costs. Sometimes benchmarking is implemented in combination with sliding-scale rate-of-return regulation. In other words, prices are adjusted if the industry's return goes outside a pre-established range. The system requires periodical price reviews and interim adjustments in line with an inflation index relevant to the sector.

The problem with benchmarking rates arises from the difficulty in agree-ing on the costs of an efficient firm. Concentration in certain sectors pre-vents competition by comparison between similar firms. Moreover, the benchmarking in Chile used an average of two estimates of an "efficient" firm: one provided by the regulator and the other by the operator. Clearly, the operator had an incentive to provide the highest possible cost estimate.[11] The controlling groups behind public utility firms acquired political and social leverage and exerted enormous influence in the definition of the ef-ficient firm. Consequently, the firm tended to reflect inefficient pre-privatization operations rather than the efficiency gains achieved since then. Failure to distribute the gains to users is the result. But this problem is essentially a reflection of the institutional weakness of the regulators.

The Limits of Sector-Specific Political Regulators

The responsibility for implementing these rules has been left to a sector-specific regulator. This regulatory body is also responsible for granting li-censes and monitoring service quality. Responsibility for setting tariffs is shared with the Economics Ministry. This co-responsibility is typical of the political nature of the regulatory role in Chile. Regulatory institutions are in fact government bodies. This reduces their autonomy. Some also argue

---

11. In 1997 a change in the assessment of those estimates improved the incentive for the operator to report a more accurate figure. A "final offer arbitration" scheme was implemented. An arbitrator now selects one of two estimates (the operator and the regulator) reported. The arbitrator chooses the one he thinks is closer to the correct value. This eliminates incentives by the operator to greatly exaggerate its costs.

that it limits technical expertise. It is difficult to attract the best regulatory specialists to agencies subject to public sector wages that are relatively low. Staff turnover is fairly high in these agencies. Officials who prove to be productive often migrate to the regulated firms where wages are several times higher. Since the regulators may see their work in the regulating body as a gateway to employment in the regulated industry, the risk of regulatory capture is high.

This threat to independence is exacerbated by the need to coordinate with other government agencies working in overlapping areas but with different concerns. Coordination is needed with the antitrust agencies and the judiciary. Furthermore, a new strong player is emerging in the utilities regulatory arena: the environmental regulators. Coordination with these multiple partners is not an easy task.

Coordination with Antitrust Agencies

Responsibility for the implementation of the regulatory framework is shared with the antitrust agencies and the judiciary. Deregulation of public services has led to a rise in the number and complexity of disputes between operators and between operators and regulators, as well as with users. This is not surprising because a competitive system implies the coexistence of conflicting interests, and this gives rise to disputes that cannot always be solved administratively.

A 1973 Law Decree (DL 211) classifies as an infraction any act tending to impede free competition. Multiple agencies are in charge of defending and promoting free competition: two antitrust commissions known as the *Preventive Commission (Comisión Preventiva)* and the *Resolution Commission (Comisión Resolutiva)*, along with *the National Economic Prosecutor's Office (Fiscalía Nacional Económica)*. The prosecutor is appointed by the president of the Republic. Each antitrust commission has five members who hold unpaid office for a two-year term. None of these entities seems to have the required technical or political capability to be watchdogs or enforcers of competition in network industries because they suffer from many of the same problems that the regulators have.

Prima facie, the staffing of these institutions seems reasonable. The Central Preventive Commission, headed by a representative of the Economics Ministry, is comprised of a representative of the Finance Ministry, two university professors (a lawyer and an engineer nominated by the Council of University Rectors), and a representative of the Neighborhood Associations chosen by the presidents of the Borough Neighborhood Associations

Union in the Metropolitan Region. The Resolution Commission, in turn, is headed by a Supreme Court judge, assisted by two heads of the Public Service Administration (one nominated by the Economics Ministry and the other by the Finance Ministry), and two university deans drawn by lots, one from an economics faculty and the other from a faculty of law.

The assignment of responsibilities seems to be reasonable on paper as well. The prosecutor has to ensure compliance with the rulings made by the Resolution Commission or the law courts on issues of free competition, and it must issue reports requested by the commissions. The prosecutor also has the authority to order investigations as she or he sees fit. The Preventive Commission can propose measures to correct situations harmful to free competition. The Resolution Commission has wide powers to hear, investigate, and sanction cases of conduct that may act against free competition. It can terminate contracts, order the prosecutor to take criminal action against conduct tending to hinder free competition, order the modification or dissolution of legal entities, and impose fines. The last two types of sanctions alone can be appealed before the Supreme Court.

The National Economic Prosecutor's Office is the only one that suffers obviously from its institutional set up. Since it is a government agency, it is subject to the restrictions of the public sector. The budget for 1996 was approximately US$1 million, and low wages prevent hiring skilled professionals and keeping them. Perhaps the greatest failing is in the composition of the antitrust agencies, whose members are seldom experts on competition issues. Furthermore, the agencies' links with the administrative authorities diminish their autonomy.

The main problem, however, is the collective indecisiveness of the antitrust agencies. This may be because the commissions are excessively attached to the letter rather than to the spirit of law (Paredes 1995). The scope of antitrust legislation is too broad. Serra (1995) implies that the antitrust agencies are reluctant to apply sanctions or adopt strong preventive measures because of the technical complexity of the issues involved in the conflicts. The excessively large number of players could be another contributing factor.

Coordination with Judicial Institutions

Under the 1980 Constitution, the judiciary has the responsibility to protect the property rights of private individuals from legislative and administrative abuses by the state. It is similarly responsible for resolving disputes between private agents. This situation would seem to be positive in general for a regulator otherwise subject to institutional limitations to its independence. Given the judiciary's independence from the other powers of the state, effective coordination would allow the regulator to contribute to the achievement of an independent defense of competition. Unfortunately, coordination is hard to achieve in practice. Legal processes are slow—especially litigation involving regulatory problems. In addition, for lack of specific knowledge, the judicial authority does not always have the capacity to solve such conflicts, which frequently involve intricate technical or economic issues.

The boundary between administrative and judicial jurisdiction is not always clearly drawn, and there is often a perception that the regulatory authority is weakened when the judiciary suspends or reverses regulatory decisions, or else confirms them after such a long period has elapsed that they become sterile. Judicial claims by firms in the telecommunications sector, which were resolved at the time in the authorities' favor, delayed calls for bidding on the personal communication systems by approximately eight months.

Coordination with Environmental Regulatory Agencies

As if the imbroglio just described were not enough, popular concern for the environment is bringing new players into Chile's regulatory game. Since its creation in 1994, the National Environment Commission (CONAMA) is playing an increasing role in the country. It monitors compliance with environmental standards and approves the environmental impact studies of large projects, such as hydroelectric plants that may have a significant effect on the environment. But this commission is not the only player in the field. Hydroelectric projects that will flood legally protected indigenous lands require approval from the National Commission for Indigenous Development (CONADI). The power sector includes multiple stakeholders with multiple agendas and little incentive to coordinate. Since none of these agencies is strictly independent from political forces, rents are up for grabs, and regulatory decisions are unlikely to achieve the transparency needed to ensure the most efficient outcomes.

Sector-Specific Regulatory Experiences

This section reviews private sector participation and regulation in the electricity, telecommunications, and water sectors. Reform of the water sector is ongoing, but it seemed useful to take stock of the outstanding regulatory issues. The regulatory framework, the regulatory pitfalls, and their impact on the performance of the sectors are reviewed. In each case the analysis concludes with a comparison with the U.K. and Argentinean experiences.

The Electricity Industry

The reforms were preceded by price controls, service rationing, overstaffing, and large deficits in the public electricity utilities.[12] The reforms were fitted into a general attempt to deregulate while maximizing fiscal revenue or minimizing revenue losses characterizing the first wave of privatization. Concentration of the control of former public companies was also considered an acceptable strategy at the time. Competition was the main goal, but the philosophy of the first wave was still quite prevalent. In fact, the restructuring of the sector was done in two stages. The first, between 1974 and 1979, was intended to adjust prices to allow the public utilities to achieve self financing and to prepare the ground work for private sector participation. The second stage, between 1979 and 1990, dealt with, in addition to the main institutional changes discussed below, the restructuring and privatization of the sector. Generation and transmission were, in principle, separated from distribution.

The two existing utilities, Endesa and Chilectra, were decentralized and regionalized. Endesa, the largest company, was divided into 14 companies. Six of the fourteen were generation companies: Edelnor (with 240MW of capacity), Endesa (1832MW), Colbun (490MW), Pehuenche (585MW), Pilmaiquen (35MW), and Pullinque (49MW). Six were distribution companies: Emelari, Eliqsa, and Elecda (combining 18,000 customers in the North), Esmelat (5,000 clients), Emec (143,000), and Emel (122,000 clients). Two companies combined generation and distribution: Edelaysen (15,000 clients) and Edelmag (35,000). Chilectra was divided into three firms: a generating company (Chilgener with 756MW capacity) and two distribution companies (Chilectra with 1,064,000 clients and Chilquinta with 322,000 clients).

Privatization per se started in 1986, after the introduction in 1982 of the regulatory framework described below. By 1990 only two generation companies were left to be privatized, and this has been accomplished since

---

12. This section on the electricity industry builds on Bitran and Serra (1997) and Berstein (1996).

then. Three main mechanisms were used to privatize the electricity industry: the sale of the smallest companies through public auctions (awarding the deal to the highest price bidder), the auction of share packages on the stock market for the largest companies, and the sale of small packages of shares in the largest companies (popular capitalism).[13] Endesa and its transmission system, the largest one in the country, were privatized as a package. The main reason was that the transmission pricing rules had not yet been fully defined. This erroneous decision is continuing to haunt Chile's regulators.

Since 1992, Chilean electricity companies have become major players in other privatizations in the region. They are present in Argentina, Bolivia, and Peru in electricity, and they have been actively diversifying into other sectors such as real estate, water, telecoms, and cable TV. Currently, both Endesa and Gener generate more energy through their foreign affiliates than through their domestic companies. For instance, Endesa's installed power is distributed as follows: 3,001 MW in Chile, 2,998 MW in Colombia, 1,320 MW in Argentina, 809 MW in Peru, and 658 MW in Brazil.

THE REGULATORY FRAMEWORK. The legislation introduced in 1982 attempted to maximize social welfare by establishing conditions that would promote efficient operations in the electricity sector. The legislation distinguishes three separate segments in the sector: generation, transmission, and distribution. It spells out the main rules for the regulation of these three segments and addresses other issues, such as the allocation of licenses, pricing, investment, quality, and safety. It also makes clear the obligations and rights of all players involved: the service providers as well as the government institutions.

The role of the government players. Before privatization occurred, three government institutions were established: the National Energy Commission (NEC), created in 1978; the Economic Load Dispatch Center (ELDC), created in 1982; and the Superintendency of Electricity and Fuels, created in 1985.

The National Energy Commission was established to develop medium- and long-term guidelines for the sector free from the influence of the large utilities. It is managed by a board of directors composed of seven ministers, and it has an executive secretariat, technical staff, and resources to

---

13. In addition, shares were given as a way of returning the financial deposits users had to make when connected to the service.

recruit special advisers as needed. The NEC proposes policies to be implemented through laws. It sets tariffs. It also grants licenses to public service distributors for specific areas.

Another governmental role is to extend coverage of the service to rural populations. Broadly speaking, the government subsidizes private sector projects that have a positive social rate of return but are not profitable from a private sector point of view. The government subsidy is for an amount equal to the negative net present value corresponding to the private evaluation of the project. The program finances self-generation projects as well as projects to extend the distribution network, and the aim is to achieve 100 percent electrification coverage among rural homes by the year 2005. Between 1995 and 1997, 55,603 rural houses were electrified, increasing rural coverage from 57 percent to 67 percent. At the end of 1997, 173,828 rural homes were still without electricity. This program, administered by the Under-Secretariat for Regional Development in the Interior Ministry, with technical support from the NEC, has had a yearly budget of approximately US$24 million since 1985.

The electricity law obliges all generating and transmission companies operating an electricity system to coordinate their activities through the Economic Load Dispatch Center. Only generators with an installed capacity below 2 percent of total installed capacity within the system are excluded. Chile currently has two electricity grids: the Central Interconnected System (CIS) and the Northern Interconnected System (NIS). Actual dispatch is handled by the transmission company; the ELDC is essentially a generators' pool. Inside the ELDC, decisions are taken unanimously. Divergences are arbitrated by the Minister of Economics, subject to a prior report from the NEC.

The ELDC has three specific objectives: to achieve the minimum total operating cost for the system as a whole, to guarantee the right of generators to sell energy at any point in the system, and to ensure the safety of the service. The ELDC plans the daily operation of the system, coordinates the maintenance of plants, and computes instantaneous marginal costs. Plants and service delivery are programmed on a merit basis according to production costs from lowest to highest. All power plants must make themselves available, unless they have been programmed previously for maintenance. In this respect the Chilean model is more dirigiste than, say, the British regulatory framework. It leaves no room for strategic behavior on the part of generators.

Each member of an ELDC is entitled to make direct supply contracts with clients for amounts up to its available firm capacity. Any shortfall must be purchased from other members at the marginal cost of peak power. The peak power price is computed as the annual cost of increasing the power during peak hours using the most economic generation sets. This cost is increased to take into account the reserve margin in the electric system. The ELDC plans daily production independent from any direct supply contracts there may be. This situation gives rise to energy transfers between generators, and these are priced at the systemic instantaneous marginal cost of energy. The marginal cost of energy is computed ex-post for each hour. The marginal cost is only used to value transactions among generators. Conflicting interests among generators probably ensure that the marginal cost is properly computed.

Distributors need to have contracts, the same as large clients. Hence, every customer is covered by a contract. Generators must ensure they have the capacity to supply their demand during each hydrological year. For thermoelectric plants, availability is computed considering average maintenance periods; for hydroelectric plants, availability is computed considering generation in the worst year obtained, discarding the 10 percent years with lowest generation. The thermoelectric generation company (Gener and its affiliate Guacolda) usually sells more energy than it produces. The difference is bought from hydroelectric generators at the marginal cost.

The CIS generated 20,505 GWh in 1995, which represents about 73.1 percent of the national power generation. Generation in the CIS is mainly hydroelectric (90 percent in 1995), supplemented by thermoelectric generation. Hydrology is a major source of uncertainty. Since tariffs are fixed (all demand is under contract), a prolonged drought may require the rationing of electricity. In fact, in 1989 and 1990 the electricity supply was subject to a 10 percent restriction for approximately 45 days. During these years hydroelectricity provided about 65 percent of total power generation in the CIS. The Chilean law mandates an equiproportional curtailment of all clients. However, utilities must compensate their customers for each unit of energy that they reduce below their normal consumption during an energy shortage. The compensation equals the net marginal outage cost. Hence, when an energy shortage occurs, generators have incentives to reduce it as much as possible. At the beginning of 1997, a severe energy shortage was anticipated. Additional generators were installed to deal with the emergency and reduce its exposition to compensation payments.

What ensures the long-run availability of energy in a country where demand grew at a 7 percent annual rate from the mid-1980s to the mid-1990s? Considering demand forecasts, existing installations, and plants under construction, the government determines a ten-year investment plan for generation and transmission that minimizes the present value costs of investment, operation, and rationing the system. The plan considers an optimal combination of hydroelectricity and thermoelectricity. Although the plan is only a guideline for the sector, companies tend to follow it. Overcapacity could have a tremendous impact on the profitability of firms. Firms tend to compete for the same "slot" in the plan, but so far all but one had finally given up. What ensures companies' interest in building new plants? So far the rate of return has been moderately high in the Central Interconnected System. However, stronger competition could lower the rate if more capacity is built. This occurred in the Northern Interconnected System. In the CIS, where there is one dominant firm, and two medium-size generators, the development has been orderly. Firms tend to maintain their market shares. However, in NIS, where there is no dominant firm, the rates of return for generators have been much lower.

The Superintendency of Electricity and Fuels was set up as an administrative branch of the Economics Ministry. It supervises compliance with the law and regulation and monitors the quality of services. It also deals with users' and suppliers' complaints and prepares the information for the price-setting process carried out by NEC.

The multiplicity of the institutional actors and their lack of independence may be the most salient feature of these institutional arrangements. The only apparent form of independence in the whole system stems from the role of the antitrust agencies. The Resolution Commission and the Preventive Commission seem to have the required independence but may lack the required technical skills to make the most of their independence.

Price regulation. Competition is the norm in generation and in the supply to large users, those requiring more than 2MW of power. (It could be argued that this is too large a number to be able to achieve effective competition.) Distribution (to small users) and transmission are considered natural monopolies. The price system thus consists of regulated charges for small customers and freely negotiated rates for large customers whose maximum power demand exceeds 2MW. The regulated rates must be within a 10 percent band of the average price of freely negotiated contracts. These contracts represent about 40 percent of the total consumption.

Generators supplying large customers negotiate toll fees with the transmission company and the distribution company, if needed. If no agreement is reached, a mandatory arbitrage process is triggered. As can be seen, there is no intervention of the regulator in the supply of large customers. On the other hand, the tariff for small customers is highly regulated. The regulated price has two components. The first is the node price at which distribution companies buy energy from generators. The second is the value added tariff, which rewards the services provided by the distribution company. This second charge will be analyzed later.

The node price is equal to the sum of the marginal cost of energy, the marginal cost of peak power, and the marginal cost of transmission. It is designed to approximate long-run marginal costs. The Economics Ministry, with technical support from the NEC, is responsible for calculating node prices. Marginal costs do not fully cover total transmission costs. The law states that the difference is charged to generating firms according to their "area of influence." In practice, the charges end up being negotiated between the owner of the grid and the generators. This is a recurrent source of conflict since the owner of the grid is also one of the generators.

The node price in turn has two components: the energy tariff and the peak power tariff. The energy price is computed every six months by the government as an average of the expected marginal costs for the next 48 months. The purpose of the averaging is to smooth the price for regulated energy consumers. The computation of the node price considers the indicative plan prepared by the NEC. A provision of the law states that the node price for regulated customers has to be inside a deadband, centered around the average price of freely negotiated prices for large customers. The width of the band is 10 percent below and 10 percent above the average price of contracts negotiated between generators and large customers. This provision shows the reliance of lawmakers on market forces. However, the situation has evolved in an unexpected way: most freely negotiated contracts have been set around the regulated price. In fact, they tend to specify a price equal to the regulated price plus or minus a given percentage.

The distribution charge is recalculated every four years. A procedure determines the operating costs of an efficient firm and sets rates to provide a 10 percent real return on the replacement value of assets. These rates are then applied to existing companies to ensure that the industry average return on the replacement value of assets does not exceed 14 percent or fall below 6 percent. If the actual average industry return falls outside this range, rates are adjusted to the nearest bound. The operating costs of an efficient firm and the replacement value of assets are obtained as a weighted average of estimates made by the NEC and by consultants hired by the industry. The weight of the NEC estimate is two thirds.

Competition and access rules. There are no limits to vertical or horizontal integration. To limit the risks from integration, competition to supply large users is allowed. A toll must be paid to the local distribution company, and this is a source of difficulties as discussed in the next section.

The access rules are different for generation, transmission, and distribution. The law says that the use of property for the generation of electricity requires a concession. This implies that entry is free for thermal generation, while it is not for hydro and geothermal generation. Although some firms can operate without a license, most will want to have one since a license provides some implicit exclusive rights. Licenses are given through a competitive process. The NEC ranks projects according to costs. Each year it assesses the minimum cost expansion plan for the system and clears the conditions for entry. For transmission, entry is free. For distribution, concessions are needed for systems larger than 1500kW. These licenses are granted for an indefinite period, but they can be withdrawn when service quality falls below the legal standard. It is possible for the service areas of two or more operators to overlap to further promote competition in the sector. Figure 8-1 shows the price of electricity from 1982 to 1997.

REGULATORY PITFALLS. Most consumers are under long-term contracts where the energy price changes only every six months. In fact, the purpose of the law was to smooth the cost of energy for regulated consumers. Price smooth-

Figure 8-1. The Price of Electricity, 1982–97

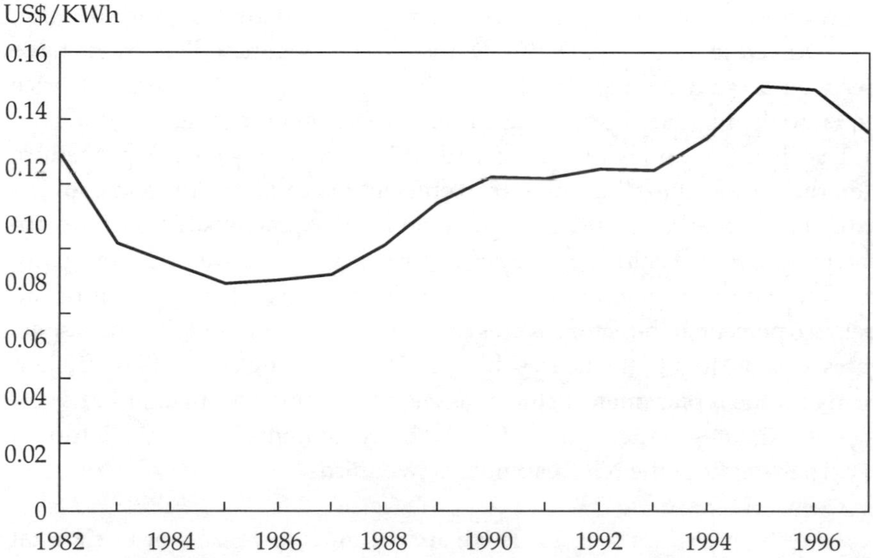

US$/KWh

Source: Authors' compilations.

ing is achieved at the cost of isolating clients from actual marginal costs. In the short run this does not seem to be a serious problem in the SIC. Marginal costs tend to remain fairly constant over days and weeks, due to the existence of considerable regulatory capacity in the Laja reservoir. However, there is an obvious disadvantage to price smoothing: customers do not face the actual cost of energy.

At the beginning of 1997, because of a prolonged drought, the marginal cost was a multiple of the node price paid by regulated customers. The clause specifying that the regulated price must be inside a band around the free prices adds to price rigidity. For instance, the import of gas from Argentina that began in August 1997 should have reduced the regulated price by about 17 percent in the September 1997 price calculation. Because of the band, the price reduction was much lower.

The problem of not facing marginal costs also occurs with large customers. As mentioned earlier, freely negotiated long-term contracts tend to mimic regulated prices. Even large customers seem to reveal a strong preference for price smoothing. However, a different explanation can also be advanced for large customers: using the regulated price as a yardstick lowers transaction costs. One solution would be to reduce the forward-looking orientation of the regulated price. For instance, the energy price could be computed every quarter as the expected value for the marginal cost during the next three months. This is likely to reap the most benefits for consumers by stabilizing prices without unduly complicating the costs of running the system.

Although the regulatory framework assumes competition in generation and supply to large users, concentration is a problem. Endesa, the dominant firm in the system, together with its affiliates has 60 percent of installed capacity. It also owns the transmission grid (which it manages through a subsidiary), and it has links to 40 percent of the distribution sector through Enersis, an investment group that controls Endesa. The concentration problem, however, is a more generic one. The second generating firm, Gener, and the third one, Colbún, own 22 percent and 11 percent of installed capacity, respectively, which gives a Herfindahl Index for the three largest generators of 0.43. Moreover, Endesa holds 60 percent of allocated nonconsuming water rights, of which it has developed 13 percent. Most of these rights belonged to Endesa prior to its privatization when it was the only major hydroelectric generator, and it is safe to assume that they represent the most profitable investment opportunities. By postponing the development of these projects, Endesa can obtain rents on its existing capacity.

This industry structure, and ambiguities in the regulatory framework, increase the risk for new firms that might consider investing in the generating sector. For instance, the law is not sufficiently explicit about how transmission grid development costs should be allocated between generating companies. Generators pay marginal transmission costs. Since these costs do not fully cover total transmission costs, the law states that the difference should be charged to generating firms according to their "area of influence." The law, however, is not sufficiently explicit to do this, and the charges end up being negotiated between the owner of the grid and the generators.

Endesa's market power is limited by the fact that the project plan it uses in calculating node prices is one that minimizes the cost of the system in present value terms. For example, when the National Energy Commission considered combined-cycle power stations coming on line, the node price looking forward four years went down substantially, thereby giving a clear signal for the sector.

Moreover, the import of natural gas from Argentina, which began in August 1997, lowered entry barriers in the generating sector. Although gas transportation has natural monopoly characteristics, ex-ante competition between two consortia willing to build a pipeline to transport gas from Argentina and anti-price-discrimination clauses drafted into the regulatory framework have brought transport prices down to a competitive level. In fact, to obtain financing, the consortia needed to have contracts signed with large customers, and this led to open competition for customers. The combined-cycle gas turbine electricity power plants that will be built close to demand centers, in conjunction with Colbún's decision to build a transmission line between its generating units and the main demand node, will diminish the impact of the transmission monopoly. Although more stringent environmental rules will have to be satisfied in the construction of dams, hydroelectricity is still the most attractive option. According to the NEC (1997), the generating cost of a hydroelectric plant is US¢1.87 per KWh; that of a combined-cycle gas turbine power plant is US¢2.63. In any case, this represents a significant reduction with respect to the cost of coal power generation, which is US¢3.60 per KWh.

There are also problems in supplying unregulated customers located in the franchise areas of distribution firms, which in 1995 represented 23 percent of all sales to unregulated customers. Indeed, when a generator gains a free-price customer from a distribution firm, it has to negotiate with the latter a toll for using its electricity cables. If they can't agree, arbitration follows. There is enough uncertainty in this procedure for some generating firms to desist in their attempt to supply such clients directly. A firm may not want to participate in the process of bidding to supply potential customers unless it knows how much it will have to pay in transmission costs.

In addition, the distributors are generating firms' main customers, so taking clients from them is bound to be costly. A claim by Colbún against Chilectra in September 1996 focused on this aspect. The lack of competition in supplying unregulated customers also affects regulated customers because the regulated node price has to be adjusted within a 10 percent band centered on the average of unregulated prices.

There are also significant problems in establishing electricity distribution value-added. The fact that the costs of the simulated efficient firm are calculated as a weighted average of studies carried out by the NEC and the firms themselves is problematic. It gives rise to obvious incentives for each party to bias the estimates. In the 1992 price-setting process, discrepancies in estimating distribution costs and the replacement value of assets in some cases exceeded 50 percent. A better solution would be for an arbitrator to decide which study in his or her judgment best reflects the costs of a model firm.

The Resolution Commission was asked by the National Economic Prosecutor to rule on the vertical disintegration of the group of firms controlled by Enersis (the Endesa group). In June 1997 the Commission ruled against compulsory disintegration, but issued instructions that recognized market imperfections in the electricity sector. Firstly, it asked the government to introduce legal amendments to clarify the mechanisms for determining transmission and distribution charges. Secondly, it instructed distributors in the future to put their energy requirements out to tender among all generating firms. It was hoped that this would end the suspicion that distribution companies favor related generators and reduce costs to final consumers. Finally, it resolved that, within a "prudent" time, the Endesa transmission subsidiary (TRANSELEC) should become a joint stock company operating exclusively in electricity transmission. This would open the company up for parties other than Enersis to participate in ownership (box 8-2).

SECTORAL PERFORMANCE AND REGULATION. The generation industry is highly concentrated in the SIC; the Herfindahl Index is 0.4. More importantly, the largest generator owns most water rights for building the most profitable hydroelectric projects. One reference that can be used to evaluate the conduct of generators is the regulated price. Free contracts tend to shadow the regulated price. Of course, the regulated price is an adequate yardstick if it is properly computed. As is the case with any regulated price, the industry will lobby to raise it. In the first years after privatization, the average price for free customers was above the regulated price, which reveals that some market power was being exercised. Lately, the free price

---

Box 8-2. Privatizing an Electricity Monopoly: Chile's Endesa

The notion that generation, transmission, and distribution functions should be undertaken separately contests the privatized structure of Endesa. The options that could be applied to Endesa were limited. The country's geography requires that most transmission lines be shared among generators, so a structure characterized by vertically integrated firms, each serving well-defined territories, was not possible.

Two factors impede competition in the electricity industry. First, Endesa, the main industry generator, was privatized with an important share in the generation market and most water rights. Chilean legislation states that to be granted a concession on water rights, the interested party must submit a development project to the firm holding the water rights. Since Endesa holds the water rights and therefore has a relatively low cost structure for development, it could delay the project or use the rights as an entry deterrent. Second, Endesa became a monopolist from the outset. It was privatized with 100 percent of the transmission in the Interconnected Transmission System (ITS).

The distance between the hydrological plants and consumption centers makes transmission costs important in Chile. Although transmission costs as a share of the total cost of electricity in Spain and England are 4 percent and 7 percent respectively, in Chile they are 25 percent. Endesa, as sole owner of the transmission system, can either increase transmission costs for its generation competitors or give privileged access to its subsidiaries, hence limiting competition.

Source: Paredes (1994).

---

has been below the regulated price, an indication that probably the node price is overestimated or that competition has taken free prices below their long-run equilibrium.

A better benchmark is the instant marginal cost computed by the Economic Load Dispatch Center, since the right incentives are built into its calculation. From September 1995 to August 1996 the node price averaged 10 percent higher than the marginal cost. Although the calculation methods are quite distinct, both should coincide in the long run. What explains the difference? The most likely explanations are two. First, the model used by the regulator is less precise, leaving less room for optimization. Second, the regulated price for energy considers the possibility of an energy shortage, in which case the marginal cost is set equal to the outage cost. However, during energy shortage periods the marginal cost equals the variable cost of the most expensive plant being used, which is below the outage cost.

Despite the two anchor prices, barriers to entry in generation (the ownership structure of the sector as well as regulatory ambiguities) might lead to high rates of return. Endesa's rate of return on equity was 5.2 percent in 1987, 13.7 percent in 1988, 7.7 percent in 1989, 6.4 percent in 1990, 10.4 percent in 1991, 13.4 percent in 1992, 11 percent in 1993, 15.6 percent in 1994, 14.5 percent in 1995, 12.7 percent in 1996, and 9.9 percent in 1997. The less profitable years correspond to a drought period. In addition, the arrival of gas from Argentina impacted profitability in 1997. While Endesa's profitability has been increasing since its privatization, the information would not seem to point to the abuse of monopoly power in the sector. A review of the behavior of Endesa by Paredes (1995) found no analytical evidence of monopoly pricing. There was, however, some evidence of strategic behavior by Endesa in its negotiation of transmission charges. Charges are negotiated between the owner of the grid and the generators, and lack of agreement leads to a compulsory arbitration process. By delaying its interactions and decisions with other generators, Endesa can favor its own generation companies.

Problems arise in the regulation of electricity distribution companies. The average rate of return for the industry as a whole in 1995 was 30 percent, while average operating profits as a percentage of assets (fixed and current) stood at 20 percent—a high figure considering that it is an underestimate because not all current assets are related to the main business. Such rates of profitability are way above those being earned by generating companies, which are subject to a greater degree of uncertainty because they do not have a secure market and because they face periods of drought and competition. The most recent rate-setting process for electricity distribution was interrupted when three distribution companies filed suits in the law courts, and this delayed the new rates coming into force from October 1996 until mid-1997. To prevent consumers from suffering from these delays, in early 1997 Congress passed a law obliging the distributors to compensate their consumers for the difference in tariffs between the date when the new rates should have come into force and the date when they did so. (Of course, the law did not take effect retroactively.)

In the Northern Interconnected System, four generating companies are competing, two of them foreign; one has a share in the ownership of the recently privatized firm Colbún, the third operator of the Central Interconnected System. The NIS expanded at a rate of 15 percent from 1993 to 1995, mainly because of the rapid growth of mining. In 1998 two consortia were competing for the construction of a gas pipeline to Argentina, which would make it possible to reduce generating costs with combined-cycle gas power plants. Moreover, Gener is building a transmission line that will join the NIS with Salta, an Argentine province where a combined-cycle power plant has been built with a capacity of more than 1,000 megawatts. Excess capacity will be generated in the Chilean-Argentine north. In order to reduce this, it is hoped that the north will be interconnected with the center of the country to make greater competition possible, since concentration will be reduced by incorporating new operators into the system (Edelnor and Tocopilla). Also anticipated in the future is electrical interconnection with the Neuquen zone of Argentina, which will result in more competitive generation supply. However, insufficient regulation of the transmission rates and vertical integration with the main generating company will continue to affect competition.

COMPARISON WITH ARGENTINA AND THE UNITED KINGDOM. Approaches to reform differ depending on a country's industry structure and regulatory framework. Norway, the United Kingdom, Argentina, Peru, and now Colombia have opted for an unbundled sector with mostly separate generation, transmission, and distribution functions, allowing private ownership of these functions. They seek to establish a highly competitive generating subsector through the use of contracts between generators and consumers or distributors to establish market prices for electricity at the bulk level. Price regulation is reserved for open access transmission and distribution grids and for retail tariffs for "captive" consumers. Other countries, like the United States, Jamaica, and Costa Rica, have opted for limited competition in generation. Independent power producers supply bulk power through a competitive bidding or contract process to a monopoly grid owner.

In Argentina there are 35 generating firms belonging to 8 independent groups. The Herfindahl Index for the three largest firms is 0.15, which results in a highly competitive market. Large customers pay up to 30 percent less for electricity than do their Chilean counterparts.[14] The price difference is partly explained by the location of gas fields in Chile, but the situation should become more equal as the pipeline bringing gas from Argentina comes on stream. In Argentina there is an independent body responsible

---

14. This considers all the generating plants in which Enersis has participation. The same is done for generating plants in which Chilgener has participation. By considering grouped firms, concentration is overestimated. Although Chilgener and Endesa participate in the ownership of more than one plant, they do so with different partners and percentages.

for administering the sector (CAMMESA), owned jointly by the government and the associations of generators, distributors, transmission firms, and large-scale users.

Although the Argentine price system has similarities with the Chilean one, generators are paid the instantaneous marginal cost on regulated sales to distributors. Distributors pay the seasonal price, equivalent to the node price in Chile. A stabilization fund has been set up to manage surpluses or deficits generated from revenues earned from sales to distributors and the instantaneous marginal cost payments made to generating firms. Differences produced during the season between the spot price and the seasonal price, calculated *ex-ante*, have to be compensated in the following period through the price charged.

The other difference is that distribution franchises, as well as the transmission concession, are granted for 95 years, divided into 10-year management periods (except for the first period, which lasts 15 years). At the start of each period, the regulating entity (ENRE) sets the tariff regime and calls for competitive bidding for the majority of the firm's shares. If the current holder submits the highest price, it retains ownership. Otherwise, the investor offering the highest bid obtains the concession and pays the current owner the asking price. This mechanism of periodic competition for the franchise is designed to give the incumbent incentives to maintain assets and invest when appropriate to do so.

A final difference between Chile and Argentina is institutional. Argentina has a single sector-specific regulator managed by a commission of experts for transmission and distribution under federal responsibility.[15] This entails fewer coordination problems and also increases the accountability for decisions. The funding and the staffing of the agency also provide some guarantee of independence, which may be of some relevance to the next wave of regulatory reforms in Chile.

In the United Kingdom there are three main generating firms. At the beginning of 1996, the two main firms together held 45 percent of installed capacity.[16] The third firm, a thermo-nuclear plant, had more than 20 per-

---

15. Although Argentina has problems stemming from decentralized responsibility for regulating distribution services, this aspect is not relevant to the debate in Chile at this time.

16. However, this percentage underestimates the real market power of the firms because 80 percent of the time, the spot price corresponds to the supply price of a power plant belonging to one of these firms!

cent of capacity, which resulted in a Herfindahl Index for the three largest firms of less than 0.1. The big generating companies are not allowed to participate in either the transmission or the distribution segments, while distribution firms can self-generate up to 15 percent of their sales. Transmission was initially left in the hands of the 12 regional distribution companies. They subsequently decided to hive this segment of the business off.

The rate system in the United Kingdom differs from the Chilean one in that the spot price (or "pool" price) is determined on the basis of the price offers made by firms per generation unit on a half-hourly basis. These prices do not necessarily correspond to generating plants' variable costs. In addition, a large share of transactions is carried out at the spot price. The least maximum demand needed to be considered an unregulated customer is 100KW, and this regime was extended to all customers in 1998. Several second-tier electricity suppliers compete with the distribution companies for the provision of unregulated customers. These suppliers buy energy at the spot price from generators, pay transmission and distribution firms the respective tariffs, and then sell at an unregulated price to final consumers. There is a price-cap system for transmission and distribution tolls.

The regulatory institutional arrangements in the United Kingdom are closer to Argentina's than to Chile's. Instead of being managed by a commission, the agency in the United Kingdom is managed by a single regulator. Many in the United Kingdom are now arguing in favor of a commission as in the United States or Argentina.

In summary, the Argentinian and U.K. systems are far less concentrated than the Chilean one and, unlike the latter, not vertically integrated. The spot price plays a greater role in these two countries than in Chile. The lowest maximum power demand to be considered an unregulated customer is less in the United Kingdom and in Argentina (1MW in Argentina) than in Chile, and it is less difficult for generators to gain access to unregulated customers located in distributor franchise areas. Finally, both Argentina and the United Kingdom have a simpler institutional arrangement to ensure the regulation of the sector. While both have their problems, they have a smaller number of players than Chile and hence more accountable decisionmaking.

OUTSTANDING CHALLENGES FOR CHILE. To enhance competition, Chile should substantially reduce the power demand needed to be considered an unregulated customer (a reduction to 100KW, for example). This would permit the appearance of supply firms competing for clients. A solution like this would considerably diminish the role of the state. While the authority would still retain responsibility for setting transmission and distribution rates, it would play more of an intermediary role between trading firms and transmission and distribution companies. This increased competition would also provide for better opportunities for overlapping concessions in electricity distribution to meet their purpose.[17]

To ensure that consumers share in the efficiency gains, regulators should be granted jurisdiction to set tariffs. Transmission and distribution tariffs need to be based on more transparent incentive-based formula. The issues of pricing and terms of access and interconnection remain. The current structure favors the incumbent integrated firm and thus does not facilitate competition.

With regard to transmission, the lessons from the international experience are less promising. Argentina did separate transmission from generation and distribution, but its pricing rules are not as efficient as one would want, and they fail to achieve dynamic efficiency (limited incentives for investment in network expansion). The main challenge for Chile is to decide whether it should go one more step in the direction of restructuring and keeping dispatch and transmission joint. Strengthening the institutional capability to monitor the behavior is a backup strategy. The best strategy would involve a new restructuring of Endesa, something much more politically challenging.

The Telecommunications Sector

At the beginning of the 1970s, three publicly owned companies dominated Chile's telecommunications sector. CTC (Compañía de Telefonos de Chile) provided local telephony throughout most of the country. Entel (Empresa Nacional de Telecomunicaciones) provided some national and all international long-distance service. Correos and Telegrafos provided domestic and telegram services, sharing the international market with ITT and Transradio. All of these companies lacked the resources needed to expand and adopt new technologies. Cross-subsidies between local and long-distance services were the norm; price controls were often adjusted below inflation. Regulation, operation, and to some extent policymaking were in the hands of these public companies. These were the conditions at the time the government

---

17. If overall competition rules are not effective in the sector, the overlap in concession areas impedes the ability of companies to take advantage of economies of scale (Paredes 1995).

decided to deregulate and reregulate the Chilean telecoms sector through a regulatory law introduced in 1982, before the actual privatization of the sector. The law was amended in 1987 and in 1993 to allow for competition in long-distance telephone services.

Chile reformed its telecommunications and electricity sectors at the same time. Indeed, the philosophical foundations of the reforms were the same: freedom of entry into all areas of the sector, licenses required only for the taking of public or private property (and, in the case of telecommunications, for the use of the spectrum), very minimal obligations to serve, and minimal government intervention in the sector. There were, however, two main differences in the implementation. Believing that telecommunications was an inherently competitive sector, the writers of the 1982 legislation did not introduce any stipulation concerning the regulation of prices. Although interconnection was required, the legislation left the terms of interconnection to be decided by the parties. Second, the government did not change the initial market structure of the telecommunications sector, unlike the electricity sector. It did not restructure the two main telephone companies. Thus, competition in telecommunications started with two monopoly companies: one a local service (CTC) and the other a domestic and international long-distance provider (Entel).[18]

Although the privatization process started in 1985, control of these two companies passed to private hands in 1988. Telex Chile provided telegraph services, which were hived off from Correos and Telégrafos in 1982 and privatized in 1985. Two small regional local service companies, CNT and Telcoy, were privatized in 1981.

THE LONG AND WINDING ROAD TO RESTRUCTURING. In 1982 Chile was the first country to introduce open competition in all sectors of telecommunications with minimal governmental regulation and with no restructuring of the sector.[19] Such path-breaking status, however, did not last long. In 1987 a major revision of the telecommunications law introduced a tariff-setting process.[20] Following a determination by the Antitrust Commission that nei-

---

18. A third government company, Telex Chile, was formed in 1982; it took over the telex activities of the post office. Several other private companies were formed during the late 1970s and early 1980s, but they held less than 5 percent of the overall revenue.

19. Recently, New Zealand followed the same policy.

20. Cellular and other services were specifically exempted from the possibility of price regulation.

ther local service nor long-distance services were competitive, the regulatory agency SUBTEL started the price-setting process that culminated a year later, in September 1989, with the first regulated telecommunications tariffs.[21] From a "free-market perspective" the 1987 reforms seem to have been a backward movement toward price regulation.

A closer examination, however, suggests otherwise. Although CTC and Entel, the main telecommunications operators, had been allowed since 1982 to set prices freely, in fact they set their prices following informal consultations with SUBTEL and the Economics Ministry (Galal 1994).[22] Furthermore, competition in both local and long-distance services did not develop rapidly. Since the opening of the telecommunications markets, five local companies had been created, but they tended to locate in areas where CTC did not have a license, or where it provided relatively bad service.[23] The latter companies, however, faced growing difficulties, and by 1994 they had achieved only 2 percent of the market. Some of these growing difficulties could be related to normal market conditions, but others are related to the fact that interconnection agreements were not easy to develop even though the law provided for interconnection agreements by the parties. Indeed, all three companies obtained their interconnection agreements only following orders by the Antitrust Commission.[24]

Thus, by 1987 it was clear that competition did not exist in the telecommunications industry. Furthermore, from the passage of the 1982 act until

---

21. The telecommunications law specified that if a sector is determined by the Resolution Commission to be noncompetitive, SUBTEL can regulate its prices according to a particular process determined in the law.

22. Until the privatization of CTC and Entel, their shares were held by CORFO, the government's development corporation. CORFO implemented a policy of segmentation of the two companies' activities, moving CTC mostly to local service and Entel to long-distance services.

23. Compañía de Telefonos de Coyhaique (TELCOY) and Telefonica del Sur S.A (CNT) operate in areas where CTS has no operating license. The five companies are Complejo Manufacturero de Equipos Telefónicos (CMET), which operates in parts of the metropolitan region and in other regions; Compañía Teléfonica Manquehe (CTM), which operates only in parts of the metropolitan region; and SERTEL, which operates elsewhere. CTM, CMET, CTC, TELEDUCTOS, and others provide fiber optic services around the metropolitan region.

24. Each time, though, the Antitrust Commission castigated CTC with undertaking "activities that have tended to limit free competition in the telecommunications market and tended to limit entry." See Resolution 151 of July 18, 1983.

1987, the network grew only slightly faster (at a rate of 6.5 percent per annum in terms of numbers of lines) than prior to the passage of the 1982 act (a 3 percent rate). After 1987, however, the sector grew very fast (at more than 20 percent per annum). Indeed, by 1991, only three years after its privatization, CTC doubled its number of lines. More specifically, since privatization, the number of lines in service has increased from fewer than 600,000 in 1988 to over 2.6 million in 1997, and phone density has increased from 6.7 percent per 100 persons in 1987 to 16 percent in 1997.

The free-market approach to telecommunications regulation did not help develop the sector before 1987. This cannot be explained by the different spread of privatization. The main generating companies (Chilgener and Endesa) were privatized at roughly the same time as CTC and Entel. Nevertheless, competition and network growth characterized the wholesale electricity sector from the beginning. Macroeconomic circumstances also do not seem to be behind the differential performance, as electricity generation capacity grew rapidly even during the early 1980s, a period characterized by slow economic growth.[25] Chile suffered one of the worst recessions in 1982 and 1983.

Although other explanations for the lack of dynamism in the telecommunications sector could be offered, one feature seems important: the regulatory framework based on pricing freedom was not credible, particularly when the government also owned the two main telecommunications entities. The 1987 reforms, by formalizing the price-setting process, reduced the government discretion in the determination of telecommunications prices, providing a more credible framework in which to invest. CTC aggressively responded to those incentives.[26]

----

25. We are aware, though, that electricity projects are lumpy and have a relatively long life. On the other hand, the deregulation of electricity generation has drastically reduced the gestation life of new projects.

26. At the time, the government required a 100 percent dividend payout from all public companies, including CTC. This, however, cannot be a full explanation for the slow performance of the sector. First, by 1987 CTC's debt equity ratio was a mere 65 percent. Even under public ownership, it could have doubled its debt by increasing its debt equity ratio to 125 percent, a ratio that it had in the past without too much of a problem. Such an increase in debt would have allowed a rapid increase in assets. Second, if the pre-1987 regulatory framework was so credible, such investment could have been undertaken by the private sector. The fact that the private sector did not invest much prior to 1987 suggests that the pre-1987 regulatory framework did not provide it with enough investment incentives. The

Although the 1987 reforms influenced the incentives to invest by both CTC and Entel, they do not seem to have drastically affected their ex-post performance. Both companies' profitability improved following the passage of the 1982 law, although it seems that the main beneficiary was Entel: its return on net worth reached almost 40 percent by 1986. The 1987 reforms also benefited Entel: its profitability exceeded 40 percent in 1988 and 1989. CTC's profitability increased a bit, but remained below 20 percent. In fact, the companies' ex-post performance started to improve not in 1987 but in 1982 (Galal 1994).

INTERACTION BETWEEN REGULATION AND SECTOR PERFORMANCE. The reforms of 1987 and the subsequent privatization had all the predicted effects. The network expanded, prices for long-distance services fell more rapidly, while those for local service increased more rapidly, thus tending to eliminate the extent of cross-subsidization from long distance to local service (table 8-2). Currently, multiple telecoms services are provided by many firms, of which the most important are CTC, Entel, Telex Chile, VTR, and Bell South. The largest of these, CTC, owns about 95 percent of all telephone lines, owns the largest cellular phone company, has a long-distance subsidiary with the second largest market share, and controls the company providing cable TV to almost half of all subscribers. The Chilean telecoms sector is totally open to foreign investors, who participate in the ownership of most telecoms companies: Telefónica de España controls CTC; the Italian company STET and Samsung respectively own 19.5 percent and 12.5 percent of Entel; Southwestern Bell owns 49 percent of VTR.

In spite of good progress in telephone density (table 8-3), universality of service is for the moment a distant goal, although it is realistic to consider gradual improvements in universal access. A decision has been made to subsidize public and community telephone service solutions in remote and poor areas, financed out of the Telecommunications Development Fund. SUBTEL prepares a needs list and draws up the corresponding projects, which are put out to tender among interested firms and awarded to those seeking the lowest subsidy. The fund will provide approximately US$5 million per year over four years. This figure is not particularly high, so it is unclear whether after four years of operation of the fund the problem of social telephony will be resolved.

---

vagueness of the regulatory framework as it relates to interconnection was one important factor, but also the uncertainty about the future evolution of prices may have provided a strong disincentive for private sector development.

Table 8-2. Domestic Local and Long-Distance Tariffs, 1970–92

	Local service flat rate (1985 Ch$ per line)		Domestic long distance (without taxes, in June 1988 Ch$)								
			80 kilometers			400 kilometers			3,250 kilometers		
	Residential tariff	Commercial tariff	Operator 3 min.	Operator 1 min.	Domestic direct dial 1 min.	Operator 3 min.	Operator 1 min.	Domestic direct dial 1 min.	Operator 3 min.	Operator 1 min.	Domestic direct dial 1 min.
Year											
1970	1,243.9	3,342.2	175.03		557.04			1,799.71			
1971	971.7	2,610.8	175.03		557.04			1,799.71			
1972	778.7	2,092.5	175.03		557.04			1,799.71			
1973	360.9	1,575.6	174.41		555.25			971.77			
1974	906.4	3,063.3	191.32		620.89			984.20			
1975	842.6	2,848.0	163.37		530.82			841.67			
1976	576.0	1,942.7	131.76		429.43			679.14			
1977	694.1	2,346.1	144.94		445.79			691.35			
1978	848.6	2,868.0		80.15			246.44			382.20	
1979	785.0	2,653.2		86.21			265.09			411.23	
1980	830.3	2,806.3		80.11			180.90			243.66	
1981	788.0	2,663.3		83.14			177.32			209.00	
1982	870.9	2,945.1		83.14			177.32			209.00	
1983	1,034.5	2,413.9		83.14			184.03			216.89	
1984	983.1	1,994.7		56.60			125.29			147.68	
1985	1,390.7	2,387.1		49.65			109.92			129.56	
1986	1,384.2	2,048.2		40.17			85.17			93.20	
1987	1,498.1	2,433.7		35.97			76.49			79.39	
1988	1,486.1	2,511.3		32.00			68.27			70.77	
1989	1,653.5	2,576.7			24.12[a]			44.72[a]			84.52[a]
1990	1,845.0	2,700.6			19.74			32.65			67.53
1991	2,079.0	2,892.6			18.54			29.2			62.76
1992	2,305.8	3,079.7			16.69			23.89			55.2

a. In 1989 there were changes in the distance bands.
Source: Galal (1994).

Table 8-3. Lines in Service, Density, and Waiting List, 1987–95

Year	Lines in service (thousands)	Density (lines/100 people)	Waiting list (thousands)
1987	581	4.65	232
1988	631	4.93	236
1989	689	5.40	284
1990	864	6.56	308
1991	1.956	8.02	241
1992	1.279	9.56	314
1993	1.516	11.10	198
1994	1.657	11.97	117
1995	1.894	13.42	52

a. Cifras de CTC solamente.
Source: SUBTEL, memorias de la empresas.

THE REGULATORY FRAMEWORK. Since 1977 the regulatory body has been the Under-Secretariat for Telecommunications (SUBTEL) at the Ministry of Transportation and Telecommunications. SUBTEL shares responsibilities for rate setting with the Economic Ministry. Its other main duties are to present proposals for national policies in the area, develop and update technical standards, ensure compliance with regulation and legislation, administer and control the use of the radio-magnetic spectrum, process franchise applications, and run the procedures for rate setting. Its decisions are also subject to the rulings of the Antitrust Commission. SUBTEL is a public sector agency subject to public-sector salary scales. These are not very competitive, and many of SUBTEL's most able staff end up working for the regulated firms.

The 1982 telecoms law establishes total separation between the regulatory function and the operation of services. The services that are subject to price setting are determined by the Resolution Commission, according to a broad legal criterion regarding services provided under insufficiently competitive conditions. This regulation has two clear goals: (i) providing the incentive for firms to minimize long-term marginal costs, as identified through hypothetical efficient firms; and (ii) ensuring that the efficiency gains are passed on as benefits to consumers. Most of the telecom services, however, are regulated to some degree, either through licenses that regulate entry, or technical standards (including those covering the obligation to establish and accept interconnections), or rate-setting mechanisms affecting monopoly services.

Price regulation. The price-setting process designed for the telecommunications sector is almost identical to that in the electricity sector. There are, however, two important exceptions. First, the capital asset pricing model is used to compute the cost of capital of the efficient telecommunications firm. Second, disputes among the companies and the regulator are settled via a binding arbitration rather than through a fixed formula as in the electricity sector.

Thus, again in 1987, the reformers chose to limit regulatory discretion at the expense of regulatory flexibility Prices are based on the long-run marginal costs of putatively efficient firms. Currently, only the local telephone service and access to long-distance services are subject to price regulation. Price reviews are supposed to take place every five years with indexation in the interim years. The resulting prices are supposed to ensure that the firms earn a fair rate of return on revalued assets. The procedure involves estimating demand for each service, zone and firm bundle, the incremental cost based on a benchmark efficient firm, and a fair return for the firm. Rules are spelled out quite specifically. Disputes are resolved through a three-member arbitration commission. The specific pricing rules for local telephony are discussed next to illustrate some of the outstanding regulatory problems.

Local telephone rate setting. Local phone rates are set so that the net present value of expansion projects equals zero, when discounted at a rate reflecting sectoral risk. The local service is metered, and the billing has two components: a fixed monthly charge for connection and a variable charge per minute. There are two per-minute rates, corresponding to peak and off-peak hours. Rates are adjusted every five years, on the basis of cost studies prepared by the phone companies in accordance with government-set guidelines. Once a study is completed, regulators have 120 days to object and draw up counterproposals. Differences are brought before a panel of experts. Although the final decision rests with the regulators, they usually follow the panel's advice, in view of the fact that companies can take them into court.

Despite big efficiency gains in the sector, local phone charges have not fallen since privatization: on the contrary they have gone up. According to the National Institute of Statistics, in April 1989 an average family's bill was Ch$2,825, rising to Ch$3,814 by May 1996 at constant prices (table 8-4).[27] Some of the rise is explained by the partial abolition of the subsidy

---

27. The exchange rate was then 252 pesos/US$.

paid by long-distance carriers to local phone firms and by the abolition of the surcharge on phone line installation. However, the main explanation is that CTC has not passed efficiency gains on to its clients. Indeed, CTC's rate of return on equity, 14.8 percent in 1990, climbed to 22.5 percent by 1993. In 1995 it dropped back to 16.9 percent because of strong competition in the long-distance market. The rate rebounded to 18.4 percent in 1996.

The rates from the second rate-setting process that occurred in 1994 appear to have been more the result of bargaining between the authorities and the firm than the outcome of rigorous technical analysis. Reaching agreement on what the costs of a model firm are is not easy. This situation, together with the difficulty the regulator faces in obtaining precise information and the antagonistic nature of the process, lead to a continuous bargaining game. The problem is specially acute when there is only one large firm, because its costs influence the definition of the efficient firm. (Of course, the firm itself will claim to be efficient.) Even efficient-firm regulation requires actual data from firms, since costs depend among other things on customer density and traffic per line. It is therefore difficult for regulators to build a credible counterproposal when they do not have full access to the regulated firm's data. (There is no specific sanction for denying information.) However, the concept of the model firm has had the virtue of creating a framework around which to conduct negotiations.

Regulatory action also is made difficult by the publicity campaigns launched by the regulated firms. During the most recent rate-setting process, CTC launched fierce attacks on the regulatory agencies through the communications media. It also made apocalyptic announcements regarding the impact of the new rates on its profits, which caused a sharp fall in its share price. This obliged the Superintendency of Securities and Insurance to suspend trading in CTC shares for a short period. Of course, the CTC predictions did not come true.

In certain areas there have been overlapping franchises in local telephony since the early 1980s. These arose mainly as a result of the inability of CTC —at that time in state hands—to satisfy demand. However, they never represented real competition for CTC. Weaknesses in the legislation, especially as regards interconnection norms, inhibited true competition. The situation was resolved when the 1993 law was passed introducing regulated access tolls, a change that facilitated competition in fixed telephony. As with the introduction of long-distance competition, competition at the local exchange will require further refinements in the regulatory framework, which, given the constraints involved in the regulatory scheme, will have to wait the results of litigation before the antitrust authorities and the courts. Currently, competitors are positioning to compete in that market via the

Table 8-4. Monthly Local Residential Phone Rates
(fixed charge plus variable rate with tax, in $ as of April 1989)

Date	Tariff
April 1989	2.825
July 1991	3.278
December 1991	3.197
June 1992	3.349
December 1992	3.341
June 1993	3.718
December 1993	3.623
June 1994	3.921
December 1994	3.885
June 1995	3.773
December 1995	3.834
May 1996	3.814

Source: Instituto Nacional de Estadisticas, Serie de Precios.

construction of facilities, since Chile does not require unbundling or resale. Already there are six local exchange providers within the greater Santiago area, including CTC; three long-distance carriers (Entel, Telex Chile, and VTR); and the two original competitive small local exchange carriers in Santiago (CMET and Manquehue). As a result, in a number of areas in Santiago, consumers already have a choice of local providers. This strategy to integrate is a consequence of the level of competition induced in the sector.

Entry rules. Concessions are required for operation and exploitation of local public phones, national and international long-distance services, and radio broadcasting. These concessions are granted by SUBTEL and are free (except for rights to the radio electrical spectrum). They are granted for an indefinite term on a first-come-first-served basis (although more than one can be granted for each area), and they spell out service obligations. What they imply for long-distance calls and mobile telephony is discussed next.

Long-distance calls. Following privatization of the long-distance monopoly, regulatory ambiguities generated legal entry barriers to the industry, which combined with inappropriate rate-setting schemes to keep prices significantly above marginal costs for several years. In practice, the long-distance company achieved average rates of return on capital above 30 percent. Legislation passed in 1993 unambiguously eliminated legal barriers to competition in long-distance services, paving the way for a multicarrier system launched in October 1994. Long-distance callers could choose their carrier for each phone call by dialing two digits. The new legislation also facilitates competition by allowing long-distance carriers to have access to final clients directly through private circuits. But that was not to be an easy road.

Until the beginning of the 1990s, telecom services were dominated by two firms: CTC and Entel. CTC had a virtual monopoly of fixed telephony throughout the country, while Entel monopolized long-distance services. Their high rates of return on net worth are shown in table 8-5. The antitrust agencies' decision in 1992 directing Telefónica to divest its 20 percent share in Entel was essential in spurring competition, which would have been impossible if both the CTC and Entel firms had been controlled by Telefónica. By 1998, eight firms were competing in the long-distance market. The rates of return on equity of CTC and Entel are shown in figure 8-2.

The opening of the sector to competition eliminated the need to fix and regulate rates, and these are now market determined. Because a carrier needs access to and from local networks to provide long-distance services, regulation of this aspect has become crucial. The law obliges all local tele-

Table 8-5. Rates of Return on Net Worth, CTC and Entel, 1960–91
(percent)

Year	CTC	Entel
1960	7.9	n.a.
1965	14.1	n.a.
1970	10.7	n.a.
1975	−8.6	n.a.
1979	1.68	12.31
1980	4.45	12.14
1981	2.61	11.23
1982	−15.14	11.53
1983	11.89	13.05
1984	9.17	16.79
1985	−15.29	19.97
1986	21.02	35.37
1987	10.91	38.98
1988	12.31	45.54
1989	17.22	45.63
1990	13.46	38.76
1991	15.17	38.93

n.a. Not available.
Source: Galal (1994).

Figure 8-2. Rates of Return on Equity, CTC and Entel, 1990–95

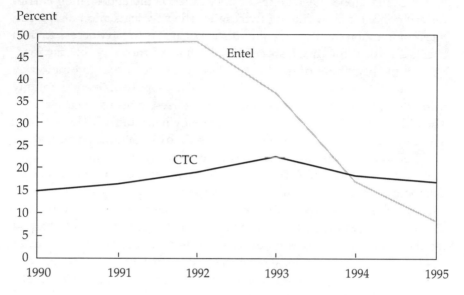

Source: Guasch and Spiller (forthcoming).

phone franchise-holders to give access to carriers on a nondiscriminatory basis, and the cost of interconnection between the public network and long-distance carriers is set by the regulator. This access toll approximately re-flects costs (two-thirds of a local call, for each origin-destination end point). However, the access toll for incoming international calls clearly exceeds the cost of providing this service. (It is 14 times the local peak rate.)

The profitability of the long-distance market provided a strong signal for potential competitors, and in 1989 CTC and other local exchange operators attempted to enter the long-distance market by requesting from SUBTEL licenses to build and operate long-distance facilities.

Here is where Chile's institutional framework starts to have an impact on the sector's development in an unexpected way. Opposed to the entry of the local exchange companies into the long-distance market, SUBTEL in 1989 asked the Central Preemptive Commission to consider whether entry of local exchange companies into long distance was in the public interest.[28]

---

28. SUBTEL's opposition to the local exchange companies' integration into long distance was based on the anticompetitive impact CTC could have on the long-distance market. See Resolution Commission's Resolution No. 389 of April 16, 1993.

Table 8-6. Market Share Restrictions in the Long-Distance Markets, 1995–98

(percent)

Year	Domestic long distance		International long distance	
	Affiliated	*Nonaffiliated*	*Affiliated*	*Nonaffiliated*
1995	35	80	20	70
1996	45	70	30	65
1997	55	60	40	60
1998	60	60	n.a.	n.a.

Source: Law 3-A.

Although the Central Preemptive Commission sided with the government, the decision was rapidly reversed on appeal by the Resolution Commission, which ordered that local and long-distance services should not be segmented and requested the introduction of a multicarrier system whereby customers could choose their long-distance provider. Thus, by 1989 Chile could have moved directly to long-distance competition.

Entel, however, appealed to the Supreme Court, which in 1990 requested from the Resolution Commission a more in-depth study of the technical conditions that would allow for fair playing conditions, including the supervision of interconnection quality. The Resolution Commission took three years to study this issue anew, and in 1993 it upheld its prior decision[29] and asked the government to implement the multicarrier system in less than 18 months. The system was introduced in late August 1994 outside Santiago and a month later in Santiago. Before then Congress amended the General Telecommunications Act. To some extent reflecting the strong pressure exercised by Entel, Congress amended this act to limit for the next five years each operator's market share in the domestic and international long-distance markets. Those carriers affiliated with local exchange companies (mostly CTC) were subject to more stringent restrictions.

Table 8-6 shows the nature of the bargain: CTC is initially limited to 35 percent of the long-distance market, while Entel is initially required to relinquish at least 30 percent of the market. But the market share restrictions also provide CTC with some protection from competition from Entel. To enter into local service in 1995, Entel had to relinquish 80 percent of its current

---

29. See, for example, *El Mercurio,* January 10, 1994, at B1, *New Competition in the Market for Telecommunications.*

Table 8-7. Telecommunication Companies and Services Offered

Firm	Associated foreign operations	Services offered						
		Local service	Long-distance services (national and international)	Business and value added services	Mobile services	Equipment and terminals	Cable television	Internet access
CTC	Telefonica	x	x	x	x	x	x	x
Entel	STET-Italia	x	x	x	x	x		x
Telex-Chile		x	x[a]	x	x	x		x
VTR	SBC-EE.UU.	x	x[a]	x	x[a]	x	x	
Bell South	Bell South	x	x		x			x
CIA. Telef. Manquehue		x						x
CMET		x						x
FirstCom			x					x
Transam			x					

a. Services were sold to CTC.

Source: Authors' compilations from firms' annual reports.

Table 8-8. Domestic Long-Distance Phone Service: CTC\Entel, 1997

Service	Price per minute (US$)
Domestic	0.17
To USA	0.34
From USA	0.51

Note: The basic rate for the typical domestic long-distance call and an international call to the United States, expressed in U.S. dollars at the current exchange rate.
Source: Spiller and Cardilli (1997).

long-distance market share, or 50 percent more than if it stayed out of the local service market. Thus, Law 3-A in table 8-6 reflects a particular bargain struck among the companies that allowed the implementation by the Resolution Commission. Although Entel lost at the Commission, litigation provided it with five years of delay and the corresponding monopoly rents. (See table 8-7 for the services offered by the telecommunication companies.)

The decision led to a flurry of entrants. Following a hectic advertising campaign by all the long-distance operators, prices of long-distance services fell by more than half of Entel's prices prior to September 1994. For example, on prices carriers charge on calls to the United States, at the beginning of 1997 the normal rate was about US¢90 per minute, with one carrier charging less than US¢40 (carriers charge their large customers even lower rates). By late 1997 that charge had dropped to US¢34 (table 8-8). By way of comparison, in 1998 AT&T in the United States charged US¢51 per minute under its One Rate Plan.

These prices can be contrasted with the pre-multicarrier regulated rates: if the rate-setting scheme in force after 1988 had been maintained, a call to the United States today would cost US$2.40 per minute. The drop in prices led to a substantial increase in traffic: international calls per month rose from about 6 million minutes before the multicarrier in September 1994 to around 19 million minutes by March 1997. Entel's market share declined by more than half overnight. Even without including public telephones, its market share did not to reach 50 percent by December 1994.[30]

---

30. Without counting public phones (CTC has the majority of the outgoing calls) and private lines, Entel has 46.2 percent of the market, CHILESAT, 30.6 percent; CTC-Mundo, 11 percent; VTR, 7.4 percent; Bell South, 2.4 percent; and CNT-Carrier, 2.4 percent.

So far, the fear that CTC will capture a large percentage of the market has not materialized. CTC is still the third largest long-distance carrier with less than 30 percent of the market. The introduction of the multicarrier system completed the first round of reforms that started in 1987 when the Resolution Commission determined that both local and long-distance services were not competitive. While the multicarrier system fosters competition in the long-distance market, it does not affect the extent of competition in local services. This is the next battlefront in the Chilean telecommunications wars.

The counterpart of the consumers' gain is a reduction in the industry's profits: in 1993 Entel made profits of about US$80 million, whereas the total profits of all carriers in the new system in 1995 amounted to US$31 million. These meager results are explained by three factors: (i) the dissipation of monopoly rents aggravated by a price war during the first quarter of 1995; (ii) high but transitory restructuring costs to cope with a competitive environment, and (iii) a narrowing of the imbalance between incoming and outgoing traffic. International carriers settle their traffic imbalances at so-called accounting rates, which are a multiple of the actual cost of providing the service. A carrier handling more incoming than outgoing traffic receives significant revenue from foreign carriers. In 1993 international traffic coming into Chile was approximately 1.3 times outgoing traffic. Estimates put incoming traffic at 160 million minutes during 1996, 15 million minutes fewer than the outgoing traffic in the same year.

Mobile telephony. In 1988 the government set up the rules for mobile telephony. Three franchise zones for cellular phones were established, with two companies operating in each zone. Prices are freely determined by the firms. By the end of 1997 there were about 410,000 cellular phone subscribers, of which 223,000 were clients of Startel, 142,000 were clients of Bell South, and the rest were with Entel. About 60 percent of all subscribers concentrate in one zone (Region Metropolitana and V Región), which was served by CTC and Bell South. Most of the remaining subscribers belong to the second zone, which was served by VTR and Entel. The last zone, corresponding to the southern part of the country, had fewer clients and was served by CTC and VTR. At the beginning of 1996 VTR and CTC merged their cellular phone companies and set up a new enterprise —Startel— serving the whole country. The Preventive Commission asked Startel to sell one of the licenses that it held in the third zone. The license was acquired by Entel in December 1996. Initially, CTC owned 55 percent of Startel, with the other 45 percent belonging to VTR. In December 1997 VTR sold to CTC its shares of Startel.

Mobil telephony prices (Ch$120 per minute in peak periods) are significantly higher than fixed telephony prices (Ch$13 per minute), reflecting higher operating costs. The biggest part of the cost of communicating from or to a mobile phone is always paid by the mobile service subscriber, although mobile phone companies argue that the party initiating the call should pay for this. CTC has opposed such a change, arguing that fixed telephony subscribers should not have to pay for the development costs of cellular telephony. What probably explains CTC's opposition is that the change would make mobile telephony a closer substitute to fixed telephony.

In November 1996 SUBTEL auctioned three nationwide franchises for personal telephony (PCS), with geographical coverage as the auction variable. This process was postponed by more than a year because of a series of lawsuits filed by CTC and Bell South to delay its introduction. Franchises were awarded in March 1997, with two franchises awarded to Entel and the third to Chilesat. These long-distance companies, with small local-phone operations, see PCS as a chance to gain direct access to final users, which seems to be increasingly important in their development strategies in a context of integrated firms offering all services. SUBTEL disregarded a recommendation by the Preventive Commission that no company should possess more than one mobile phone franchise in the same geographical area. The Commission argued that competition among potential competitors is an important factor in market discipline. Entel finally ended up with two PCS franchises and a cellular phone concession covering nearly the whole country, except the two regions where the greatest demand is concentrated. Bell South, which holds a concession in those two regions but not in the rest of the country, has ended up worse off because it is the only mobile telephony provider that does not have national coverage.

The coming into operation of Entel personal telephony in January 1998, like the case of the multicarrier system, has generated a publicity war between the companies. Mobile telephony companies have substantially lowered their rates. For example CTC-Startel made an offer through which it requires a monthly charge of Chilean $7,080, allowing up to 60 minutes of calls in a normal period; additional minutes are charged at a rate of Ch$124 at normal times and Ch$80 at off-peak times. In addition, those who sign a contract for 24 months receive the telephone as a gift. These rates are sharply lower than the rates before the entry of Entel-PCS.

CTC-Startel offered a system known as "calling party pays plus" (CPPP): the person making the call from a fixed telephone pays the fixed telephone charge (as had been the case), but the recipient of the call on the cellular phone pays no charge. This change would have meant a significant fall in the company's revenues, because approximately 40 percent of calls are incoming, a percentage that would have increased substantially due to call-back. CTC-Startel indicated that it hoped to compensate for this drop in revenues with a substantial increase in the number of clients.

At the request of the National Economic Prosecutor, the Resolution Commission decided to suspend this offer indefinitely, although it maintained it for people who had contracted the service during the week in which it was operational. The Commission's argument is that it could represent predatory pricing. Although it is hard to probe predatory pricing in advance, at least one would have to recognize that it would have been an obstacle to the introduction to the calling party pays system. Moreover, the strategic importance of mobile telephony for CTC is quite clear: this firm paid US$425 million to Startel for 45 percent of Startel.

REGULATORY PITFALLS: INTERCONNECTION, ACCESS, VERTICAL INTEGRATION, AND COMPETITION. In spite of many good features, the Chilean regulatory framework had a number of deficiencies. First, let us consider access issues. The right and terms of interconnection to the fixed link were completely neglected, with serious adverse consequences. Unnecessary lengthy delays in competition resulted with the associated welfare losses to telephone users, and years passed on interconnection-related lawsuits, highly costly to entrants. The deadlock was eventually broken through legislation and intervention by the Supreme Court. Similarly, on equal access (to the network), the legislation did not specify it, leading to the expected delays and restraints by the provider and lengthy litigation and delays of the benefits from competition. The pattern was that CTC would contract for wholesale long-distance service and would assign outbound calls randomly to long-distance carriers in proportion to the size of that carrier's contract. Again the deadlock was eventually broken by a Supreme Court decision to let customers choose their own long-distance carrier. The Court put all carriers on an equal basis by allowing the customer to dial the carrier's unique access code. Likewise with unbundling (the incumbent provides entrants with basic network elements and services individually, such as lines, switching, and transport), the legislation was mute.

A second deficiency was the rigidity of the regulatory framework with its embedded checks and balances. Not unexpectedly, this had costs. The introduction of the multicarrier is an excellent example of how the original design of a system of checks and balances in utility regulation limits the ability of the government to tightly control the evolution of the industry. Indeed, the participation of the antitrust authorities reversed an original position of the regulator against vertical integration. The participation of the Supreme Court, another part of Chile's complex system of checks and balances, delayed the de-facto deregulation of long distance by four years.[31] This seems to be another example of the reformers' choice of credibility over flexibility. This time, as may often be the case, credibility came at a cost.

In order to take advantage of economies of scale and scope, the authority chose competition between firms providing a multiplicity of services. The concept of one-stop shopping is highly attractive to users. Firms in competitive segments (such as long distance) now realize that it is essential for them to integrate services and have direct access to the client. As mentioned, five companies recently started providing local phone services through subsidiaries in areas overlapping with the CTC area. Thus, competition that had been opened up in other areas is now promoting competition in the local service.

However, achieving competition between providers of multiple services confronts SUBTEL with a real challenge. A single company holds about 90 percent of all local telephone subscribers, and SUBTEL's own resources are limited. Is there any chance of achieving real competition in basic phone services? In certain areas there have been overlapping franchises in local telephony since the early 1980s. These arose mainly as a result of the inability of CTC—at that time in state hands—to satisfy demand. However, they never represented real competition for CTC. Weaknesses in the legislation, especially as regards interconnection norms, inhibited true competition. The situation was resolved when the 1993 law was passed introducing regulated access tolls, a change that facilitated competition in fixed telephony.

Personal telephony may provide cost-effective alternatives in the future, but joint provision of cable TV and basic phone services is nowadays a more realistic possibility. VTR, which controls a company holding about 50 percent participation in the cable TV market, is experimenting with the joint provision of local phone and cable TV services. Unfortunately, the parent companies of VTR and CTC are considering merging the two firms, and if this happens the possibility of competing via joint operation with cable TV would disappear. In the meantime, the Preventive Commission has stated that any merger between CTC and VTR would have to obtain its prior approval.

---

31. Recall that the law explicitly said that decisions of the Resolution Commission could be appealed to the Supreme Court in a few specific cases, involving, among other issues, changes in the statutes of companies, as seems to have been the case here. CTC complained bitterly about what seemed to have been the manipulation of the system by Entel.

Thus, competition in basic phone services still seems a remote possibility. It remains to be seen whether CTC's dominance of basic services will allow for competition in other telecom services. One example of the risks involved in vertical integration is illustrated by a special joint-service offer made by CTC and its subsidiary CTC Cellular (before it merged with VTR Cellular). Their clients were offered a so-called "super-phone." Callers trying to reach the owner of a super-phone would call the subscriber's basic phone number. If nobody answered the call, it would automatically be transferred to the subscriber's mobile phone. Bell South complained to the Resolution Commission about this type of bundling and also about subsidies made by CTC, a regulated company, to CTC Cellular, an unregulated company. The commission sanctioned CTC with a fine of 2,500 UTM (equivalent to US$142,500). It also asked the government to introduce legislation requiring that subsidiaries of basic phone companies providing other communication services be organized as common stock companies supervised by the Securities Commission (a requirement of long-distance carriers that were subsidiaries of basic phone companies).

The current legislation allows local phone companies to enter the long-distance market through subsidiaries. But while competition consolidates, the law has set limits on the main firms' market share during the first three years. In addition, local telephone companies are obliged to supply any relevant information on long-distance traffic to all carriers, because discrimination in favor of an affiliated long-distance carrier is always a possibility while the local phone service remains a natural monopoly. So far, the long-distance market has worked comparatively well; it remains to be seen whether these conditions will continue in the future.

More worrisome is CTC's expansion policy. Through acquisition and merger, CTC has gained control (owns 40 percent) of a cable TV company providing services to 256,500 of the nation's 626,500 TV cable subscribers. (The rest are serviced by VTR.) The merger of CTC's and VTR's cellular operations created the largest mobile phone company in the country. In early 1997 CTC and VTR announced merger plans that would have led in the short run to the absorption of VTR by CTC. The VTR holding controls VTR Larga Distancia, which provides long-distance services; Telefónica del Sur, which provides local phone services in the southern part of the country; CNT Carrier, a minor regional company; VTR Hipercable, which services about 59 percent of cable subscribers; and VTR Telefónica, which provides local services in Santiago. Most auspicious for competition, VTR Telefónica, a subsidiary of VTR Hipercable, is experimenting with the joint provision of local phone and cable television services.

The Preventive Commission stated that any merger between CTC and VTR required its prior approval. Both the Preventive Commission and SUBTEL hinted that the merger of cable television and local service operations would not be allowed. In December 1997 both companies announced that VTR was selling to CTC its long-distance operation and its participation in Startel. This sale is still waiting approval by the Preventive Commission, so it remains to be seen how the regulatory agencies will react to CTC´s merger drive.

COMPARISON WITH ARGENTINA AND THE UNITED KINGDOM. Prior to privatization in 1990, Entel, the Argentine telecom company, was broken up into four companies: two provide basic domestic services in disjoint geographical areas, while the other two provide value-added and long-distance services, respectively. Ownership of the latter two companies was divided equally between the two basic service providers. These four companies now monopolize most telecom services in Argentina, having been awarded a ten-year (seven years initially with an extension of three) guarantee of exclusivity in basic, value-added and long-distance services.

The charges for basic services were negotiated after the companies had submitted their bids and the franchises had been awarded, but before the companies signed the license agreements in November 1990. Between December 1989 and September 1990 the price of a pulse went up from US¢0.58 to US¢3.32, and it was established that the rate would remain constant in real terms for two years, then decline by 2 percent per year over the following three years. In November 1991, the tariff-setting scheme was modified: prices were fixed in U.S. dollars after an initial increase of 1.3 percent. In 1994 the rate per call unit stood at US¢4.13. Price regulation of Argentine telecoms adhered to an RPI-X scheme, where the efficiency factor (X) was set at 2 percent until 1997 and 4 percent between 1998 and 2000.

According to Petrazzini (1995), the explanation for such favorable treatment of private investors is that privatizations were largely a financing instrument for stabilization policies. The economic and political instability in Argentina would have prevented liberalization and the sale of the companies arising from Entel at the floor price set by the government. Investors would not consider purchasing Entel, the first utility privatization in Argentina, unless the market was protected for an extended period of time. The Argentine government had initially planned a sweeping liberalization of the telecoms sector.

In the United Kingdom the Post Office until 1981 held a virtual monopoly on licenses to operate telecom services: only when the Post Office was unable to provide a service was another operator allowed to do so. In 1981 Post Office telecom services were hived off to a new company, British Telecommunications (BT), which was privatized in 1984. In 1981 the firm Cable & Wireless (C&W), which provided telecommunications services in the ex-colonies, was privatized, and a new company, Mercury, was formed that became a competitor in 1982 to BT. BT's license includes price controls and an obligation to provide interconnection facilities at predetermined prices and service quality. A regulatory agency (OFTEL) was also set up. OFTEL regulates prices using an RPI-X formula for a basket of services. Initially a productivity increase factor of 3 percent was considered, but this was raised to 7.5 percent in 1993.

In 1991 it was concluded that this duopoly had not been successful in terms of reducing concentration in the sector, because Mercury's participation was marginal, and consequently the restriction on telecom licensing was lifted. Moreover, BT was prohibited from entering mobile telephony and cable TV, and it was also ruled that BT and Mercury had to provide circuits to other operators. Following the ending of the duopoly, new companies were born. The main competitors to BT at the local level are cable companies offering television and telecom services. Energesis, owned by the National Grid Group, has built a digital network using power transmission lines.

In 1995, 14 years after the introduction of deregulation, BT was invoicing 87 percent of the basic telephony market (local and long distance), with the rest mainly in the hands of Mercury. All vestiges of competition would disappear if a merger between BT and C&W—owner of Mercury—occurred, and currently the only real threat to BT comes from cable TV companies. BT's license includes price controls on calls and exchange line services, an obligation to offer standard interconnection facilities at predetermined prices, and service quality.

In general the market structure in Chile is more competitive than in Argentina and the United Kingdom, for the following reasons. In the first place, franchises have not been awarded on an exclusive basis since before the privatization process. Secondly, at the time of privatization there were two large companies, one in basic telephony and the other in long distance, which the antitrust agencies prevented from falling into the hands of a single owner. Thirdly, competition was facilitated by the way the multicarrier system was implemented.

REGULATORY CHALLENGES. The main regulatory challenges facing Chile can be divided into two areas (with some inevitable overlap): improving equity and improving efficiency. To improve equity, Chile must ensure that efficiency gains (from allocative and technological innovations) are passed to users and not captured as additional rents. An incentive-based and nondistortionary universal system obligations (USO) is needed. A salient choice is the use of competitive bidding of the minimum subsidy to provide the service. The alternative, a direct targeted subsidy to the appropriate income groups, is often too administratively costly.

Access pricing and terms of that service should be revisited to ensure alignment of (efficient) costs and prices and equal treatment of service quality to all providers. Chile should consider facilitating viable alternatives to the fixed link network and a more effective implementation of the antitrust legislation in the sector.

A key issue is defining a proper role for antitrust legislation in the framework for interconnection negotiations. The introduction in Chile of a multicarrier long-distance telecommunications service, second only to that in the United States in the choices offered, has not proceeded without problems. The country has experienced total shutdowns of networks, occasional blockage of competitors' dialing codes by the main basic carrier, CTC, and longer delays in dialed calls getting through.

The example of Mexico in implementing interconnection is enlightening. In Mexico the Telmex monopoly in long-distance service expired in 1996. As a result, the terms for interconnection to the local exchange are being hotly contested. Regulators from the Communications and Transportation Ministry recently rejected, quite appropriately, the Telmex plan for ten interconnection points. Instead, the regulators approved a plan for 200 such points, to be available by the year 2000. The key issue is to define the terms under which the privatized Telmex faces competition. The reluctance of incumbent operators to open the network to external users is not surprising, given the decreases in revenues expected from such a move. In the telecommunications sector, estimates of the loss in revenue induced by an equal access policy—incremental loss of 5 percent in traffic due to ease in switching operators—are around 20 percent; or a low interconnection rate causing a 15 to 25 percent loss in international traffic can induce decreases in revenues over 50 percent (Beardsley and Patsalos-Fox 1995). In summary, the setting of standards for interconnection is essential to foster parity and effective competition and reap its benefits.

The Water and Sewerage Sector

A lot of work is in progress in the water and sewerage sector, but its recent history deserves a summary. The sanitation services sector underwent significant changes at the end of the 1980s and the beginning of the 1990s. Up to the end of the 1980s, the provision of drinking water, drainage, and sewage treatment was the responsibility of a centralized public service (SENDOS). In this period charges covered only operating costs and a minor fraction of investment costs, which were financed mainly through fiscal transfers. In 1989 and 1990 separate laws were passed allowing the state to undertake entrepreneurial activities in this sector. Under the new legislation, 13 regional joint-stock companies affiliated with the state development corporation (CORFO) were created out of SENDOS, initiating processes of "entrepreneurialization" and regionalization in the sector.

In 1988 a regulatory framework was established for the sector, based closely on the framework for electricity. Franchises are granted for an indefinite period and are transferable. Four stages are recognized in the sanitation service: production, distribution, collection, and treatment. Franchises may be granted independently for each stage. The legislation (i) establishes the obligation to provide the service within the franchise area; (ii) defines rules of service continuity and quality; and (iii) imposes mandatory interconnection with other sanitation firms as the regulating body deems necessary. In 1989 the Superintendency of Water and Sanitation Services (SWSS) was created—the entity responsible for regulating service quality and setting prices. The SWSS is an administrative dependency of the Ministry of Public Works.

The rate system set up in the new regulatory framework allows for self-financing, including capital costs, among efficient firms. The new system was used for the first time in 1990, and until early 1994 rates were raised gradually. During this period charges increased an average of 80 percent. The CORFO subsidiary companies on average achieved a 6.3 percent return on capital in 1994, although profitability by firm ranged from -4.5 percent to 13.2 percent that year. In 1996 the profitability on capital for the public sanitation companies ranged from 2.2 percent to 14.3 percent with an average of 9.2 percent.

The private firms have consistently secured higher rates of return on assets than have the state-owned-firms and better performance indicators (table 8-9), although some adjustments for the lower costs of the private firms because of their source location should be made. A targeted subsidy was introduced for the poorest families up to a maximum consumption of 20 cubic meters and 85 percent of their bill. Financed directly by the government, it replaced the old subsidy that was inefficient (users were not confronted with the real cost of the water) and regressive (it benefited more the families of high consumption). With the targeted subsidy, arrears di-

Table 8-9. Rates of Returns on Assets and Performance: Comparison of Public and Private Firms, 1988–95

Firms	1988	1989	1990	1991	1992	1993	1994	1995
Public (CORFO)	–1.4	–1.6	–1.1	–0.2	0.9	3.4	5.1	5.9
Private	-0.1	13.1	3.9	1.6	4.0	6.5	7.2	9.9

	1995	
	Water losses (percent)	*Average tariff ($/cubic meter)*
Public	31.1	237.8
Private	26.8	182.5

Source: Authors' compilations from companies' annual reports.

minished from 7.9 percent in 1990 to 2.9 percent in 1994, as a result of better commercial management, incentives for prompt payment, and authority granted to firms to suspend services to clients with unpaid bills.

The methodology for calculating rates is established by law. The rate is determined as the incremental development cost, defined as the rate that gives a zero present value on investments needed to satisfy demand increases over a 35-year horizon. The discount rate used is that which is relevant to the sector. Rates calculated in this way are then corrected so that expected revenue matches total costs in the period between successive rate settings. The charges at each stage of the service and for each firm are calculated every five years on the basis of studies carried out separately by the SWSS and the corresponding firms, and the SWSS formulates the basis for undertaking such studies. Discrepancies between studies are resolved by a three-member panel, two of whom are designated by the SWSS and the third by the firm. Rates are adjusted between tariff calculations whenever the price index relevant to one of the charges accumulates an increase of more than 3 percent.

PRIVATIZATION OF WATER AND SEWERAGE COMPANIES. In order to take advantage of private-sector managerial capabilities and overcome a long period of underinvestment, the government decided to privatize CORFO's water and sewerage subsidiaries, evaluating different privatization schemes for this purpose.[32] The analysis led the government to conclude that scope for

---

32. Investment increased threefold between 1990 and 1993 but is still inadequate.

competition in this sector was limited. First, competition in water production is restricted by natural resource availability. Second, an interconnected system, such as in the electricity sector, is unlikely to be established for water transportation, since quality problems can arise if water from different sources is mixed. Although competition is possible in water supply and sewage treatment, the benefits are not sufficient to compensate for the transaction costs that would result from the breakup of the vertically integrated firms. Therefore, it was decided to allow vertical integration in the water sector.[33]

Originally, the government opted for the full privatization of existing firms, rejecting the alternative of retaining ownership of water and sewerage firms and granting fixed-term franchises. However, for political reasons it decided to consider the latter, at least as an alternative.

The main reason for the initial decision was that finite-horizon franchises would have required legislative amendment, at a time when some concessions had already been awarded. In addition, there was a perception that end-point problems in fixed-term franchises were difficult to deal with, especially when significant investments were required close to the end of the franchise. Furthermore, long-term franchises would require periodical rate reviews, given the dynamics of the sector, thereby eliminating their main advantage over full privatization. Short-term concessions did not seem to be the solution either: labor costs represent a significant proportion of total costs in water and sewerage services, so transferring the labor force between different concessionaires would pose significant problems.

Based on these considerations, the government in 1995 sent a bill to Congress that would permit the sale of up to 65 percent of sanitation companies to the private sector. The bill also modified the dispute settlement procedure to give both the SWSS and the regulated firms incentives to tell the truth. In the event of discrepancies between the rate subsidies made by the firm and the regulator, an arbitrator chooses the one closest to the norm. In addition, the legislation enhanced the enforcement capacity of the SWSS and raised sanctions; set limits on horizontal concentration to allow for competition by comparison; and raised wages and improved hiring practices for qualified personnel in the SWSS.

In the Senate, where the right-wing opposition had a majority, the bill passed after significant changes. Clauses were eliminated that retained 35

---

33. The interconnectivity conditions imposed on the concessionaires would allow the appearance of independent water producers if the case arose.

percent ownership in state hands and prohibited concentration in the same hands of electricity distribution and the sanitation business in any given geographical area. In the lower chamber, which is dominated by a center-left coalition supporting the government, discussion has come to a halt. After the bill had been sent to Congress, new developments on the regulatory front, particularly in the water sector, made it less palatable for the center-left coalition to approve the legislation passed by the Senate.

Two private franchise-holders provided the worst service—including rationing—during the severe drought that affected the country in 1995 and 1996. Unlike public-sector firms, these firms failed to undertake the investments that would have made it possible to ensure normal provision in drought periods. Moreover, the regulator was unable to prevent this situation mainly because nonfulfillment of the investment plan would have implied very weak sanctions on franchise-holders. The rainfall deficit led to a strict rationing of consumption during the summer months in the zone supplied by the private-sector water company, Lo Castillo, where the highest-income families, with the greatest willingness to pay, live. Enersis, the dominant firm in the electricity sector, has acquired control of Lo Castillo. Rate-setting problems in electricity distribution have made clear to politicians the difficulties of regulating natural monopolies in the judicial, political, and institutional framework existing in Chile.

Parliamentarians in the government coalition want incorporation of the private sector to be achieved without transferring ownership of firms or infrastructure. In response, the government has decided to include in the legislation an article to allow one option of private participation via a management-investment scheme. This situation has led to a reassessment of the option of fixed-term franchises.

How can investment right up to the end of the franchise period be encouraged without affecting the transparency of the system? One of the options that has been considered is setting up a central auctioneer for local franchises, to deter opportunistic behavior on the part of a franchise-holder. Firms that have performed poorly in maintaining assets could be precluded from participating in future auctions. The chance of participating in several franchise auctions generates incentives to eschew opportunistic behavior.

Setting up a central auction is not an easy task, however. A black-listed entrepreneur could bid for future franchises by using a different legal front. The auction also would not deter opportunistic behavior by one-period concessionaires. These problems are resolved by the requirement that prior experience is needed to apply. But if the entry of new participants is not allowed, established firms would obtain monopoly rents.

Another possibility is the formula used for regulating electricity distribution in Argentina: in the auction rates are set by the state and the auction variable is the payment to the outgoing franchise-holder. The disadvantage of this form of franchise is that it keeps market forces from determining rates, thereby making it possible for very high rates to be perpetuated. A variant of this approach is to set an upper bound on the payment to the outgoing operator, which could correspond to the residual value of the assets. If some bidders consider the value of the franchise higher than this ceiling, the franchise would be awarded to the bidder paying the ceiling price and seeking the lowest rate.

Another factor that reduces the seriousness of the incentives problem is the significant advantage held by the incumbent firm at the time of re-auction. International experience shows that the firm actually operating has a significant advantage: in France more than 90 percent of franchises are re-awarded to the same operators, and this provides incentives to maintain assets in good working order. Despite this advantage for the incumbent, the latent threat of competition generates some degree of market discipline.

Chile has not been a pioneer in the privatization of sanitation services as it has been in other public services. This has allowed it to take other countries' experiences in this sector into account in defining the regulatory setup, as well as its own experience in other public services. Domestic experience shows that regulated rates are higher than under competition—hence the concern to introduce competition ex-ante when involving the private sector in sanitary services. The big problem with short-term franchises is that, when franchise-holders need to make new investments, the rates have to be renegotiated and all the benefits of the initial competition are lost. Unfortunately, the experience of France and Argentina is not encouraging in this regard. Analysis is needed on possible improvements to systems currently in operation.

INTERNATIONAL EXPERIENCE. Private-sector participation in the sanitation sector has expanded significantly in recent years in both developed and developing countries. The huge financial requirements involved in improving environmental and sanitation standards, as well as the need to enhance management and service quality, are the main factors explaining this trend. Most of the schemes existing in the world to bring private capital into the sanitation sector are fixed-term franchise contracts between a local regional authority and a firm with experience in this sector. These contracts oblige the franchise-holder to administer and undertake the investments necessary to meet demand over periods varying between 10 and 30 years, depending on the size of the investments. Usually, when the concession contract is short, the government retains asset ownership, and when it is long, asset ownership is transferred to the operator. The usual auction variable is the rate of charge.

In France, where the municipalities have responsibility for water provision, renegotiation of the terms of the contract has been allowed if unanticipated investments turn out to be necessary. This has led to a high degree of discretion and a lack of transparency in the sector. Consequently, the national government set mandatory objective standards for re-auctioning. The municipalities renegotiated the periods of current contracts before the new standards came into force, so it is not yet known how re-auctioning will work.

In 1989 the ten regional sanitation firms in the United Kingdom were privatized. In this case it was decided to transfer ownership of vertically integrated regional firms. There is the possibility that the regulator could renew franchises after 25 years. However, the conditions for franchise renewal have not been clearly established. Price control over the water industry involves a variant on the standard RPI-X formula, where X is a composite of the efficiency factor X and a special provision for the investment needs of the industry. Privatization of the sanitation sector caused great controversy in Britain, because charges to consumers had to be raised drastically to comply with the higher environmental requirements of the European Community. Bills to domestic customers have risen by over 40 percent since privatization.

Argentina has also undertaken programs to bring private-sector capital into the sanitation field. The province of Buenos Aires awarded (free of charge) a 30-year franchise to the firm charging the lowest rate and willing to fulfill a pre-established investment program and increase of coverage. At the end of the period all capital invested will revert to the federal government. Regular price adjustments are implemented every five years, based on five-year service obligation and investment plans. Extraordinary adjustments are initiated when the cost indices of the tariff formula rise by 7 percent or more. The franchise was won by a consortium headed by one of the main French operators with vast experience in France and in other parts of the world. Initially, the franchise meant a 27 percent reduction in charges, but modification of the investment program just one year after the franchise had been auctioned obliged the authorities to authorize an increase in rates.

After the franchise was in operation for three years, the coverage of drinking water provision expanded by 10 percent and sewerage services by 8 percent, while the drinking water production capacity rose by nearly 30 percent. Similarly, all efficiency indicators have improved: for example, the number of employees per connection has been cut to half. At the end of the franchise, the state can re-auction without paying compensation to the incumbent firm. The authorities consider that the advantage obtained by the operator winning the re-auction is a sufficient incentive to maintain assets adequately. However, the choice of technologies for treating waste-water has raised doubts concerning distortions that could be caused by the existence of a finite evaluation horizon.

Conclusion

The inefficient operation of state-owned infrastructure, resulting from political constraints, caused significant welfare losses, and the perceived difficulties in attaining managerial efficiency in state-owned enterprises (SOEs) was the driving force behind their privatization. Privatization, however, does not automatically ensure a firm's internal efficiency: agency theory shows that there is always some sacrifice of the profit-maximization goal in the presence of random events affecting firms' results, as well as risk aversion on the part of managers. However, ensuring internal efficiency is not the most critical issue in privately owned monopolies: profit maximization leads unregulated monopolies to charge higher prices and produce less than what is efficient, so natural monopolies need to be regulated in order to avoid welfare losses. We believe that better regulation of public utilities is required for both efficiency and equity reasons.

Three lessons can be drawn from Chile's experience with regulation of privatized public utilities. First, whenever possible, the attainment of competitive conditions should be the main goal before, during, and after privatization. In particular, restructuring enterprises before privatization should take into account the regulatory problems that will ensue. The second lesson is the need for developing unambiguous regulatory legislation before privatization. Third, a successful regulation of public utilities requires strong, autonomous, and technically proficient institutions, something that is hard to come across in developing countries. Thus, the speed at which the privatization process is carried out should depend on the degree of progress achieved by regulatory legislation and institutions.

Better regulation usually means less regulatory activities. When privatization leads to a competitive industry, there is no need for regulation, although in some circumstances an active policy is required to achieve competition. Clearly worded regulations lessen the likelihood of conflict between the regulated and regulators and between the regulated entities themselves. The existence of autonomous and proficient regulatory agencies reduces the steadfastness of monopolies' abuse of their market power. Finally, regulation should allow for new entrants. Actual natural monopolies could lose this condition as a result of technological advances.

Competition as a Goal

The privatization of Chilean infrastructure in the 1980s retained monopolies that had no economic justification whatsoever. The lack of consideration of regulatory aspects before and after privatization led to the monopolization of activities that could have been developed under the discipline of competition. Authorities should have been careful not to make extensive the exclusive rights that benefited SOEs over private firms. These exclusive rights created, in some cases, legal barriers to entry, thus maintaining the monopolistic characteristics of the sector. As the pioneer in the region, Chile lacked experience in privatizing public utilities, and this could be the explanation.

The property structure in the electric sector is the most illustrative case. Although the regulatory framework assumes competition in electric power generation and in supplying large customers (those with a demand exceeding 2 megawatts), the dominant firm in the Central Interconnected System and its affiliates provide more than 60 percent of the power generation, own the transmission grid and its controlling company (Enersis), and own the largest distribution firm, which is responsible for about 50 percent of distribution in the CIS area.

The restructuring of enterprises before privatization fell short of what was needed to ensure competition. Endesa could have been further broken up into two or three firms before privatization. The transmission grid could have been set up as a separate company. Consideration should have been given to two alternative schemes: (i) turning the grid into a common carrier jointly owned by all generating and distribution firms and open to newcomers and (ii) setting up a separate company without links to generators. Moreover, the water rights should have been returned to the state before privatization; then the state could have granted the rights based on the timely development of new projects by existing firms or newcomers. Right now the policy options are limited. Endesa was allowed to buy another generator, Pehuenche, in the 1980s. In the early 1990s Enersis, which already owned Chilectra, gained control of Endesa. The long-distance telephone company was awarded licenses guaranteeing its monopoly in international calls for at least five years. The maintenance of a single major local phone company owning more than 90 percent of all phone lines has prevented the development of competition by comparison.

The last round of privatization has been implemented with the clear intent to increase competition. For example, the sale of the last important generating company (Pehuenche) was geared to bring in a new large foreign company. This increased the number of active players and added some heterogeneity to the club. In the privatization of sewage companies, participation in more than one zone is prohibited in order to facilitate performance comparisons for regulatory oversight. The change in the telecommunications procedures approved in 1997 should improve competition. Requiring the calling party to pay in mobile telephony will make this service a closer substitute for fixed telephony, where competition is in principle limited. Finally, a decision by the Resolution Commission further reveals determination to establish a competitive environment. This decision forces Endesa to transform its transmission subsidiary into an open common stock company and compels distribution companies to publicly bid their purchases of energy.

Defining a Regulatory Framework

Even though Chile's regulatory framework for privatized public utilities is comparatively advanced and attempts to balance the conflicting needs for low cost-service and for reinvestment, it still is incomplete and somewhat ambiguous. The framework creates the possibility for opportunistic behavior by the regulator as well as by the regulated firms. The problem of asymmetry of information was made explicit by the rate-setting episodes. The regulatory scheme should stress the regulator's prompt access to the monopolies' production cost data. The best way to disassemble the monopoly of information, however, is to create competition by comparison among similar local monopolies.

The Chilean experience shows that rate-setting schemes, and regulatory frameworks in general, constitute incomplete contracts between regulators and regulated firms. For instance, the law allows the electric companies to require reimbursable financial contributions from customers requesting new services. However, the law does not say anything about the way in which the money is reimbursed. Rulings 792 and 793 of the Preventive Antitrust Commission have asked the government to modify the law specifying the ways in which the reimbursements have to be made. The overlapping of distribution concessions is another source of conflict. Ambiguities in the rate-setting schemes generate uncertainty over the property rights that are being acquired. Consequently, investors highly discount the value of companies being privatized.

The regulatory process has increasingly become a bargaining process. The outcome greatly depends on the relative power and influence of interest groups. This environment has led to the development of rent-seeking activities. Considerable resources are spent to affect favorably the regulators' decisions and to settle disputes between regulators and firms and among the firms themselves. In this climate where everyone is attempting to cultivate influence, regulated public utilities earn high returns on capital.

The government is not completely pleased with how the regulation of privatized public utilities has worked out. The problems in rate setting in electricity distribution and local telephony have made clear to politicians how difficult it is to regulate natural monopolies in the juridical, political, and institutional framework now existing in Chile. Therefore, the authorities have decided to strengthen the regulatory framework of the water and sewerage sector before proceeding to the privatization of the sanitation firms. In 1995 the government sent a bill to Congress that reinforced the regulatory framework of the sector. Congress approved a diluted version of the bill in November 1997.

From this experience another lesson can be drawn: the regulatory framework should be as unambiguous as possible, and it should be completed before privatization. Otherwise, privatizations can cause undesired income redistributions and welfare losses. The regulatory framework should include disclosure rules ensuring regulators easy and prompt access to all relevant cost data, and it should specify sanctions for profit transferring. On the other hand, very restrictive regulations could result in efficiency reducing rigidities. The regulatory framework will not solve all the issues. Highly technical and autonomous regulatory institutions are required.

Strengthening the Regulatory Institutions

The privatization experience in Chile revealed three undesired traits of regulatory agencies that probably are shared by agencies in many other countries: regulated firms' technical advantage over regulatory agencies, regulatory agencies' closeness to the political system, and the inadequacy of the regulatory structure. Regulatory institutions sometimes overlap and sometimes leave important aspects unregulated.

Regulatory agencies are part of the public sector, so their wages are limited by public wage scales. Because of the low wages in the public sector, professionals with little or no experience are hired, and turnover is high. Those employees who turn out to be productive quickly learn the nature of the business and with few exceptions migrate to the regulated firms where wages are several times higher. Thus, the negotiating power of the regulator and the professional capacity of the regulated firms are not balanced. Regulators see their labor in the regulating entity as a transition to the regulated industry. Therefore, the risk of regulators being captured by the industry is high.

In Chile, regulatory bodies are very dependent on the Ministries. The autonomy of regulatory agencies could be increased by (i) paying competitive salaries that will attract and retain able professionals and (ii) reducing the political pressures that public utility firms exert on the political system. However, autonomy does not eliminate the risk of capture of the regulatory institutions by the regulated firms. Autonomy has to be balanced by stronger control on the part of the comptroller's office and Parliament. Regulatory institutions should be accountable to the public, and their decision-making process should be transparent.

The existence of a well-staffed and endowed regulatory agency does not solve all problems. Conflicts still can be expected between public utility firms and regulators. The regulatory agency cannot be a party and an arbitrator at the same time; hence, there is a need for a highly technical arbitrage process, which certainly is not provided by the judiciary system. The antitrust commission could play an important role by solving disputes between regulators and regulated firms and by penalizing those who intentionally manipulate cost data. The cornerstone of any competition policy is the antitrust institutions. To succeed, these institutions must be independent from political pressures. The antitrust commissioners should work full time and have a solid background in regulatory economics and law, characteristics not met by most of the current antitrust commissioners.

Most persons on the antitrust commissions have no previous experience in the field. This is particularly the case on the Resolution Commission: members belong because of their other positions, not because of their knowledge of antitrust theory and practice. Chile needs to make a significant effort to strengthen the technical capacity of regulatory and antitrust institutions. The regulatory agencies need to hire more qualified staff, promote on the basis of merit instead of years of service, and change the law to allow inefficient personnel to be fired. In addition, officials in regulatory agencies should be prohibited from working for firms in the corresponding regulated industry for a number of years after leaving the agency. Obviously, this strategy needs a policy for remunerations and training in accordance with these new requirements.

References

Beardsley, Scott, and Michael Patsalos-Fox. 1995. "Getting Telecoms Privatization Right." *The McKinsey Quarterly*, no. 1.

Berstein, D. 1996. "Electricity Policy in Chile from 1980 Onwards: Analysis and Results." Economic Development Institute, World Bank, Washington, D.C.

Bitrán, Eduardo, and F. Saez. 1994. "Privatization and Regulation in Chile." In B. Bosworth, R. Dornbush, and R. Labán, eds., *The Chilean Economy: Policy Lessons and Challenges*. Washington, D.C.: The Brookings Institution.

Bitrán, Eduardo, and Pablo Serra. 1994. "Regulatory Issues in the Privatization of Public Utilities: The Chilean Experience." *Quarterly Review of Economics and Finance 34*.

———.1997. "Regulation of Privatized Utilities: Lessons from the Chilean Experience." In *OECD Proceedings, Privatisation of Utilities and Infrastructure: Methods and Constraints*. Paris: OECD.

Engel, E., R. Fischer, and A. Galetovic. 1998a. "Infrastructure Franchising and Government Guarantees." Working Paper 29, Centro de Economía Aplicada, Universidad de Chile, Santiago.

———.1998b. "A New Mechanism to Auction Highway Franchises." Working Paper 13, Centro de Economía Aplicada, Universidad de Chile, Santiago.

El Mercurio. 1994. "New Competition in the Market for Telecommunications." January 10 (Chile).

Galal, A. 1994. "Regulation and Commitment in the Development of Telecommunications in Chile." Policy Research Working Paper 1294, Policy Research Department, World Bank, Washington, D.C.

Galal, Ahmed, and others. 1994. *Welfare Consequences of Selling Public Enterprises: An Empirical Analysis*. Washington, D.C.: World Bank.

Guasch, J. L., and Pablo Spiller. Forthcoming. *Managing the Regulatory Process: Concept, Design and the Latin America and Caribbean Story*. Washington, D.C.: World Bank.

Hachette, Dominique. 1994. "Comment on Bitran and Saez." In B. Bosworth, R. Dornbush, and R. Labán, eds., *The Chilean Economy: Policy Lessons and Challenges*. Washington, D.C.: The Brookings Institution.

Hachette, Dominique, and Rolf Luders. 1993. *Privatization in Chile*. San Francisco: International Center for Economic Growth.

Luders, Rolf. 1991. "Massive Divestiture and Privatization: Lessons from Chile." *Contemporary Policy Issues* 9 (October): 1–19.

Munoz, O., ed. 1993. *Despues de la Privatizacion: Haciael Estado Regulador*. Santiago: CIEPLAN.

NEC (National Energy Commission). 1997. "El Sector Eléctrico Chileno." Santiago.

Paredes, Ricardo D. 1993. "Privatización y Regulación: Lecciones de la Experiencia Chilena." In O. Muñoz, ed., *Despues de la Privatización: Haciael Estado Regulador.* Santiago: CIEPLAN.

_____. 1994. "Privatization and Regulation in a Less Developed Economy: The Chilean Case." Universidad de Chile, Santiago.

_____. 1995. "Evaluating the Cost of Bad Regulation in a Newly Privatized Sector: The Chilean Case." *Revista de Analisis Economico* 10 (2): 89–112.

_____. 1996. "Competition Policies in an Economy without Market Tradition." Economic Development Institute, World Bank, Washington, D.C.

Petrazzini, B. 1995. "Telephone Privatization in a Hurry: Argentina." In Ravi Ramamurti, ed., *Privatizing Monopolies*. Baltimore: The Johns Hopkins University Press.

Serra, P. 1995. "La Politica de Competencia en Chile." *Revista de Analisis Economico* 10 (Noviembre): 63–88.

Spiller, Pablo, and Carlo G. Cardilli. 1997. "The Frontier of Telecommunications Deregulation: Small Countries Leading the Pack." *Journal of Economic Perspectives* 11 (Fall): 127–38.

Spiller, Pablo, and Luis Viana. 1992. "How Not to Do It: Electricity Regulation in Argentina, Brazil, Chile, and Uruguay." Department of Economics, University of California, Berkeley.

political and ideological trust had to be reestablished between the Christian Democrats and the left-wing parties that had constituted the Popular Unity government. Second, the Concertación had to gain the trust of supporters and opponents of the military government.

BUILDING TRUST BETWEEN THE CENTER AND THE LEFT. The recomposition of the political ties between the center and the left took some time and started in the early 1980s. Academics and intellectuals, as well as politicians, played a crucial role.

Academics and intellectuals who opposed the military government created research centers and think tanks. Since political parties were banned, these centers (supported by international organizations and governments) soon became the main voice of the opposition. Policies were intensely debated, and individuals from the different opposition parties created strong personal and intellectual ties.[2] By the early 1980s, these centers had won some degree of social recognition and, most importantly, had caught the attention of political party leaders.

Party leaders began discreetly to gather around different initiatives.[3] Union leaders, professional organizations, and political parties worked together on them. Encounters between old political adversaries of the center and the left led to the identification of a common political goal and debate about how to achieve it.

This rapprochement in the political arena was made possible to a large extent by changes in the views of the political parties themselves. Two complementary factors contributed to the process of ideological convergence. First, the Christian Democrats rejected their "camino único" thesis, which had guided the party's political strategy throughout the 1960s and early 1970s. Second, the Socialist Party experienced a "renewal" that led it to support a system of representative democracy without reservations and,

---

for Democracy or PPD. The rest were smaller parties, mainly factions of the old socialist party and other members of the Popular Unity coalition. It also included the radical and social democratic parties, and a small center-right party. The Concertación grew to include four more parties. After the 1988 plebiscite, the coalition was renamed Concertación de Partidos por la Democracia.

2. For a detailed analysis of the role played by academic and research centers in the formation of a consensus among intellectuals and politicians opposed to the military government, see Puryear (1994).

3. The Alianza Democrática of 1983, the Acuerdo Nacional para una Transición a la Democracia Plena of 1985, and the Asamblea de la Civilidad of 1986 are examples.

eventually, to drop its identification as a Marxist-Leninist Party.[4] Thus, the largest political parties in the opposition were able to develop a shared perception that democracy and the democratic system were something intrinsically good.

Complementing the consensus-building efforts in the academic and political arenas were initiatives directed at social organizations. The parties were able to establish a strong relationship with social organizations, particularly with labor unions, which would prove critical during the first years of the Aylwin government.

REBUILDING THE OPPOSITION PARTIES. The Communist Party, which since 1980 had been advocating "all forms of struggle," was a critical player among parties on the left and as such exercised considerable influence over that sector's political decisions. Events in 1986 isolated the Communists from their traditional allies on the left and paved the way for an agreement between the Christian Democrats, Socialists, and several other minor parties. The Socialist Party, once it broke ranks with the Communist Party, decided to form a political group with other left-wing parties, the "Izquierda Unida." Thus, the Socialist Party and the Christian Democratic Party, along with the Party for Democracy (Partido por la Democracia–PPD), became the axis around which all negotiations on political strategy moved.[5]

These developments led to the creation of the Concertación, the broadest political coalition in the second half of the twentieth century. The creation of the Concertación signals the acceptance by the opposition of the institutional design drawn by the military government.

The Concertación before the Aylwin Government

As the Concertación emerged victorious from the 1988 plebiscite and a triumph in the 1989 elections became more likely, the military government agreed to negotiate with the Concertación two important issues: (1) a package of constitutional reforms and (2) changes in the composition of the Central Bank's Board.

---

4. For an analysis of the evolution of the Chilean party system, see Scully (1992), Valenzuela (1978), and Walker (1990).

5. Ricardo Lagos, a socialist, designed the PPD as an "instrumental political party" or umbrella organization that would include a wide range of opponents to the military government. The PPD allowed the socialists to circumvent the prohibition of Marxist parties.

In the first case, the government understood that it would be better to reform some aspects of the Constitution while it was still in power and avoid a broader reform once the Concertación took over. A negotiating group of representatives from the government, Renovación Nacional (RN) and Unión Demócrata Independiente (UDI), and the Concertación drafted the 1989 constitutional reform proposals.[6] The proposals were submitted to the electorate and approved by plebiscite on July 30, 1989.

In the case of the Central Bank, the military government thought it was important to establish the legitimacy of the Bank's Board by negotiating its members. Thus, the Concertación, which had expressed doubts during the campaign about the law that granted the Bank autonomy, tacitly supported the new law by agreeing to appoint two of the Board's five directors.[7] This guaranteed that the Concertación would have some input in the Bank's policymaking process. Simultaneously, the Concertación used the occasion to signal to the markets and economic actors its willingness to conduct economic policy in a nonpartisan way.

Both issues were significant because they were perceived as an early recognition on the part of the government of the Concertación's likelihood of winning the December 1989 elections.

The Concertación in Power: The Political Challenges

On December 11, 1989, Patricio Aylwin was elected president with 55 percent of the votes.[8] The political agenda of the first Concertación government was delicate compromise. The plebiscite and the presidential election

---

6. The group produced a list of 49 specific reforms including elimination of article 8 (which banned Marxist parties and ideologies); a change in the composition of the National Security Council and limitation of its powers; an increase in the number of elected senators; and elimination of the requirement of two successive Congress's to approve constitutional reforms. All international agreements ratified by Chile on human rights were given constitutional rank.

7. The government appointed two members, and a fifth member was appointed by consensus. The five-member Board was appointed in a staggered way, for ten-year terms.

8. The complete results of the 1989 elections were Patricio Aylwin, 55.2 percent; Hernán Büchi, 29.4 percent; and Francisco Javier Errázuriz, 15.4 percent. At the Lower Chamber of Congress, the Concertación received 51.5 percent of the votes; Democracia y Progreso (the right-wing coalition), 34.2 percent. In the Senate the Concertación had 55.5 percent and Democracia y Progreso, 34.9 percent.

showed that the sector supporting the military government, despite losing both electoral contests, had significant support. Furthermore, the composition of Congress and the army's commitment to "protect the legacy of the military government" set strong de facto limits on the government's prerogatives. It was clear that a "maximalist" approach to political reform would not succeed.

However, the social and political majority that had voted for change took a different view. It expected clear signs that the Concertación government would provide a clean break from the past.

The Concertación government determined that its most critical objective was to ease the way to true national reconciliation. It was convinced that the goal of national reconciliation had to be built on two pillars: truth about human rights violations (and justice as politically feasible); and a strong commitment to greater social justice (as Aylwin called it, "growth with equity").

Given the distribution of political power and the restrictions set by the 1980 Constitution, the government chose to pursue what the right called a "politics of agreements" (*la política de los acuerdos*). Every important piece of legislation or government program was broadly discussed with the parties of the government coalition and, more importantly, with the parties of the opposition and the relevant social organizations. In most cases the government was able to achieve important agreements. Examples include tax reform, tariff reduction, the minimum wage, municipal and regional government reform, and labor reform. The government was unable to achieve its goals concerning reform of the teachers' statute, the more substantial constitutional reforms, the more ambitious judicial reforms, and the so-called "Aylwin law" on issues involving human rights.

This consensus-building strategy worked well for the Concertación government. The general public recognized its ability to move forward its agenda in a climate of social peace and economic growth.[9]

Boeninger (1997) identifies the following as the government's initial goals:

1. Achieve the full return of the military to its professional duties;
2. Confront the problem of human rights violations, combining justice and prudence as a contribution to national reconciliation;

---

9. The lowest support received by the Concertación in an election was 53.2 percent of the votes in the 1992 municipal elections. The highest was achieved in the 1993 presidential election when Eduardo Frei, the Concertación candidate, got more than 58 percent of the votes.

3. Ensure the country's governance; and
4. Finish the process of institutional legitimacy and construction of basic consensus in areas not covered by the 1989 reforms.

Thus, the Aylwin administration set forth a narrow, but clear and specific, political agenda.[10] The most salient policy issues, which it felt ought to be addressed in the short term, were human rights, constitutional reforms, municipal elections, electoral reform, and judicial reform.

MILITARY AND HUMAN RIGHTS. Clearly, the most difficult challenge on the new government's agenda was human rights. Three issues needed to be addressed: (1) the problem of crimes (disappearances, executions, and victims of political violence); (2) the rights of individuals that had suffered exile; and (3) the rights of public sector employees fired for political reasons (*exonerados*)?

The first issue was the most delicate. The government appointed a high-level commission to investigate, in a limited time frame, the disappearances and deaths caused by political violence. The Commission for Truth and Reconciliation (known as the Rettig Commission) was composed of lawyers from diverse political sectors, including a former minister of the Pinochet government and a former executive secretary for Amnesty International. In its lengthy report the Commission said the state was responsible for the disappearance of 1,198 individuals and had violated the human rights of nearly 3,000 people.

On the basis of the report, President Aylwin went on national television to admit state responsibility for those human rights violations, and to formally ask forgiveness from the victims and their relatives. The report had no legal value, but its investigations could be used to open formal judiciary investigations. Finally, the government established a fund to compensate, in a symbolic manner, the victims and their relatives.

In the case of individuals who had suffered exile or arbitrary destitution from public employment, the government set up two independent commissions to gather information. These commissions provided support for Chileans in exile who wanted to return to their country, and they helped the *exonerados* to reestablish their legal rights.

As for the relations with the military, once Aylwin became president, General Pinochet stayed as commander in chief of the army. This setting

---

10. The main issues of the economic agenda are discussed in a separate section.

provided the basis for a cold, formal, and at times very tense relation between the government and the army. These tensions reached their peak on two occasions: the "Ejercicio de Enlace" of December 1990 and the "Boinazo" of May 1993.[11] These military exercises had as much to do with institutional issues, as with financial scandals involving relatives of General Pinochet. In both cases, the army provided an administrative justification for its activities, and thus avoided creating a major constitutional and political affair. The events were of short duration and never received support from other branches of the armed forces or from RN and UDI.[12]

CONSTITUTIONAL REFORMS. The 1989 reforms cleared some obstacles in terms of acceptance of the 1980 Constitution by the political parties and electorate in general. However, for the Concertación, and important sectors of the population, the 1989 reforms were not enough. According to them, the Constitution maintained a strong balance in favor of executive power over legislative power and kept a large degree of autonomy for the armed forces vis-à-vis civilians.

Therefore, during the Aylwin government there was another attempt to reform the Constitution. Among the reforms that the Concertación proposed were elimination of nonelected senators; elimination of the life tenure of commanders in chief; reestablishment of presidential authority to retire military officers; and reform of the appointment mechanism for members of constitutional courts.

All of these reform proposals were strongly opposed by UDI and RN. They interpreted the reforms of military institutions as an attempt to politicize the military. The elimination of nonelected senators, they feared, would establish a government completely run by political parties. Their flat rejection of these proposals seemingly shattered the possibilities for a new political agreement.

---

11. Another incident occurred during the early days of the Frei government, when the Supreme Court decided to uphold a lower court's prison sentence for two military officers accused of masterminding the assassination of Orlando Letelier and Ronnie Moffit in 1976. These officers, one retired and the other in active duty, had headed the DINA (secret police) during the early Pinochet years. After some tense days caused by the officers' rejection of the sentence and refusal to comply with the prison terms, both officers were sent to Punta Peuco, a new reclusion site for high-risk prisoners involved in political crimes.

12. For a detailed explanation of these events, see Boeninger (1997, 408–23).

MUNICIPAL GOVERNMENT. During the military government, all local and regional authorities were appointed by the president, and they reported directly to him through the Minister of the Interior. A reform in 1988 determined that the president would appoint the mayors of the nine largest cities in Chile, and the other mayors would be chosen by local councils appointed by the central government.

In 1992 Congress approved the Municipal Governments Law governing all municipal authorities. The law was an important step giving local communities greater control over their affairs. All political parties supported it since it opened new areas of power to party competition.

ELECTORAL SYSTEM. The military government designed an electoral law that established two-member voting districts. In these districts any single party can present a ticket with two candidates or can form a pact or list with other parties of similar programmatic orientation, in which case each party presents one of the two candidates on the list. When a single list receives more than two-thirds of the total district votes, or doubles the number of votes of the second-highest list, both candidates from that list are elected. If the result is lower, the second-highest plurality obtains the second seat.

This system has forced the creation of coalitions. In order to maximize the number of seats, parties must agree on a coalition and a single slate of candidates. This has meant that parties have to sacrifice particular interests in favor of the overall coalition. As a result of this exercise, the law has ended up favoring the formation of two large voting blocs.

Since 1990 several attempts by Concertación governments to reform the electoral law have failed. In essence the Concertación governments proposed systems of proportional representation that would provide a distribution of parliamentary seats more in line with the preferences of the electorate. Arguments against such a system are based on the positive effects of having a party system that needs to establish coalitions (hence moderating their goals), and on the benefits of parliamentary representation that is not tied to the will of small parties that can hold the deciding votes.[13]

JUDICIAL REFORM. The initial proposal for judicial reform was an ambitious and broad effort to modify the structure, composition, and procedures of

---

13. For a detailed description of Chilean electoral law and its implications, see Scully (1995).

the judiciary. Until 1990 the members of the judiciary were appointed by the executive, which seriously hindered its independence. Furthermore, incentives for early retirement from the Supreme Court offered by the military government in the last months of its tenure allowed it to appoint younger judges that could serve longer.

When the Aylwin administration took office, one of its initial proposals was to modify the composition of the Supreme Court by increasing the number of members. The government also proposed the creation of a Superior Council of Magistrates as an entity responsible for judicial sector policy and administration. The Council would be composed of representatives of executive, legislative, and judicial powers.

These proposals did not receive the support of the judiciary or of political parties on the right. Therefore, the government lacked the votes to approve them and had to settle for a more moderate approach. Its new strategy emphasized modernizing and strengthening the judiciary by reforming some procedural codes; promoting open and quick access to justice by creating new courts or reorganizing some of the lower level courts; and limiting the powers of the military courts.

The Operation of the Aylwin Government

By March of 1990, the Concertación had become a coalition of 17 different political parties. To strengthen order and discipline, the parties agreed to give President Aylwin full responsibility and authority over government appointments and policy decisions. At the same time the parties maintained a strong sense of discipline and loyalty to their leaders.

The close ties knit during the military government among members of research centers, social organizations, and political parties helped build bridges across political parties. Purely partisan positions on policy issues were thus avoided. This process of integration and consensus across party lines was soon described as the work of the "transversal party," a group of individuals, from different parties within the Concertación, who shared a strong consensus on how policy ought to be conducted and prioritized.

Executive power was structured under a very strong axis composed of four ministers: Interior (as head of the cabinet), Presidency, Government, and Finance. Their personalities strongly influenced its operation. The ministers had established their technical and political credentials before the election, and they had the president's full confidence. This core of ministers constituted the main articulators of policy. The "La Moneda" ministers (the Interior, Presidency, and Government ministers who worked at the presidential palace) knew from the beginning that the Finance minister would need a strong political shield in order to contain what was likely to be an avalanche of demands. Hence, Finance was a close fourth member of this group.

As a matter of general practice, the full Cabinet rarely discussed and decided specific policy issues. From the beginning the Aylwin administration favored a strongly technical and sectorial approach to policymaking. This approach limited the margin for political pressure from political parties and other social actors.

Relations between the executive and the other actors in the policymaking process were conducted according to a clear division of labor. The Presidency, Interior, and Government ministers conducted political and legislative relations. Legislative projects were drafted at the Presidency ministry, which gave the minister clear authority in the policy debate. Economic policy was the responsibility of the Finance ministry, which coordinated with the Central Bank on matters of monetary policy. On social policy issues the Finance ministry, working with the sectorial ministry, conducted relations with the leaders of social organizations.

This mode of conducting policy debate and implementation sought to decrease the mistrust and skepticism of some political leaders and social organizations. The system worked on the basis of reaching the strongest possible consensus on policy issues. When consensus was not possible, the Aylwin government was ready to pursue its own proposals as far as it could, which usually meant intense negotiations in Congress.

President Aylwin maintained a Cabinet that reflected the relative strength of the members of the coalition. As a general principle, he tried to appoint a minister from a center party (mainly PDC) and an undersecretary from a leftist party (PS or PPD), or vice-versa. This ensured a political balance. To maintain a certain equilibrium in the parties' representation at the Cabinet level, he introduced a criteria of shared responsibility for government policy. Once policy was approved at the Cabinet level, no major party of the Concertación could argue it had not participated in the process.

The Institutional Dimensions of the Political Process

In order to understand the political process in Chile since 1990, one must understand the strength of its party system. The literature has broadly recognized the importance of political parties in the country's political development.[14] Garretón (1989, xvi) notes that political parties constitute the backbone of the country's political process. Early on they emerged as the main venue to access political power. All social actors soon recognized political parties as the determining players in the political field. The parties became the main articulators between social demands and the state's policy responses. They also acquired a strong ideological component, which set clear lines among different parties. Sartori (1976) has described the pre-1973 Chilean party system as one of polarized pluralism.[15] As the ideological discussion in the 1960s heated up, divisions within Chilean society intensified. By September 1973 the process exploded.

Despite the military government's efforts to end political parties, they showed an amazing ability to survive and reorganize themselves. By the early 1980s the political party system, although banned, was back in place and configured in a way very similar to the pre-coup setting. However, one important element had changed. As a direct and indirect consequence of the military coup, the political parties in opposition to the military government had experienced an important change in their ideological platforms. As Sartori (1976) observes, the ideological distance between the parties decreased significantly. This made possible a substantial change in their relationships and the establishment of political agreements.

Simultaneously, the electoral law forced political parties to minimize their differences in order to establish coalitions that would increase their electoral chances. This electoral framework worked in favor of the center and left-wing parties, given the greater political and ideological proximity that characterized their relations.

Another institutional determinant of Chile's political process is the 1980 Constitution and the legal framework that emerged from it. By accepting the 1988 plebiscite, the Concertación accepted the 1980 Constitution and limited its own ability to question constitutional norms in the future. Furthermore, once the Concertación won the plebiscite, the coalition agreed with the military government on a package of reforms that further confirmed the Concertación's tacit acceptance of the Constitution of 1980. (Elements of the Constitution are analyzed in detail in the economic policy section of this chapter.)

---

14. According to Scully (1995, 100), "Chilean parties, from the earliest days in the mid-nineteenth century, have been highly and deliberately intrusive institutions, seeking to reach deeply into the workings of civil society." For an account of the role played by the Chilean political party system, see also Garretón (1989), Scully (1992), Gil (1966), and Valenzuela (1977, 1985).

15. According to Sartori (1976), the main feature of such a system is a large number of relevant parties (at least five parties) and a strong ideological component.

The Political Economics of Chile's Transition to Democracy

There are, to be sure, many reasons why events unfolded as they did—the people, the ideas at the time, the external conditions, the internal economic situation, the institutional setup, and so on. We study here how changes in the institutional setup may have affected behavior during the transition, and also how institutional arrangements may help to preserve such economic performance in the future.

In political economics literature, institutions are relevant only if they impose constraints on the behavior of actors. They have to meet two conditions: diminish the discretion of the government in the administration and implementation of its policy objectives and/or the ability of the government to undertake unilateral changes in governmental policies.

The institutional reforms that are important for our purposes are only those that limit government discretion and make drastic shifts in policies difficult, thus providing a more stable and credible investment environment. Understanding these reforms will help us understand the continuity in economic policy from the military government to the democratic government in Chile.

Flexibility versus Credibility

The two conditions are similar to the mechanisms that provide credibility and effectiveness to a regulatory framework (Levy and Spiller 1994). The main purpose of these mechanisms should be to restrain arbitrary administrative action. As Levy and Spiller point out, to choose this route is to choose policy credibility over policy flexibility. (This replicates the choice at the level of macro policy between rules and discretion.)

Opinions differ concerning the weights to assign to both objectives. Those that have utmost confidence in public institutions prefer flexibility since they expect these institutions to pursue the population's welfare at every turn. They find the restraints unnecessary, suboptimal, and in some cases even undemocratic.

Political Economics: The Theoretical Literature

Which policymaking institutions produce the best policy outcomes? According to Persson and Tabellini (forthcoming, 3), "the general approach of the political economics literature is to explain deviations in observed economic policies from a hypothetical social optimum by appealing to specific incentive constraints in the decision problem of optimizing policy makers.

The positive analysis focuses on identifying the relevant incentive constraints, while the normative analysis focuses on institutional reforms which may relax them."

Credibility suffers when the government has incentives to be time inconsistent—that is, promise something and then renege on that promise. Lack of credibility may lead to economic policies or results that are suboptimal. (For example, equilibrium average inflation or wealth taxation may be too high.)

The "lack of credibility" problem has implications for institutional design. In particular, it makes it desirable to restrict the discretion of the policymaker. This insight has been exploited in monetary policy to advocate the benefit of an independent and "conservative" central bank. It also explains why it may be convenient for a central bank to issue debt in foreign currency (or, in the case of Chile, in UFs). [16] In sum, institutions that tie the hands of politicians ex ante may result in better policy and better outcomes.

Capital controls or international tax agreements that limit tax competition exacerbate credibility problems and thus can be counterproductive (Persson and Tabellini 1995). The more open a country is the more it tends not to adopt suboptimal policies because negative effects are widely enlarged by open trade and capital accounts.[17] Other research shows that institutions that can moderate political conflict and policy extremism result in better outcomes. This literature also has normative implications that are useful to our examination of the Chilean case.

Institutions lay down fundamental rules of the game that cannot be changed easily. For example, once an independent central bank has been set up, changing the institution is costly.[18] However, an institution does not need to last a long time to be effective. In the model that dominates the literature on credibility issues in monetary policy, for example, what is

---

16. The UF or Unidad de Fomento is a unit of account adjusted daily according to the inflation rate. (The rate of the previous month is used.) The UF is widely utilized in Chile in financial or real estate operations. For example, debt or prices are quoted in UFs.

17. See Sapelli (1992) for an analysis of how the openness of an economy constrains the ability of the state to influence it.

18. This premise is questioned by critics such as McCallum (1996). The critics argue that the institutional remedies do not fix the dynamic inconsistency at the core of this literature since the institutions are assumed to enforce a policy that is ex post suboptimal from the incumbent government's point of view. Hence, the government has a temptation to renege on the institution.

needed is a high cost for changing the institution within the time horizon of existing nominal contracts. If the costs of changing it are lowered, there will be effects as the population evaluates the increase in the temptation to renege on the institution. Merely lowering the costs may weaken credibility and lead to a loss in welfare. The real question is what costs are sufficiently high to make the institution credible. In this chapter we assume that an institution with "enough" costs can be designed.[19]

FISCAL POLICY. In the case of fiscal policy, a number of stylized facts give credence to the assumption that institutions matter. Large deficits and debts have been more common in countries with proportional rather than majoritarian electoral systems; with coalition governments and frequent government turnover; and with lenient rather than stringent government budget processes (Persson and Tabellini forthcoming).

The correlations between policies and political institutions suggest that political and institutional factors play an important role in shaping fiscal policy. Although the literature concentrates on analyzing credibility problems in capital taxation, the credibility problems are not found only there and should be considered the norm rather than the exception when policy is analyzed in a dynamic context.

In the case of capital taxation, the dynamic inconsistency is very clear. Since the ex post optimal tax structure differs dramatically from the ex ante optimal structure (as ex ante and ex post elasticities differ substantially), it is optimal for the government to renege on its announced tax structure and dramatically increase the taxes on capital.[20] If the government is unable to commit to the initial tax structure, the economy is trapped in a third-best, or worse, allocation. The resulting policy uncertainty is another consequence of the discretionary policy environment.

MONETARY POLICY. Well-designed monetary institutions can lessen the distortions created by credibility problems and political cycles. Crosscountry data for industrial countries show a strong negative correlation between

---

19. Jensen (forthcoming) studies a model in which a government can renege on the initial institution at a cost. In this setting, institutional design improves credibility but does not remove the credibility problem completely.

20. Hence, in a simple two-period model, the government finds it ex post optimal to set either a fully expropriating capital tax rate of 100 percent or a tax rate sufficiently high to finance all of public consumption with capital taxes, driving labor taxes to zero. Anticipating this, nobody invests.

measures of central bank independence and inflation, but no correlation between output or employment volatility and central bank independence. Thus, central bank independence seems to be a free lunch: it reduces average inflation at no real cost.[21]

In monetary policy, institutional reforms can raise the credibility of desirable policies. With fiscal policy such reforms (for example, delegation to a conservative policymaker or international tax competition) are less effective, since the tasks of a sovereign legislature cannot be narrowly defined.

DEBT POLICY. Models yield the empirical prediction that political polarization and political instability lead to larger debt accumulation. Political instability causes government to behave myopically. The result is general and can be applied to any intertemporal aspect of public policy, such as the level of public investment or the implementation of tax reforms.

The overissue of debt is obviously caused by a flawed government budget process. Each group in the coalition is given decisionmaking authority over part of the budget, but nobody is given decisionmaking authority over the aggregate outcome. Which institutional reforms could address this problem? A natural idea is to centralize decisionmaking authority in one of the parties (or reform the electoral system to make majority governments rather than coalition governments more likely). If the same party completely controlled all spending decisions, it would appropriately internalize the cost of overspending and of debt issue. Centralization of decisionmaking power can be abused, however. Checks and balances, as Persson, Roland, and Tabellini (1997) note, can mitigate the problem.

The Chilean Case: Economic Policy during the Transition

After 16 years of military rule, the first democratically elected government in Chile inherited a very successful economy. This stands as a major contrast to other experiences of transition in the region. It is very important because economic growth can reduce the frustrations derived from distributional inequalities. Economic growth increases social mobility and provides the material base for social compromises. A long record of successful

---

21. The formal theoretical literature on central bank independence starts with Rogoff (1985). He concludes that society is better off electing a conservative (tough on inflation) central banker. But the treatment of society's problem as a principal agent problem is anticipated by Barro and Gordon (1983b).

economic performance can strengthen citizens' beliefs in the effectiveness and legitimacy of the system as a whole.

Chile's democratic legitimization of the free-market economic model was crucial, however. The political actors at the time were extremely conscious of the legitimacy issue and hence designed an agenda to deal with it. To make the permanence of the market economy viable, the government had to gain the support for policy continuity from those who were hardest hit during the prolonged adjustment process of the 1980s—namely, workers (in particular those earning the minimum wage) and beneficiaries of social spending programs (for example, family allowances, public sector pensions, and the subsidy for extremely poor families). Moreover, they had to gain this support quickly.

During its first year the Aylwin administration made the important political decision to propose two critical economic reforms: it introduced a package to fund new social programs, and it recommended reform of the labor law, which had been much criticized by union leaders. Government officials were careful to explain that these two pieces of legislation were the only important changes in the economic model of the military government. By tackling these issues early, the government sought to minimize possible negative effects on private investment associated with policy uncertainty. As E. Boeninger, Minister of the Presidency, explained on April 25, 1991: "The administration first undertook the task of implementing reforms producing either uncertainty or cost increases in the economy (tax reforms and changes in labor legislation). These have now been mostly completed, enabling the government to guarantee full stability of the rules of the economic game for the rest of its term, thus facilitating dynamic behavior by business" (Boeninger 1992, 35).

Another reason the reforms had to be implemented quickly was the fear that the government, pressed by special interests, would return to populist politics. Some feared that import tariffs would be increased selectively and that an increase in fiscal deficits and in wages would lead to a surge in inflation, and capital flight. As it turned out, these fears were not warranted. The government cut import tariffs further and pursued a prudent fiscal policy that included fiscal surpluses and an acceptable increase in wages (as gauged by the nonexistent effect on unemployment).

The Aylwin administration was able to achieve a climate of consensus in the conduct of economic policy around four points: (1) market allocation of resources, (2) the importance of macroeconomic stability, (3) the need for a substantial increase in social spending, and (4) the desirability of an open economy. It avoided a conflict between points 2 and 3 by shifting the composition of government spending toward social spending and implementing a tax.

In addition, the government sent to Congress in 1990 a labor reform proposal, partly intended to balance negotiating power, and it raised the minimum wage, the family allowance, and the subsidy for low-income families during 1990–92. National agreement between the government, the Central Unitaria de Trabajadores (the main trade union), and the Confederación de la Producción y el Comercio (the main employers' association) allowed for a 21.9 percent increase in the real minimum wage (March 1990–92).[22]

It was necessary to be cautious to implement a wage increase that was sustainable. The experience of other countries in Latin America helped Chile. Aggressive wage adjustment above productivity gains proved short lived in Argentina, Brazil, and Peru in the 1980s. After a few years, wages were substantially below the starting point in all of these countries. This is what Dornbusch and Edwards (1991) have called the populist cycle. It is clearly in the interest of workers and trade unions to prevent such a pattern. After the agreement was implemented, economic growth and external conditions continued to be extremely favorable. Real wages increased on average by 3.7 percent annually during President Aylwin's administration and the minimum wage by more than double that. At the end of 1993 the unemployment rate was below 5 percent, almost 2 percentage points lower than in 1989. And public social spending rose by almost 50 percent between 1990 and 1993. The government was able to satisfy most of its requirements in terms of wages and social spending, while not affecting growth, inflation, or the balance of payments.

To signal its commitment to the goal of an open economy, the Aylwin administration made the significant decision to reduce import tariffs by one third in June 1991 (from 15 percent to 11 percent). However, the benefits of this strategy were in some ways jeopardized by bilateral agreements that increased effective protection for many sectors and abandoned the worthy goal of giving all sectors the same degree of protection.

Since the 1960s, the political economy of trade protection and exchange rate policy has changed drastically. After 20 years of a very open trade regime in Chile, the constituency in favor of low tariffs is dominant, since

---

22. An agreement had been made to link further increases in the minimum wage to gains in labor productivity and future expected inflation. This agreement, however, was violated in 1998 when a three-year increase in the minimum wage clearly surpassed any possible increase in productivity plus expected inflation.

the export sector grew from 15 percent of GDP in 1965 to 35 percent in 1990–94.

MONETARY POLICY. The new authorities thought that Chile could not sustain the high rates of GDP expansion it had experienced in 1988 and 1989 (about 9 percent per year on average). They also considered the rate of expansion of private money (about 40 percent per year) and domestic expenditure (11 percent per year) unsustainable. Not surprisingly, inflation was pushing toward 30 percent.

In early 1990 the newly independent Central Bank engineered a sharp monetary contraction aimed at reducing aggregate expenditures. This moderated the rise of imports and helped to control inflation. The adjustment was costly in terms of GDP (GDP growth dropped to 3.3 percent in 1990), but it demonstrated the government's willingness to pay a cost to fight an overheated economy and thus preserve macroeconomic equilibrium.

It is important to note that the economy had been slowing down since the third quarter of 1989. Many analysts think the adjustment inaugurated cyclical policy changes by the authorities that recurred during the 1990s. The Central Bank had a reputation to establish and could not risk making a mistake. It wanted to signal it would be committed to keeping inflation low and hence had to be tough.

FISCAL POLICY. Another conflict during Chile's transition to democracy was over spending and taxes. A sharply increased awareness of the costs of budget deficits and money creation moderated the spending demands of ministers, legislators, and local governments.[23] The budget rules also helped keep the process running smoothly.

With the creation of the Copper Stabilization Fund, the Finance Ministry sought to manage demands to expand spending when copper prices were high. Since copper exports generate fiscal revenues, those revenues increase when prices are high. Because the price of copper fluctuates, the revenues

---

23. According to Edwards (1993, 23), "a combination of factors" was responsible for the transformation in economic views. These included "the failure of the heterodox programs in Argentina, Brazil, and Peru in the mid-1980s and the general sense that the state-based development strategy of the previous decade had run out of steam." Edwards notes that "the collapse of the Soviet Union pulled the rug out from under the Marxist camp that had long advocated replacing markets with central planing. The Spanish experience with economic reform under socialist leader Felipe González also became an important factor."

are temporary and should be saved. The Copper Stabilization Fund was the mechanism created to achieve this.

All revenues generated by any increase in the price of copper above the estimate used for the budget would be deposited directly into the Fund. If, however, the price fell below a specific level, the Fund could be used to cover the deficit. Thus, two goals were achieved: in times of surplus, the additional revenues were not incorporated into the government budget and hence were not available to be spent; when prices fell below the expected level, the resulting deficit could be covered without requiring new spending cuts.

Fiscal revenue increased significantly during 1990–93 because of several factors: the tax reform of 1990, a strong expansion of economic activity and imports, a relatively high price for copper, and a reduction in tax evasion. This progress together with low international interest rates made it possible to increase social spending and have a budget surplus of between 1.5 and 2.5 percent of GDP every year between 1990 and 1994.

The Central Bank's losses in current open market operations and inherited losses from the rescue operation of banks in the early 1980s created an important quasi-fiscal deficit. The first Concertación government contributed to a reduction in this deficit by making extraordinary prepayments to the Central Bank. This achieved several objectives. First, the government was able to support the public sector surplus reducing debt and hence future expenditures. Second, by increasing expenditure through prepayments, the government lowered the nonfinancial public sector surplus. This was important since it was politically costly for the government to show a high nonfinancial public sector surplus given the many demands for further spending. In this way the government utilized what it considered nonpermanent surpluses in the most reasonable way: to retire debt and not to increase current expenditure that in the future could not be financed.

TAX REFORM. An agreement between the government and the main opposition party, Renovación Nacional, won legislative approval of the tax reform law. The corporate tax base went from only distributed earnings to total earnings, and the rate was increased from 10 percent to 15 percent. Narrowing the income tax brackets but not changing the tax rates (the highest marginal tax rates remained at 50 percent) raised personal income taxes, and the value-added tax was increased from 16 percent to 18 percent. It is estimated that the tax reform package raised fiscal revenue by 2.8 percent of 1991 GDP. Legislated as temporary at first, the tax increase in the end became permanent.

LABOR REFORM. The government had two major goals with this reform: to balance negotiating power, which the authorities thought was biased in favor of employers, and to legitimize the labor legislation, which was largely opposed by trade unions.

The reform that was finally approved by Congress represented a compromise with the main opposition party. The labor reform eliminated the right of employers to fire workers with no expression of cause, but it allowed an open category called "in the needs of the company." Severance payments remained at one month per year of work, but the maximum was increased from five to eleven months (there was no maximum in the original reform proposal), and workers could appeal in court. If the courts found the firing unjustified, severance payments had to be increased 20 percent.

The other reforms applied to collective bargaining and unionization. Groups of nonunionized workers were allowed to participate in collective bargaining. Negotiations became permissible at the industry level, but only by common agreement between employers and employees. Strikes, which had been limited to 60 days, were allowed of indefinite duration.

The Institutional Foundations of the Economic Process

The deep economic chaos of the Allende period (1970–73) destroyed the special interest groups that sustained the clientelistic state and allowed a more autonomous state to emerge, one in which technocratic considerations had greater policy weight. As Velasco (1994, 382–83) says: "The demise of the clientelistic state is expressed in the institutional arrangements that emerged." These included "the uniform tariff which limits the scope of private sector lobbying for import protection; the technification of the state's activities as regulator; the privatization of social security and consolidation of changes in budgeting procedures, both of which limit the amount of lobbying on fiscal matters; and the independence of the Central Bank that both ends the partial control that private sector interests had on credit policies and also limits severely the ability of the bank to finance fiscal deficits. These institutional reforms changed the nature and policymaking capacity of the Chilean state and therefore the way resources are allocated in the Chilean economy."

This institutional setup is credible only if it cannot be reversed with the stroke of a pen. In all cases the legislation affecting private interests appears difficult to change. In some cases (for example, the prohibition against nontariff barriers), the new legislation took on a quasi-constitutional status by increasing the costs associated with attempted reversal. (This prohibition is contained in the Central Bank Organic Law, which requires a three-fifths majority in Congress for amendments.)

Tariffs are no longer the domain of presidential decrees but are uniformly levied across all goods, and nontariff barriers are banned. Both of these changes severely limited the space available for producers to lobby for protection. The need to discuss tariff changes in Congress brings the issue out of the back rooms of bilateral political deals and into the open arena of competitive politics. And the common tariff makes it more difficult for certain sectors to ask for special deals.[24] The reforms limited the access of business groups to state protection and the benefits of relative price manipulation by the government.

Consider also the area of social security. Under a pay-as-you-go system, the incentives were all there for congressional representatives and pressure groups to demand increases in benefits to be financed by borrowing (or taxes on future generations with no current political representation).[25] With the creation of an individually funded system, the range of social security issues on which the government can be lobbied is much narrower, and the political incentives point in the direction of preserving the accumulated savings of individuals, not spending them away.

Two other aspects of the institutional environment are significant. One is the budget process. Although Chile's 1925 Constitution endowed the executive with ample powers in many areas, governments often found it hard to negotiate and obtain approval of their annual budgets in a timely and reasonably effective way. Reforms introduced in 1970 and retained in the 1980 Constitution and in the current budget procedure legislation greatly limit the scope for vested interests to lobby on fiscal affairs. First, only the executive can initiate bills involving the allocation of public resources; the role of Congress is limited to approving, amending, or turning down the legislation. Second, there are strict limits on the time allocated to congressional discussion of the budget. If 60 calendar days after the reception of the bill the legislature has not approved an alternative to it, the executive's proposal is automatically approved (box 9.1).

The final change has to do with Central Bank independence. The 1980 Constitution prohibits the Central Bank from financing government defi-

---

24. See Rodrik and Panagariya (1991) for a review of the political economy arguments for a common tariff.

25. See Alesina and Tabellini (1990) and Velasco (1994) for models in which the possibility of borrowing creates incentives for systematic government deficits. See Tabellini (1990) for an analysis of the politics of intergenerational redistribution through social security.

Box 9.1 Chile's Fiscal Institutions

Baldez and Carey (1998) examine Chile's fiscal institutions. A key hypothesis of their paper is that the Chilean budget deficits should be low relative to regimes with other budget procedures. The hypothesis reflects the insight of a spatial model that concludes that on each policy dimension, the Chilean budget process favors whichever institutional actor (Congress or the president) prefers less spending. If the president prefers less spending than does Congress on a particular item, the president's proposal sets the spending ceiling; if Congress prefers less spending, it can amend the budget to its ideal level. By prohibiting Congress from creating new programs or transferring funds among programs, Chile's budget rules limit the potential for legislative logrolls that push spending up. The hypothesis also assumes that tax and revenue policy is fixed, so that the direct effect of policymakers on deficits is through expenditures.

Article 64 of the Chilean Constitution establishes the procedure for making government spending policy as follows:

> The Budgetary Law Bill must be submitted to the National Congress by the President of the Republic at least three months prior to the date on which it should become effective; should it not be passed by Congress within sixty days of its date of submittal, the proposal submitted by the President of the Republic shall enter into force. The National Congress may not increase or diminish the estimate of revenues; it may only reduce the expenditures contained in the Budgetary Law Bill, except for those established by permanent law. Estimation of the returns of resources stated in the Budgetary Law and other resources established by any other proposed law shall be the exclusive right of the President, following a report to be submitted by the respective technical agencies. Congress may not approve additional expenditures by charging them to the funds of the Nation without indicating, at the same time, the sources of the funds needed to meet such expenditures. In case the source of funds granted by Congress were insufficient for financing any additional expenditures approved, the President of the Republic upon promulgating the law, subject to favorable report from the service or institution through which new returns are collected, countersigned by the Comptroller General of the Republic, must proportionately reduce all expenditures, regardless of their nature.

The president's agenda control over fiscal policy is not limited to the annual budget bill; it extends generally to all spending and tax policy. Article 62 states, in part: "The President of the Republic holds the exclusive initiative for proposals of law related to . . . the financial or budgetary administration of the State, amendments to the Budgetary Law. . . ."

(Box continues on the following page.)

Box 9.1 *(continued)*

The president of the Republic shall also hold the exclusive initiative for

> imposing, suppressing, reducing or condoning taxes of any type or na-
> ture, establishing exemptions or amending those in effect and determin-
> ing their form, proportionality or progression.... The National Congress
> may only accept, reduce or reject the services, employment, salaries,
> loans, benefits, expenditures and other related proposals made by the
> President of the Republic.

The Chilean fiscal year is concurrent with the calendar year. Thus, under
Article 64, the president proposes a budget to Congress by the end of September, and Congress, in turn, must promulgate a budget law by November
30, one month before it is to take effect. The first public sector budget created
under the current process was for 1991. It was passed by the newly elected
president and Congress in 1990.

---

cits by purchasing treasury securities. In December 1989 an organic law
was passed to insulate the monetary authority from executive branch pressures. Its new independence has ended the Central Bank's age-old vulnerability to private sector demands for direct credit.

In sum, businesspeople, public enterprise managers, middle-class groups
linked to the state apparatus, and trade unions have had their power to
lobby for special treatment curtailed. The dire predictions of chaos, populism, fiscal deficit, inflation, and capital flight did not materialize to a large
extent because of the institutional reforms.

The Relevance of Institutions for Economic Policy: The Political Science Literature

The case study literature on the politics of adjustment suggests repeatedly
that governmental elites and state institutions are pivotal to launching reforms (Grindle 1989) and that their influence on the government is medi-
ated by the structure of political institutions. Political institutions, like
markets, structure the incentives for political action and can profoundly
influence the relative standing and power of different groups.

Once an institutional framework is in place that permits deep reform,
this becomes the key question: Can that same framework guarantee the

reforms will not be overturned some time down the road? This is a problematic paradox: the institutions that finally permit reform may not be adequate to provide a credible long-term horizon to the new rules of the game. Hence, there is a need to give signals of the permanence of the new rules once they are in place. This second step, the consolidation of reform, involves stabilizing expectations around a new set of incentives and convincing economic agents that the reforms cannot be reversed at the discretion of individual decisionmakers.

THE PARTY SYSTEM AND ELECTORAL RULES. The study of inflation (Haggard and Kaufman 1992) suggests that a number of democratic regimes, in particular those based on catchall two-party systems, have a successful record of macroeconomic management. On the other hand, fragmented party systems increase the risks of unstable coalitions, populist appeal, favoritism, and wide swings in policy. Fragmented party systems can result in perverse incentives that undermine not only macroeconomic stability but democratic governance as well. The engineering of the political and electoral system can have important consequences for the stability of electoral and legislative majorities, and thus for their capacity to mobilize support for credible policy initiatives.

Most electoral systems give large parties a more than proportional share of seats. The larger the big-party bias, the greater the incentive to form electoral alliances. This incentive can be understood by examining the number of viable parties under a given system. Political scientists estimate the "threshold of exclusion" as the largest vote share that a party can win in a given electoral district and still not be guaranteed a seat. In Chile, it is 33 percent of the vote.[26] This threshold is often taken as a rough estimate of the minimum viable size of a party, and taking its reciprocal gives an upper bound on the number of viable parties in a given district. In Chile this number is three. While the percentage of votes remains as is, close to 50/50 between the two alliances, there are no incentives for a third party to ap-

---

26. Both the Chamber and Senate are elected from two-member districts. The two-member electoral system is unique to Chile. Under this system, parties or coalitions present lists of two candidates, and voters indicate a preference for one candidate within one of the lists. The votes of both candidates are totaled and the two seats allocated. The first seat is allocated to the candidate from the list with the most total votes, after which the lists' vote total is divided by two. If this quotient is still higher than any other lists' vote total, the second candidate gets the second seat. Otherwise, the second seat goes to the first candidate on the second-place list.

pear. However, if one of the alliances were to achieve a dominant majority, there would be incentives for it to split.

The Chilean system is unique in its tendency to overrepresent second-place finishers. It also encourages the formation of broad coalitions. The imperative to coalesce is formidable enough that Chile's traditional multi-party system now performs much like a two-party system.

Adopting the terminology of Sartori (1976), we can say that systems are "strong" when they provide substantial electoral incentives to coalesce and "feeble" when they provide little or no such incentives. Systems with low district magnitudes of winner-take-all seat allocation formulas are strong; systems with high district magnitudes and proportional seat allocations are feeble. Strong systems put meaningful upper bounds on the number of parties. Hence, the current system in Chile could be called strong.[27]

Party systems that promote intraparty competition for seats promote candidate-based electoral politics; systems that hinder that competition promote party-oriented elections. The current electoral system in Chile, like the U.S. system, promotes few decentralized parties. The 1925 Chilean Constitution, however, promoted *many* decentralized parties.

The decisiveness of the system depends on whether the executive and legislative powers are aligned. The presence of a misalignment produces the phenomenon of divided government. Divided government was imposed, at least for a time, by the 1980 Constitution and the institution of appointed senators. Divided government fosters a degree of indecisiveness and favors the status quo. Such indecisiveness would negatively affect fiscal policy were it not for the budget rules, which impose order and direction even in the context of divided government. In the current legislature most of the appointed senators have been designated by the government. This may make it easier for the Concertación to pass laws in the Senate even with opposition from the center-right coalition. What the cost will be in terms of the government's credibility remains to be seen. It could be high.

----

27. Corbo, Lüders, and Spiller (1995) argue that the Chilean system has a strong set of checks and balances based on diffusion of power. This is related to the incentive for divided government. They conclude that electoral rules lead to party and regional fragmentation. Hence, the legislature will not respond to a single party, and the parties themselves will not be very homogeneous. The Chilean system may create gridlock since legislation may not pass easily (Shugart and Carey 1992). Given that the initial conditions before the resumption of constitutional rule in 1989 were pro market, the potential gridlock may translate into a strong signal of stability.

PRESIDENTIALISM VERSUS PARLIAMENTARISM. We turn now to analyzing the presidential nature of the Chilean system. Does it provide any of the beneficial institutional effects we have been discussing?

Policymaking in presidential systems depends on the electoral rules and party systems those rules foster and cannot be analyzed without reference to them (Shugart and Haggard 1998). Policymaking is likely to be impeded by electoral laws that foster multiparty systems in which presidents have difficulty forming legislative coalitions. Does the president have agenda-setting powers and exclusive rights of introduction of bills to parliament on certain topics? This is an important question.

Republic of Korea, Taiwan (China), Brazil, Colombia, and Peru—like Chile—have constitutional provisions limiting Congress's authority to increase the amounts allocated to items in the budget submitted by the president. These provisions enhance the capacity of the president to obtain outcomes closer to his preferences (Baldez and Carey 1998). In Chile these provisions tend to minimize pork and restrain spending to the level advocated by the most restrictive of the two powers: executive or legislative. However, this does not guarantee a stable fiscal stance if both powers agree to an expansive fiscal policy. The constellation that leads to the greatest overall authority—decree power, a strong veto, and exclusive powers of agenda setting—is present in Chile on fiscal matters.

One key issue is whether a presidential system provides more credibility to the policy status quo than does a parliamentary system. Moe and Caldwell (1994) argue that it does. Presidential systems typically have more vetoes in the policymaking process than do parliamentary systems, in which the majority in a single legislative house is usually sovereign. Policies, therefore, tend to endure. In a parliamentary system, if the majority shifts, the new winners are able to rule unencumbered by preestablished rules, and policies are easier to change. Though some think this is more democratic (and it may be), it is clearly less efficient. Since under a parliamentary system the state cannot commit to any policy rule, policies are less credible, investment lower, interest rates higher, and so on.

In Chile the president's main powers are in the realm of budgetary policy. Only the president can introduce legislation concerning taxes, expenditures, public debt, social security schemes, new public services, and collective bargaining. Moreover, in budgetary expenditure or employment legislation, the legislature cannot increase any proposed appropriation. The legislature, however, can delete or reduce any item in the proposed bill. Chile's Constitution also requires a partially balanced budget, since it prohibits the legislature from approving an expenditure increase without determining the sources of the additional funds needed. Also the Executive Power is the only one who can provide an estimate of revenues.

Conclusion

Chile's economic performance since the mid-1990s has been outstanding. By the end of the first Concertación government in March 1994, the country had enjoyed a decade of uninterrupted growth at almost 7 percent per year. The macro situation was solid, inflation was going down, and a surplus showed in the balance of payments. Several reasons account for this success. The strong initial position of the economy was a crucial asset.

In addition, broad consensus on economic matters helped a lot. But Chile's institutions were the key to its success. They significantly reduced the profitability of rent-seeking activities, so pressure on economic policy was sharply reduced.

Policymaking involves the interplay of large and small institutions. Small institutions are the agencies that undertake day-to-day policymaking. Recently, great hope has been placed on the design of such institutions. The literature on economic reform stresses that it is not enough to get policies right; it is also important to get institutions right. The technocratic approach to this problem is the creation of independent agencies: independent central banks, autonomous regulatory agencies, independent judiciaries, and so forth. The creation of such agencies contributed importantly to the practically nonexistent credibility costs in Chile's transition to democracy.

On the political side, two factors smoothed the transition: the strength of the political party system and the context provided by the 1980 Constitution and the electoral legislation. Although the Constitution has placed important restrictions on the authority of the executive on certain issues, it has granted that office great latitude in the policymaking process, including the legislative aspects of it. Chile's weak Congress is attributable to its constitutionally defined functions, its electoral system and the presence of nonelected members. No party or coalition has been able to establish a clear majority in Congress, and this has underscored the powers of the presidency even further.

In this unbalanced scheme, the critical actors have been the political parties. Their strength, discipline, and degree of penetration of Chilean society have helped to ease the executive-legislative relationship, thus ensuring a remarkable degree of governance. Political parties have succeeded in reestablishing some consensus across the political, economic, and social arenas. They have acted as an efficient bridge between policymakers in the executive and the legislative branches. They have also contributed to improved working relations between the presidency and social organizations. All of this has been achieved without undermining the authority of the president and the attributes of that office.

Finally, there is the question of the replicability of the Chilean "model." The Chilean case has very country-specific elements, which should warn against an open and unquestioned application to other countries. Chile's historical development and context, the weight of its political institutions throughout its history, and the framework within which the transition process has taken place are, to say the least, uncommon.

As we have argued throughout this chapter, the role of institutions is critical. Without a strong institutional framework, recognized by the relevant players, efforts by the government to implement policies are severely limited.

References

Alesina, Alberto, and Guido Tabellini. 1990. "A Political Theory of Fiscal Deficits and Government Debt." *Review of Economic Studies* 57 (July): 403–14.

Baldez, Lisa, and John Carey. 1998. "Budget Procedure and Fiscal Restraint in Post-Transition Chile." In *Political Institutions and the Determinants of Public Policy: When Do Institutions Matter?* edited by S. Haggard and M. McCubbins. Princeton, N. J.: Princeton University Press.

Barro, Robert, and D. Gordon. 1983a. "A Positive Theory of Monetary Policy in a Natural Rate Model." *Journal of Political Economy* 91: 589–610.

———. 1983b. "Rules, Discretion and Reputation in a Model of Monetary Policy." *Journal of Monetary Economics* 12: 101–21.

Boeninger, Edgardo. 1992. "Governance and Development: Issues, Challenges, Opportunities, and Constraints." In *Proceedings of the World Bank Annual Conference on Development Economics 1991*. Washington, D.C.: World Bank.

———. 1997. *Democracia en Chile. Lecciones para la gobernabilidad.* Santiago: Editorial Andrés Bello.

Bosworth, Barry, Rudiger Dornbusch, and Raúl Labán, eds. 1994. *The Chilean Economy: Policy Lessons and Challenges.* Washington, D.C.: The Brookings Institution.

Corbo, Vittorio, Rolf Lüders, and Pablo T. Spiller. 1995. "The Institutional Foundations of Economic Reforms: The Case of Chile." Pontificia Universidad Católica de Chile, Santiago.

Dornbusch, Rudiger, and Sebastián Edwards. 1991. *The Macroeconomics of Populism in Latin America.* Chicago: University of Chicago Press.

Drake, Paul, and Mathew McCubbins, eds. 1998. *The Origins of Liberty: Political and Economic Liberalization in the Modern World.* Princeton, N. J.: Princeton University Press.

Edwards, Sebastián. 1993. *Latin America and the Caribbean: A Decade after the Debt Crisis.* Washington, D.C.: World Bank

Garretón, Manuel Antonio. 1989. *The Chilean Political Process.* Boston, Mass.: Unwin Press.

Gil, Federico. 1966. *The Political System of Chile.* Boston: Houghton Mifflin.

Grindle, Marilee S. 1989. "The New Political Economy." Working Paper. World Bank, Country Economics Department, Washington, D.C.

Haggard, Stephan, and Mathew McCubbins, eds. 1998. *Political Institutions and the Determinants of Public Policy: When Do Institutions Matter?* Princeton, N. J.: Princeton University Press.

Haggard, Stephan, and Robert Kaufman, eds. 1992. *The Politics of Economic Adjustment: International Constraints, Distributive Conflicts, and the State.* Princeton, N. J.: Princeton University Press.

Haggard, Stephan, and Robert Kaufman. 1995. *The Political Economy of Democratic Transitions.* Princeton, N. J.: Princeton University Press.

Jensen, Henry. Forthcoming. "Credibility of Optimal Monetary Delegation." *American Economic Review.*

Levy, Paul, and Pablo Spiller. 1994. "The Institutional Foundations of Regulatory Commitment: A Comparative Analysis of Telecommunications Regulation." *Journal of Law, Economics & Organization.* October.

McCallum, B. 1996. "Crucial Issues Concerning Central Bank Independence." National Bureau of Economic Research Working Paper 5597, Cambridge, Mass.

Moe, Terry, and Michael Caldwell. 1994. "The Institutional Foundations of Democratic Government: A Comparison of Presidential and Parliamentary Systems." *Journal of Institutional and Theoretical Economics* 150 (1): 171–95.

Persson, Torsten, and Guido Tabellini. 1990. *Macroeconomic Policy, Credibility and Politics.* New York: Harwood Academic Publishers.

———. 1995. "Double-Edged Incentives: Institutions and Policy Coordination." In Gene M. Grossman and Kenneth Rogoff, eds., *Handbook of International Economics,* vol. 3. Amsterdam: North Holland.

———. Forthcoming. "Political Economics and Macroeconomic Policy." In John Taylor and Michael Woodford, eds., *Handbook of Macroeconomics.* Amsterdam: North Holland.

Persson, Torsten, G. Roland, and Guido Tabellini. 1997. "Separation of Powers and Political Accountability." *Quarterly Journal of Economics* 112: 1163–202.

Puryear, Jeffrey M. 1994. *Thinking Politics: Intellectuals and Democracy in Chile, 1973–1988*. Baltimore: Johns Hopkins University Press.

Rodrik, Dani, and A. Panagariya. 1991. "Political Economy Arguments for a Common Tariff." Working Paper. World Bank, Country Economics Department, Washington, D.C.

Rogoff, Kenneth. 1985. "The Optimal Degree of Commitment to an Intermediate Monetary Target." *Quarterly Journal of Economics* 100: 1169–90.

Sapelli, Claudio. 1992. *Tamaño del Estado, Instituciones y Crecimiento Económico*. Santiago: CERES-CINDE.

Sartori, Giovanni. 1976. *Parties and Party Systems: A Framework for Analysis*. Cambridge, U.K.: Cambridge University Press.

Scully, Timothy R. 1992. *Rethinking the Center: Party Politics in Nineteenth and Twentieth Century Chile*. Stanford, Calif.: Stanford University Press.

———. 1995. "Reconstructing Party Politics in Chile." In Scott Mainwaring and Timothy R. Scully, eds., *Building Democratic Institutions: Party Systems in Latin America*. Stanford, Calif.: Stanford University Press.

Shugart, Matthew, and John Carey. 1992. *Presidents and Assemblies*. New York: Cambridge University Press.

Shugart, Matthew, and Stephen Haggard. 1998. "Institutions and Public Policy in Presidential Systems." In S. Haggard and M. McCubbins, eds., *Political Institutions and the Determinants of Public Policy: When Do Institutions Matter?* Princeton, N. J.: Princeton University Press.

Tabellini, Guido. 1990. "A Positive Theory of Social Security." National Bureau of Economic Research Working Paper 3272, Cambridge, Mass.

Valenzuela, Arturo. 1977. *"Political Brokers in Chile."* Chapel Hill, N.C.: Duke University Press.

———. 1978. "The Breakdown of Democratic Regimes: Chile." In Juan J. Linz and Alfred Stepan, eds., *The Breakdown of Democratic Regimes: Latin America*. Baltimore: Johns Hopkins University Press.

———. 1985. "The Chilean Party System: Origins, Characteristics, and Future Prospects." Woodrow Wilson Center Working Paper 164, Washington, D.C.

Velasco, Andrés. 1994. "The State and Economic Policy: Chile 1952–1992." In Barry Bosworth, Rudiger Dornbusch, and Raúl Labán, eds., *The Chilean Economy: Policy Lessons and Challenges*. Washington, D.C.: The Brookings Institution.

Walker, Ignacio. 1990. *Socialismo y Democracia: Chile y Europa en Perspectiva Comparada*. Santiago: CIEPLAN-Hachette.

Conference Agenda

December 17–18, 1997
Washington, D.C.

Welcome
Barbara Bruns

Module I: Economic Management

Co-chairs:	Minister Eduardo Aninat *Myrna Alexander*
Presentation:	Myths and Facts of Chilean Macroeconomic Policy *Guillermo Calvo and Enrique Mendoza*
Presentation:	Chile's Takeoff: Facts, Challenges, Lessons *Klaus Schmidt-Hebbel*
Presentation:	Capital Markets in Chile, 1985–97 *Nicolas Eyzaguirre*
Panel of Discussants:	*Gerard Caprio, Ricardo Hausmann,* *Andrés Velasco, and Roberto Zahler*

Open Plenary Discussion led by Eduardo Aninat

Module II: Poverty and Social Development

Introduction: *Julian Schweitzer*

Chair: *Barbara Bruns*

Presentation: Reform of Chilean Education System
                        Cristián Cox

Presentation: Reforms of the Health Sector in Chile
                        Osvaldo Larrañaga

Panel of Discussants: *Richard Elmore and Richard Feachem*

Presentation: Poverty and Income Distribution in a High-
                        Growth Economy: Chile, 1987–95
                        Alberto Valdés

Discussants: *Dagmar Raczynski and Nora Lustig*

Module III: Governance

Introduction: *Guillermo Perry*

Chair: *Edgardo Boeninger*

Presentation: Effectiveness of the State and Social and
                        Economic Development

Discussant: *Davis Shand*

Open Discussion led by Edgardo Boeninger

Presentation: Privatizing and Regulating Chile's Utilities:
                        Successes, Failures, and Outstanding Challenges
                        Eduardo Bitrán and José Luis Guasch

Discussant: *Martín Rodriguez-Pardina*

Presentation: The Governance of the Chilean Economy
                        since 1990
                        Eugenio Lahera

Discussant: *Arturo Israel*

Open Discussion led by Edgardo Boeninger

Discussion: Relevance and Applicability of Chile
                        Lessons to Other Countries

Introduction: *Moses Naim*

Open Discussion led by Lajos Bokros

Wrap-up

Rapporteur's Report: *Guillermo Perry*

Final Remarks: *Eduardo Aninat*

Index

(Page numbers in italics indicate material in tables or figures)